PRIDE AND PREJUDICE
AND ZOMBIES

THE GRAPHIC NOVEL

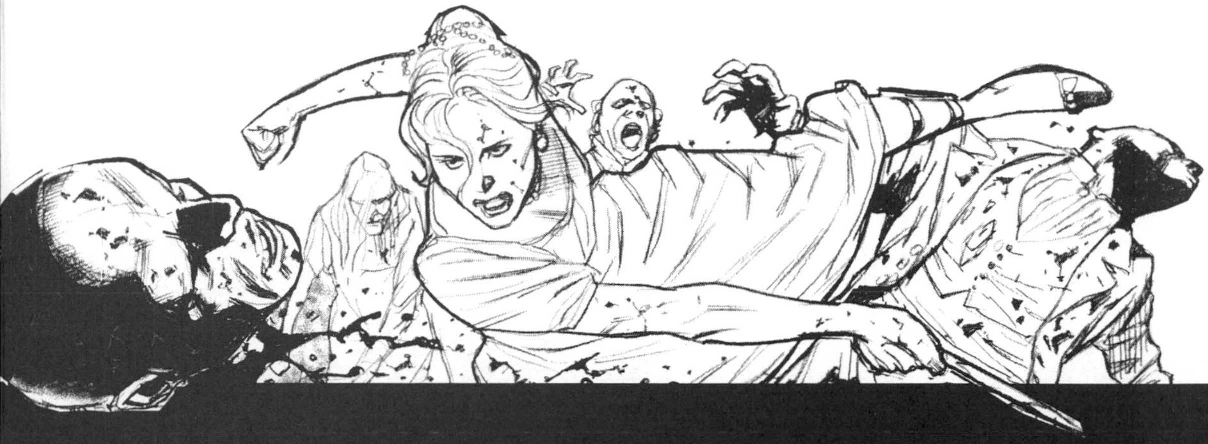

PRIDE AND PREJUDICE AND ZOMBIES

THE GRAPHIC NOVEL

Jane Austen and Seth Grahame-Smith

ADAPTED BY TONY LEE • ILLUSTRATED BY CLIFF RICHARDS

DEL REY

BALLANTINE BOOKS • NEW YORK

Pride and Prejudice and Zombies is a work of fiction.
Names, characters, places, and incidents are the products of the author's imagination or are used fictitiously.
Any resemblance to actual events, locales, or persons, living, dead, or undead, is entirely coincidental.

A Del Rey Trade Paperback Original

Published in the United States by Del Rey,
an imprint of The Random House Publishing Group,
a division of Random House, Inc., New York.

DEL REY is a registered trademark and the
Del Rey colophon is a trademark of Random House, Inc.

This graphic novel is adapted from *Pride and Prejudice and Zombies*
by Jane Austen and Seth Grahame-Smith, published in 2009
by Quirk Books, Philadelphia, copyright © 2009 by
Quirk Productions, Inc.

ISBN 978-0-345-52068-5

Printed in the United States of America

www.delreybooks.com
www.quirkclassics.com

246897531

PRIDE AND PREJUDICE
AND ZOMBIES

THE GRAPHIC NOVEL

[redacted]

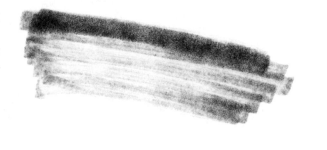

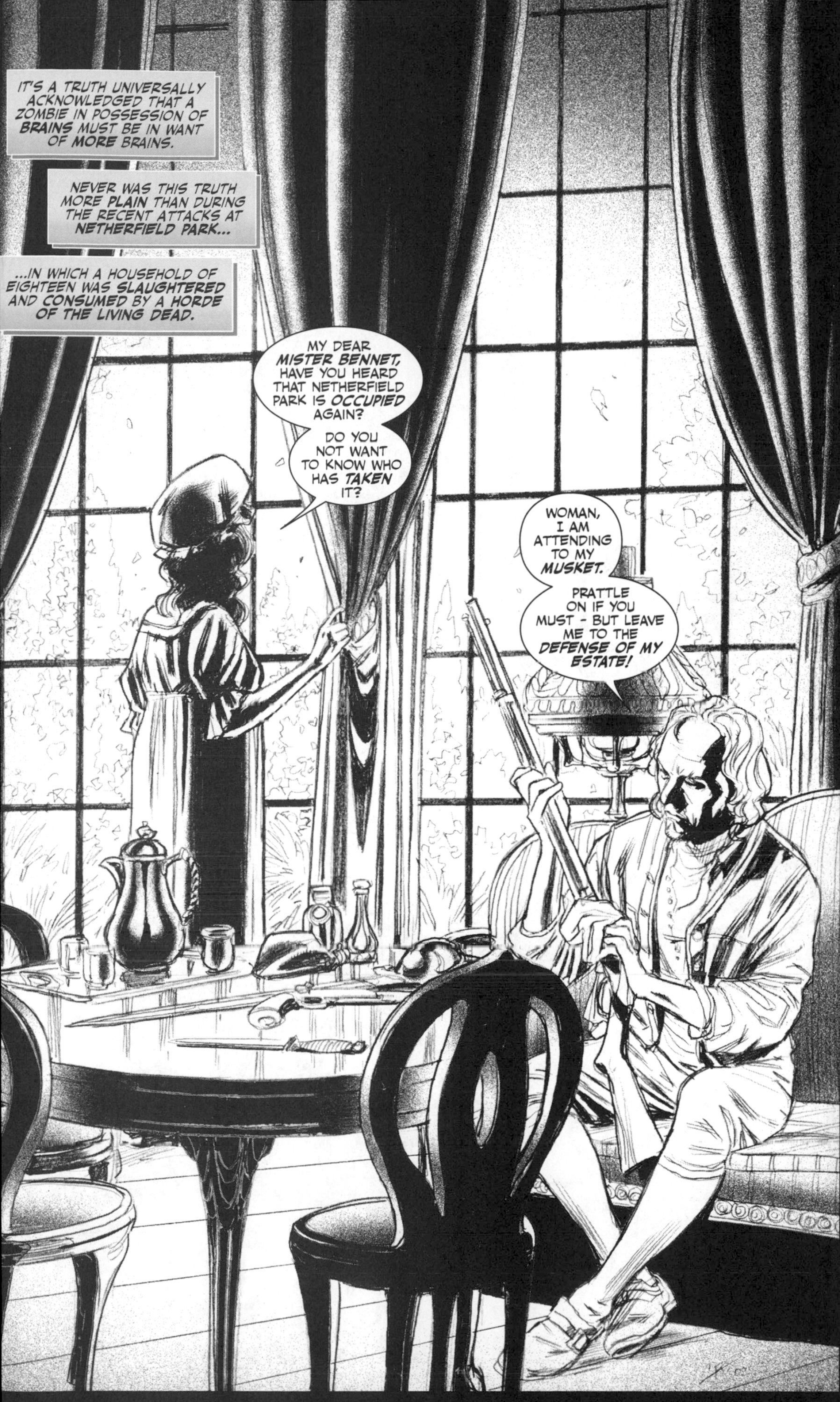
IT'S A TRUTH UNIVERSALLY ACKNOWLEDGED THAT A ZOMBIE IN POSSESSION OF BRAINS MUST BE IN WANT OF MORE BRAINS.
NEVER WAS THIS TRUTH MORE PLAIN THAN DURING THE RECENT ATTACKS AT NETHERFIELD PARK...
...IN WHICH A HOUSEHOLD OF EIGHTEEN WAS SLAUGHTERED AND CONSUMED BY A HORDE OF THE LIVING DEAD.
MY DEAR MISTER BENNET, HAVE YOU HEARD THAT NETHERFIELD PARK IS OCCUPIED AGAIN?
DO YOU NOT WANT TO KNOW WHO HAS TAKEN IT?
WOMAN, I AM ATTENDING TO MY MUSKET.
PRATTLE ON IF YOU MUST - BUT LEAVE ME TO THE DEFENSE OF MY ESTATE!

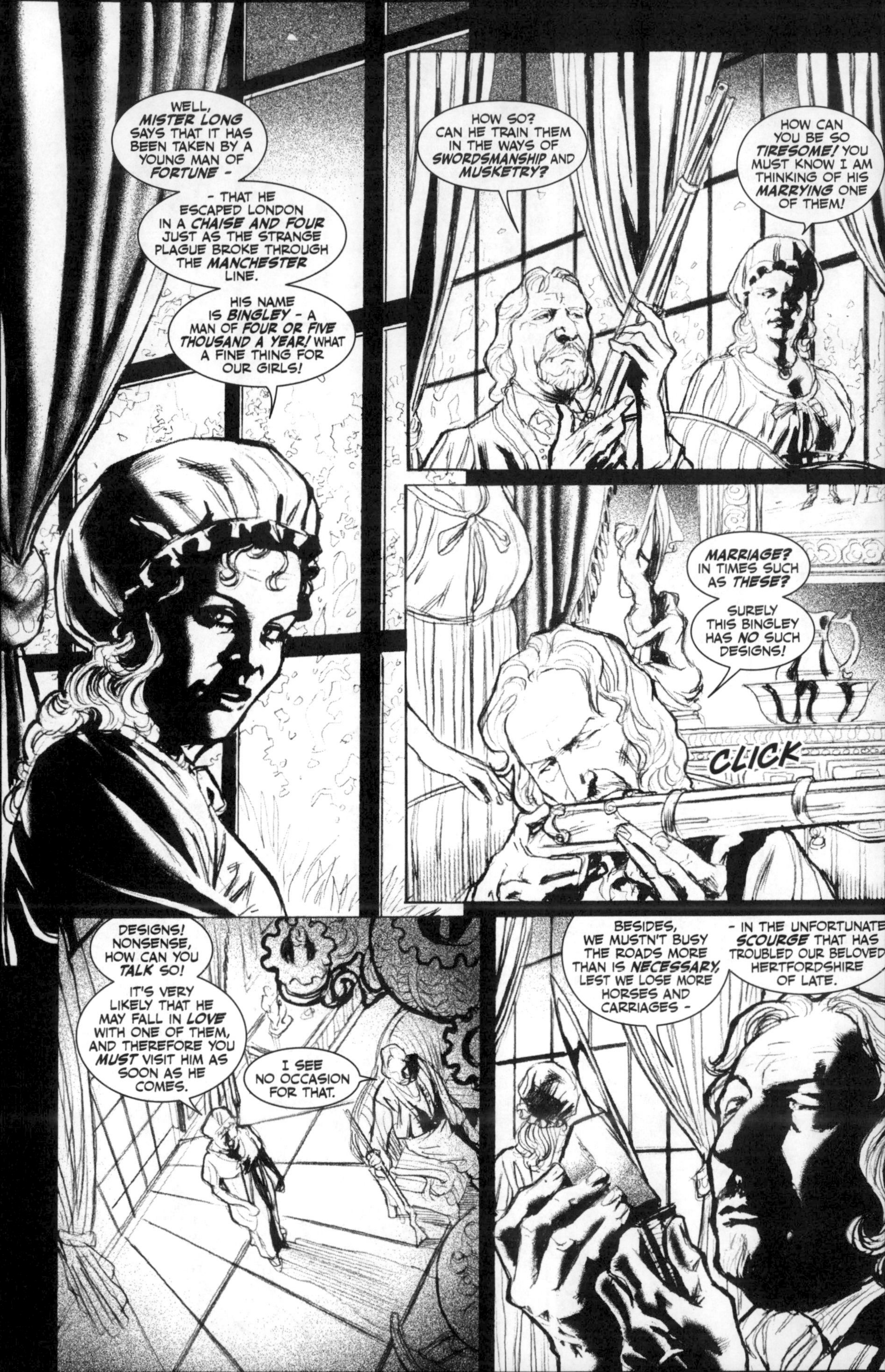
WELL, MISTER LONG SAYS THAT IT HAS BEEN TAKEN BY A YOUNG MAN OF FORTUNE -
- THAT HE ESCAPED LONDON IN A CHAISE AND FOUR JUST AS THE STRANGE PLAGUE BROKE THROUGH THE MANCHESTER LINE.
HIS NAME IS BINGLEY - A MAN OF FOUR OR FIVE THOUSAND A YEAR! WHAT A FINE THING FOR OUR GIRLS!
HOW SO? CAN HE TRAIN THEM IN THE WAYS OF SWORDSMANSHIP AND MUSKETRY?
HOW CAN YOU BE SO TIRESOME! YOU MUST KNOW I AM THINKING OF HIS MARRYING ONE OF THEM!
MARRIAGE? IN TIMES SUCH AS THESE?
SURELY THIS BINGLEY HAS NO SUCH DESIGNS!
CLICK
DESIGNS! NONSENSE, HOW CAN YOU TALK SO!
IT'S VERY LIKELY THAT HE MAY FALL IN LOVE WITH ONE OF THEM, AND THEREFORE YOU MUST VISIT HIM AS SOON AS HE COMES.
I SEE NO OCCASION FOR THAT.
BESIDES, WE MUSTN'T BUSY THE ROADS MORE THAN IS NECESSARY, LEST WE LOSE MORE HORSES AND CARRIAGES -
- IN THE UNFORTUNATE SCOURGE THAT HAS TROUBLED OUR BELOVED HERTFORDSHIRE OF LATE.

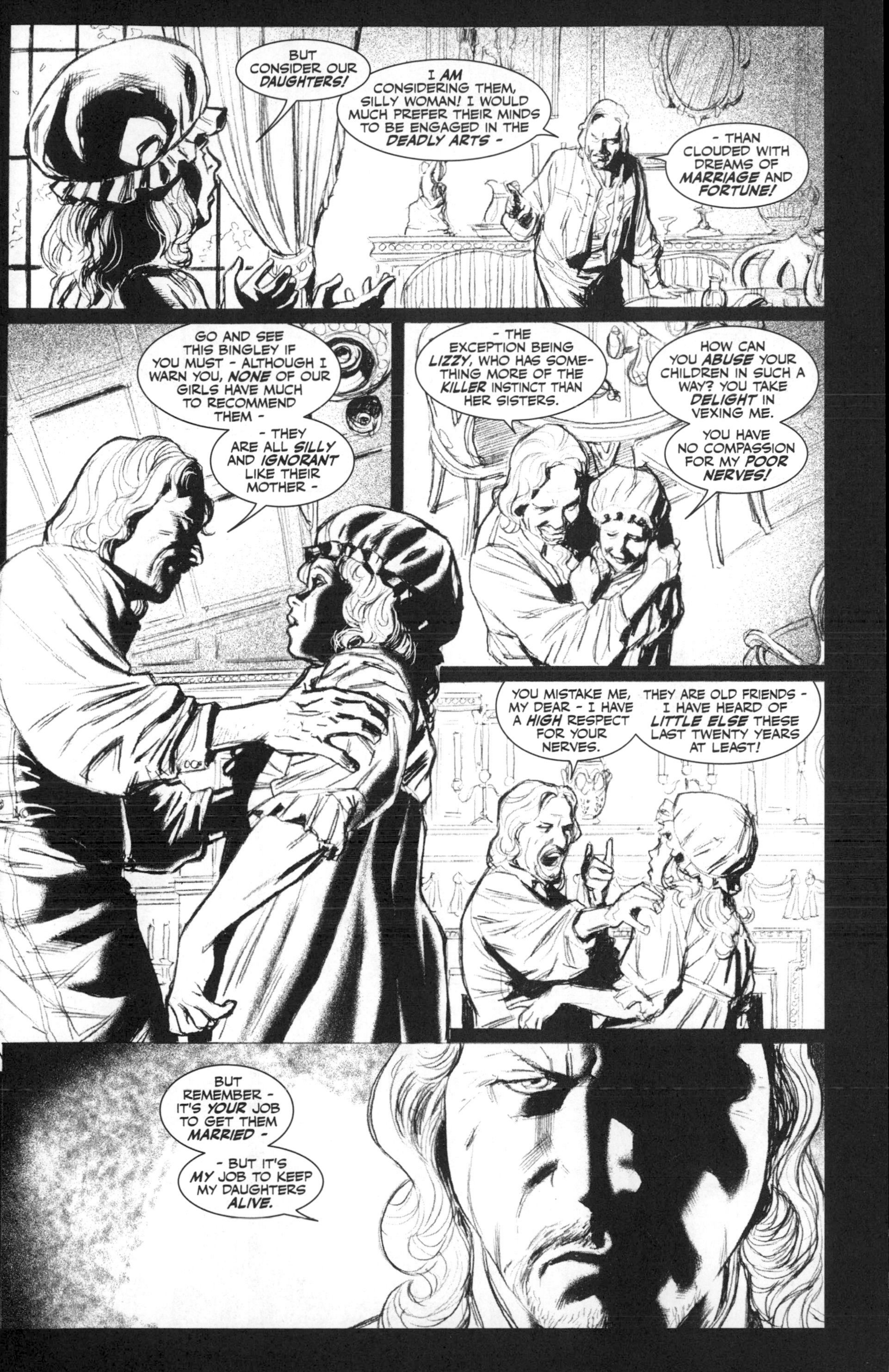
BUT CONSIDER OUR *DAUGHTERS!*
I *AM* CONSIDERING THEM, SILLY WOMAN! I WOULD MUCH PREFER THEIR MINDS TO BE ENGAGED IN THE *DEADLY ARTS* -
- THAN CLOUDED WITH DREAMS OF *MARRIAGE* AND *FORTUNE!*
GO AND SEE THIS BINGLEY IF YOU MUST - ALTHOUGH I WARN YOU, *NONE* OF OUR GIRLS HAVE MUCH TO RECOMMEND THEM -
- THEY ARE ALL *SILLY* AND *IGNORANT* LIKE THEIR MOTHER -
- THE EXCEPTION BEING *LIZZY*, WHO HAS SOMETHING MORE OF THE *KILLER* INSTINCT THAN HER SISTERS.
HOW CAN YOU *ABUSE* YOUR CHILDREN IN SUCH A WAY? YOU TAKE *DELIGHT* IN VEXING ME.
YOU HAVE NO COMPASSION FOR MY *POOR NERVES!*
YOU MISTAKE ME, MY DEAR - I HAVE A *HIGH* RESPECT FOR YOUR NERVES.
THEY ARE OLD FRIENDS - I HAVE HEARD OF *LITTLE ELSE* THESE LAST TWENTY YEARS AT LEAST!
BUT REMEMBER - IT'S *YOUR* JOB TO GET THEM *MARRIED* -
- BUT IT'S *MY* JOB TO KEEP MY DAUGHTERS *ALIVE.*

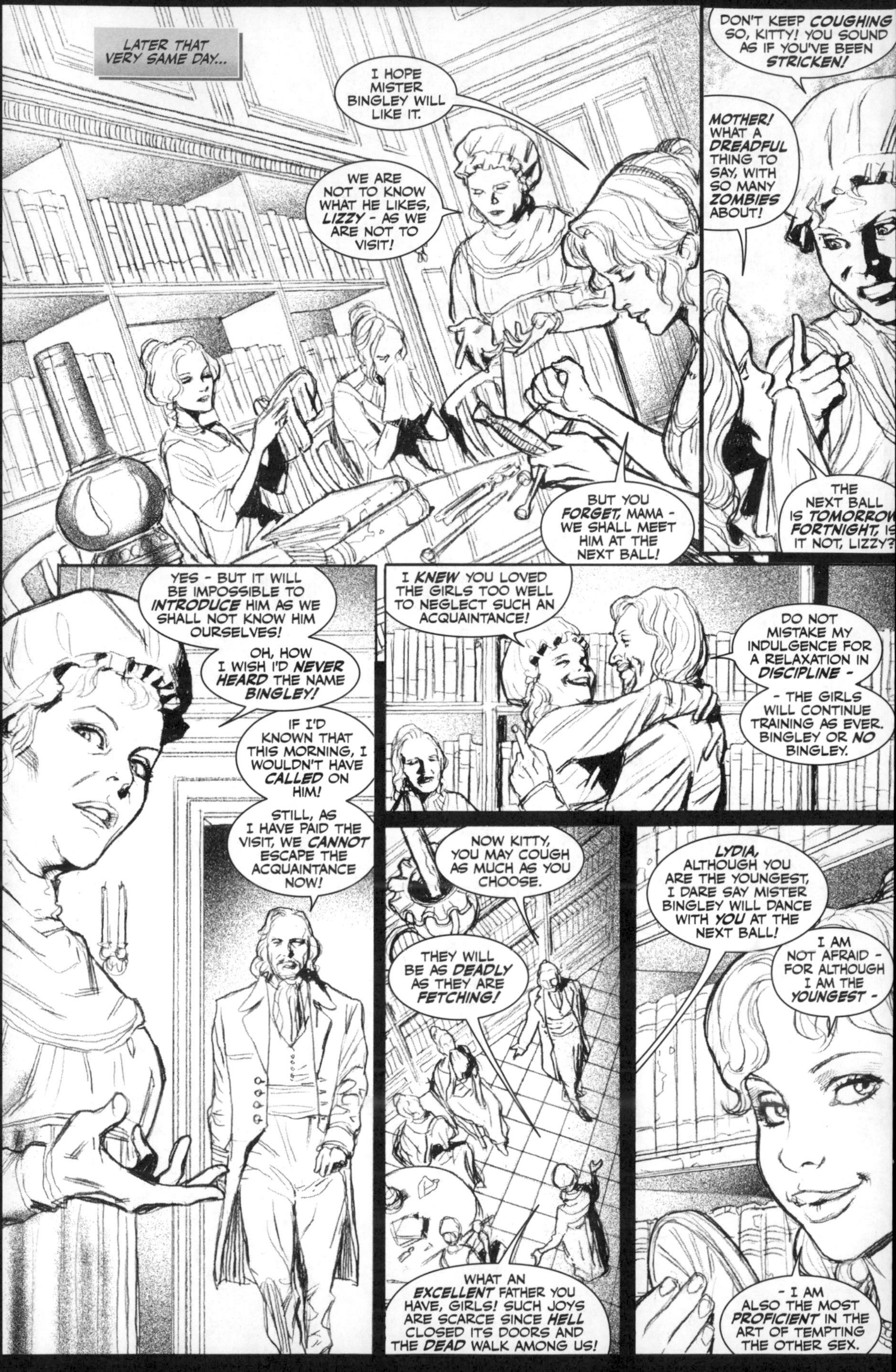
LATER THAT VERY SAME DAY...
I HOPE MISTER BINGLEY WILL LIKE IT.
WE ARE NOT TO KNOW WHAT HE LIKES, LIZZY - AS WE ARE NOT TO VISIT!
BUT YOU FORGET, MAMA - WE SHALL MEET HIM AT THE NEXT BALL!
DON'T KEEP COUGHING SO, KITTY! YOU SOUND AS IF YOU'VE BEEN STRICKEN!
MOTHER! WHAT A DREADFUL THING TO SAY, WITH SO MANY ZOMBIES ABOUT!
THE NEXT BALL IS TOMORROW FORTNIGHT, IS IT NOT, LIZZY?
YES - BUT IT WILL BE IMPOSSIBLE TO INTRODUCE HIM AS WE SHALL NOT KNOW HIM OURSELVES!
OH, HOW I WISH I'D NEVER HEARD THE NAME BINGLEY!
IF I'D KNOWN THAT THIS MORNING, I WOULDN'T HAVE CALLED ON HIM!
STILL, AS I HAVE PAID THE VISIT, WE CANNOT ESCAPE THE ACQUAINTANCE NOW!
I KNEW YOU LOVED THE GIRLS TOO WELL TO NEGLECT SUCH AN ACQUAINTANCE!
DO NOT MISTAKE MY INDULGENCE FOR A RELAXATION IN DISCIPLINE -
- THE GIRLS WILL CONTINUE TRAINING AS EVER. BINGLEY OR NO BINGLEY.
NOW KITTY, YOU MAY COUGH AS MUCH AS YOU CHOOSE.
THEY WILL BE AS DEADLY AS THEY ARE FETCHING!
WHAT AN EXCELLENT FATHER YOU HAVE, GIRLS! SUCH JOYS ARE SCARCE SINCE HELL CLOSED ITS DOORS AND THE DEAD WALK AMONG US!
LYDIA, ALTHOUGH YOU ARE THE YOUNGEST, I DARE SAY MISTER BINGLEY WILL DANCE WITH YOU AT THE NEXT BALL!
I AM NOT AFRAID - FOR ALTHOUGH I AM THE YOUNGEST -
- I AM ALSO THE MOST PROFICIENT IN THE ART OF TEMPTING THE OTHER SEX.

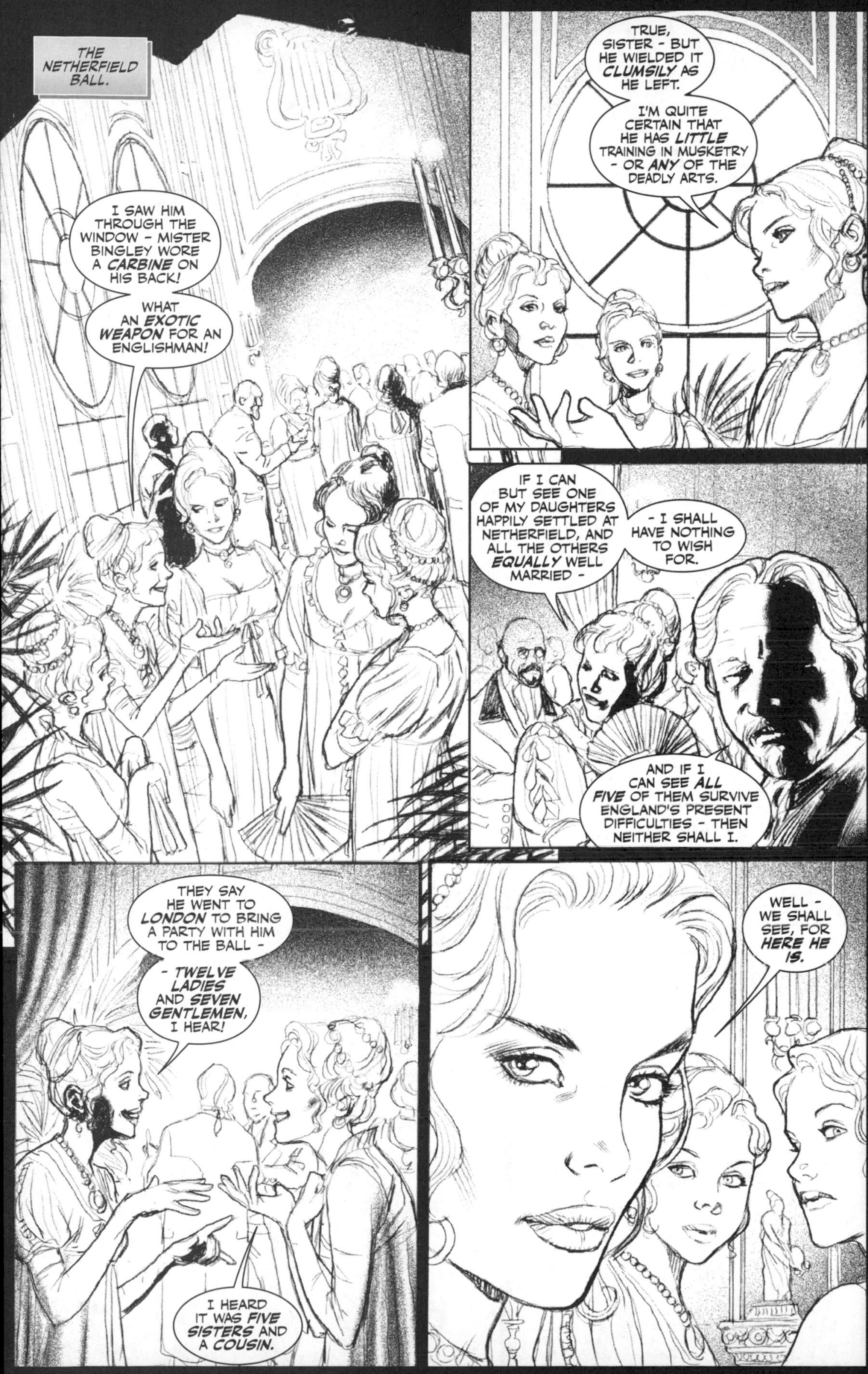
THE NETHERFIELD BALL.
I SAW HIM THROUGH THE WINDOW - MISTER BINGLEY WORE A CARBINE ON HIS BACK!
WHAT AN EXOTIC WEAPON FOR AN ENGLISHMAN!
TRUE, SISTER - BUT HE WIELDED IT CLUMSILY AS HE LEFT.
I'M QUITE CERTAIN THAT HE HAS LITTLE TRAINING IN MUSKETRY - OR ANY OF THE DEADLY ARTS.
IF I CAN BUT SEE ONE OF MY DAUGHTERS HAPPILY SETTLED AT NETHERFIELD, AND ALL THE OTHERS EQUALLY WELL MARRIED -
- I SHALL HAVE NOTHING TO WISH FOR.
AND IF I CAN SEE ALL FIVE OF THEM SURVIVE ENGLAND'S PRESENT DIFFICULTIES - THEN NEITHER SHALL I.
THEY SAY HE WENT TO LONDON TO BRING A PARTY WITH HIM TO THE BALL -
- TWELVE LADIES AND SEVEN GENTLEMEN, I HEAR!
I HEARD IT WAS FIVE SISTERS AND A COUSIN.
WELL - WE SHALL SEE, FOR HERE HE IS.

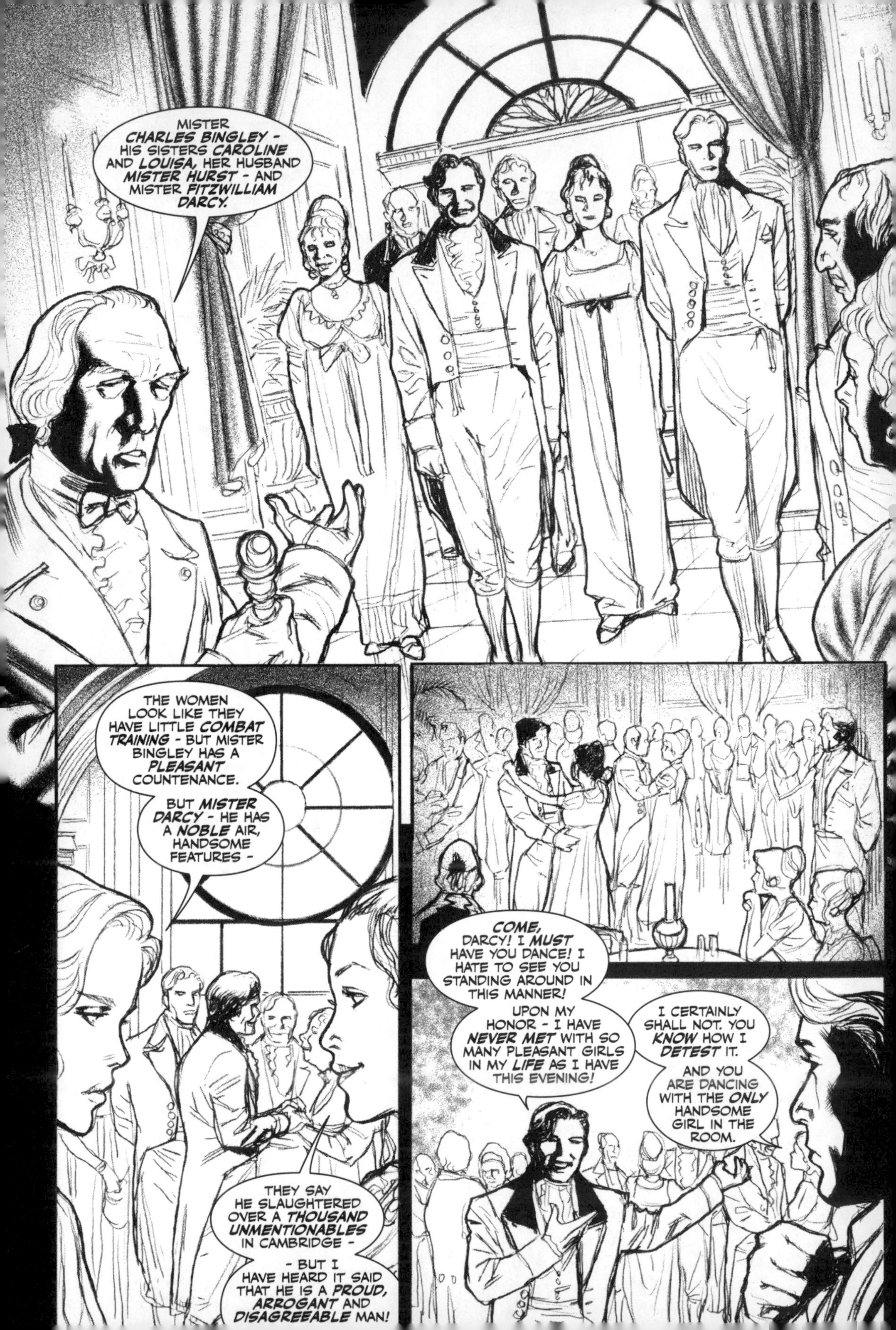
MISTER CHARLES BINGLEY - HIS SISTERS CAROLINE AND LOUISA, HER HUSBAND MISTER HURST - AND MISTER FITZWILLIAM DARCY.
THE WOMEN LOOK LIKE THEY HAVE LITTLE COMBAT TRAINING - BUT MISTER BINGLEY HAS A PLEASANT COUNTENANCE.
BUT MISTER DARCY - HE HAS A NOBLE AIR, HANDSOME FEATURES -
THEY SAY HE SLAUGHTERED OVER A THOUSAND UNMENTIONABLES IN CAMBRIDGE -
- BUT I HAVE HEARD IT SAID THAT HE IS A PROUD, ARROGANT AND DISAGREEABLE MAN!
COME, DARCY! I MUST HAVE YOU DANCE! I HATE TO SEE YOU STANDING AROUND IN THIS MANNER!
I CERTAINLY SHALL NOT. YOU KNOW HOW I DETEST IT.
AND YOU ARE DANCING WITH THE ONLY HANDSOME GIRL IN THE ROOM.
UPON MY HONOR - I HAVE NEVER MET WITH SO MANY PLEASANT GIRLS IN MY LIFE AS I HAVE THIS EVENING!

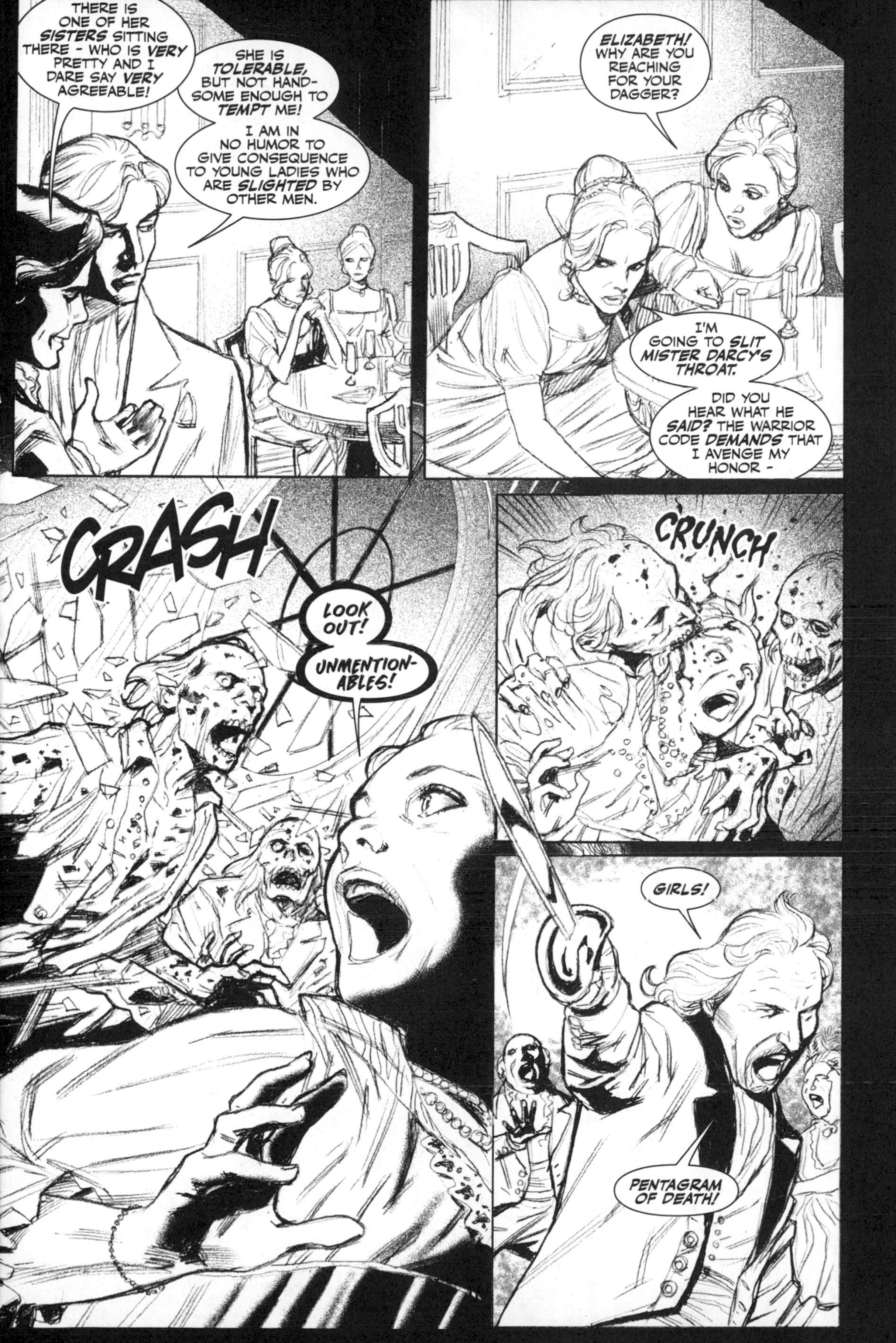
THERE IS ONE OF HER SISTERS SITTING THERE - WHO IS VERY PRETTY AND I DARE SAY VERY AGREEABLE!
SHE IS TOLERABLE, BUT NOT HAND-SOME ENOUGH TO TEMPT ME!
I AM IN NO HUMOR TO GIVE CONSEQUENCE TO YOUNG LADIES WHO ARE SLIGHTED BY OTHER MEN.
ELIZABETH! WHY ARE YOU REACHING FOR YOUR DAGGER?
I'M GOING TO SLIT MISTER DARCY'S THROAT.
DID YOU HEAR WHAT HE SAID? THE WARRIOR CODE DEMANDS THAT I AVENGE MY HONOR -
CRASH
LOOK OUT!
UNMENTION-ABLES!
CRUNCH
GIRLS!
PENTAGRAM OF DEATH!

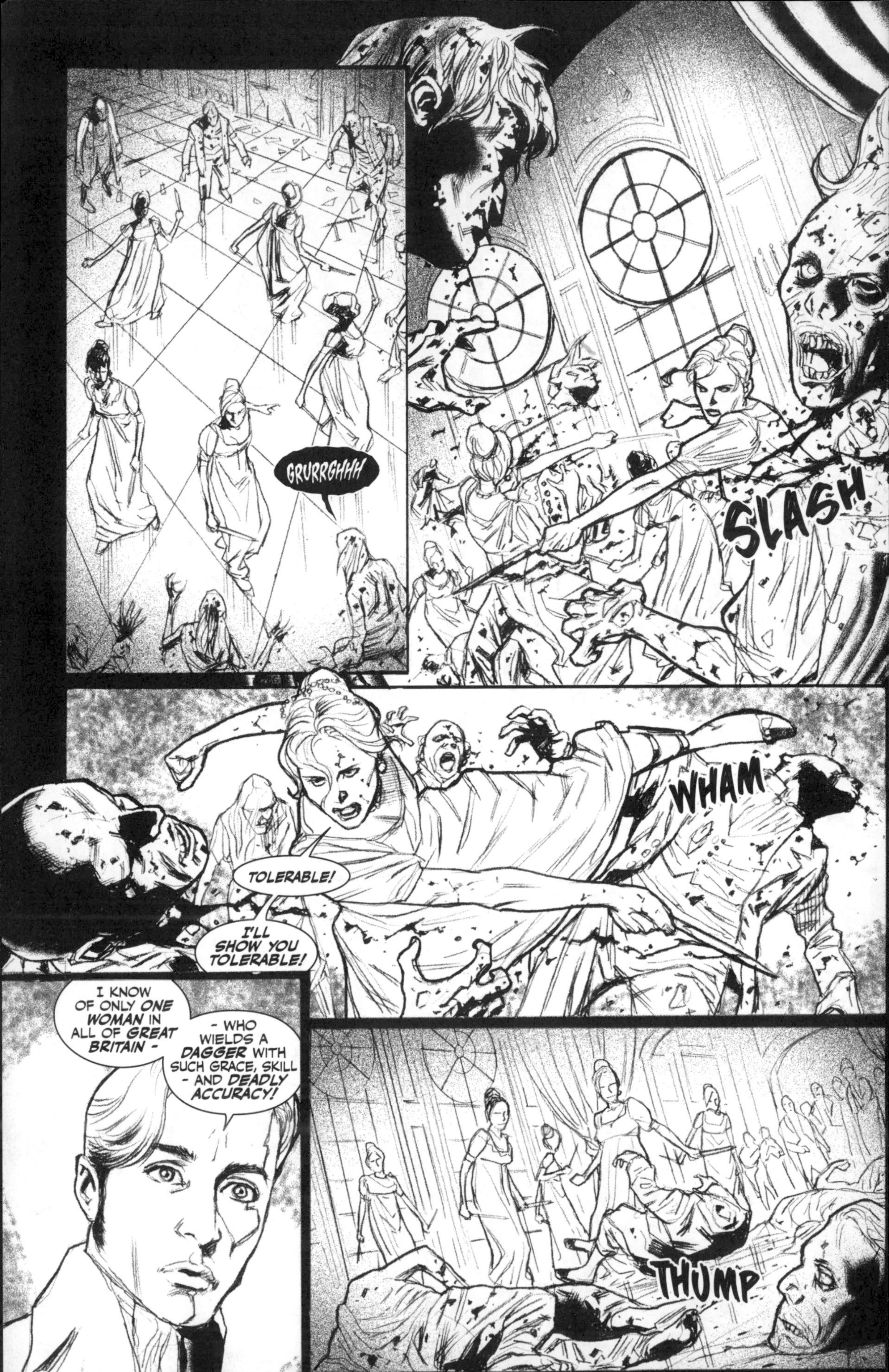
GRURRGHHH
SLASH
WHAM
TOLERABLE!
I'LL SHOW YOU TOLERABLE!
I KNOW OF ONLY ONE WOMAN IN ALL OF GREAT BRITAIN -
- WHO WIELDS A DAGGER WITH SUCH GRACE, SKILL - AND DEADLY ACCURACY!
THUMP

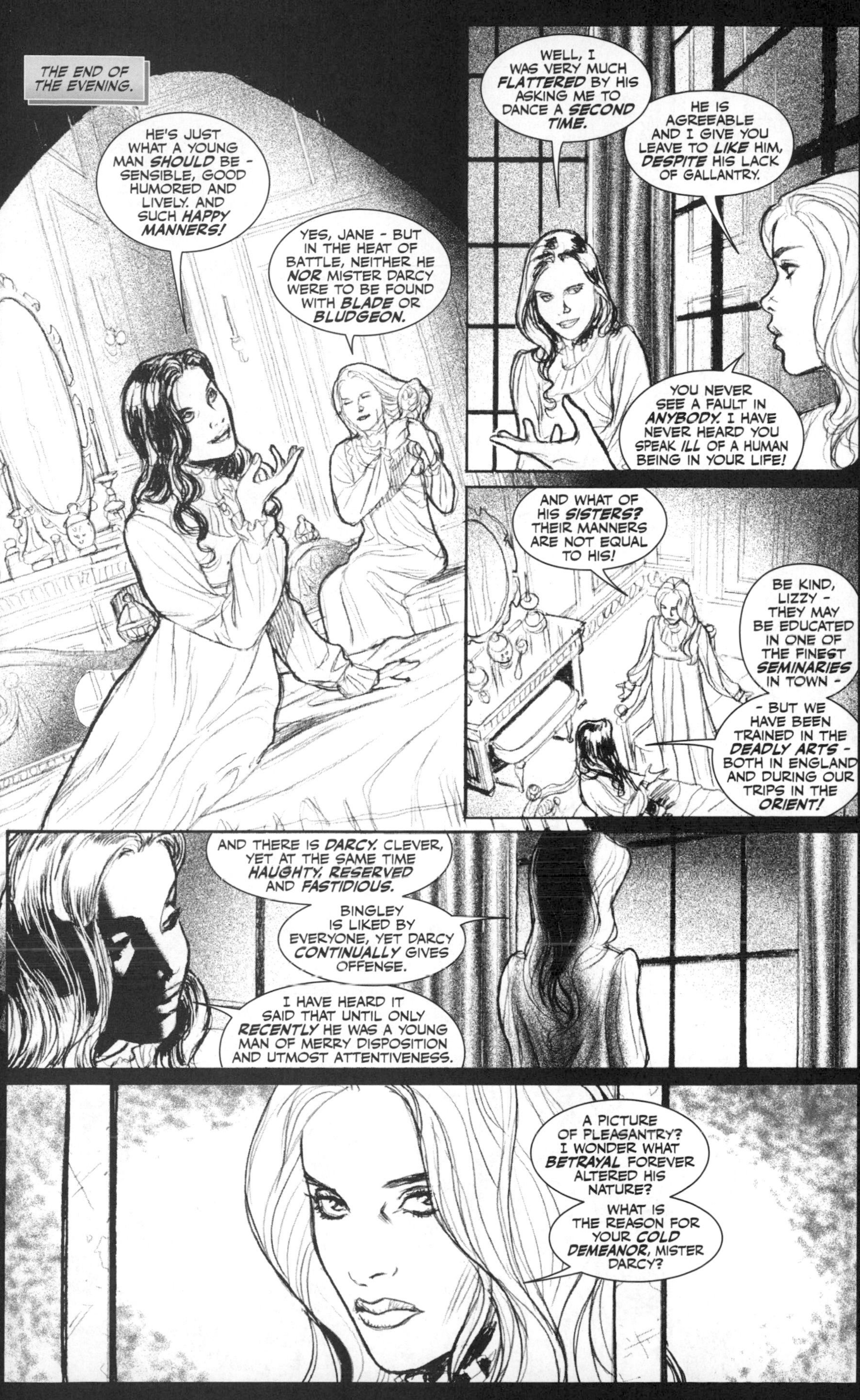
THE END OF THE EVENING.
HE'S JUST WHAT A YOUNG MAN SHOULD BE - SENSIBLE, GOOD HUMORED AND LIVELY. AND SUCH HAPPY MANNERS!
YES, JANE - BUT IN THE HEAT OF BATTLE, NEITHER HE NOR MISTER DARCY WERE TO BE FOUND WITH BLADE OR BLUDGEON.
WELL, I WAS VERY MUCH FLATTERED BY HIS ASKING ME TO DANCE A SECOND TIME.
HE IS AGREEABLE AND I GIVE YOU LEAVE TO LIKE HIM, DESPITE HIS LACK OF GALLANTRY.
YOU NEVER SEE A FAULT IN ANYBODY. I HAVE NEVER HEARD YOU SPEAK ILL OF A HUMAN BEING IN YOUR LIFE!
AND WHAT OF HIS SISTERS? THEIR MANNERS ARE NOT EQUAL TO HIS!
BE KIND, LIZZY - THEY MAY BE EDUCATED IN ONE OF THE FINEST SEMINARIES IN TOWN -
- BUT WE HAVE BEEN TRAINED IN THE DEADLY ARTS - BOTH IN ENGLAND AND DURING OUR TRIPS IN THE ORIENT!
AND THERE IS DARCY. CLEVER, YET AT THE SAME TIME HAUGHTY, RESERVED AND FASTIDIOUS.
BINGLEY IS LIKED BY EVERYONE, YET DARCY CONTINUALLY GIVES OFFENSE.
I HAVE HEARD IT SAID THAT UNTIL ONLY RECENTLY HE WAS A YOUNG MAN OF MERRY DISPOSITION AND UTMOST ATTENTIVENESS.
A PICTURE OF PLEASANTRY? I WONDER WHAT BETRAYAL FOREVER ALTERED HIS NATURE?
WHAT IS THE REASON FOR YOUR COLD DEMEANOR, MISTER DARCY?

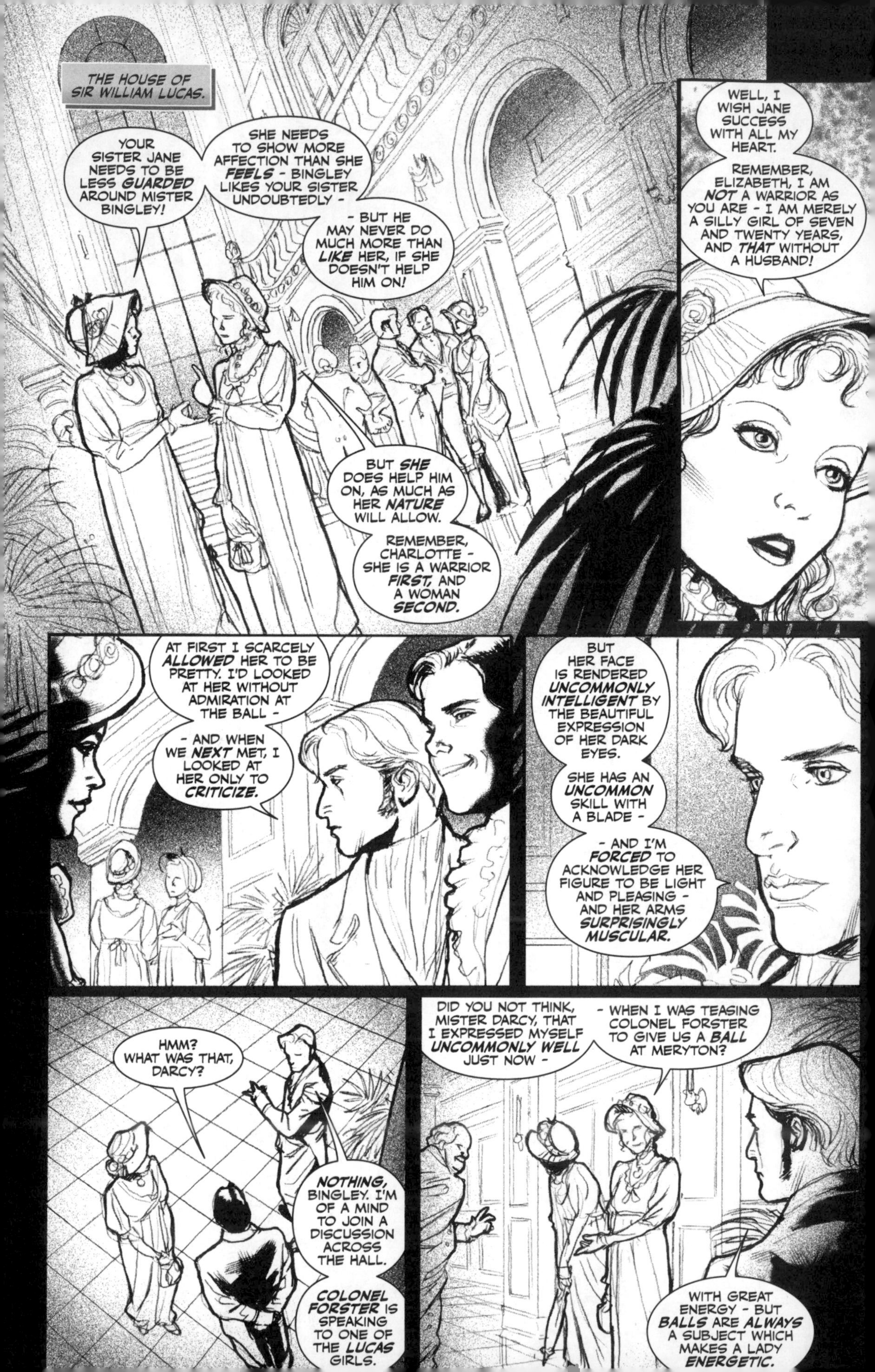
THE HOUSE OF SIR WILLIAM LUCAS.
YOUR SISTER JANE NEEDS TO BE LESS GUARDED AROUND MISTER BINGLEY!
SHE NEEDS TO SHOW MORE AFFECTION THAN SHE FEELS - BINGLEY LIKES YOUR SISTER UNDOUBTEDLY -
- BUT HE MAY NEVER DO MUCH MORE THAN LIKE HER, IF SHE DOESN'T HELP HIM ON!
BUT SHE DOES HELP HIM ON, AS MUCH AS HER NATURE WILL ALLOW.
REMEMBER, CHARLOTTE - SHE IS A WARRIOR FIRST, AND A WOMAN SECOND.
WELL, I WISH JANE SUCCESS WITH ALL MY HEART.
REMEMBER, ELIZABETH, I AM NOT A WARRIOR AS YOU ARE - I AM MERELY A SILLY GIRL OF SEVEN AND TWENTY YEARS, AND THAT WITHOUT A HUSBAND!
AT FIRST I SCARCELY ALLOWED HER TO BE PRETTY. I'D LOOKED AT HER WITHOUT ADMIRATION AT THE BALL -
- AND WHEN WE NEXT MET, I LOOKED AT HER ONLY TO CRITICIZE.
BUT HER FACE IS RENDERED UNCOMMONLY INTELLIGENT BY THE BEAUTIFUL EXPRESSION OF HER DARK EYES.
SHE HAS AN UNCOMMON SKILL WITH A BLADE -
- AND I'M FORCED TO ACKNOWLEDGE HER FIGURE TO BE LIGHT AND PLEASING - AND HER ARMS SURPRISINGLY MUSCULAR.
HMM? WHAT WAS THAT, DARCY?
NOTHING, BINGLEY. I'M OF A MIND TO JOIN A DISCUSSION ACROSS THE HALL.
COLONEL FORSTER IS SPEAKING TO ONE OF THE LUCAS GIRLS.
DID YOU NOT THINK, MISTER DARCY, THAT I EXPRESSED MYSELF UNCOMMONLY WELL JUST NOW -
- WHEN I WAS TEASING COLONEL FORSTER TO GIVE US A BALL AT MERYTON?
WITH GREAT ENERGY - BUT BALLS ARE ALWAYS A SUBJECT WHICH MAKES A LADY ENERGETIC.

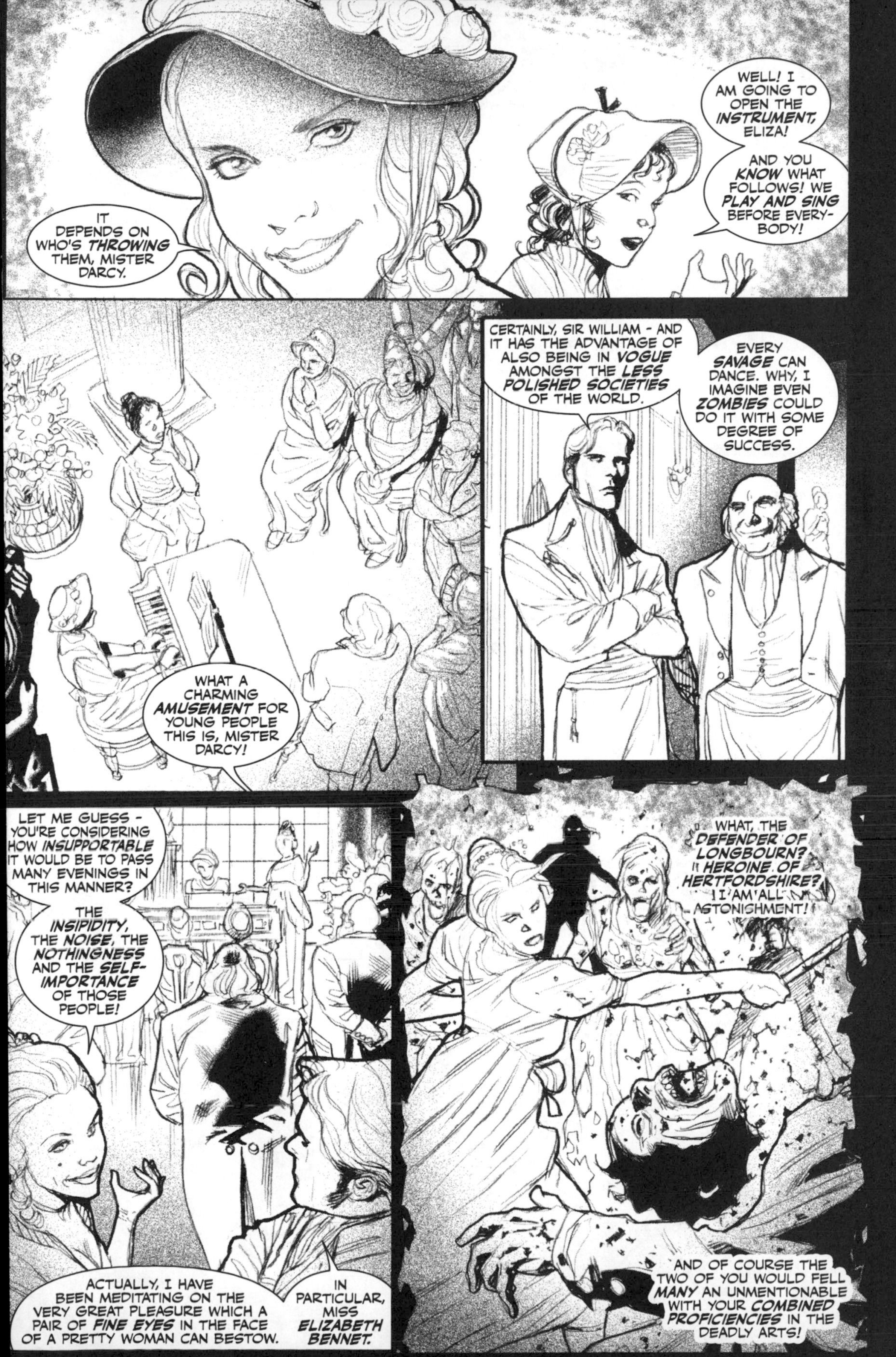
WELL! I AM GOING TO OPEN THE *INSTRUMENT,* ELIZA!
AND YOU *KNOW* WHAT FOLLOWS! WE *PLAY AND SING* BEFORE EVERY-BODY!
IT DEPENDS ON WHO'S *THROWING* THEM, MISTER DARCY.
WHAT A CHARMING *AMUSEMENT* FOR YOUNG PEOPLE THIS IS, MISTER DARCY!
CERTAINLY, SIR WILLIAM - AND IT HAS THE ADVANTAGE OF ALSO BEING IN *VOGUE* AMONGST THE *LESS POLISHED SOCIETIES* OF THE WORLD.
EVERY *SAVAGE* CAN DANCE. WHY, I IMAGINE EVEN *ZOMBIES* COULD DO IT WITH SOME DEGREE OF SUCCESS.
LET ME GUESS - YOU'RE CONSIDERING HOW *INSUPPORTABLE* IT WOULD BE TO PASS MANY EVENINGS IN THIS MANNER?
THE *INSIPIDITY*, THE *NOISE*, THE *NOTHINGNESS* AND THE *SELF-IMPORTANCE* OF THOSE PEOPLE!
ACTUALLY, I HAVE BEEN MEDITATING ON THE VERY GREAT PLEASURE WHICH A PAIR OF *FINE EYES* IN THE FACE OF A PRETTY WOMAN CAN BESTOW.
IN PARTICULAR, MISS *ELIZABETH BENNET.*
WHAT, THE *DEFENDER OF LONGBOURN? HEROINE OF HERTFORDSHIRE?* I AM ALL ASTONISHMENT!
AND OF COURSE THE TWO OF YOU WOULD FELL *MANY* AN UNMENTIONABLE WITH YOUR *COMBINED PROFICIENCIES* IN THE DEADLY ARTS!

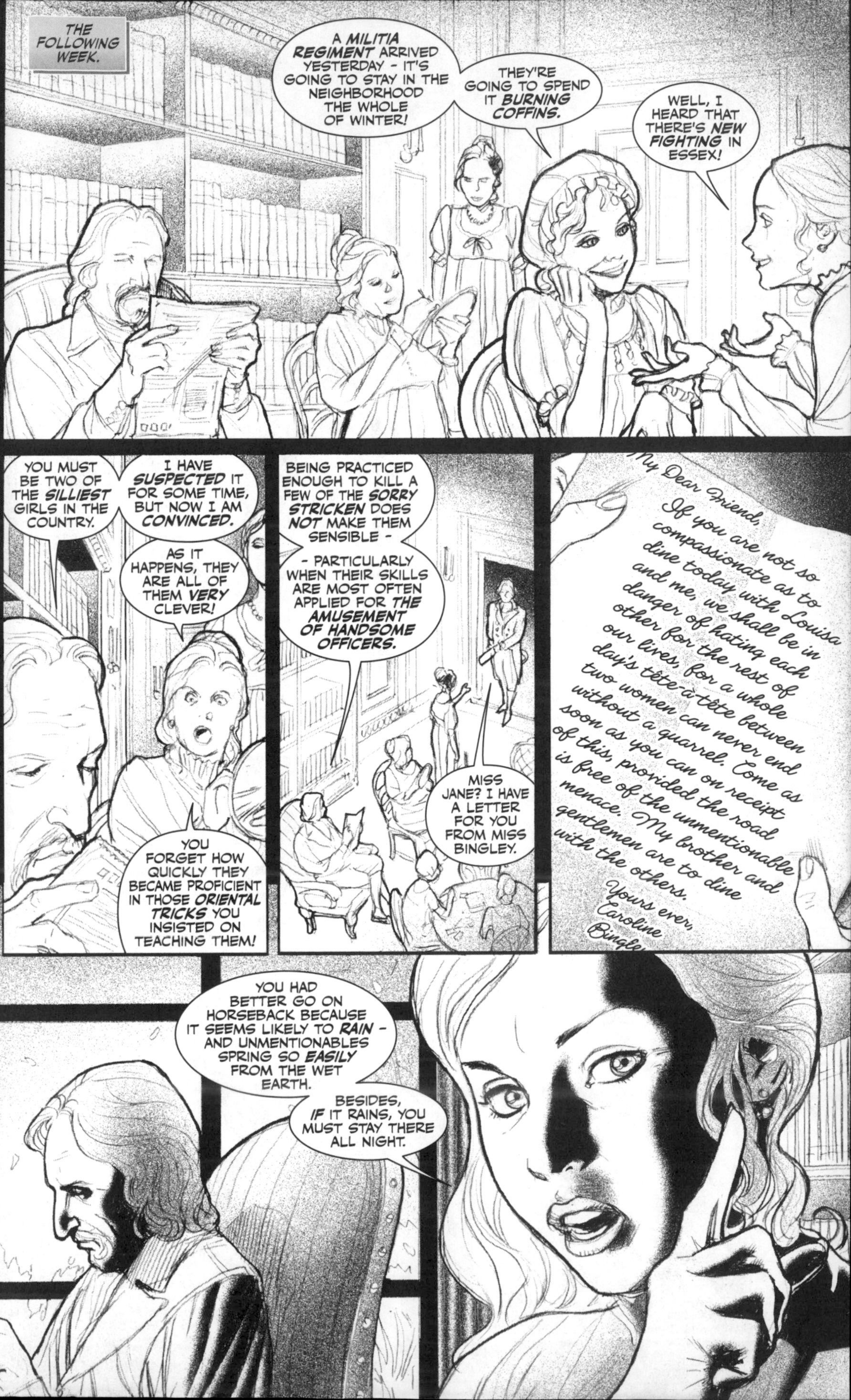
THE FOLLOWING WEEK.
A MILITIA REGIMENT ARRIVED YESTERDAY - IT'S GOING TO STAY IN THE NEIGHBORHOOD THE WHOLE OF WINTER!
THEY'RE GOING TO SPEND IT BURNING COFFINS.
WELL, I HEARD THAT THERE'S NEW FIGHTING IN ESSEX!
YOU MUST BE TWO OF THE SILLIEST GIRLS IN THE COUNTRY.
I HAVE SUSPECTED IT FOR SOME TIME, BUT NOW I AM CONVINCED.
AS IT HAPPENS, THEY ARE ALL OF THEM VERY CLEVER!
YOU FORGET HOW QUICKLY THEY BECAME PROFICIENT IN THOSE ORIENTAL TRICKS YOU INSISTED ON TEACHING THEM!
BEING PRACTICED ENOUGH TO KILL A FEW OF THE SORRY STRICKEN DOES NOT MAKE THEM SENSIBLE -
- PARTICULARLY WHEN THEIR SKILLS ARE MOST OFTEN APPLIED FOR THE AMUSEMENT OF HANDSOME OFFICERS.
MISS JANE? I HAVE A LETTER FOR YOU FROM MISS BINGLEY.
My Dear Friend,
If you are not so compassionate as to dine today with Louisa and me, we shall be in danger of hating each other for the rest of our lives, for a whole day's tête-à-tête between two women can never end without a quarrel. Come as soon as you can on receipt of this, provided the road is free of the unmentionable menace. My brother and gentlemen are to dine with the others.
Yours ever,
Caroline
YOU HAD BETTER GO ON HORSEBACK BECAUSE IT SEEMS LIKELY TO RAIN - AND UNMENTIONABLES SPRING SO EASILY FROM THE WET EARTH.
BESIDES, IF IT RAINS, YOU MUST STAY THERE ALL NIGHT.

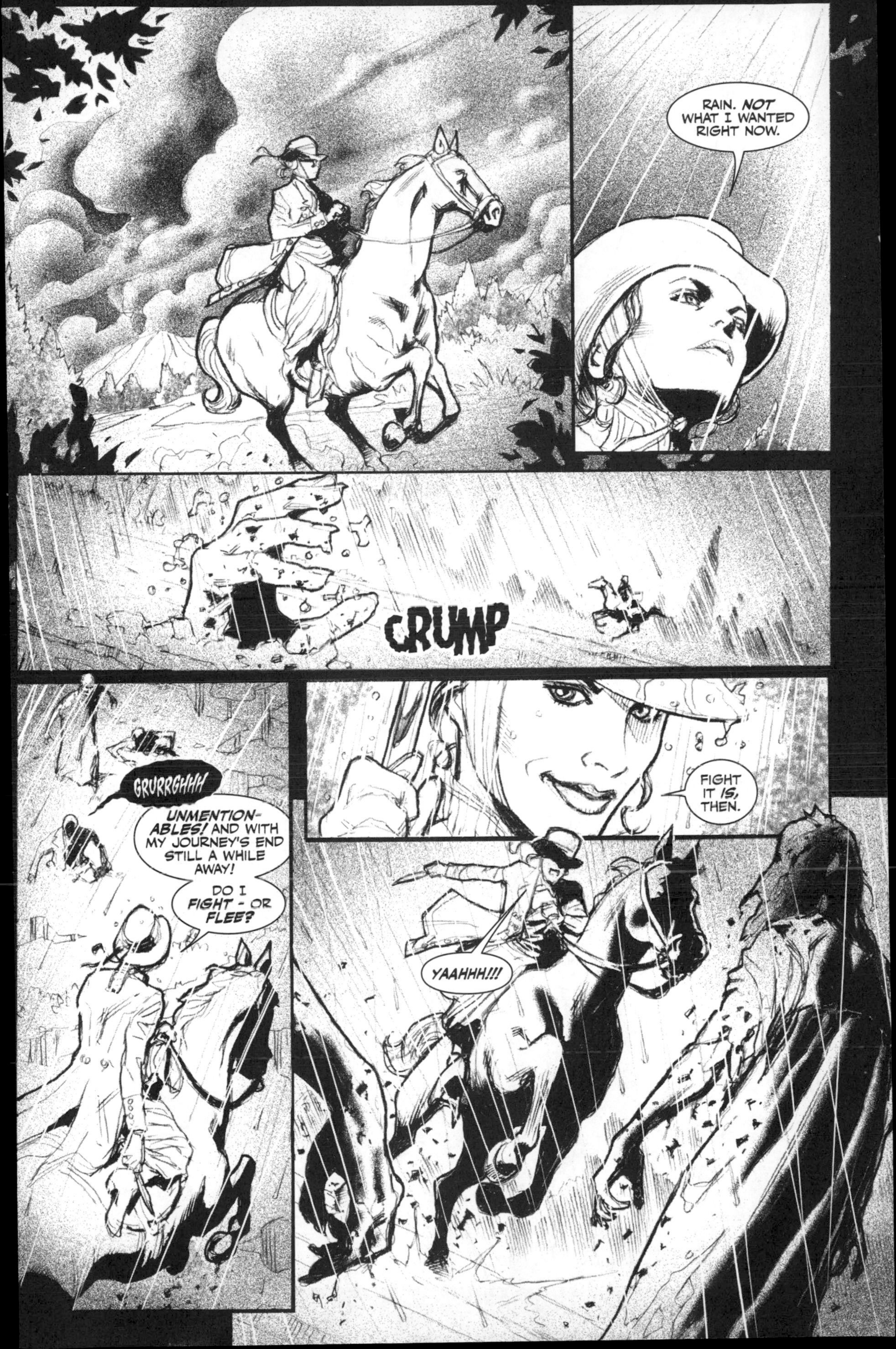
RAIN. *NOT* WHAT I WANTED RIGHT NOW.
CRUMP
GRURRGHHH
UNMENTION-ABLES! AND WITH MY JOURNEY'S END STILL A WHILE AWAY!
DO I *FIGHT* - OR *FLEE?*
FIGHT IT *IS,* THEN.
YAAHHH!!!

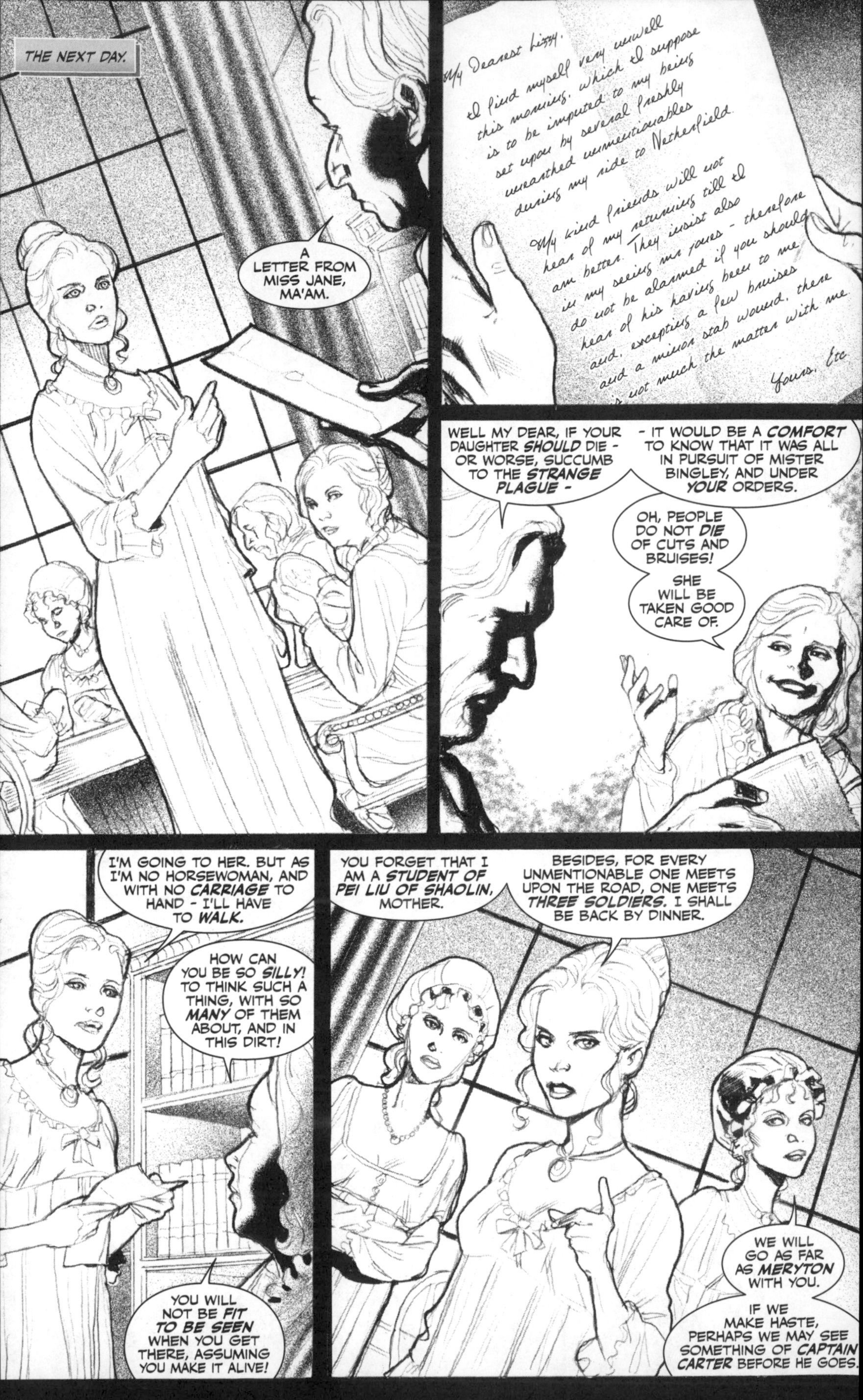
THE NEXT DAY.
A LETTER FROM MISS JANE, MA'AM.
My Dearest Lizzy,
I find myself very unwell this morning, which I suppose is to be imputed to my being set upon by several freshly unearthed unmentionables during my ride to Netherfield.
My kind friends will not hear of my returning till I am better. They insist also on my seeing Mr Jones - therefore do not be alarmed if you should hear of his having been to me and, excepting a few bruises and a minor stab wound, there not much the matter with me.
Yours, Etc
WELL MY DEAR, IF YOUR DAUGHTER SHOULD DIE - OR WORSE, SUCCUMB TO THE STRANGE PLAGUE -
- IT WOULD BE A COMFORT TO KNOW THAT IT WAS ALL IN PURSUIT OF MISTER BINGLEY, AND UNDER YOUR ORDERS.
OH, PEOPLE DO NOT DIE OF CUTS AND BRUISES!
SHE WILL BE TAKEN GOOD CARE OF.
I'M GOING TO HER. BUT AS I'M NO HORSEWOMAN, AND WITH NO CARRIAGE TO HAND - I'LL HAVE TO WALK.
HOW CAN YOU BE SO SILLY! TO THINK SUCH A THING, WITH SO MANY OF THEM ABOUT, AND IN THIS DIRT!
YOU WILL NOT BE FIT TO BE SEEN WHEN YOU GET THERE, ASSUMING YOU MAKE IT ALIVE!
YOU FORGET THAT I AM A STUDENT OF PEI LIU OF SHAOLIN, MOTHER.
BESIDES, FOR EVERY UNMENTIONABLE ONE MEETS UPON THE ROAD, ONE MEETS THREE SOLDIERS. I SHALL BE BACK BY DINNER.
WE WILL GO AS FAR AS MERYTON WITH YOU.
IF WE MAKE HASTE, PERHAPS WE MAY SEE SOMETHING OF CAPTAIN CARTER BEFORE HE GOES.

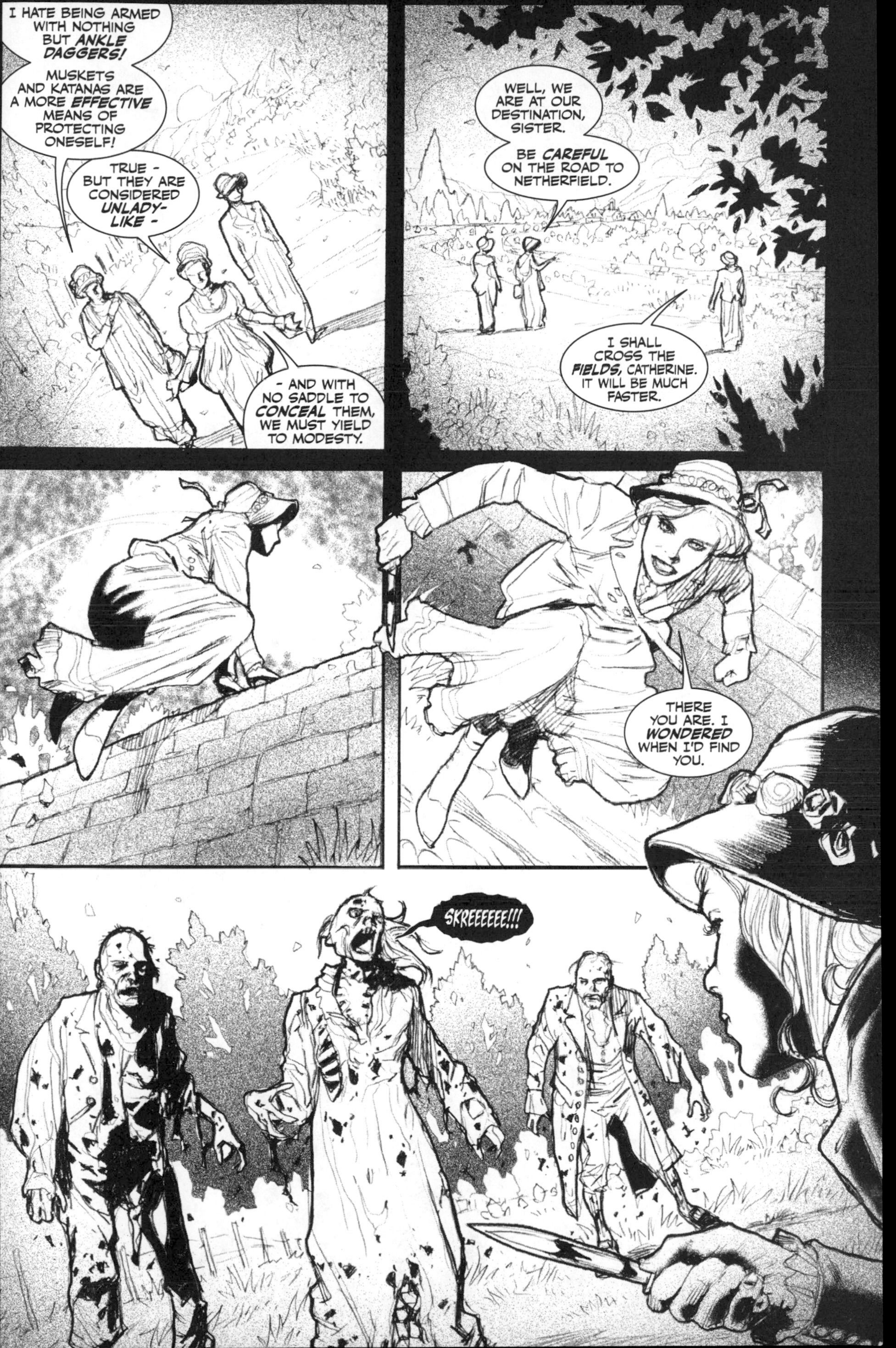
I HATE BEING ARMED WITH NOTHING BUT ANKLE DAGGERS!
MUSKETS AND KATANAS ARE A MORE EFFECTIVE MEANS OF PROTECTING ONESELF!
TRUE - BUT THEY ARE CONSIDERED UNLADY-LIKE -
- AND WITH NO SADDLE TO CONCEAL THEM, WE MUST YIELD TO MODESTY.
WELL, WE ARE AT OUR DESTINATION, SISTER.
BE CAREFUL ON THE ROAD TO NETHERFIELD.
I SHALL CROSS THE FIELDS, CATHERINE. IT WILL BE MUCH FASTER.
THERE YOU ARE. I WONDERED WHEN I'D FIND YOU.
SKREEEEEE!!!

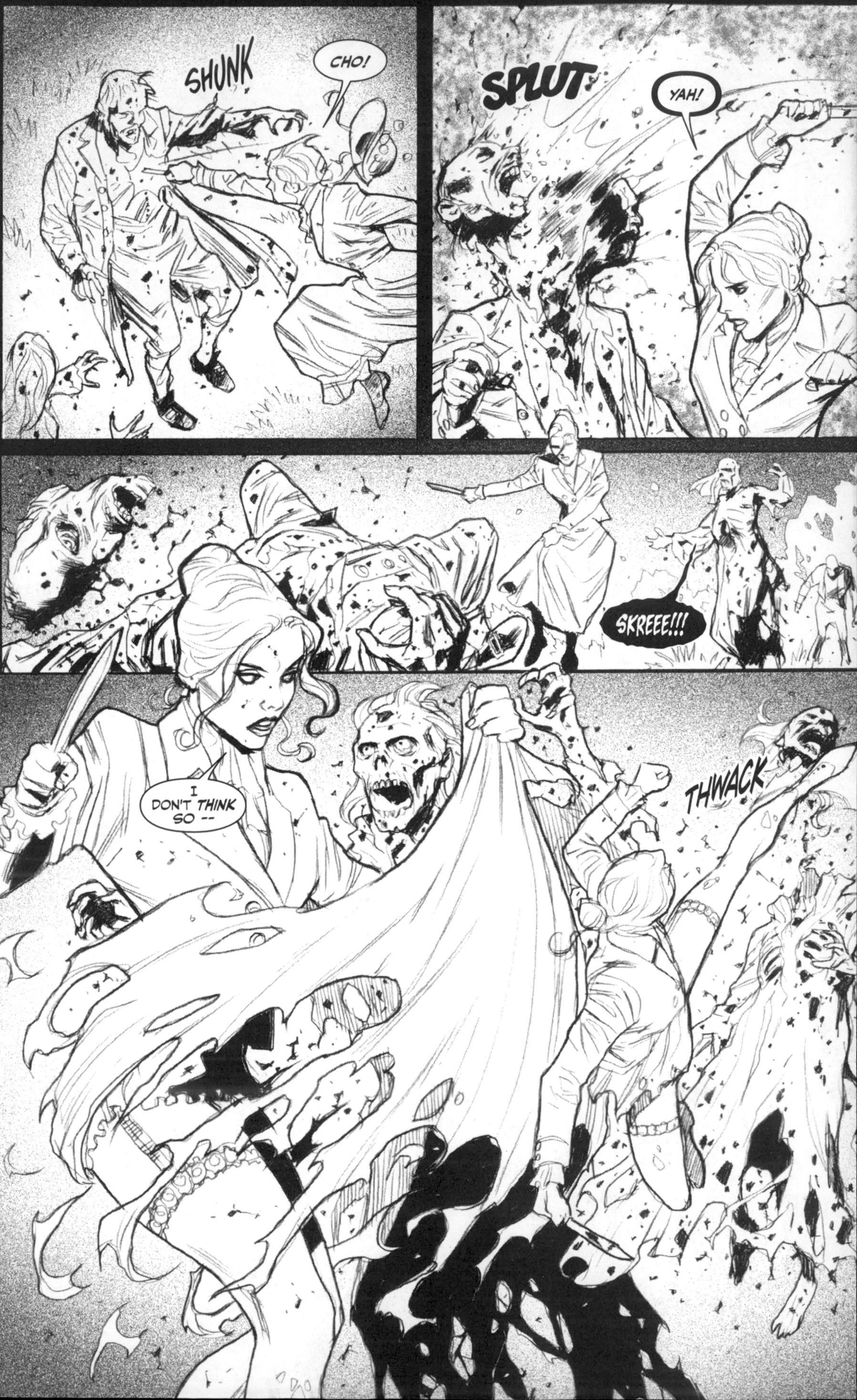
SHUNK
CHO!
SPLUT
YAH!
SKREEE!!!
I DON'T THINK SO --
THWACK

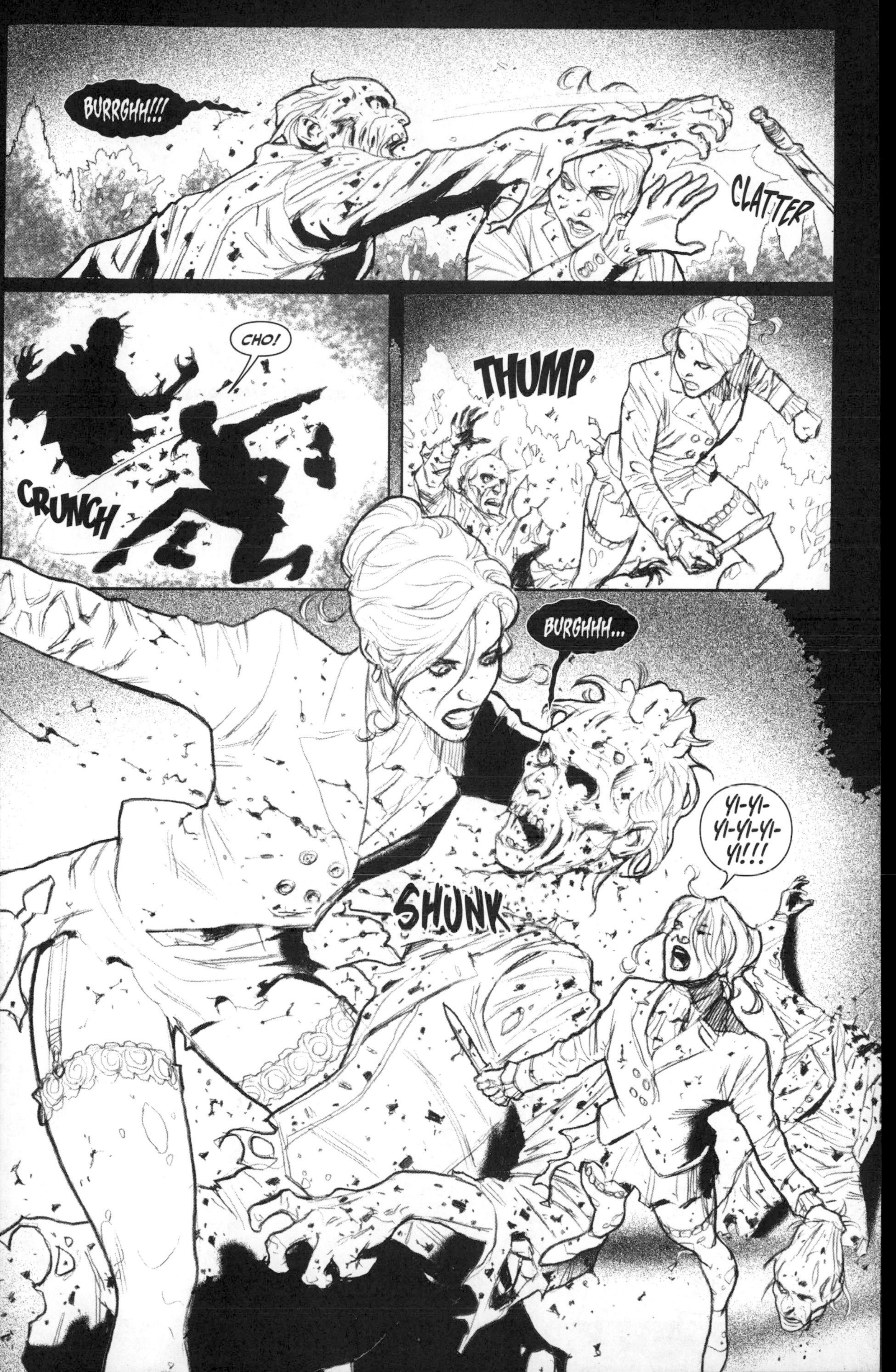
BURRGHH!!!
CLATTER
CHO!
CRUNCH
THUMP
BURGHHH...
SHUNK
YI-YI-YI-YI-YI-YI!!!

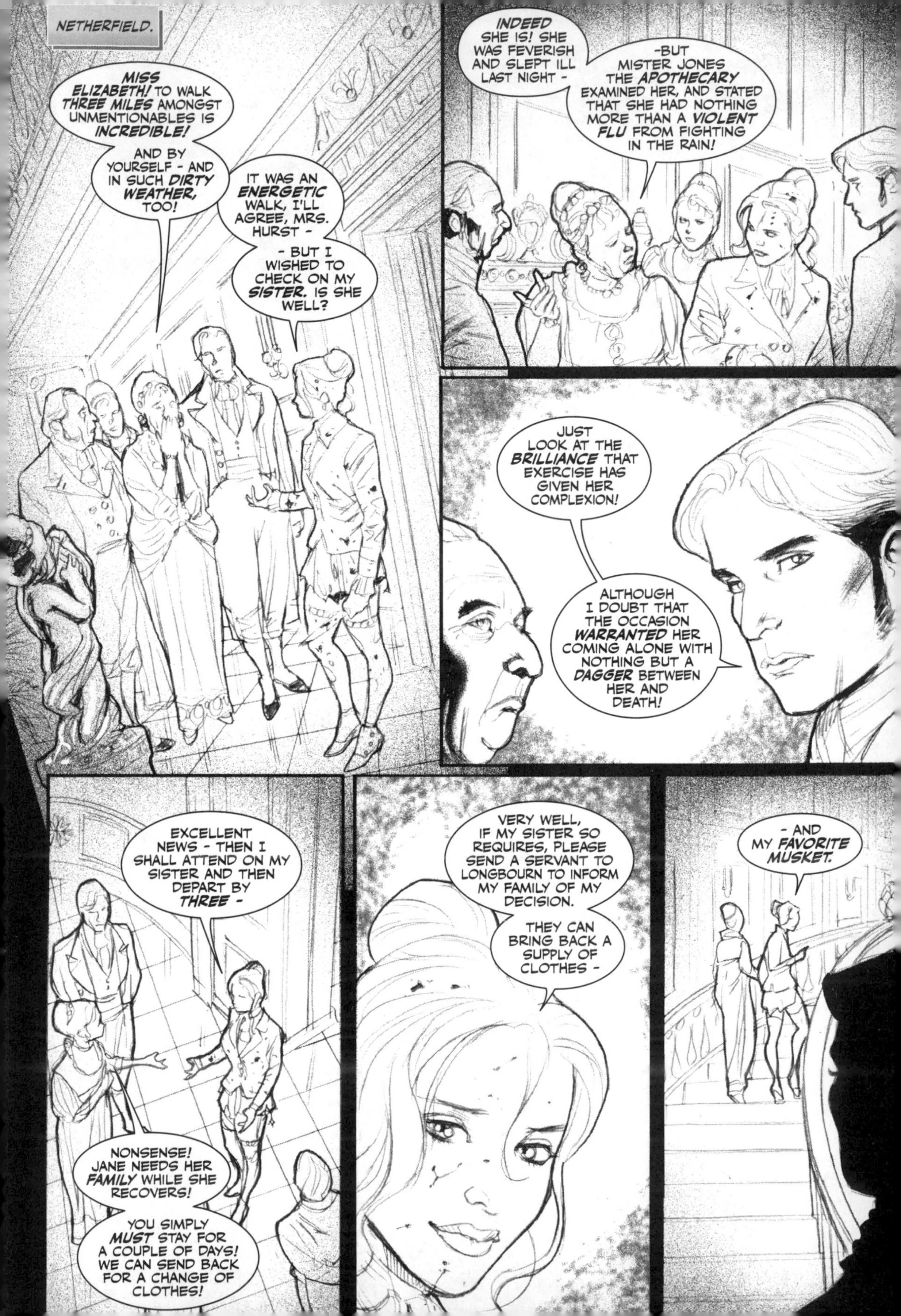
NETHERFIELD.
MISS ELIZABETH! TO WALK THREE MILES AMONGST UNMENTIONABLES IS INCREDIBLE!
AND BY YOURSELF - AND IN SUCH DIRTY WEATHER, TOO!
IT WAS AN ENERGETIC WALK, I'LL AGREE, MRS. HURST -
- BUT I WISHED TO CHECK ON MY SISTER. IS SHE WELL?
INDEED SHE IS! SHE WAS FEVERISH AND SLEPT ILL LAST NIGHT -
-BUT MISTER JONES THE APOTHECARY EXAMINED HER, AND STATED THAT SHE HAD NOTHING MORE THAN A VIOLENT FLU FROM FIGHTING IN THE RAIN!
JUST LOOK AT THE BRILLIANCE THAT EXERCISE HAS GIVEN HER COMPLEXION!
ALTHOUGH I DOUBT THAT THE OCCASION WARRANTED HER COMING ALONE WITH NOTHING BUT A DAGGER BETWEEN HER AND DEATH!
EXCELLENT NEWS - THEN I SHALL ATTEND ON MY SISTER AND THEN DEPART BY THREE -
NONSENSE! JANE NEEDS HER FAMILY WHILE SHE RECOVERS!
YOU SIMPLY MUST STAY FOR A COUPLE OF DAYS! WE CAN SEND BACK FOR A CHANGE OF CLOTHES!
VERY WELL, IF MY SISTER SO REQUIRES, PLEASE SEND A SERVANT TO LONGBOURN TO INFORM MY FAMILY OF MY DECISION.
THEY CAN BRING BACK A SUPPLY OF CLOTHES -
- AND MY FAVORITE MUSKET.

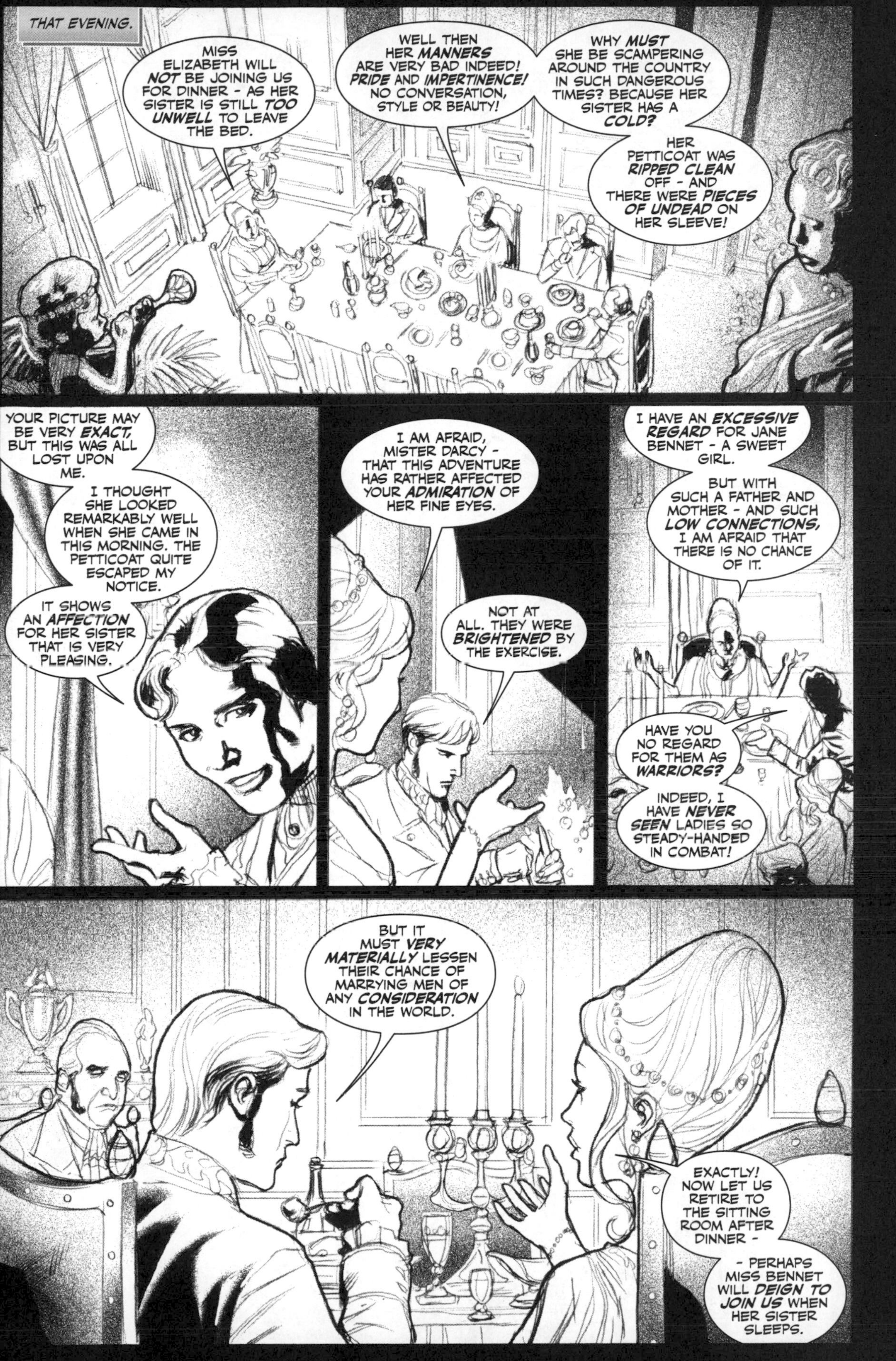
THAT EVENING.
MISS ELIZABETH WILL NOT BE JOINING US FOR DINNER - AS HER SISTER IS STILL TOO UNWELL TO LEAVE THE BED.
WELL THEN HER MANNERS ARE VERY BAD INDEED! PRIDE AND IMPERTINENCE! NO CONVERSATION, STYLE OR BEAUTY!
WHY MUST SHE BE SCAMPERING AROUND THE COUNTRY IN SUCH DANGEROUS TIMES? BECAUSE HER SISTER HAS A COLD?
HER PETTICOAT WAS RIPPED CLEAN OFF - AND THERE WERE PIECES OF UNDEAD ON HER SLEEVE!
YOUR PICTURE MAY BE VERY EXACT, BUT THIS WAS ALL LOST UPON ME.
I THOUGHT SHE LOOKED REMARKABLY WELL WHEN SHE CAME IN THIS MORNING. THE PETTICOAT QUITE ESCAPED MY NOTICE.
IT SHOWS AN AFFECTION FOR HER SISTER THAT IS VERY PLEASING.
I AM AFRAID, MISTER DARCY - THAT THIS ADVENTURE HAS RATHER AFFECTED YOUR ADMIRATION OF HER FINE EYES.
NOT AT ALL. THEY WERE BRIGHTENED BY THE EXERCISE.
I HAVE AN EXCESSIVE REGARD FOR JANE BENNET - A SWEET GIRL.
BUT WITH SUCH A FATHER AND MOTHER - AND SUCH LOW CONNECTIONS, I AM AFRAID THAT THERE IS NO CHANCE OF IT.
HAVE YOU NO REGARD FOR THEM AS WARRIORS?
INDEED, I HAVE NEVER SEEN LADIES SO STEADY-HANDED IN COMBAT!
BUT IT MUST VERY MATERIALLY LESSEN THEIR CHANCE OF MARRYING MEN OF ANY CONSIDERATION IN THE WORLD.
EXACTLY! NOW LET US RETIRE TO THE SITTING ROOM AFTER DINNER -
- PERHAPS MISS BENNET WILL DEIGN TO JOIN US WHEN HER SISTER SLEEPS.

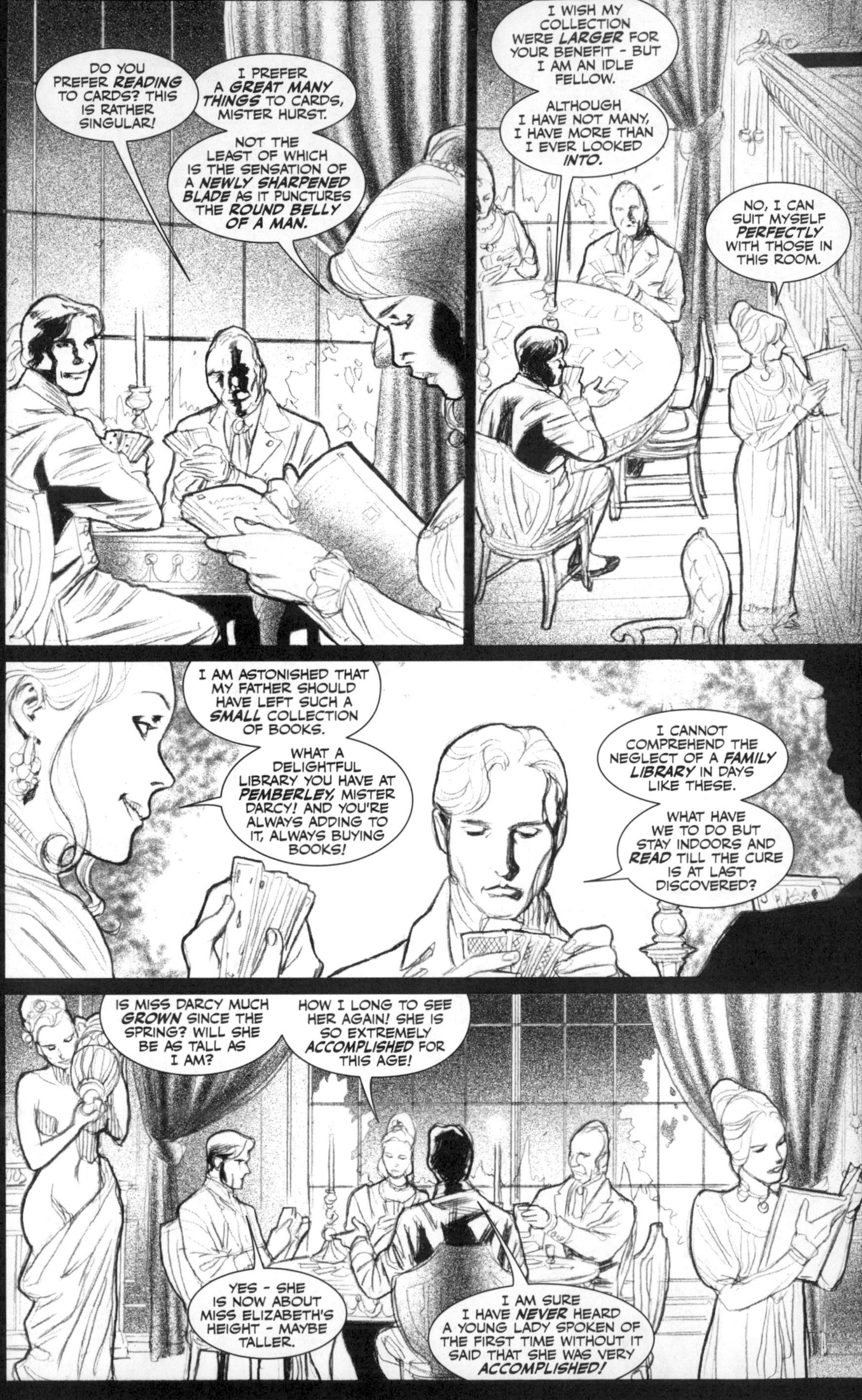
DO YOU PREFER READING TO CARDS? THIS IS RATHER SINGULAR!
I PREFER A GREAT MANY THINGS TO CARDS, MISTER HURST.
NOT THE LEAST OF WHICH IS THE SENSATION OF A NEWLY SHARPENED BLADE AS IT PUNCTURES THE ROUND BELLY OF A MAN.
I WISH MY COLLECTION WERE LARGER FOR YOUR BENEFIT - BUT I AM AN IDLE FELLOW.
ALTHOUGH I HAVE NOT MANY, I HAVE MORE THAN I EVER LOOKED INTO.
NO, I CAN SUIT MYSELF PERFECTLY WITH THOSE IN THIS ROOM.
I AM ASTONISHED THAT MY FATHER SHOULD HAVE LEFT SUCH A SMALL COLLECTION OF BOOKS.
WHAT A DELIGHTFUL LIBRARY YOU HAVE AT PEMBERLEY, MISTER DARCY! AND YOU'RE ALWAYS ADDING TO IT, ALWAYS BUYING BOOKS!
I CANNOT COMPREHEND THE NEGLECT OF A FAMILY LIBRARY IN DAYS LIKE THESE.
WHAT HAVE WE TO DO BUT STAY INDOORS AND READ TILL THE CURE IS AT LAST DISCOVERED?
IS MISS DARCY MUCH GROWN SINCE THE SPRING? WILL SHE BE AS TALL AS I AM?
HOW I LONG TO SEE HER AGAIN! SHE IS SO EXTREMELY ACCOMPLISHED FOR THIS AGE!
YES - SHE IS NOW ABOUT MISS ELIZABETH'S HEIGHT - MAYBE TALLER.
I AM SURE I HAVE NEVER HEARD A YOUNG LADY SPOKEN OF THE FIRST TIME WITHOUT IT SAID THAT SHE WAS VERY ACCOMPLISHED!

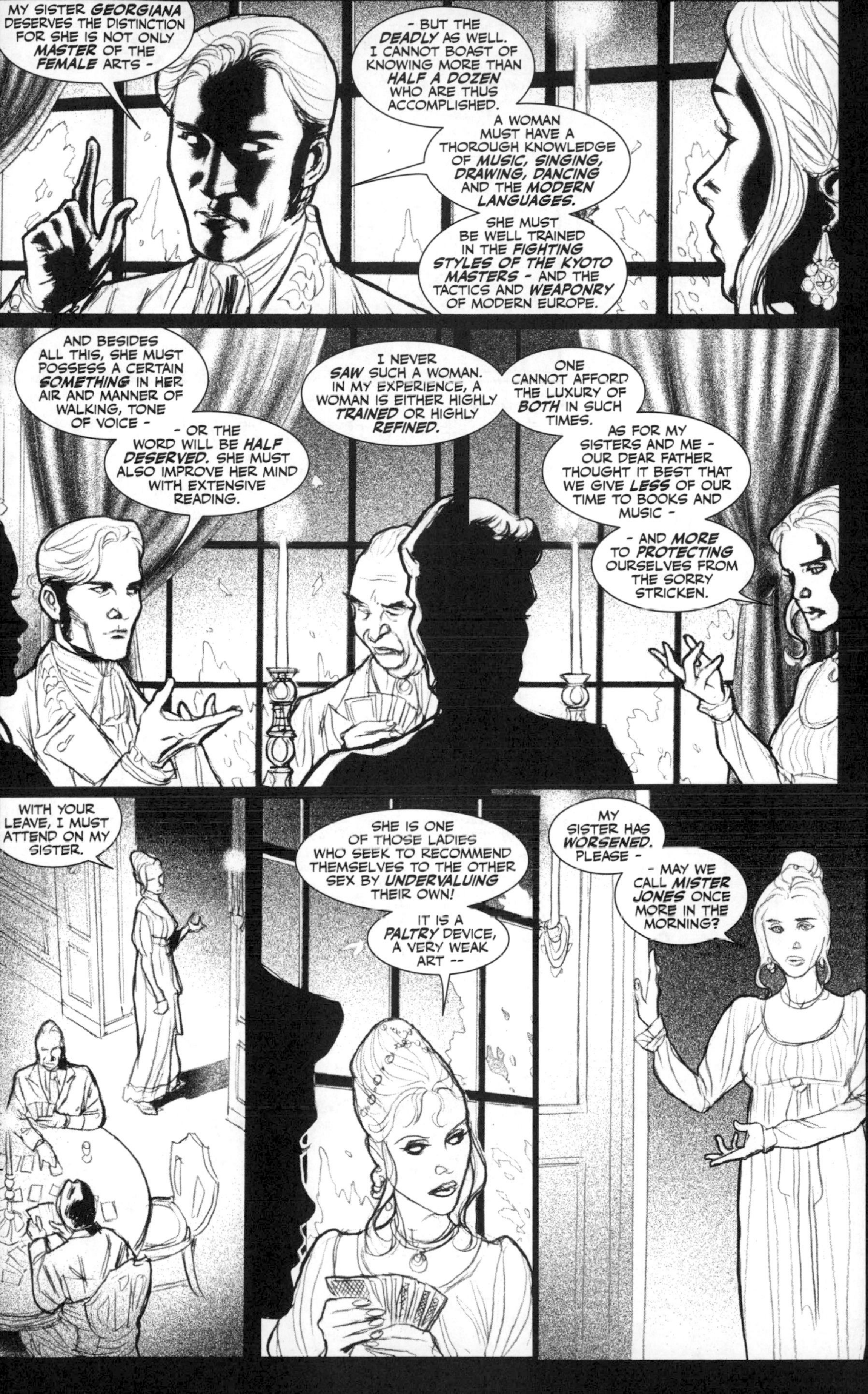
MY SISTER GEORGIANA DESERVES THE DISTINCTION FOR SHE IS NOT ONLY MASTER OF THE FEMALE ARTS -
- BUT THE DEADLY AS WELL. I CANNOT BOAST OF KNOWING MORE THAN HALF A DOZEN WHO ARE THUS ACCOMPLISHED.
A WOMAN MUST HAVE A THOROUGH KNOWLEDGE OF MUSIC, SINGING, DRAWING, DANCING AND THE MODERN LANGUAGES.
SHE MUST BE WELL TRAINED IN THE FIGHTING STYLES OF THE KYOTO MASTERS - AND THE TACTICS AND WEAPONRY OF MODERN EUROPE.
AND BESIDES ALL THIS, SHE MUST POSSESS A CERTAIN SOMETHING IN HER AIR AND MANNER OF WALKING, TONE OF VOICE -
- OR THE WORD WILL BE HALF DESERVED. SHE MUST ALSO IMPROVE HER MIND WITH EXTENSIVE READING.
I NEVER SAW SUCH A WOMAN. IN MY EXPERIENCE, A WOMAN IS EITHER HIGHLY TRAINED OR HIGHLY REFINED.
ONE CANNOT AFFORD THE LUXURY OF BOTH IN SUCH TIMES.
AS FOR MY SISTERS AND ME - OUR DEAR FATHER THOUGHT IT BEST THAT WE GIVE LESS OF OUR TIME TO BOOKS AND MUSIC -
- AND MORE TO PROTECTING OURSELVES FROM THE SORRY STRICKEN.
WITH YOUR LEAVE, I MUST ATTEND ON MY SISTER.
SHE IS ONE OF THOSE LADIES WHO SEEK TO RECOMMEND THEMSELVES TO THE OTHER SEX BY UNDERVALUING THEIR OWN!
IT IS A PALTRY DEVICE, A VERY WEAK ART --
MY SISTER HAS WORSENED. PLEASE -
- MAY WE CALL MISTER JONES ONCE MORE IN THE MORNING?

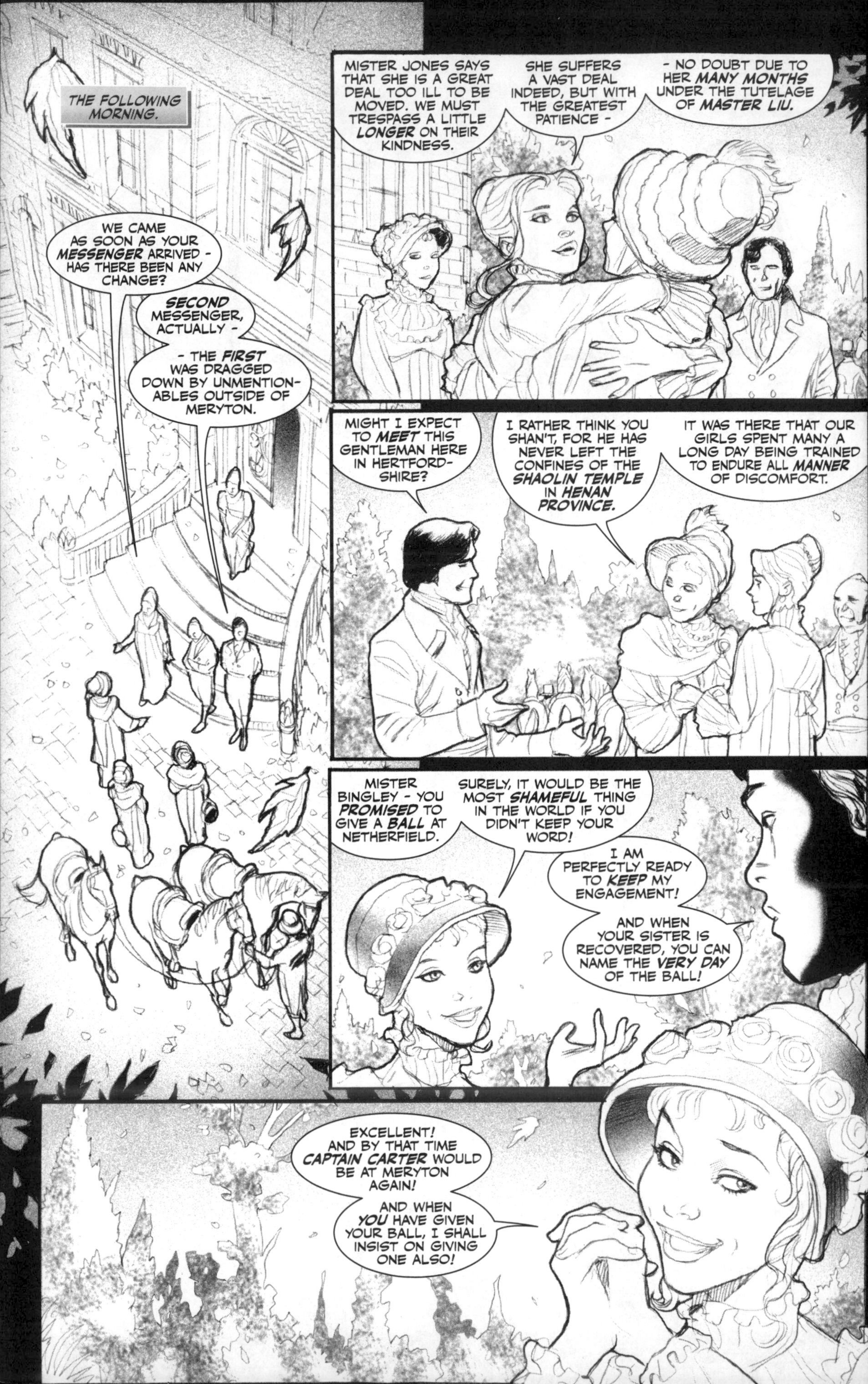
THE FOLLOWING MORNING.
WE CAME AS SOON AS YOUR MESSENGER ARRIVED - HAS THERE BEEN ANY CHANGE?
SECOND MESSENGER, ACTUALLY -
- THE FIRST WAS DRAGGED DOWN BY UNMENTIONABLES OUTSIDE OF MERYTON.
MISTER JONES SAYS THAT SHE IS A GREAT DEAL TOO ILL TO BE MOVED. WE MUST TRESPASS A LITTLE LONGER ON THEIR KINDNESS.
SHE SUFFERS A VAST DEAL INDEED, BUT WITH THE GREATEST PATIENCE -
- NO DOUBT DUE TO HER MANY MONTHS UNDER THE TUTELAGE OF MASTER LIU.
MIGHT I EXPECT TO MEET THIS GENTLEMAN HERE IN HERTFORDSHIRE?
I RATHER THINK YOU SHAN'T, FOR HE HAS NEVER LEFT THE CONFINES OF THE SHAOLIN TEMPLE IN HENAN PROVINCE.
IT WAS THERE THAT OUR GIRLS SPENT MANY A LONG DAY BEING TRAINED TO ENDURE ALL MANNER OF DISCOMFORT.
MISTER BINGLEY - YOU PROMISED TO GIVE A BALL AT NETHERFIELD.
SURELY, IT WOULD BE THE MOST SHAMEFUL THING IN THE WORLD IF YOU DIDN'T KEEP YOUR WORD!
I AM PERFECTLY READY TO KEEP MY ENGAGEMENT!
AND WHEN YOUR SISTER IS RECOVERED, YOU CAN NAME THE VERY DAY OF THE BALL!
EXCELLENT! AND BY THAT TIME CAPTAIN CARTER WOULD BE AT MERYTON AGAIN!
AND WHEN YOU HAVE GIVEN YOUR BALL, I SHALL INSIST ON GIVING ONE ALSO!

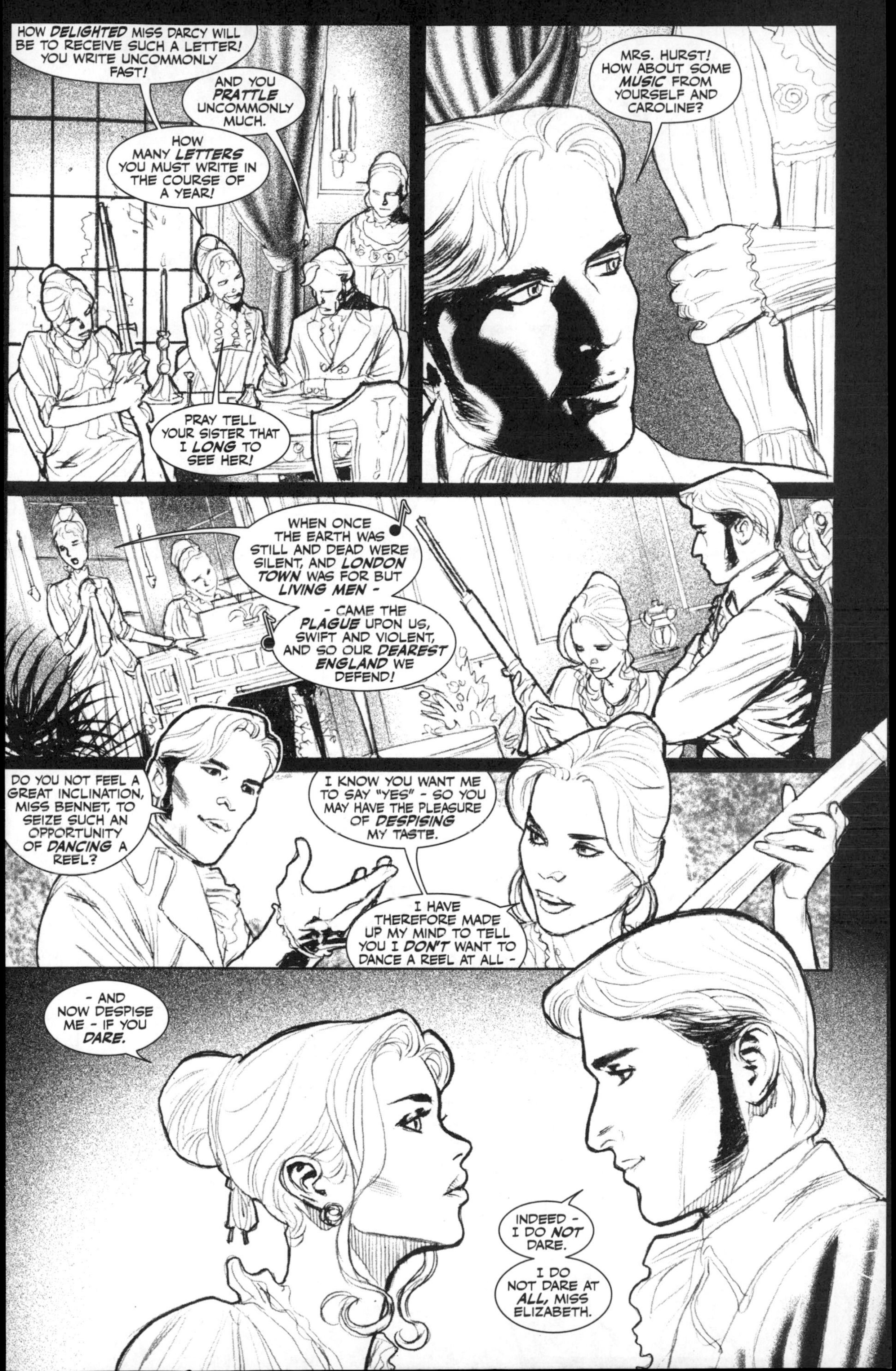
HOW DELIGHTED MISS DARCY WILL BE TO RECEIVE SUCH A LETTER! YOU WRITE UNCOMMONLY FAST!
AND YOU PRATTLE UNCOMMONLY MUCH.
HOW MANY LETTERS YOU MUST WRITE IN THE COURSE OF A YEAR!
PRAY TELL YOUR SISTER THAT I LONG TO SEE HER!
MRS. HURST! HOW ABOUT SOME MUSIC FROM YOURSELF AND CAROLINE?
WHEN ONCE THE EARTH WAS STILL AND DEAD WERE SILENT, AND LONDON TOWN WAS FOR BUT LIVING MEN -
- CAME THE PLAGUE UPON US, SWIFT AND VIOLENT, AND SO OUR DEAREST ENGLAND WE DEFEND!
DO YOU NOT FEEL A GREAT INCLINATION, MISS BENNET, TO SEIZE SUCH AN OPPORTUNITY OF DANCING A REEL?
I KNOW YOU WANT ME TO SAY "YES" - SO YOU MAY HAVE THE PLEASURE OF DESPISING MY TASTE.
I HAVE THEREFORE MADE UP MY MIND TO TELL YOU I DON'T WANT TO DANCE A REEL AT ALL -
- AND NOW DESPISE ME - IF YOU DARE.
INDEED - I DO NOT DARE.
I DO NOT DARE AT ALL, MISS ELIZABETH.

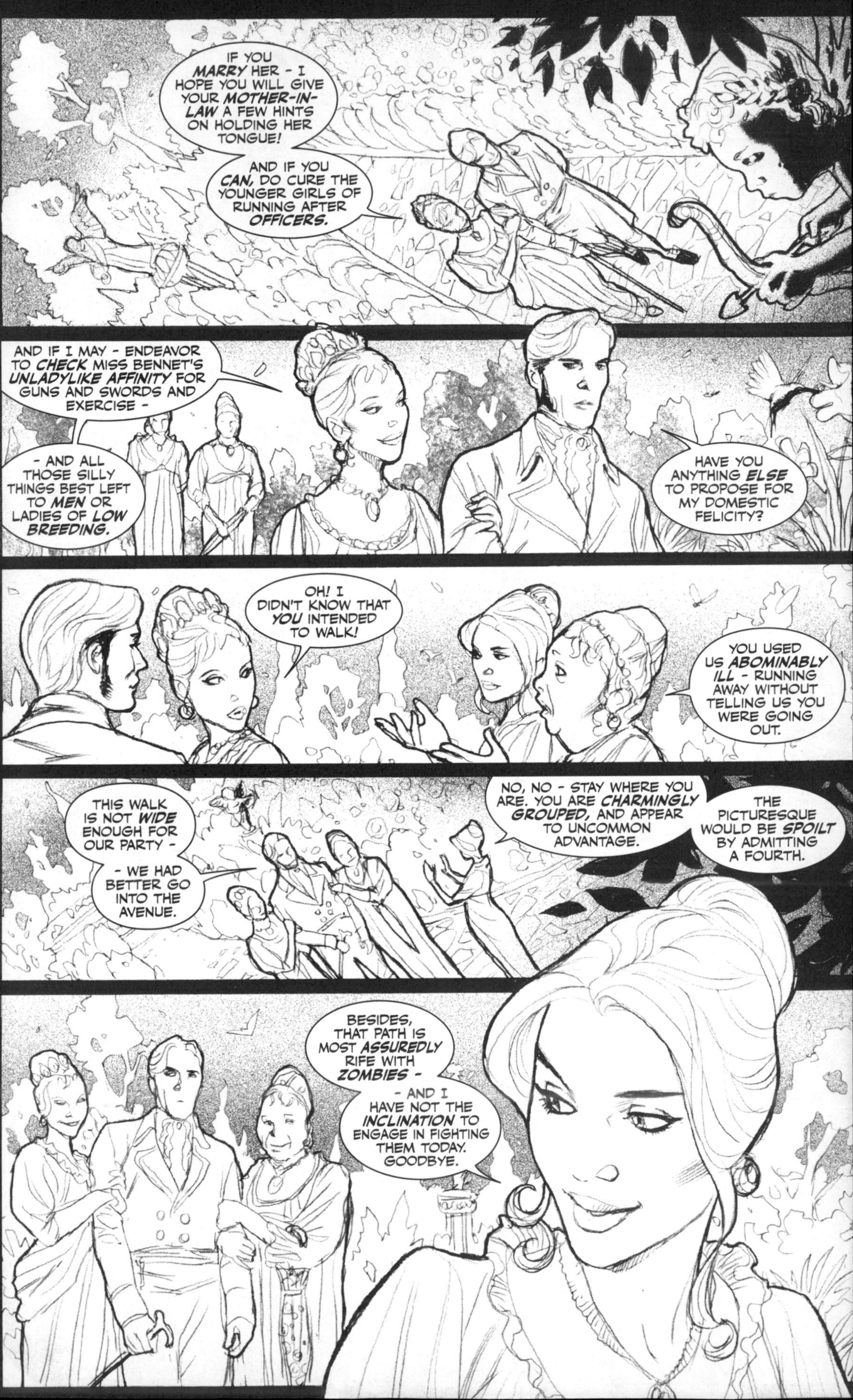
IF YOU MARRY HER - I HOPE YOU WILL GIVE YOUR MOTHER-IN-LAW A FEW HINTS ON HOLDING HER TONGUE!
AND IF YOU CAN, DO CURE THE YOUNGER GIRLS OF RUNNING AFTER OFFICERS.
AND IF I MAY - ENDEAVOR TO CHECK MISS BENNET'S UNLADYLIKE AFFINITY FOR GUNS AND SWORDS AND EXERCISE -
- AND ALL THOSE SILLY THINGS BEST LEFT TO MEN OR LADIES OF LOW BREEDING.
HAVE YOU ANYTHING ELSE TO PROPOSE FOR MY DOMESTIC FELICITY?
OH! I DIDN'T KNOW THAT YOU INTENDED TO WALK!
YOU USED US ABOMINABLY ILL - RUNNING AWAY WITHOUT TELLING US YOU WERE GOING OUT.
THIS WALK IS NOT WIDE ENOUGH FOR OUR PARTY -
- WE HAD BETTER GO INTO THE AVENUE.
NO, NO - STAY WHERE YOU ARE. YOU ARE CHARMINGLY GROUPED, AND APPEAR TO UNCOMMON ADVANTAGE.
THE PICTURESQUE WOULD BE SPOILT BY ADMITTING A FOURTH.
BESIDES, THAT PATH IS MOST ASSUREDLY RIFE WITH ZOMBIES -
- AND I HAVE NOT THE INCLINATION TO ENGAGE IN FIGHTING THEM TODAY. GOODBYE.

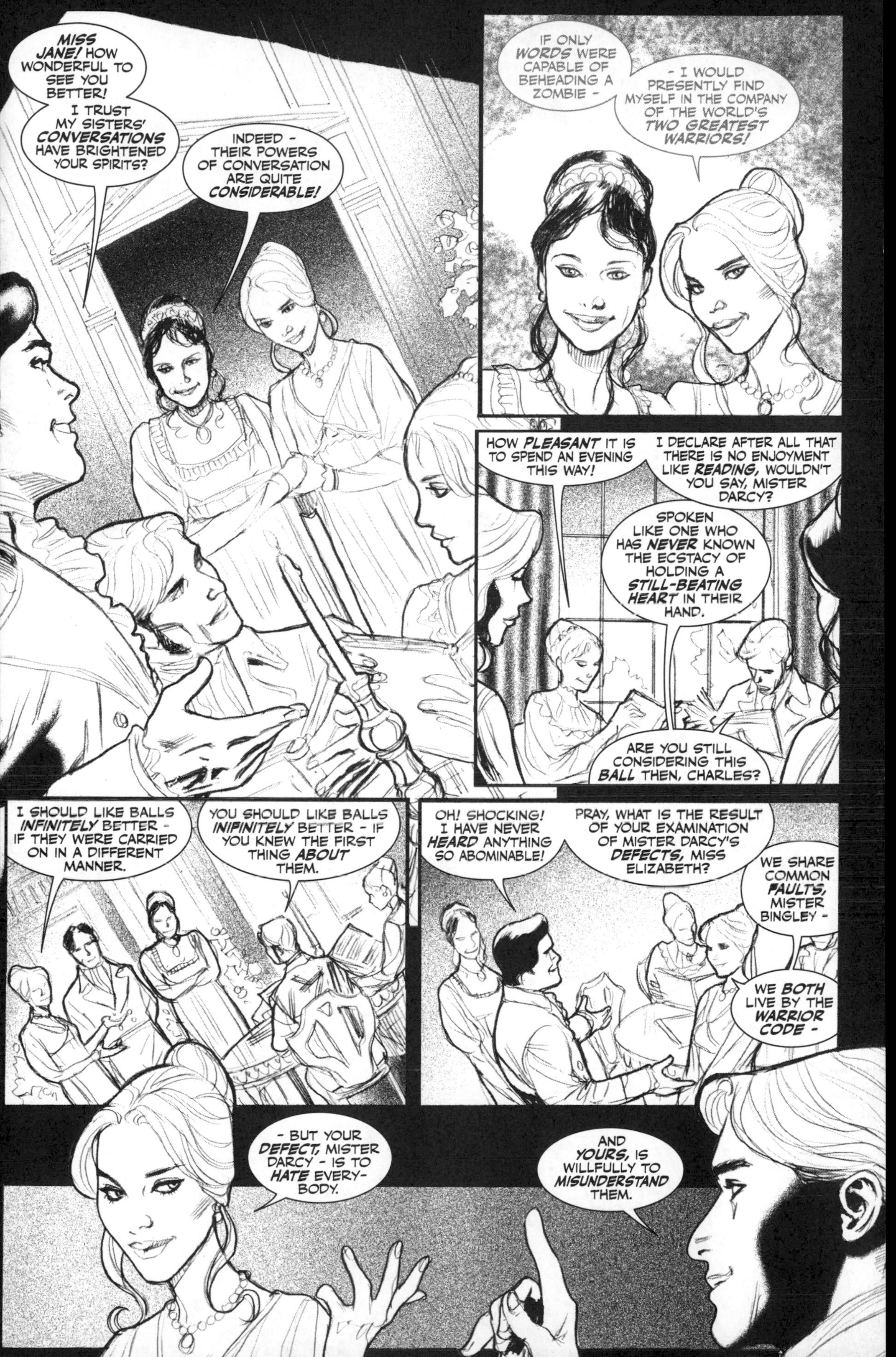
MISS JANE! HOW WONDERFUL TO SEE YOU BETTER!
I TRUST MY SISTERS' CONVERSATIONS HAVE BRIGHTENED YOUR SPIRITS?
INDEED - THEIR POWERS OF CONVERSATION ARE QUITE CONSIDERABLE!
IF ONLY WORDS WERE CAPABLE OF BEHEADING A ZOMBIE -
- I WOULD PRESENTLY FIND MYSELF IN THE COMPANY OF THE WORLD'S TWO GREATEST WARRIORS!
HOW PLEASANT IT IS TO SPEND AN EVENING THIS WAY!
I DECLARE AFTER ALL THAT THERE IS NO ENJOYMENT LIKE READING, WOULDN'T YOU SAY, MISTER DARCY?
SPOKEN LIKE ONE WHO HAS NEVER KNOWN THE ECSTACY OF HOLDING A STILL-BEATING HEART IN THEIR HAND.
ARE YOU STILL CONSIDERING THIS BALL THEN, CHARLES?
I SHOULD LIKE BALLS INFINITELY BETTER - IF THEY WERE CARRIED ON IN A DIFFERENT MANNER.
YOU SHOULD LIKE BALLS INIFINITELY BETTER - IF YOU KNEW THE FIRST THING ABOUT THEM.
OH! SHOCKING! I HAVE NEVER HEARD ANYTHING SO ABOMINABLE!
PRAY, WHAT IS THE RESULT OF YOUR EXAMINATION OF MISTER DARCY'S DEFECTS, MISS ELIZABETH?
WE SHARE COMMON FAULTS, MISTER BINGLEY -
WE BOTH LIVE BY THE WARRIOR CODE -
- BUT YOUR DEFECT, MISTER DARCY - IS TO HATE EVERY-BODY.
AND YOURS, IS WILLFULLY TO MISUNDERSTAND THEM.

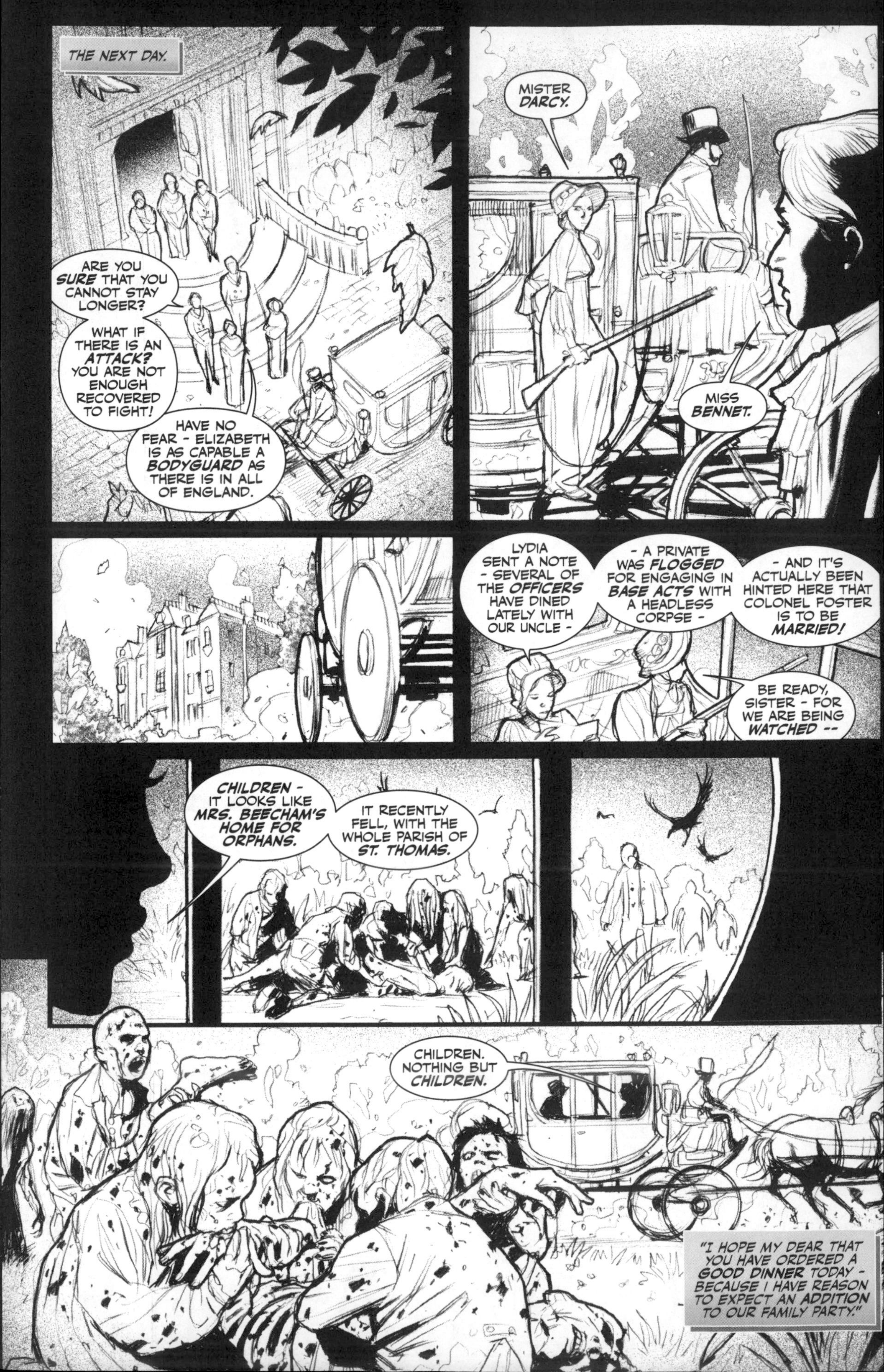
THE NEXT DAY.
ARE YOU SURE THAT YOU CANNOT STAY LONGER?
WHAT IF THERE IS AN ATTACK? YOU ARE NOT ENOUGH RECOVERED TO FIGHT!
HAVE NO FEAR - ELIZABETH IS AS CAPABLE A BODYGUARD AS THERE IS IN ALL OF ENGLAND.
MISTER DARCY.
MISS BENNET.
LYDIA SENT A NOTE - SEVERAL OF THE OFFICERS HAVE DINED LATELY WITH OUR UNCLE -
- A PRIVATE WAS FLOGGED FOR ENGAGING IN BASE ACTS WITH A HEADLESS CORPSE -
- AND IT'S ACTUALLY BEEN HINTED HERE THAT COLONEL FOSTER IS TO BE MARRIED!
BE READY, SISTER - FOR WE ARE BEING WATCHED --
CHILDREN - IT LOOKS LIKE MRS. BEECHAM'S HOME FOR ORPHANS.
IT RECENTLY FELL, WITH THE WHOLE PARISH OF ST. THOMAS.
CHILDREN. NOTHING BUT CHILDREN.
"I HOPE MY DEAR THAT YOU HAVE ORDERED A GOOD DINNER TODAY - BECAUSE I HAVE REASON TO EXPECT AN ADDITION TO OUR FAMILY PARTY."

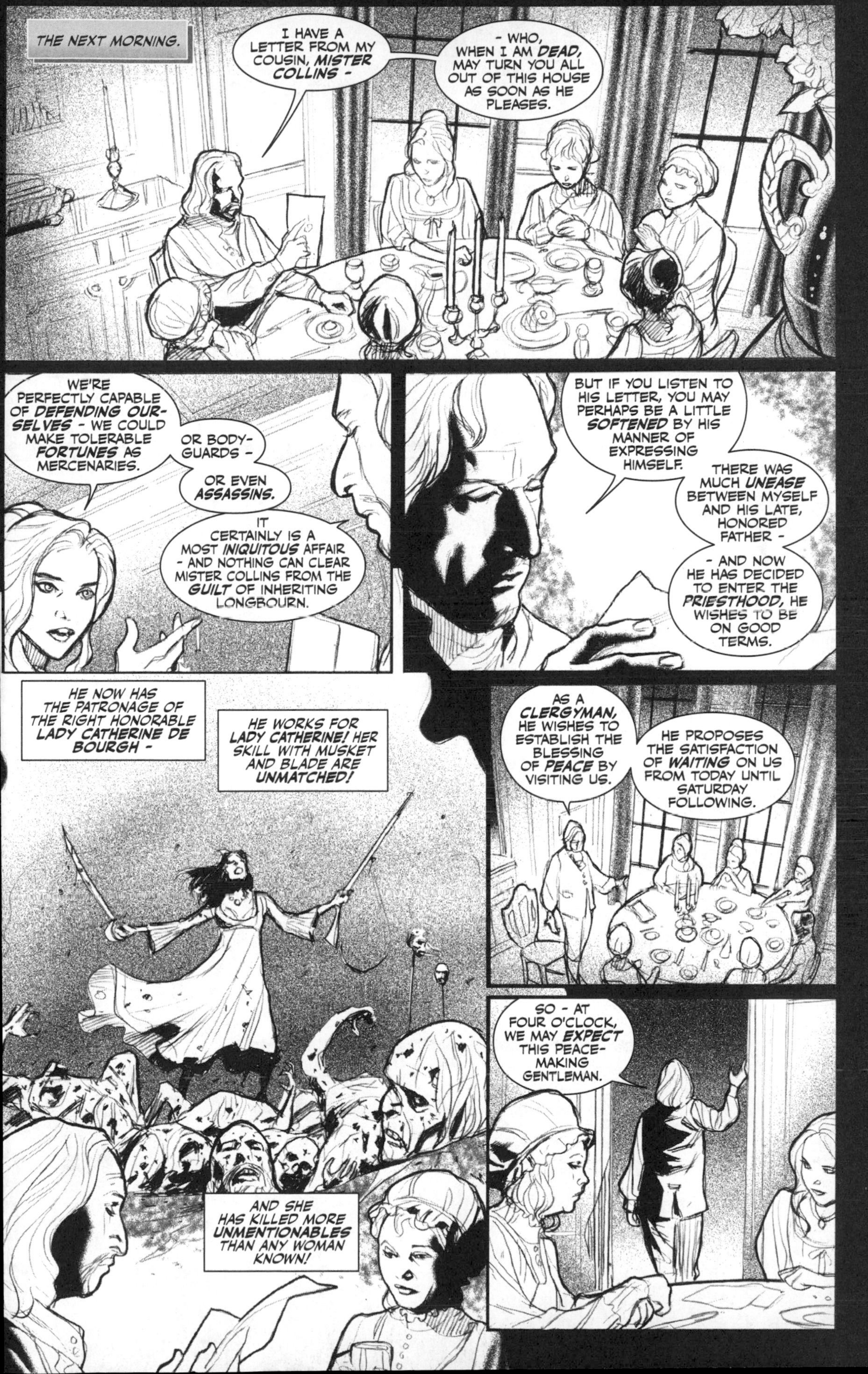
THE NEXT MORNING.
I HAVE A LETTER FROM MY COUSIN, MISTER COLLINS -
- WHO, WHEN I AM DEAD, MAY TURN YOU ALL OUT OF THIS HOUSE AS SOON AS HE PLEASES.
WE'RE PERFECTLY CAPABLE OF DEFENDING OUR-SELVES - WE COULD MAKE TOLERABLE FORTUNES AS MERCENARIES.
OR BODY-GUARDS -
OR EVEN ASSASSINS.
IT CERTAINLY IS A MOST INIQUITOUS AFFAIR - AND NOTHING CAN CLEAR MISTER COLLINS FROM THE GUILT OF INHERITING LONGBOURN.
BUT IF YOU LISTEN TO HIS LETTER, YOU MAY PERHAPS BE A LITTLE SOFTENED BY HIS MANNER OF EXPRESSING HIMSELF.
THERE WAS MUCH UNEASE BETWEEN MYSELF AND HIS LATE, HONORED FATHER -
- AND NOW HE HAS DECIDED TO ENTER THE PRIESTHOOD, HE WISHES TO BE ON GOOD TERMS.
HE NOW HAS THE PATRONAGE OF THE RIGHT HONORABLE LADY CATHERINE DE BOURGH -
HE WORKS FOR LADY CATHERINE! HER SKILL WITH MUSKET AND BLADE ARE UNMATCHED!
AND SHE HAS KILLED MORE UNMENTIONABLES THAN ANY WOMAN KNOWN!
AS A CLERGYMAN, HE WISHES TO ESTABLISH THE BLESSING OF PEACE BY VISITING US.
HE PROPOSES THE SATISFACTION OF WAITING ON US FROM TODAY UNTIL SATURDAY FOLLOWING.
SO - AT FOUR O'CLOCK, WE MAY EXPECT THIS PEACE-MAKING GENTLEMAN.

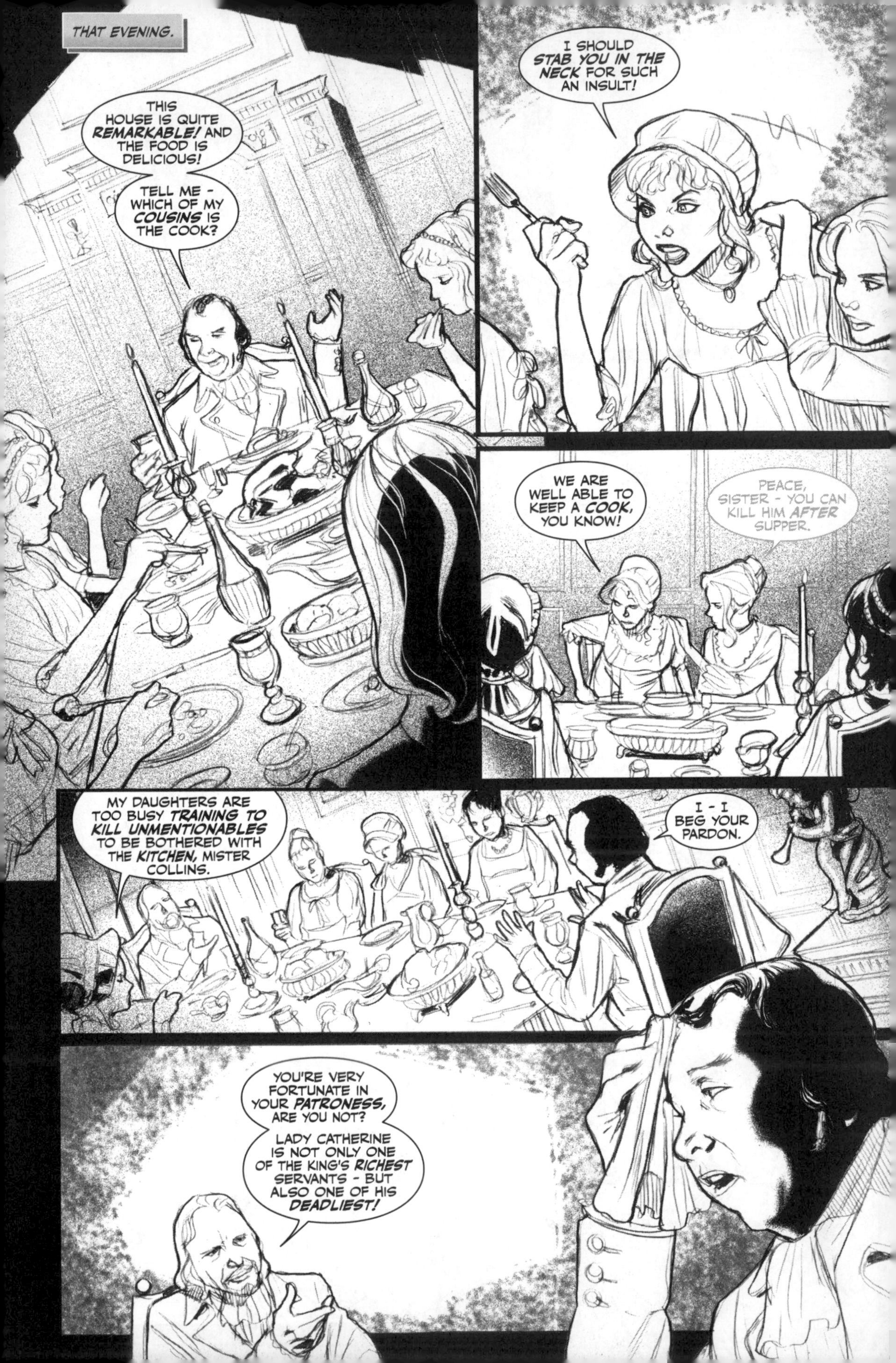
THAT EVENING.
THIS HOUSE IS QUITE REMARKABLE! AND THE FOOD IS DELICIOUS!
TELL ME - WHICH OF MY COUSINS IS THE COOK?
I SHOULD STAB YOU IN THE NECK FOR SUCH AN INSULT!
WE ARE WELL ABLE TO KEEP A COOK, YOU KNOW!
PEACE, SISTER - YOU CAN KILL HIM AFTER SUPPER.
MY DAUGHTERS ARE TOO BUSY TRAINING TO KILL UNMENTIONABLES TO BE BOTHERED WITH THE KITCHEN, MISTER COLLINS.
I - I BEG YOUR PARDON.
YOU'RE VERY FORTUNATE IN YOUR PATRONESS, ARE YOU NOT?
LADY CATHERINE IS NOT ONLY ONE OF THE KING'S RICHEST SERVANTS - BUT ALSO ONE OF HIS DEADLIEST!

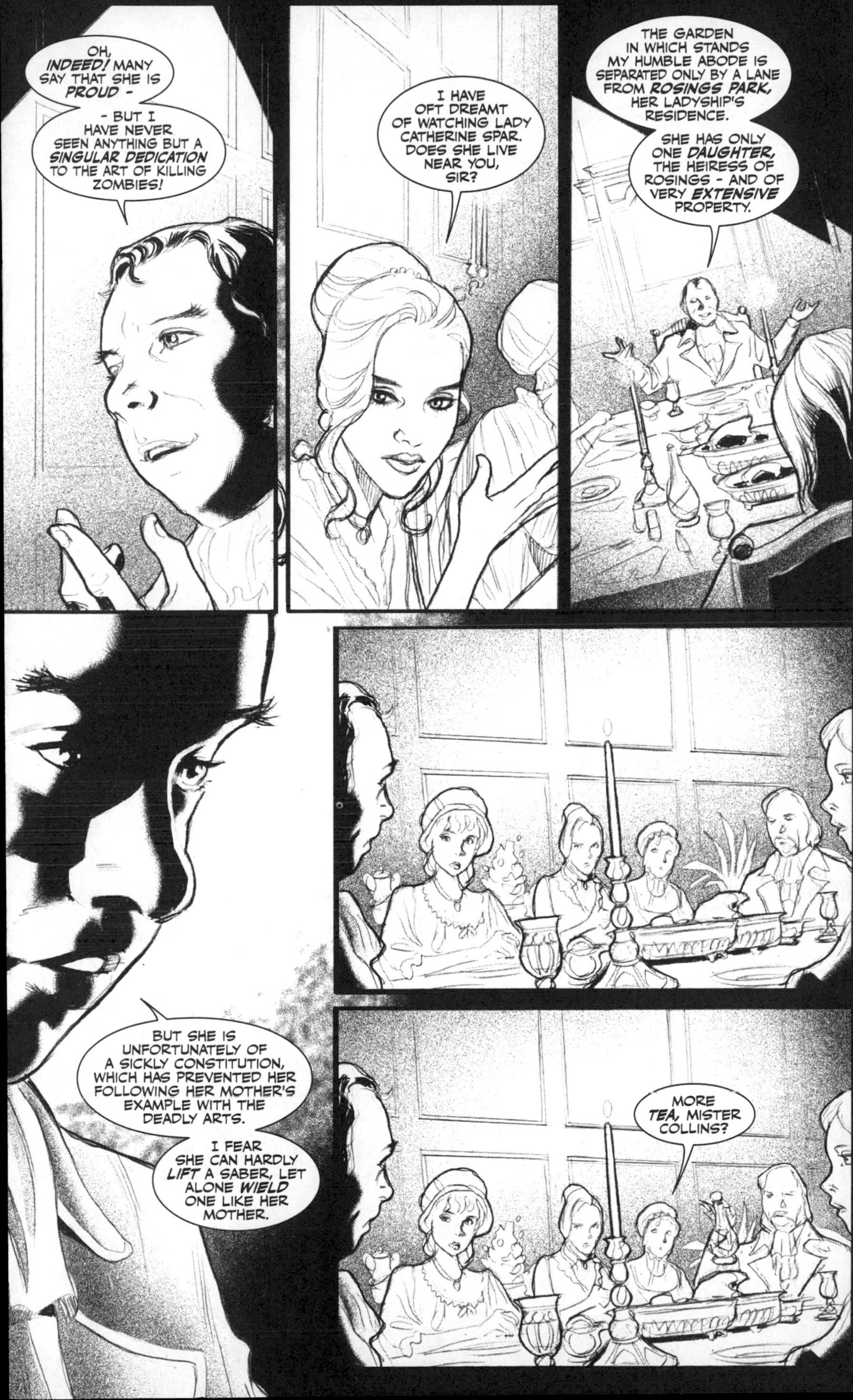
OH, INDEED! MANY SAY THAT SHE IS PROUD -
- BUT I HAVE NEVER SEEN ANYTHING BUT A SINGULAR DEDICATION TO THE ART OF KILLING ZOMBIES!
I HAVE OFT DREAMT OF WATCHING LADY CATHERINE SPAR. DOES SHE LIVE NEAR YOU, SIR?
THE GARDEN IN WHICH STANDS MY HUMBLE ABODE IS SEPARATED ONLY BY A LANE FROM ROSINGS PARK, HER LADYSHIP'S RESIDENCE.
SHE HAS ONLY ONE DAUGHTER, THE HEIRESS OF ROSINGS - AND OF VERY EXTENSIVE PROPERTY.
BUT SHE IS UNFORTUNATELY OF A SICKLY CONSTITUTION, WHICH HAS PREVENTED HER FOLLOWING HER MOTHER'S EXAMPLE WITH THE DEADLY ARTS.
I FEAR SHE CAN HARDLY LIFT A SABER, LET ALONE WIELD ONE LIKE HER MOTHER.
MORE TEA, MISTER COLLINS?

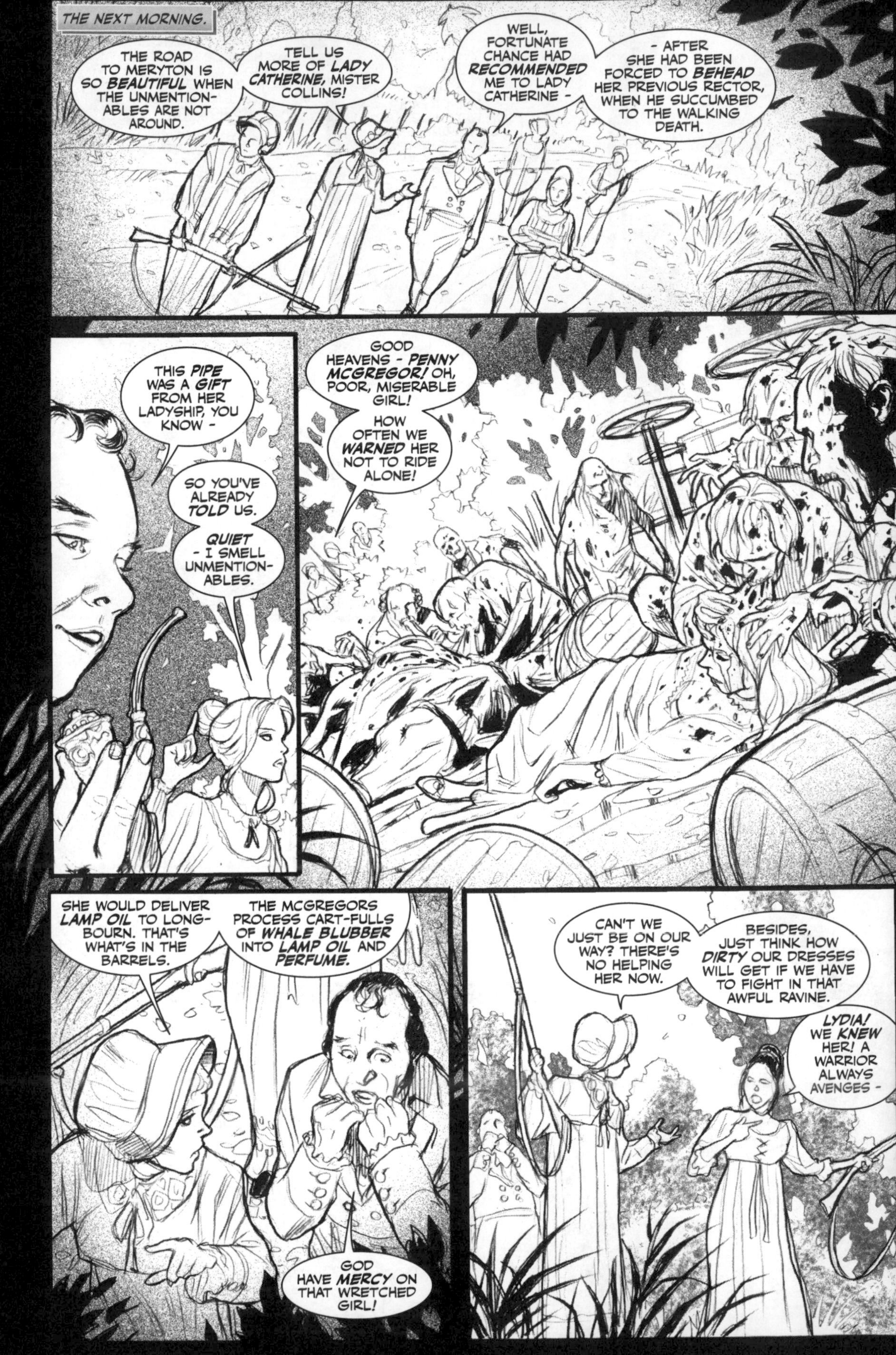
THE NEXT MORNING.
THE ROAD TO MERYTON IS SO BEAUTIFUL WHEN THE UNMENTION-ABLES ARE NOT AROUND.
TELL US MORE OF LADY CATHERINE, MISTER COLLINS!
WELL, FORTUNATE CHANCE HAD RECOMMENDED ME TO LADY CATHERINE -
- AFTER SHE HAD BEEN FORCED TO BEHEAD HER PREVIOUS RECTOR, WHEN HE SUCCUMBED TO THE WALKING DEATH.
THIS PIPE WAS A GIFT FROM HER LADYSHIP, YOU KNOW -
SO YOU'VE ALREADY TOLD US.
QUIET - I SMELL UNMENTION-ABLES.
GOOD HEAVENS - PENNY MCGREGOR! OH, POOR, MISERABLE GIRL!
HOW OFTEN WE WARNED HER NOT TO RIDE ALONE!
SHE WOULD DELIVER LAMP OIL TO LONG-BOURN. THAT'S WHAT'S IN THE BARRELS.
THE MCGREGORS PROCESS CART-FULLS OF WHALE BLUBBER INTO LAMP OIL AND PERFUME.
GOD HAVE MERCY ON THAT WRETCHED GIRL!
CAN'T WE JUST BE ON OUR WAY? THERE'S NO HELPING HER NOW.
BESIDES, JUST THINK HOW DIRTY OUR DRESSES WILL GET IF WE HAVE TO FIGHT IN THAT AWFUL RAVINE.
LYDIA! WE KNEW HER! A WARRIOR ALWAYS AVENGES -

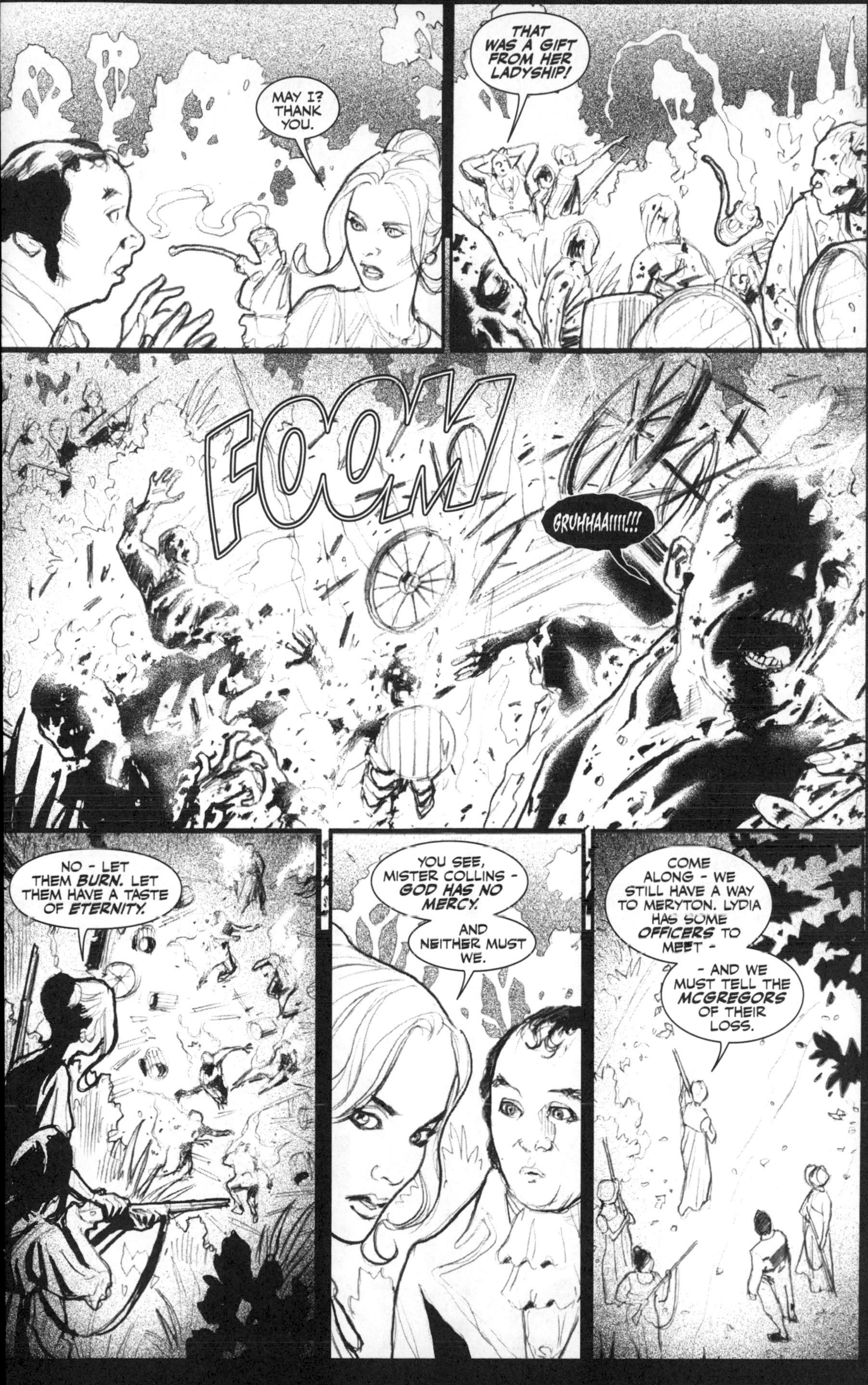
MAY I? THANK YOU.
THAT WAS A GIFT FROM HER LADYSHIP!
FOOM
GRUHHAA!!!!!!
NO - LET THEM BURN. LET THEM HAVE A TASTE OF ETERNITY.
YOU SEE, MISTER COLLINS - GOD HAS NO MERCY.
AND NEITHER MUST WE.
COME ALONG - WE STILL HAVE A WAY TO MERYTON. LYDIA HAS SOME OFFICERS TO MEET -
- AND WE MUST TELL THE MCGREGORS OF THEIR LOSS.

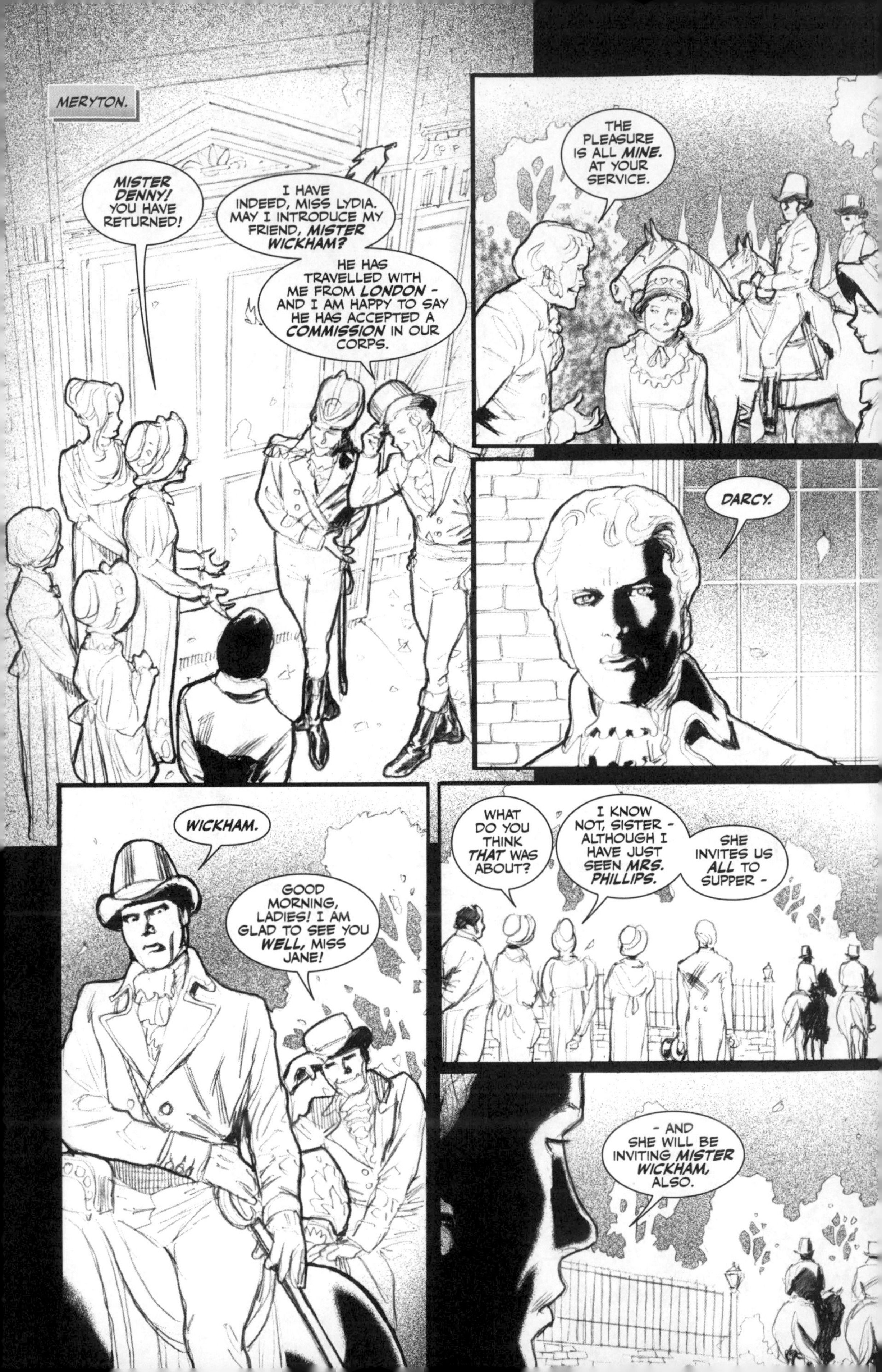
MERYTON.
MISTER DENNY! YOU HAVE RETURNED!
I HAVE INDEED, MISS LYDIA. MAY I INTRODUCE MY FRIEND, MISTER WICKHAM?
HE HAS TRAVELLED WITH ME FROM LONDON - AND I AM HAPPY TO SAY HE HAS ACCEPTED A COMMISSION IN OUR CORPS.
THE PLEASURE IS ALL MINE. AT YOUR SERVICE.
DARCY.
WICKHAM.
GOOD MORNING, LADIES! I AM GLAD TO SEE YOU WELL, MISS JANE!
WHAT DO YOU THINK THAT WAS ABOUT?
I KNOW NOT, SISTER - ALTHOUGH I HAVE JUST SEEN MRS. PHILLIPS.
SHE INVITES US ALL TO SUPPER -
- AND SHE WILL BE INVITING MISTER WICKHAM, ALSO.

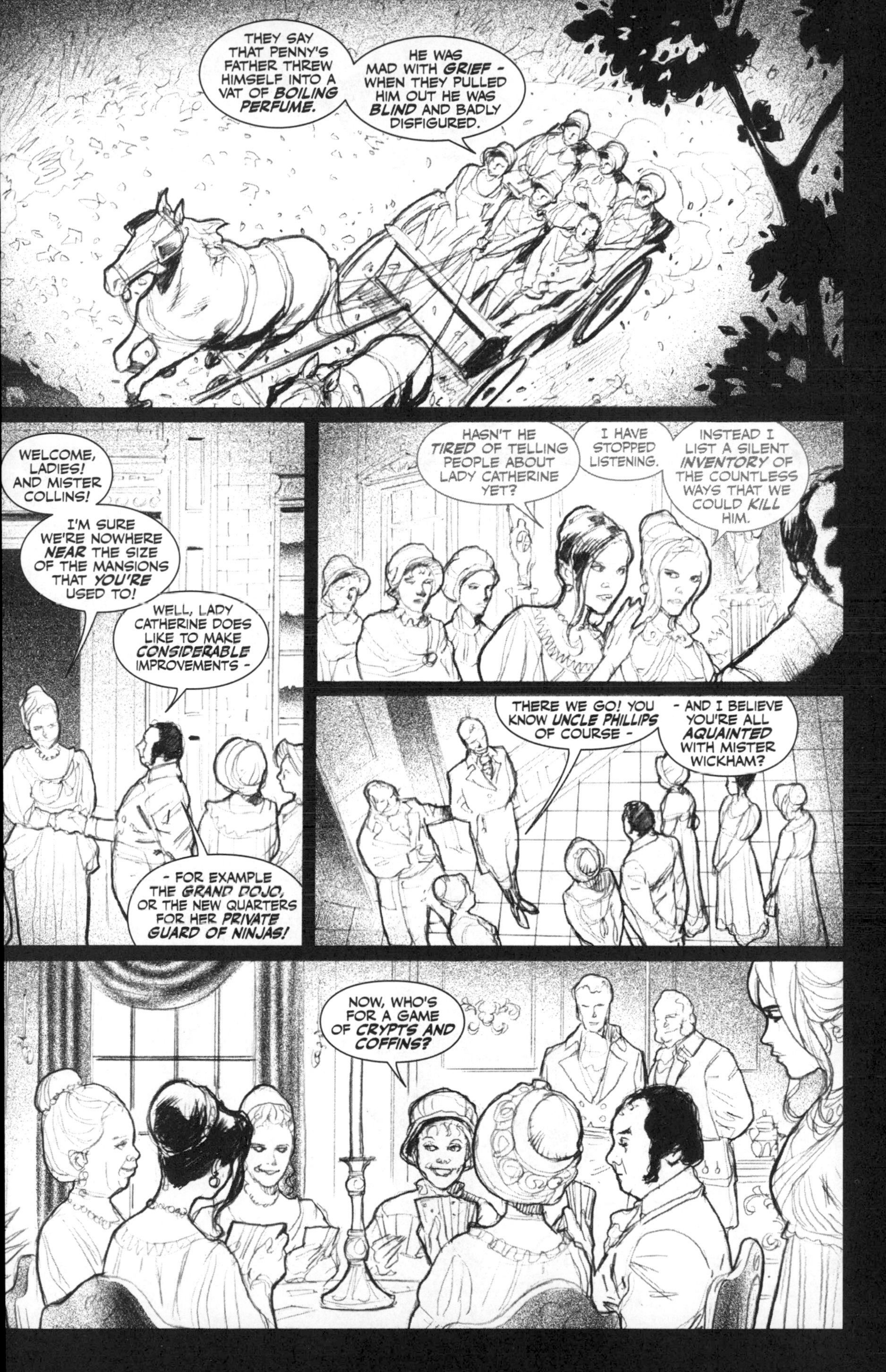
THEY SAY THAT PENNY'S FATHER THREW HIMSELF INTO A VAT OF BOILING PERFUME.
HE WAS MAD WITH GRIEF - WHEN THEY PULLED HIM OUT HE WAS BLIND AND BADLY DISFIGURED.
WELCOME, LADIES! AND MISTER COLLINS!
I'M SURE WE'RE NOWHERE NEAR THE SIZE OF THE MANSIONS THAT YOU'RE USED TO!
WELL, LADY CATHERINE DOES LIKE TO MAKE CONSIDERABLE IMPROVEMENTS -
- FOR EXAMPLE THE GRAND DOJO, OR THE NEW QUARTERS FOR HER PRIVATE GUARD OF NINJAS!
HASN'T HE TIRED OF TELLING PEOPLE ABOUT LADY CATHERINE YET?
I HAVE STOPPED LISTENING.
INSTEAD I LIST A SILENT INVENTORY OF THE COUNTLESS WAYS THAT WE COULD KILL HIM.
THERE WE GO! YOU KNOW UNCLE PHILLIPS OF COURSE -
- AND I BELIEVE YOU'RE ALL AQUAINTED WITH MISTER WICKHAM?
NOW, WHO'S FOR A GAME OF CRYPTS AND COFFINS?

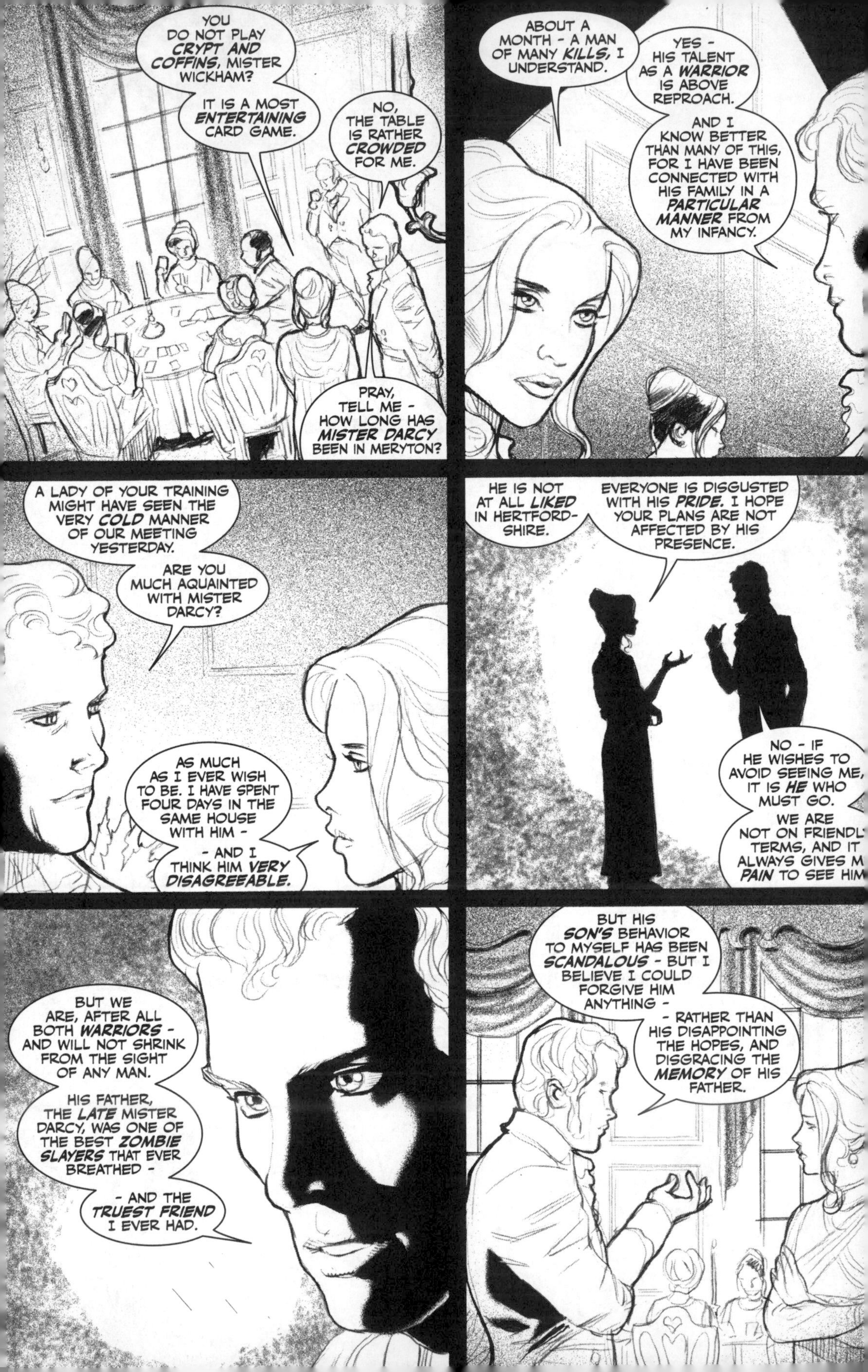
YOU DO NOT PLAY CRYPT AND COFFINS, MISTER WICKHAM?
IT IS A MOST ENTERTAINING CARD GAME.
NO, THE TABLE IS RATHER CROWDED FOR ME.
PRAY, TELL ME - HOW LONG HAS MISTER DARCY BEEN IN MERYTON?
ABOUT A MONTH - A MAN OF MANY KILLS, I UNDERSTAND.
YES - HIS TALENT AS A WARRIOR IS ABOVE REPROACH.
AND I KNOW BETTER THAN MANY OF THIS, FOR I HAVE BEEN CONNECTED WITH HIS FAMILY IN A PARTICULAR MANNER FROM MY INFANCY.
A LADY OF YOUR TRAINING MIGHT HAVE SEEN THE VERY COLD MANNER OF OUR MEETING YESTERDAY.
ARE YOU MUCH AQUAINTED WITH MISTER DARCY?
AS MUCH AS I EVER WISH TO BE. I HAVE SPENT FOUR DAYS IN THE SAME HOUSE WITH HIM -
- AND I THINK HIM VERY DISAGREEABLE.
HE IS NOT AT ALL LIKED IN HERTFORD-SHIRE.
EVERYONE IS DISGUSTED WITH HIS PRIDE. I HOPE YOUR PLANS ARE NOT AFFECTED BY HIS PRESENCE.
NO - IF HE WISHES TO AVOID SEEING ME, IT IS HE WHO MUST GO.
WE ARE NOT ON FRIENDL TERMS, AND IT ALWAYS GIVES M PAIN TO SEE HIM
BUT WE ARE, AFTER ALL BOTH WARRIORS - AND WILL NOT SHRINK FROM THE SIGHT OF ANY MAN.
HIS FATHER, THE LATE MISTER DARCY, WAS ONE OF THE BEST ZOMBIE SLAYERS THAT EVER BREATHED -
- AND THE TRUEST FRIEND I EVER HAD.
BUT HIS SON'S BEHAVIOR TO MYSELF HAS BEEN SCANDALOUS - BUT I BELIEVE I COULD FORGIVE HIM ANYTHING -
- RATHER THAN HIS DISAPPOINTING THE HOPES, AND DISGRACING THE MEMORY OF HIS FATHER.

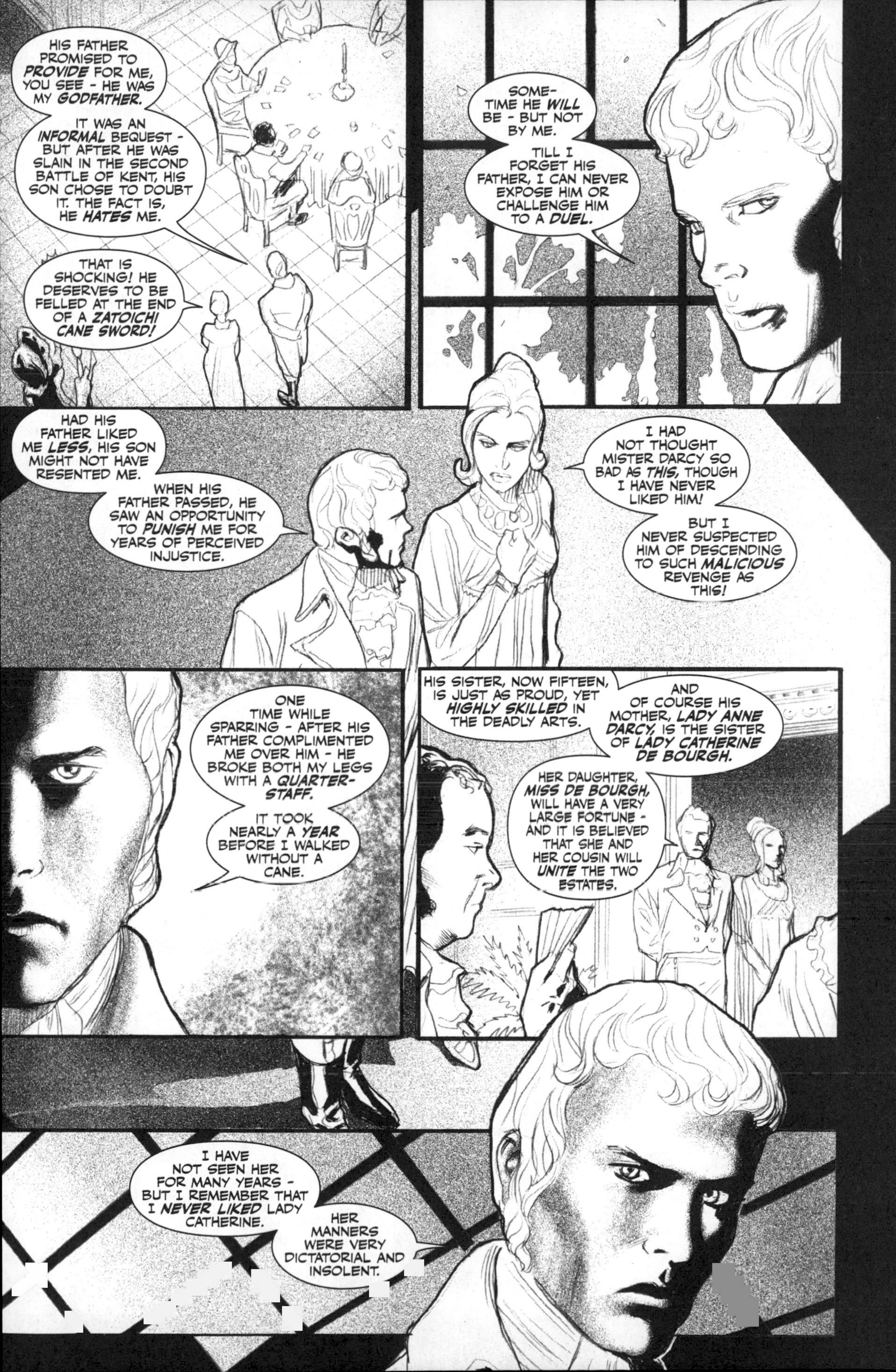
HIS FATHER PROMISED TO PROVIDE FOR ME, YOU SEE - HE WAS MY GODFATHER.
IT WAS AN INFORMAL BEQUEST - BUT AFTER HE WAS SLAIN IN THE SECOND BATTLE OF KENT, HIS SON CHOSE TO DOUBT IT. THE FACT IS, HE HATES ME.
THAT IS SHOCKING! HE DESERVES TO BE FELLED AT THE END OF A ZATOICHI CANE SWORD!
SOMETIME HE WILL BE - BUT NOT BY ME.
TILL I FORGET HIS FATHER, I CAN NEVER EXPOSE HIM OR CHALLENGE HIM TO A DUEL.
HAD HIS FATHER LIKED ME LESS, HIS SON MIGHT NOT HAVE RESENTED ME.
WHEN HIS FATHER PASSED, HE SAW AN OPPORTUNITY TO PUNISH ME FOR YEARS OF PERCEIVED INJUSTICE.
I HAD NOT THOUGHT MISTER DARCY SO BAD AS THIS, THOUGH I HAVE NEVER LIKED HIM!
BUT I NEVER SUSPECTED HIM OF DESCENDING TO SUCH MALICIOUS REVENGE AS THIS!
ONE TIME WHILE SPARRING - AFTER HIS FATHER COMPLIMENTED ME OVER HIM - HE BROKE BOTH MY LEGS WITH A QUARTER-STAFF.
IT TOOK NEARLY A YEAR BEFORE I WALKED WITHOUT A CANE.
HIS SISTER, NOW FIFTEEN, IS JUST AS PROUD, YET HIGHLY SKILLED IN THE DEADLY ARTS.
AND OF COURSE HIS MOTHER, LADY ANNE DARCY, IS THE SISTER OF LADY CATHERINE DE BOURGH.
HER DAUGHTER, MISS DE BOURGH, WILL HAVE A VERY LARGE FORTUNE - AND IT IS BELIEVED THAT SHE AND HER COUSIN WILL UNITE THE TWO ESTATES.
I HAVE NOT SEEN HER FOR MANY YEARS - BUT I REMEMBER THAT I NEVER LIKED LADY CATHERINE.
HER MANNERS WERE VERY DICTATORIAL AND INSOLENT.

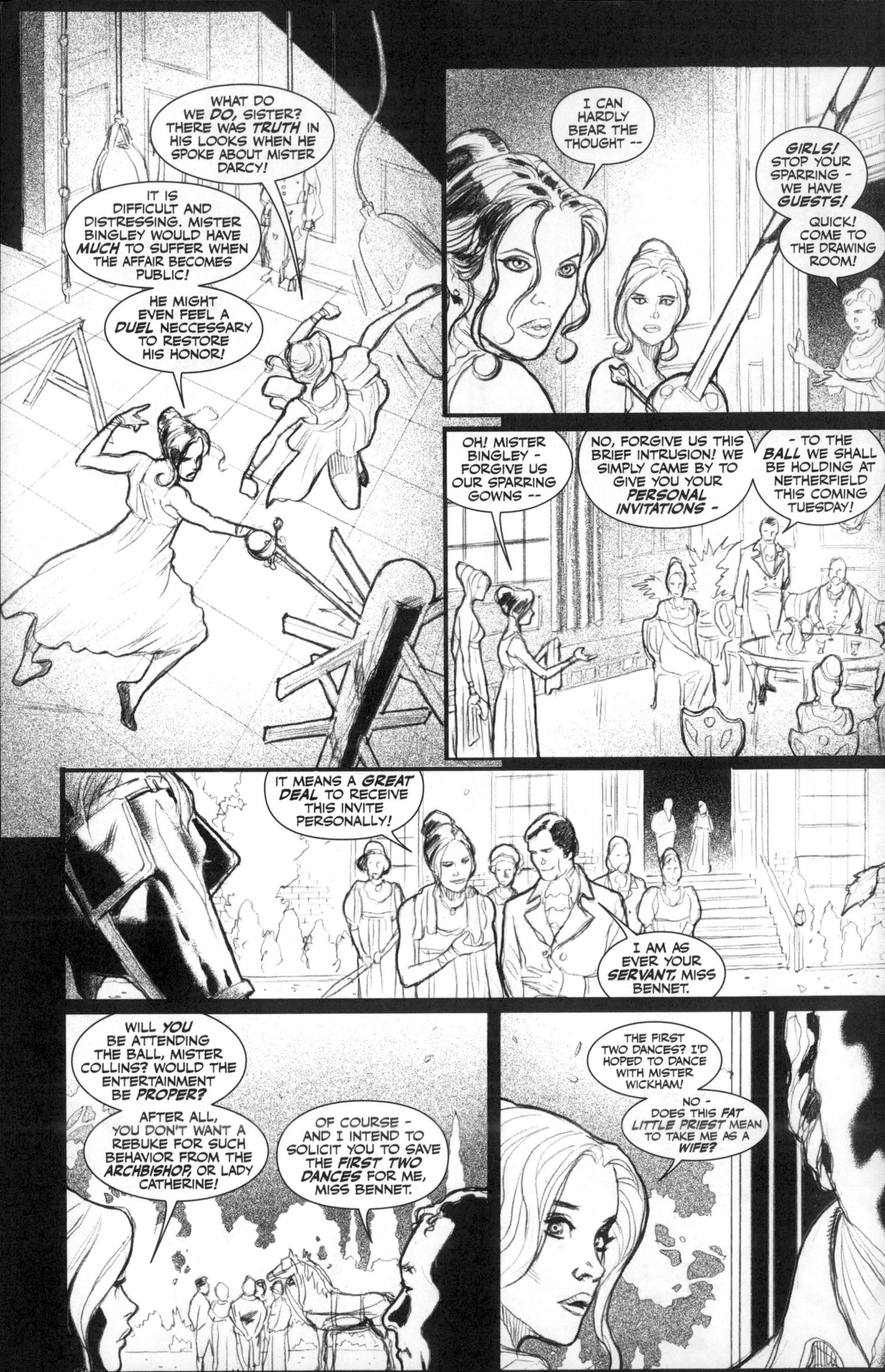
WHAT DO WE DO, SISTER? THERE WAS TRUTH IN HIS LOOKS WHEN HE SPOKE ABOUT MISTER DARCY!
IT IS DIFFICULT AND DISTRESSING. MISTER BINGLEY WOULD HAVE MUCH TO SUFFER WHEN THE AFFAIR BECOMES PUBLIC!
HE MIGHT EVEN FEEL A DUEL NECCESSARY TO RESTORE HIS HONOR!
I CAN HARDLY BEAR THE THOUGHT --
GIRLS! STOP YOUR SPARRING - WE HAVE GUESTS!
QUICK! COME TO THE DRAWING ROOM!
OH! MISTER BINGLEY - FORGIVE US OUR SPARRING GOWNS --
NO, FORGIVE US THIS BRIEF INTRUSION! WE SIMPLY CAME BY TO GIVE YOU YOUR PERSONAL INVITATIONS -
- TO THE BALL WE SHALL BE HOLDING AT NETHERFIELD THIS COMING TUESDAY!
IT MEANS A GREAT DEAL TO RECEIVE THIS INVITE PERSONALLY!
I AM AS EVER YOUR SERVANT, MISS BENNET.
WILL YOU BE ATTENDING THE BALL, MISTER COLLINS? WOULD THE ENTERTAINMENT BE PROPER?
AFTER ALL, YOU DON'T WANT A REBUKE FOR SUCH BEHAVIOR FROM THE ARCHBISHOP, OR LADY CATHERINE!
OF COURSE - AND I INTEND TO SOLICIT YOU TO SAVE THE FIRST TWO DANCES FOR ME, MISS BENNET.
THE FIRST TWO DANCES? I'D HOPED TO DANCE WITH MISTER WICKHAM!
NO - DOES THIS FAT LITTLE PRIEST MEAN TO TAKE ME AS A WIFE?

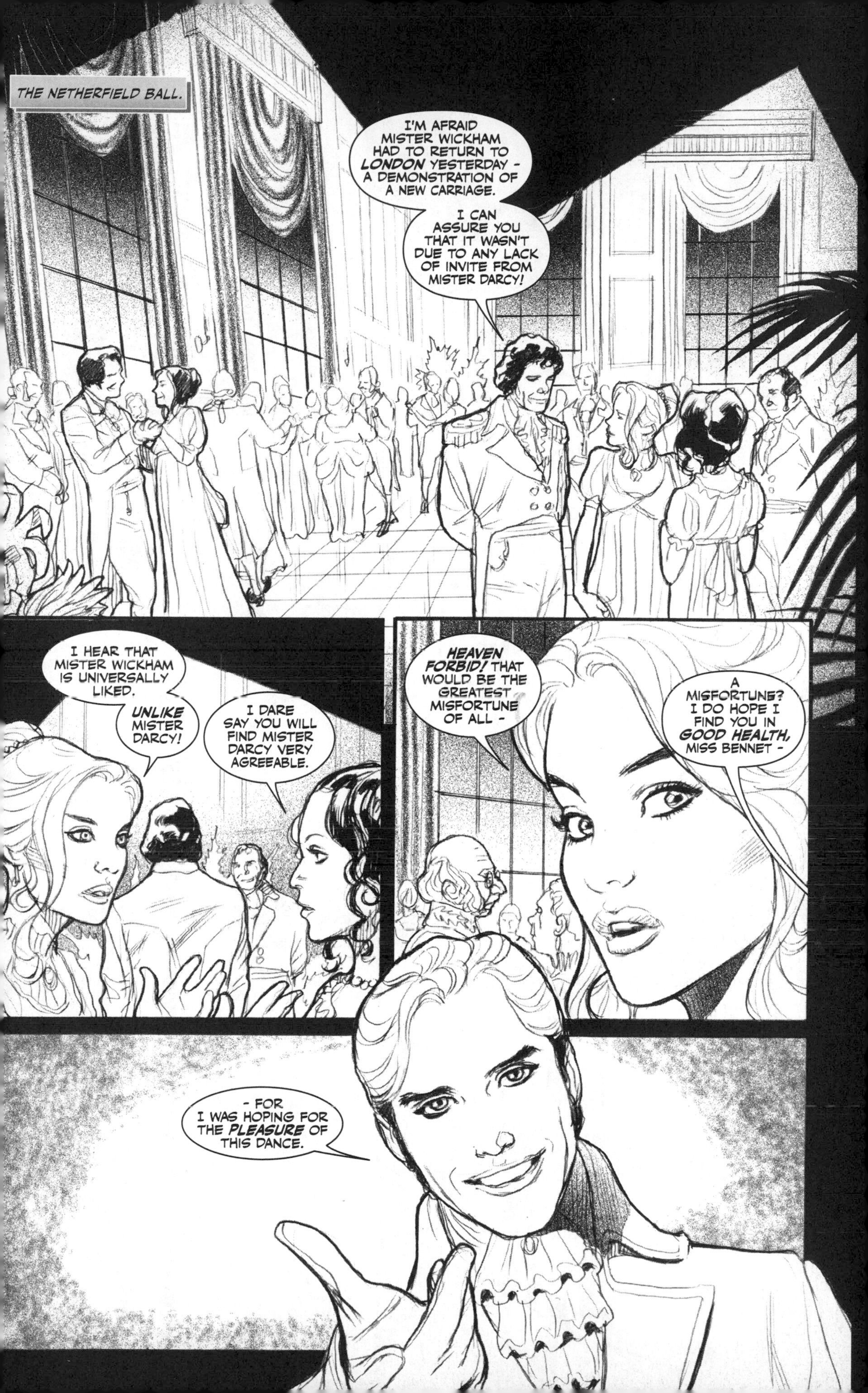
THE NETHERFIELD BALL.
I'M AFRAID MISTER WICKHAM HAD TO RETURN TO LONDON YESTERDAY - A DEMONSTRATION OF A NEW CARRIAGE.
I CAN ASSURE YOU THAT IT WASN'T DUE TO ANY LACK OF INVITE FROM MISTER DARCY!
I HEAR THAT MISTER WICKHAM IS UNIVERSALLY LIKED.
UNLIKE MISTER DARCY!
I DARE SAY YOU WILL FIND MISTER DARCY VERY AGREEABLE.
HEAVEN FORBID! THAT WOULD BE THE GREATEST MISFORTUNE OF ALL -
A MISFORTUNE? I DO HOPE I FIND YOU IN GOOD HEALTH, MISS BENNET -
- FOR I WAS HOPING FOR THE PLEASURE OF THIS DANCE.

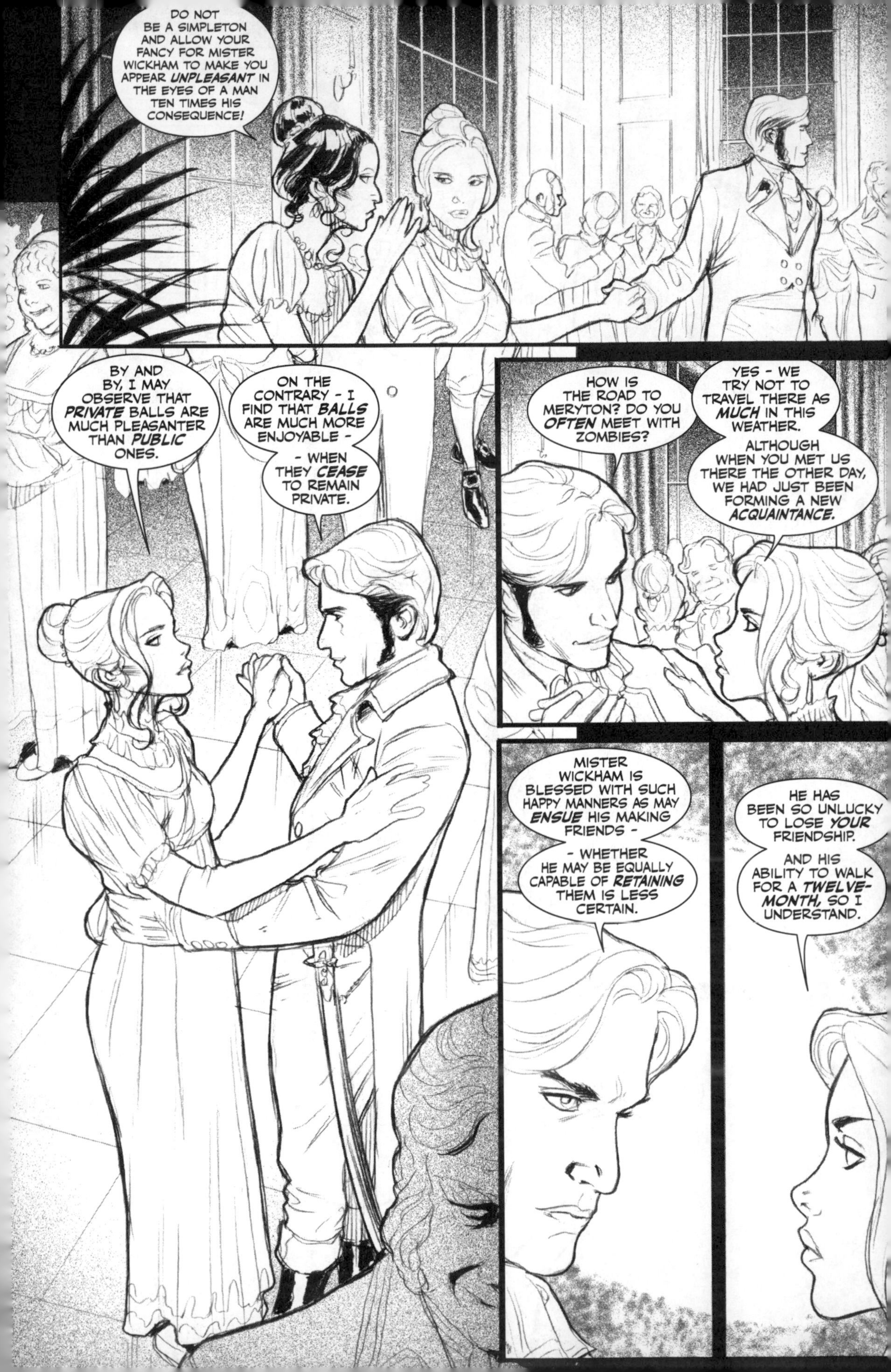
DO NOT BE A SIMPLETON AND ALLOW YOUR FANCY FOR MISTER WICKHAM TO MAKE YOU APPEAR UNPLEASANT IN THE EYES OF A MAN TEN TIMES HIS CONSEQUENCE!
BY AND BY, I MAY OBSERVE THAT PRIVATE BALLS ARE MUCH PLEASANTER THAN PUBLIC ONES.
ON THE CONTRARY - I FIND THAT BALLS ARE MUCH MORE ENJOYABLE -
- WHEN THEY CEASE TO REMAIN PRIVATE.
HOW IS THE ROAD TO MERYTON? DO YOU OFTEN MEET WITH ZOMBIES?
YES - WE TRY NOT TO TRAVEL THERE AS MUCH IN THIS WEATHER.
ALTHOUGH WHEN YOU MET US THERE THE OTHER DAY, WE HAD JUST BEEN FORMING A NEW ACQUAINTANCE.
MISTER WICKHAM IS BLESSED WITH SUCH HAPPY MANNERS AS MAY ENSUE HIS MAKING FRIENDS -
- WHETHER HE MAY BE EQUALLY CAPABLE OF RETAINING THEM IS LESS CERTAIN.
HE HAS BEEN SO UNLUCKY TO LOSE YOUR FRIENDSHIP.
AND HIS ABILITY TO WALK FOR A TWELVE-MONTH, SO I UNDERSTAND.

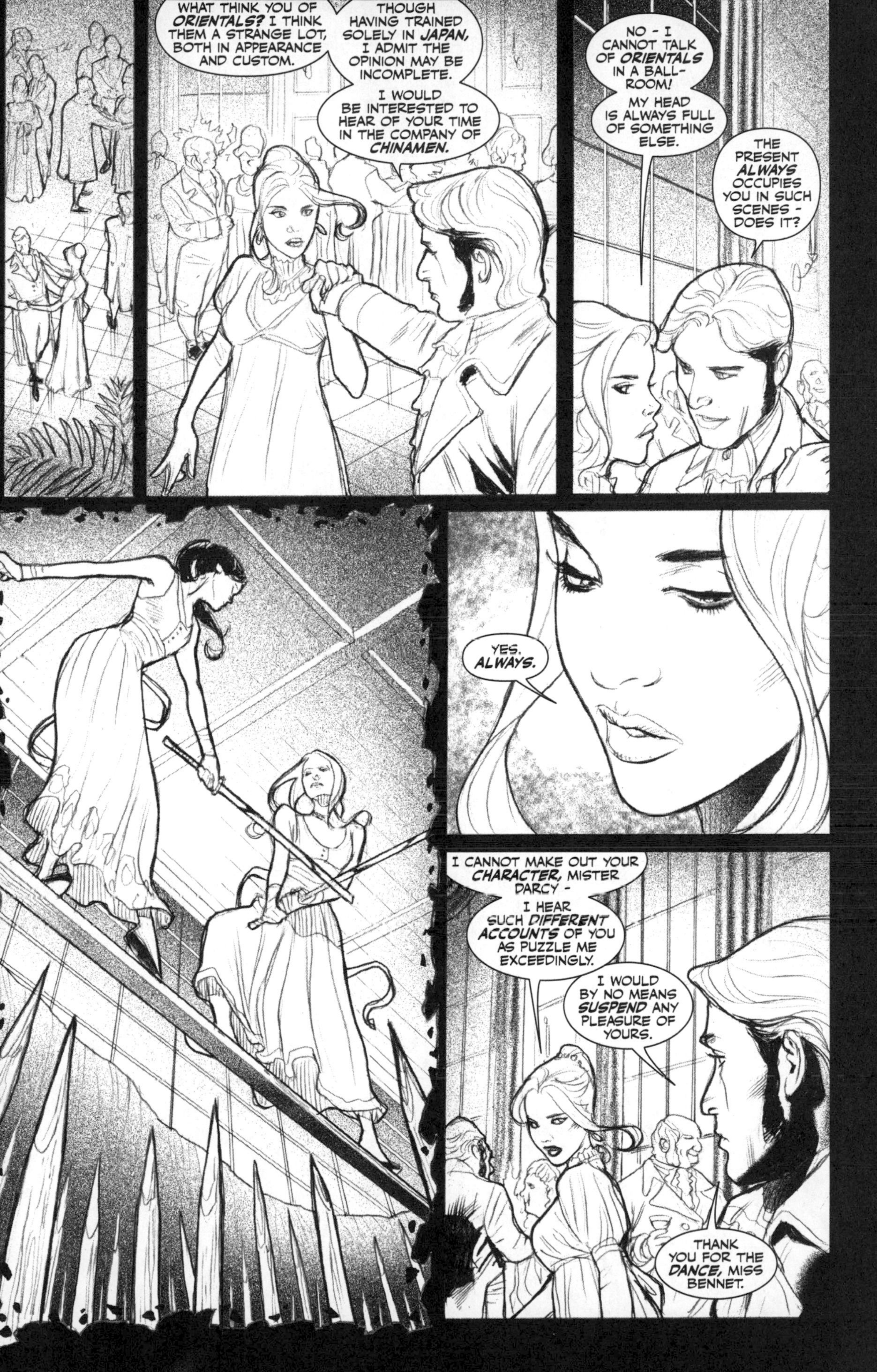
WHAT THINK YOU OF ORIENTALS? I THINK THEM A STRANGE LOT, BOTH IN APPEARANCE AND CUSTOM.
THOUGH HAVING TRAINED SOLELY IN JAPAN, I ADMIT THE OPINION MAY BE INCOMPLETE.
I WOULD BE INTERESTED TO HEAR OF YOUR TIME IN THE COMPANY OF CHINAMEN.
NO - I CANNOT TALK OF ORIENTALS IN A BALL-ROOM!
MY HEAD IS ALWAYS FULL OF SOMETHING ELSE.
THE PRESENT ALWAYS OCCUPIES YOU IN SUCH SCENES - DOES IT?
YES. ALWAYS.
I CANNOT MAKE OUT YOUR CHARACTER, MISTER DARCY -
I HEAR SUCH DIFFERENT ACCOUNTS OF YOU AS PUZZLE ME EXCEEDINGLY.
I WOULD BY NO MEANS SUSPEND ANY PLEASURE OF YOURS.
THANK YOU FOR THE DANCE, MISS BENNET.

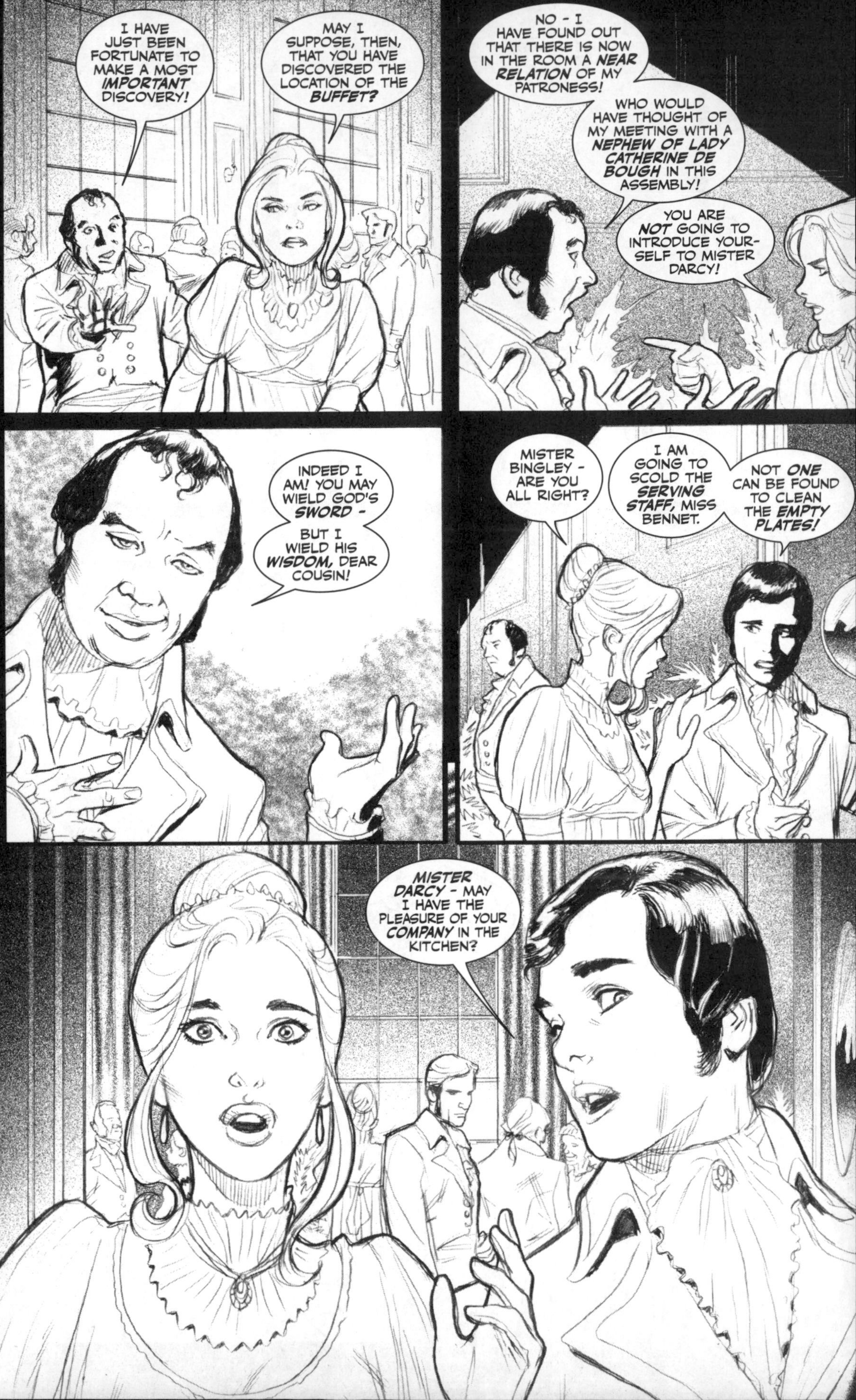
I HAVE JUST BEEN FORTUNATE TO MAKE A MOST IMPORTANT DISCOVERY!
MAY I SUPPOSE, THEN, THAT YOU HAVE DISCOVERED THE LOCATION OF THE BUFFET?
NO - I HAVE FOUND OUT THAT THERE IS NOW IN THE ROOM A NEAR RELATION OF MY PATRONESS!
WHO WOULD HAVE THOUGHT OF MY MEETING WITH A NEPHEW OF LADY CATHERINE DE BOUGH IN THIS ASSEMBLY!
YOU ARE NOT GOING TO INTRODUCE YOURSELF TO MISTER DARCY!
INDEED I AM! YOU MAY WIELD GOD'S SWORD -
BUT I WIELD HIS WISDOM, DEAR COUSIN!
MISTER BINGLEY - ARE YOU ALL RIGHT?
I AM GOING TO SCOLD THE SERVING STAFF, MISS BENNET.
NOT ONE CAN BE FOUND TO CLEAN THE EMPTY PLATES!
MISTER DARCY - MAY I HAVE THE PLEASURE OF YOUR COMPANY IN THE KITCHEN?

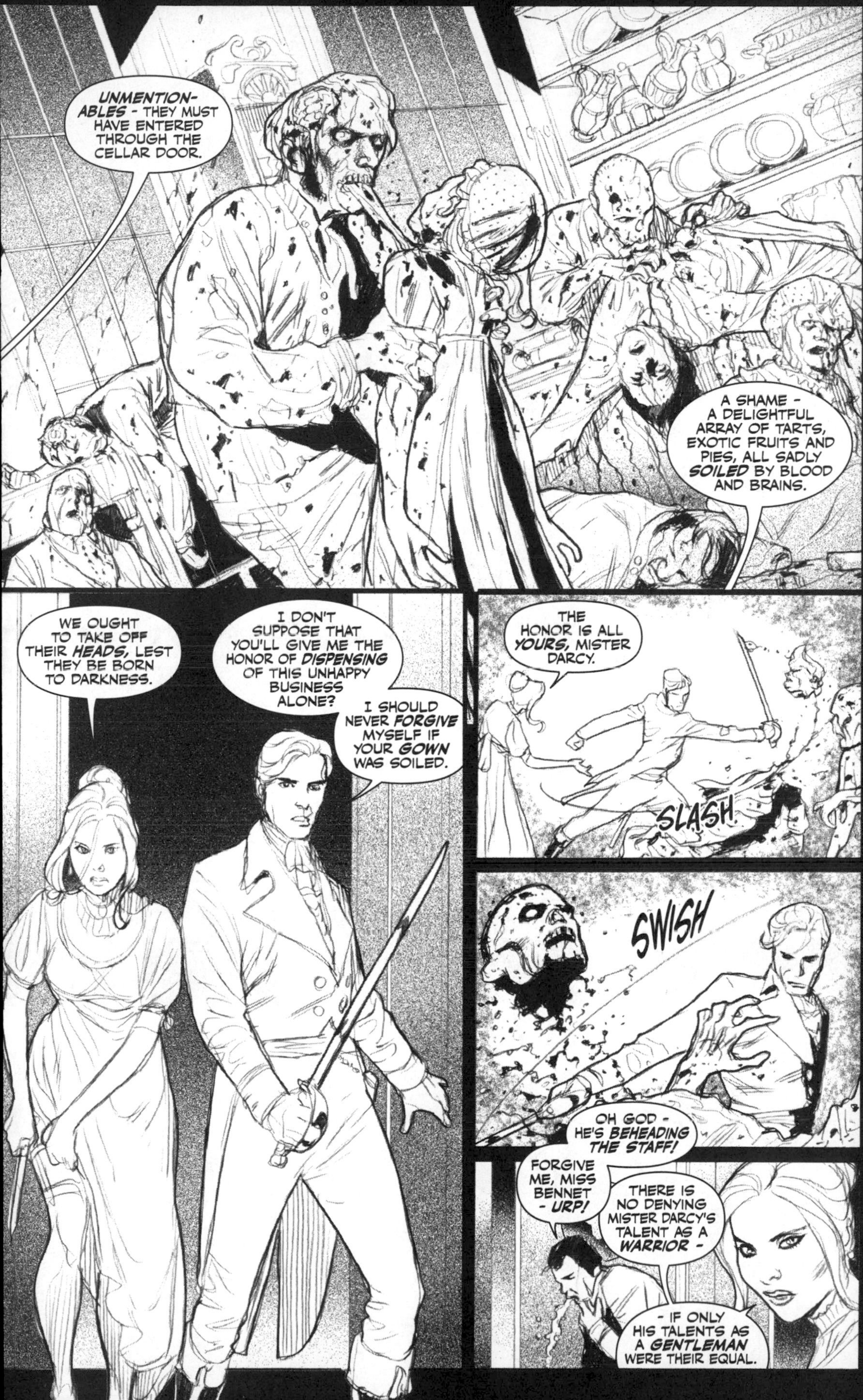
UNMENTIONABLES - THEY MUST HAVE ENTERED THROUGH THE CELLAR DOOR.
A SHAME - A DELIGHTFUL ARRAY OF TARTS, EXOTIC FRUITS AND PIES, ALL SADLY SOILED BY BLOOD AND BRAINS.
WE OUGHT TO TAKE OFF THEIR HEADS, LEST THEY BE BORN TO DARKNESS.
I DON'T SUPPOSE THAT YOU'LL GIVE ME THE HONOR OF DISPENSING OF THIS UNHAPPY BUSINESS ALONE?
I SHOULD NEVER FORGIVE MYSELF IF YOUR GOWN WAS SOILED.
THE HONOR IS ALL YOURS, MISTER DARCY.
SLASH
SWISH
OH GOD - HE'S BEHEADING THE STAFF!
FORGIVE ME, MISS BENNET - URP!
THERE IS NO DENYING MISTER DARCY'S TALENT AS A WARRIOR -
- IF ONLY HIS TALENTS AS A GENTLEMAN WERE THEIR EQUAL.

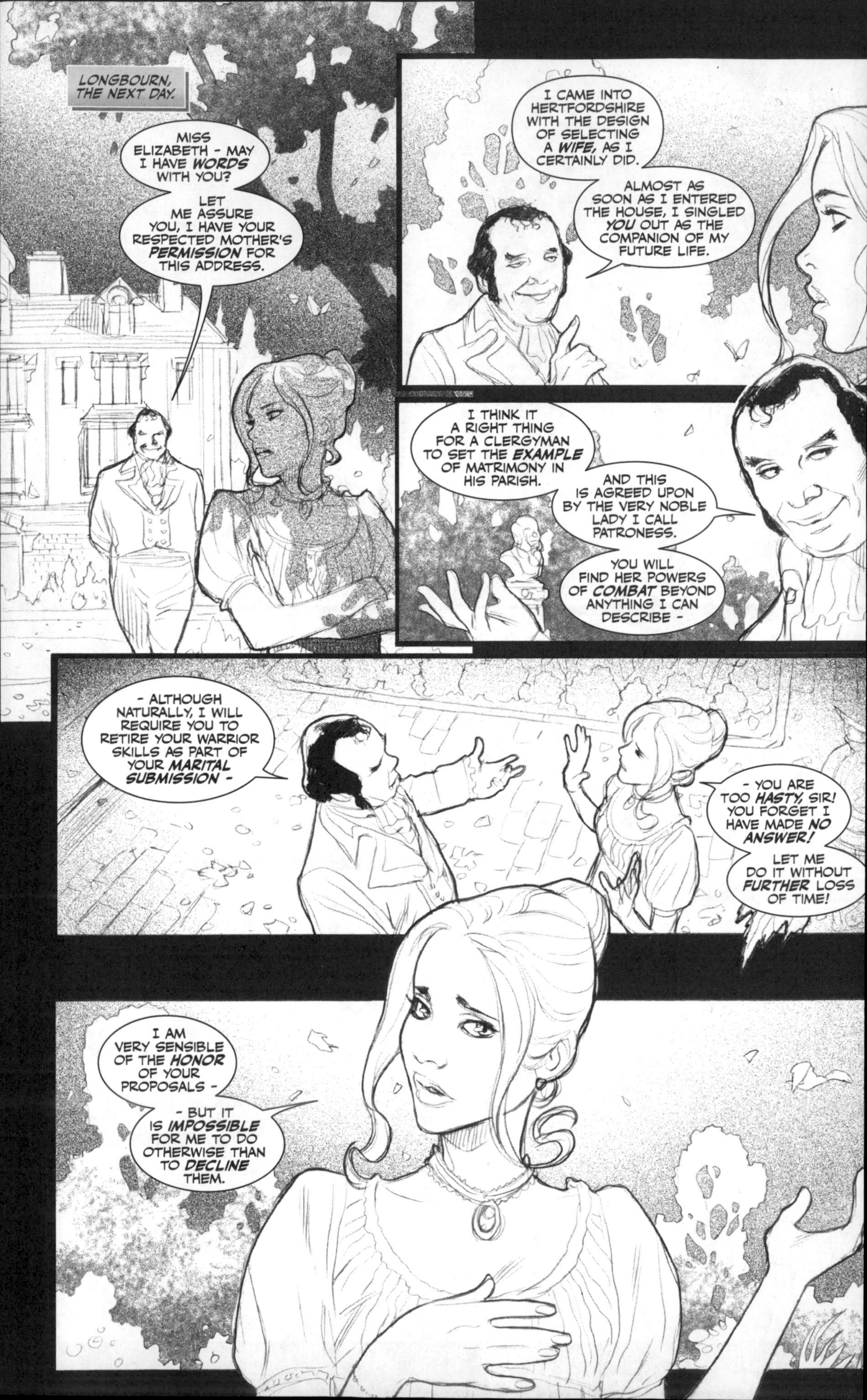

LONGBOURN, THE NEXT DAY.
MISS ELIZABETH - MAY I HAVE WORDS WITH YOU?
LET ME ASSURE YOU, I HAVE YOUR RESPECTED MOTHER'S PERMISSION FOR THIS ADDRESS.
I CAME INTO HERTFORDSHIRE WITH THE DESIGN OF SELECTING A WIFE, AS I CERTAINLY DID.
ALMOST AS SOON AS I ENTERED THE HOUSE, I SINGLED YOU OUT AS THE COMPANION OF MY FUTURE LIFE.
I THINK IT A RIGHT THING FOR A CLERGYMAN TO SET THE EXAMPLE OF MATRIMONY IN HIS PARISH.
AND THIS IS AGREED UPON BY THE VERY NOBLE LADY I CALL PATRONESS.
YOU WILL FIND HER POWERS OF COMBAT BEYOND ANYTHING I CAN DESCRIBE -
- ALTHOUGH NATURALLY, I WILL REQUIRE YOU TO RETIRE YOUR WARRIOR SKILLS AS PART OF YOUR MARITAL SUBMISSION -
- YOU ARE TOO HASTY, SIR! YOU FORGET I HAVE MADE NO ANSWER!
LET ME DO IT WITHOUT FURTHER LOSS OF TIME!
I AM VERY SENSIBLE OF THE HONOR OF YOUR PROPOSALS -
- BUT IT IS IMPOSSIBLE FOR ME TO DO OTHERWISE THAN TO DECLINE THEM.

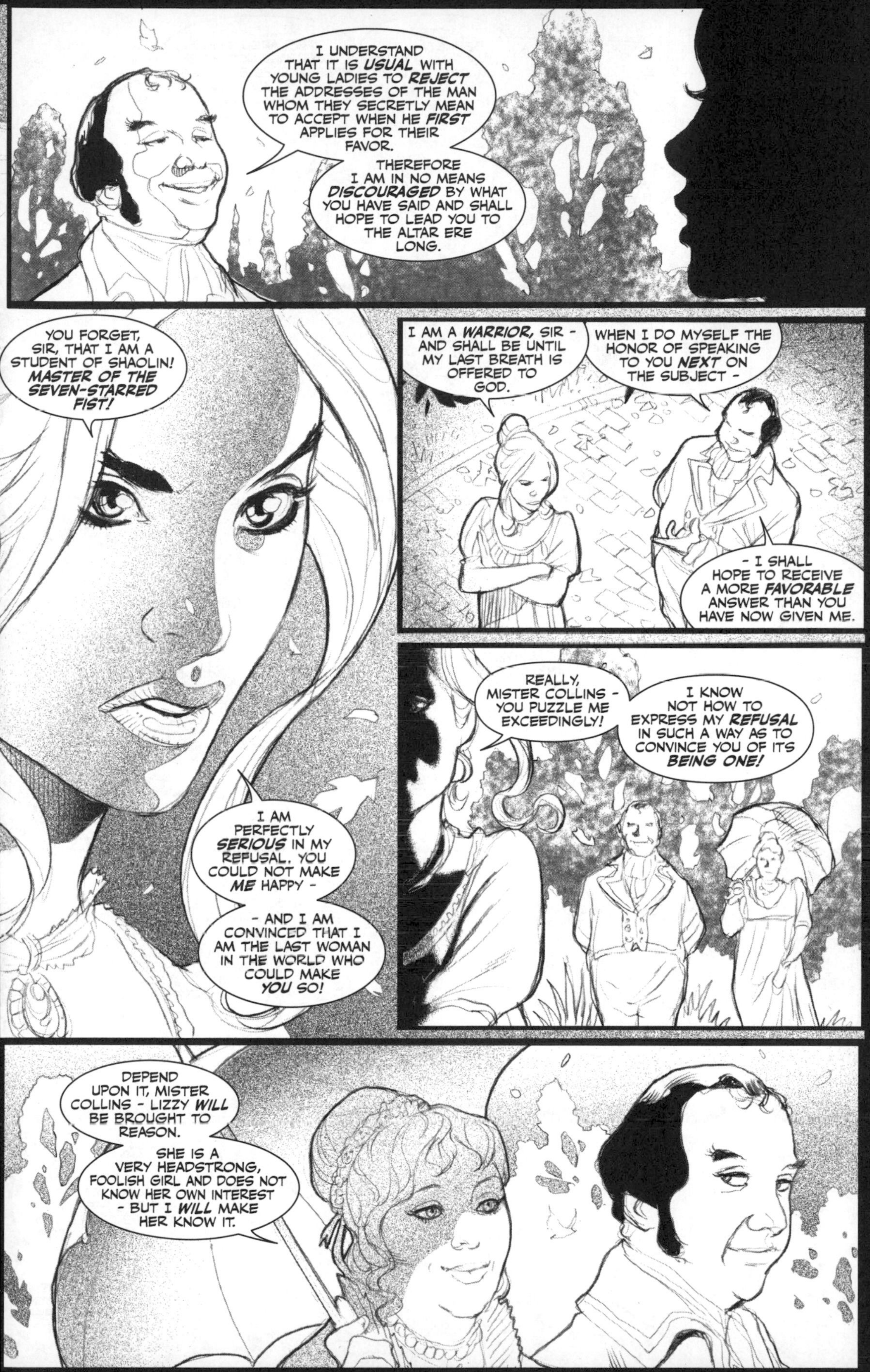
I UNDERSTAND THAT IT IS USUAL WITH YOUNG LADIES TO REJECT THE ADDRESSES OF THE MAN WHOM THEY SECRETLY MEAN TO ACCEPT WHEN HE FIRST APPLIES FOR THEIR FAVOR.
THEREFORE I AM IN NO MEANS DISCOURAGED BY WHAT YOU HAVE SAID AND SHALL HOPE TO LEAD YOU TO THE ALTAR ERE LONG.
YOU FORGET, SIR, THAT I AM A STUDENT OF SHAOLIN! MASTER OF THE SEVEN-STARRED FIST!
I AM A WARRIOR, SIR - AND SHALL BE UNTIL MY LAST BREATH IS OFFERED TO GOD.
WHEN I DO MYSELF THE HONOR OF SPEAKING TO YOU NEXT ON THE SUBJECT -
- I SHALL HOPE TO RECEIVE A MORE FAVORABLE ANSWER THAN YOU HAVE NOW GIVEN ME.
I AM PERFECTLY SERIOUS IN MY REFUSAL. YOU COULD NOT MAKE ME HAPPY -
- AND I AM CONVINCED THAT I AM THE LAST WOMAN IN THE WORLD WHO COULD MAKE YOU SO!
REALLY, MISTER COLLINS - YOU PUZZLE ME EXCEEDINGLY!
I KNOW NOT HOW TO EXPRESS MY REFUSAL IN SUCH A WAY AS TO CONVINCE YOU OF ITS BEING ONE!
DEPEND UPON IT, MISTER COLLINS - LIZZY WILL BE BROUGHT TO REASON.
SHE IS A VERY HEADSTRONG, FOOLISH GIRL AND DOES NOT KNOW HER OWN INTEREST - BUT I WILL MAKE HER KNOW IT.

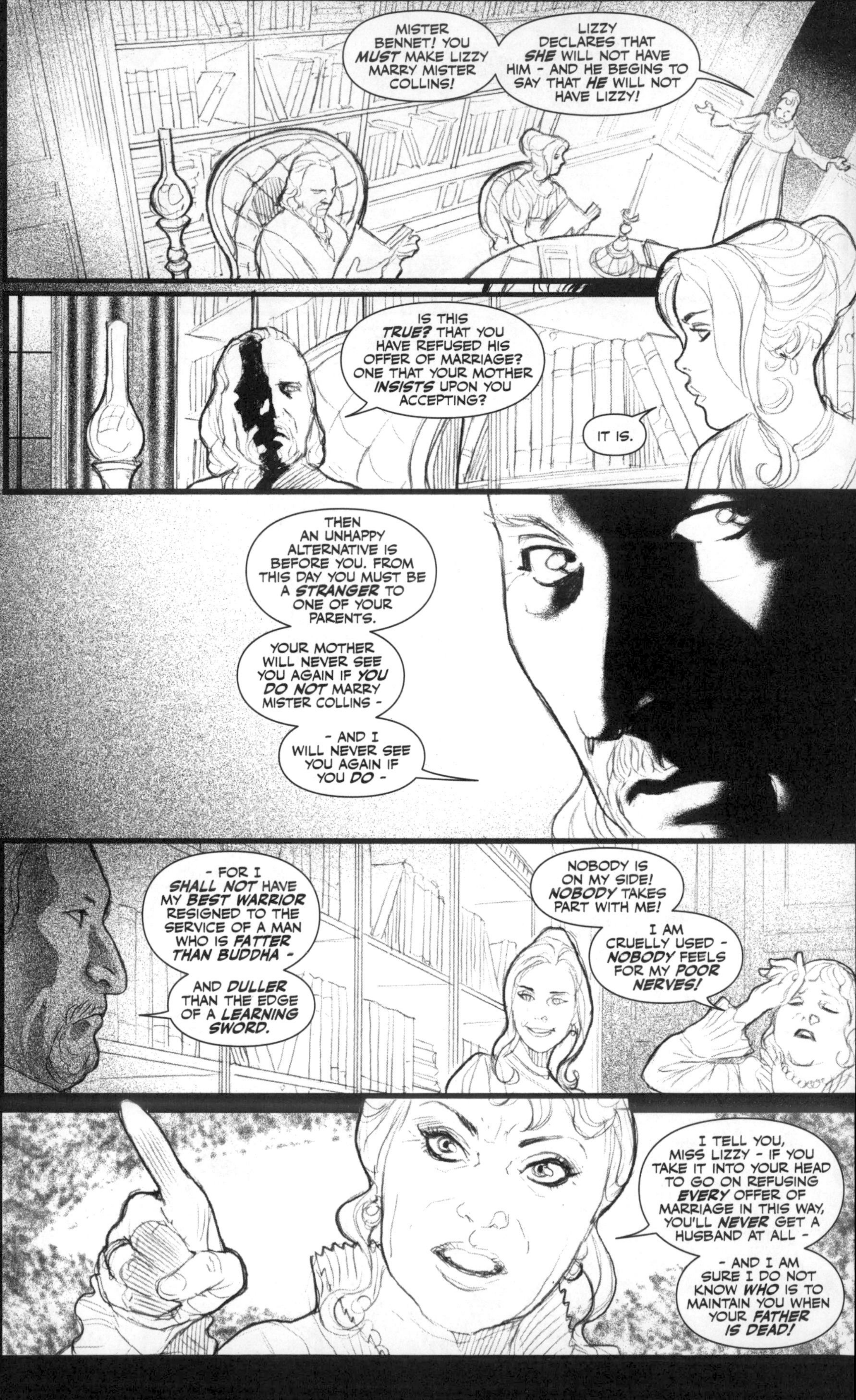
MISTER BENNET! YOU MUST MAKE LIZZY MARRY MISTER COLLINS!
LIZZY DECLARES THAT SHE WILL NOT HAVE HIM - AND HE BEGINS TO SAY THAT HE WILL NOT HAVE LIZZY!
IS THIS TRUE? THAT YOU HAVE REFUSED HIS OFFER OF MARRIAGE? ONE THAT YOUR MOTHER INSISTS UPON YOU ACCEPTING?
IT IS.
THEN AN UNHAPPY ALTERNATIVE IS BEFORE YOU. FROM THIS DAY YOU MUST BE A STRANGER TO ONE OF YOUR PARENTS.
YOUR MOTHER WILL NEVER SEE YOU AGAIN IF YOU DO NOT MARRY MISTER COLLINS -
- AND I WILL NEVER SEE YOU AGAIN IF YOU DO -
- FOR I SHALL NOT HAVE MY BEST WARRIOR RESIGNED TO THE SERVICE OF A MAN WHO IS FATTER THAN BUDDHA -
AND DULLER THAN THE EDGE OF A LEARNING SWORD.
NOBODY IS ON MY SIDE! NOBODY TAKES PART WITH ME!
I AM CRUELLY USED - NOBODY FEELS FOR MY POOR NERVES!
I TELL YOU, MISS LIZZY - IF YOU TAKE IT INTO YOUR HEAD TO GO ON REFUSING EVERY OFFER OF MARRIAGE IN THIS WAY, YOU'LL NEVER GET A HUSBAND AT ALL -
- AND I AM SURE I DO NOT KNOW WHO IS TO MAINTAIN YOU WHEN YOUR FATHER IS DEAD!

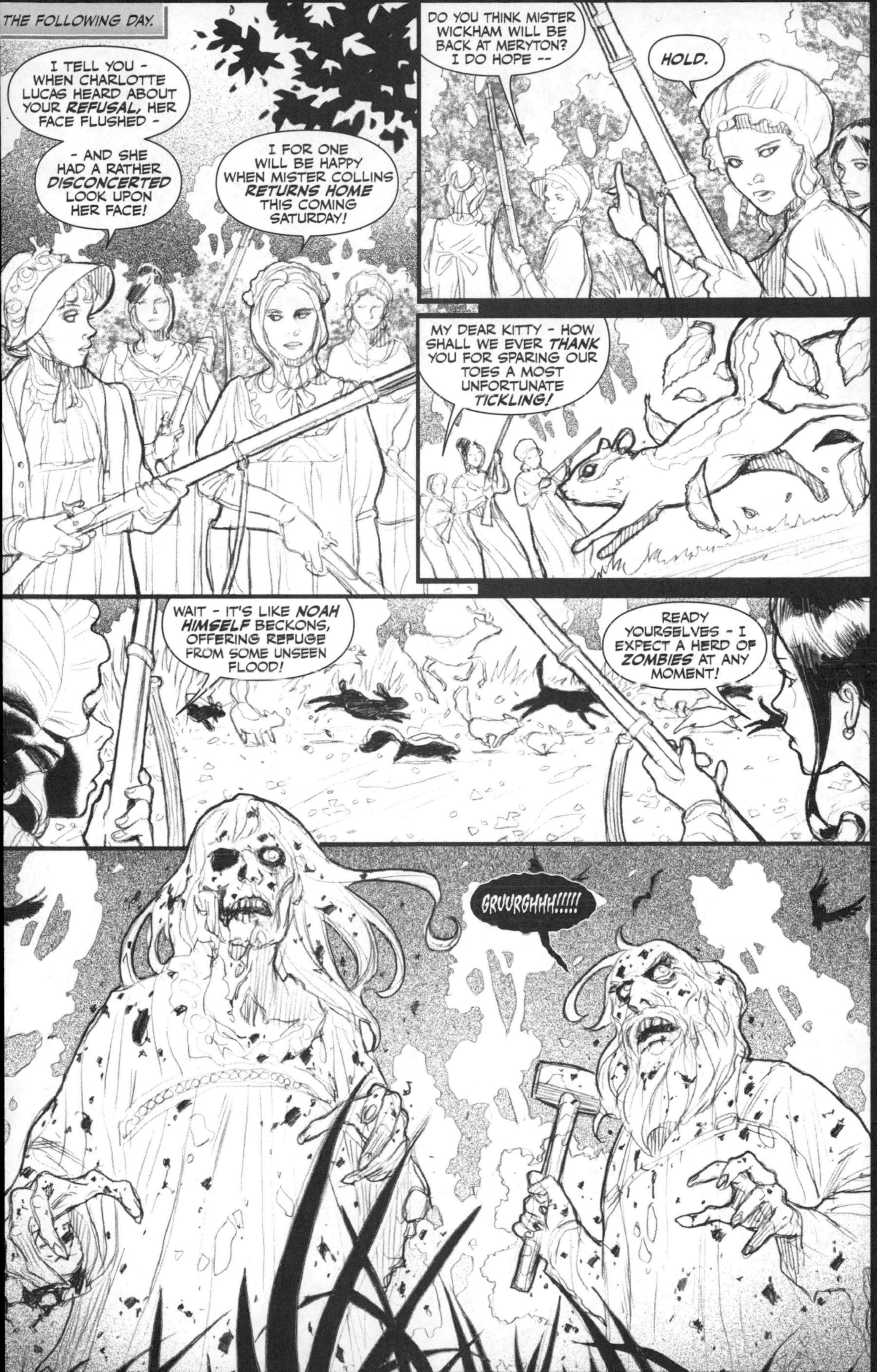
THE FOLLOWING DAY.
I TELL YOU - WHEN CHARLOTTE LUCAS HEARD ABOUT YOUR REFUSAL, HER FACE FLUSHED -
- AND SHE HAD A RATHER DISCONCERTED LOOK UPON HER FACE!
I FOR ONE WILL BE HAPPY WHEN MISTER COLLINS RETURNS HOME THIS COMING SATURDAY!
DO YOU THINK MISTER WICKHAM WILL BE BACK AT MERYTON? I DO HOPE --
HOLD.
MY DEAR KITTY - HOW SHALL WE EVER THANK YOU FOR SPARING OUR TOES A MOST UNFORTUNATE TICKLING!
WAIT - IT'S LIKE NOAH HIMSELF BECKONS, OFFERING REFUGE FROM SOME UNSEEN FLOOD!
READY YOURSELVES - I EXPECT A HERD OF ZOMBIES AT ANY MOMENT!
GRUURGHHH!!!!!

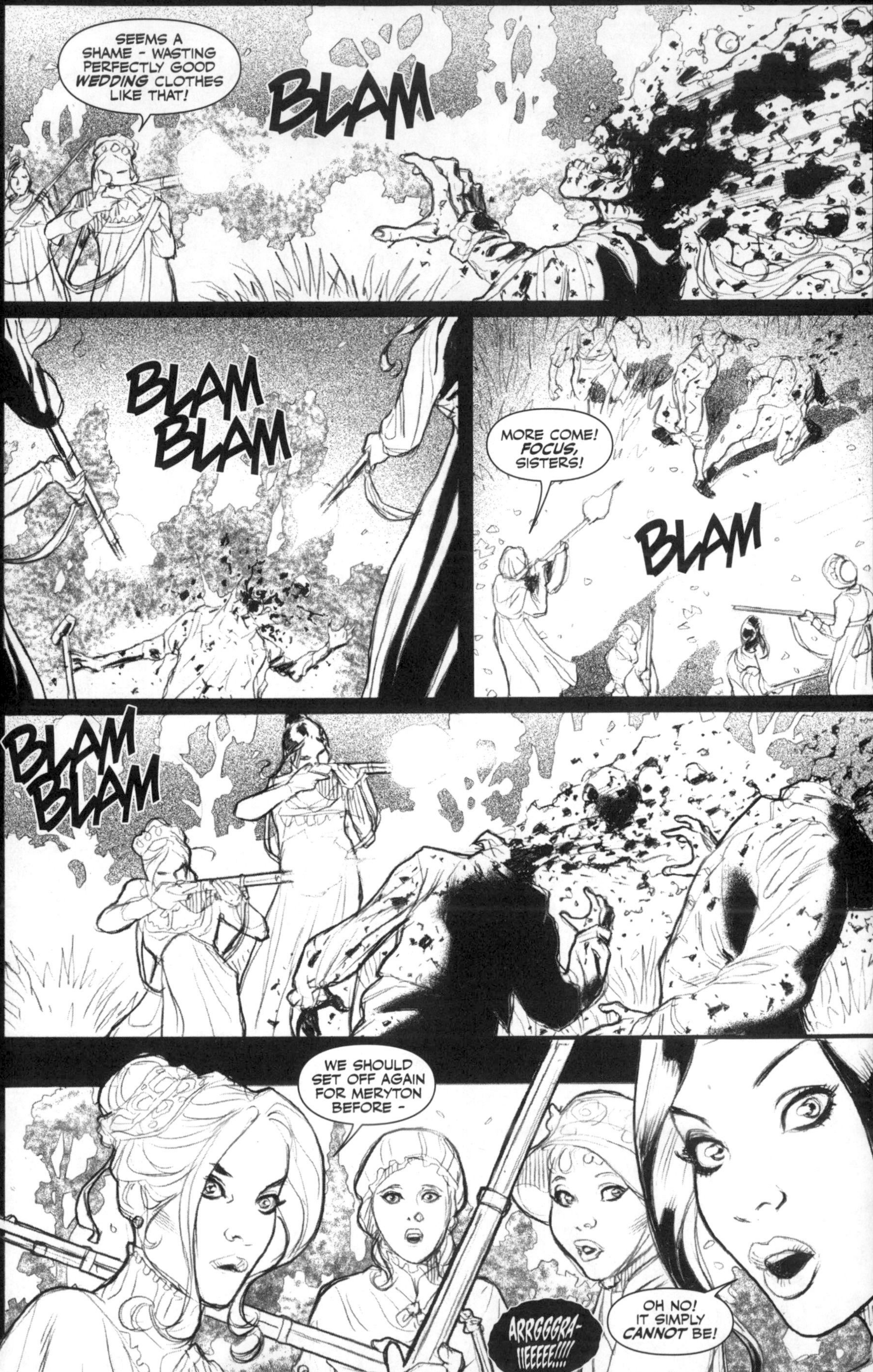

SEEMS A SHAME - WASTING PERFECTLY GOOD *WEDDING* CLOTHES LIKE THAT!
BLAM
BLAM BLAM
MORE COME! *FOCUS,* SISTERS!
BLAM
BLAM BLAM
WE SHOULD SET OFF AGAIN FOR MERYTON BEFORE -
ARRGGGRA-IIEEEEE!!!!
OH NO! IT SIMPLY *CANNOT* BE!

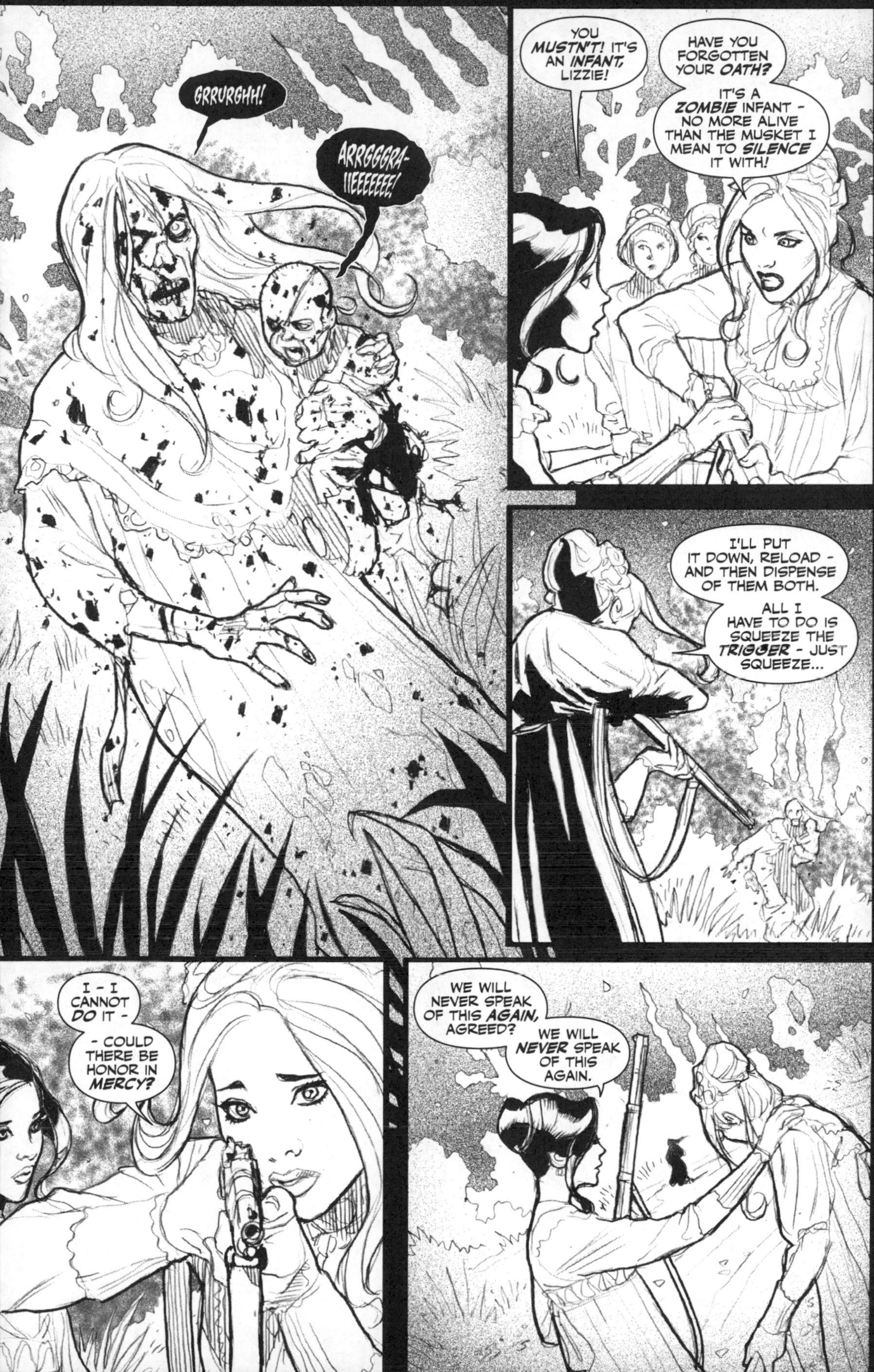
GRRURGHH!
ARRGGGRA-IIEEEEEEE!
YOU MUSTN'T! IT'S AN INFANT, LIZZIE!
HAVE YOU FORGOTTEN YOUR OATH?
IT'S A ZOMBIE INFANT - NO MORE ALIVE THAN THE MUSKET I MEAN TO SILENCE IT WITH!
I'LL PUT IT DOWN, RELOAD - AND THEN DISPENSE OF THEM BOTH.
ALL I HAVE TO DO IS SQUEEZE THE TRIGGER - JUST SQUEEZE...
I - I CANNOT DO IT -
- COULD THERE BE HONOR IN MERCY?
WE WILL NEVER SPEAK OF THIS AGAIN, AGREED?
WE WILL NEVER SPEAK OF THIS AGAIN.

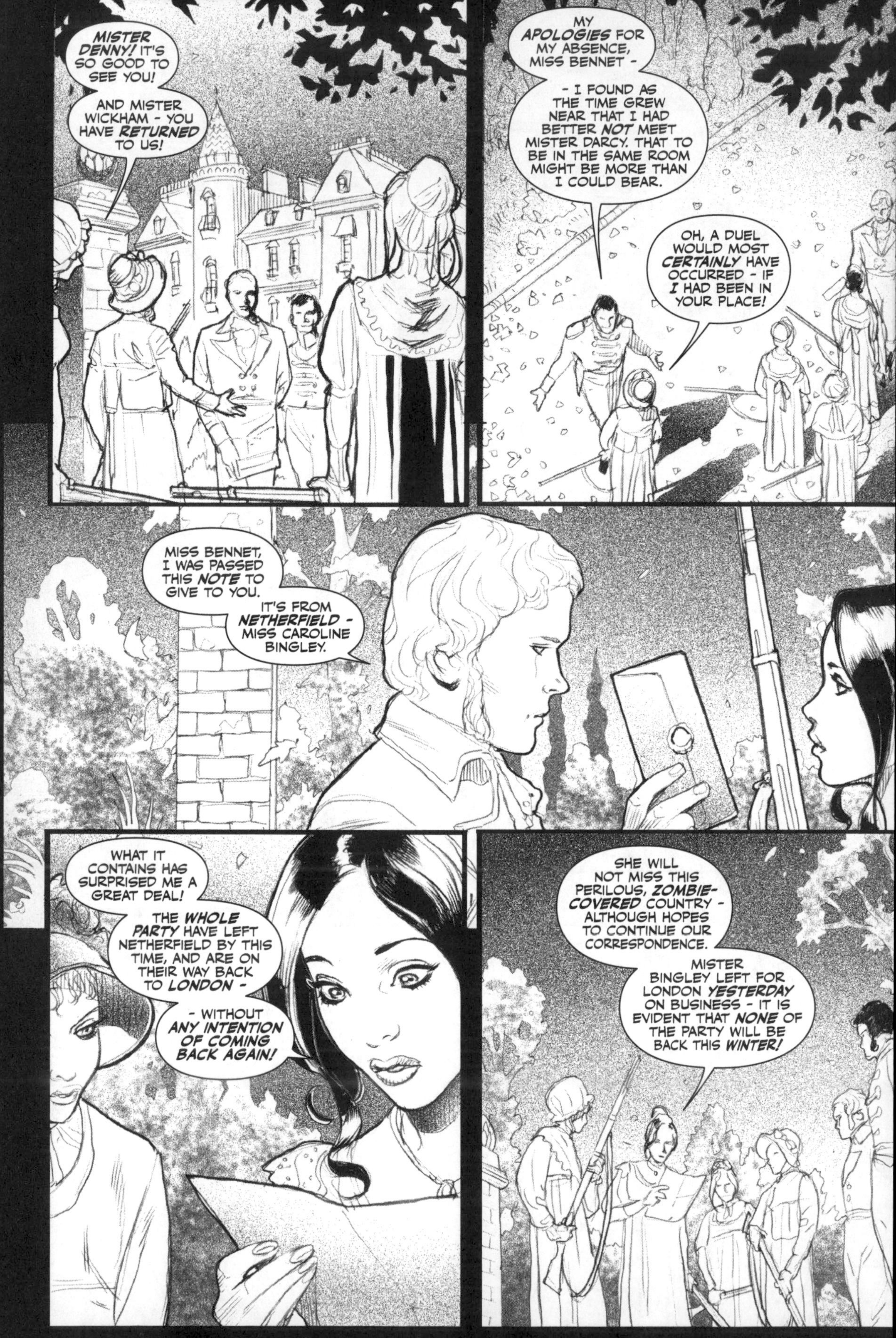
MISTER DENNY! IT'S SO GOOD TO SEE YOU!
AND MISTER WICKHAM - YOU HAVE RETURNED TO US!
MY APOLOGIES FOR MY ABSENCE, MISS BENNET -
- I FOUND AS THE TIME GREW NEAR THAT I HAD BETTER NOT MEET MISTER DARCY. THAT TO BE IN THE SAME ROOM MIGHT BE MORE THAN I COULD BEAR.
OH, A DUEL WOULD MOST CERTAINLY HAVE OCCURRED - IF I HAD BEEN IN YOUR PLACE!
MISS BENNET, I WAS PASSED THIS NOTE TO GIVE TO YOU.
IT'S FROM NETHERFIELD - MISS CAROLINE BINGLEY.
WHAT IT CONTAINS HAS SURPRISED ME A GREAT DEAL!
THE WHOLE PARTY HAVE LEFT NETHERFIELD BY THIS TIME, AND ARE ON THEIR WAY BACK TO LONDON -
- WITHOUT ANY INTENTION OF COMING BACK AGAIN!
SHE WILL NOT MISS THIS PERILOUS, ZOMBIE-COVERED COUNTRY - ALTHOUGH HOPES TO CONTINUE OUR CORRESPONDENCE.
MISTER BINGLEY LEFT FOR LONDON YESTERDAY ON BUSINESS - IT IS EVIDENT THAT NONE OF THE PARTY WILL BE BACK THIS WINTER!

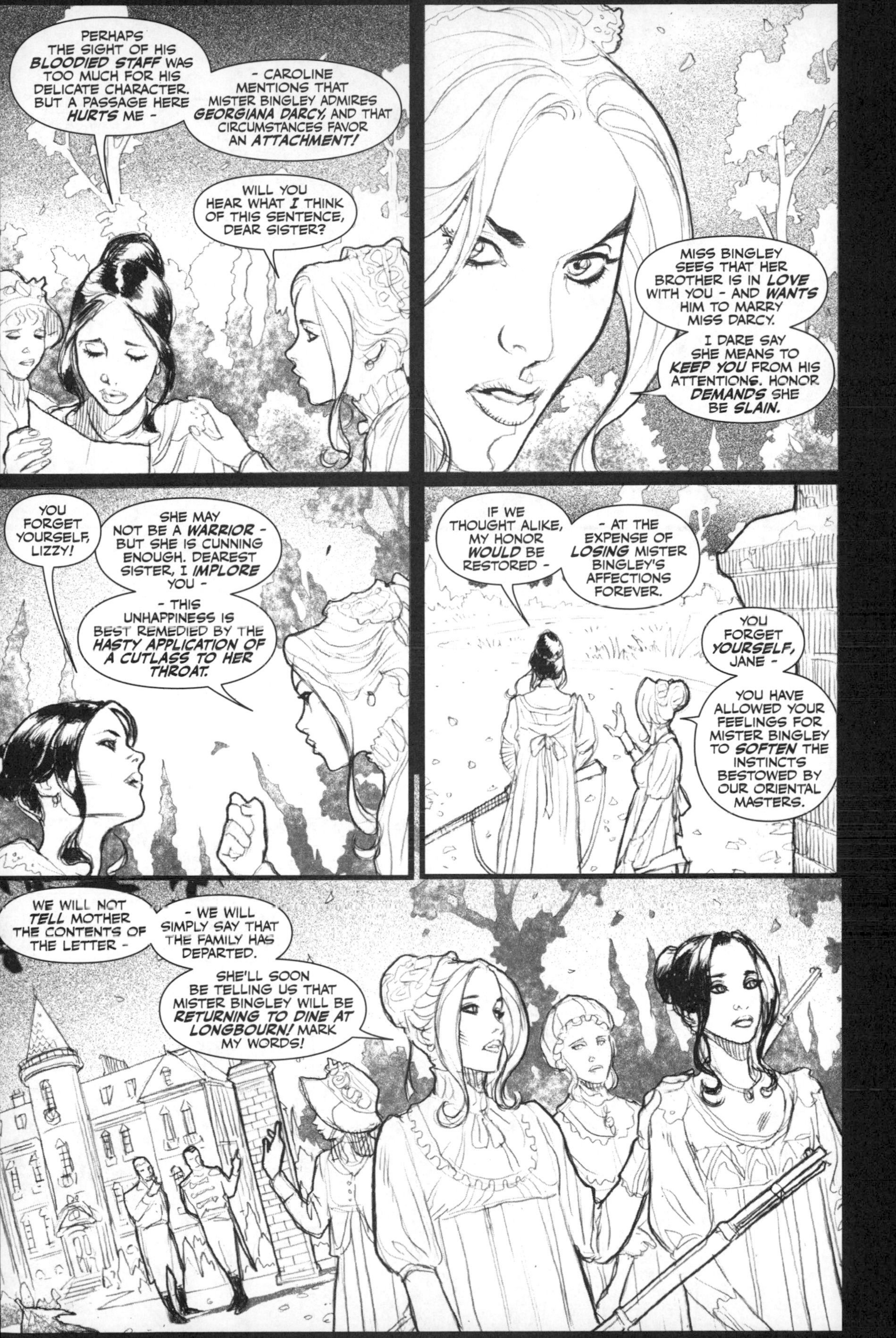
PERHAPS THE SIGHT OF HIS BLOODIED STAFF WAS TOO MUCH FOR HIS DELICATE CHARACTER. BUT A PASSAGE HERE HURTS ME -
- CAROLINE MENTIONS THAT MISTER BINGLEY ADMIRES GEORGIANA DARCY, AND THAT CIRCUMSTANCES FAVOR AN ATTACHMENT!
WILL YOU HEAR WHAT I THINK OF THIS SENTENCE, DEAR SISTER?
MISS BINGLEY SEES THAT HER BROTHER IS IN LOVE WITH YOU - AND WANTS HIM TO MARRY MISS DARCY.
I DARE SAY SHE MEANS TO KEEP YOU FROM HIS ATTENTIONS. HONOR DEMANDS SHE BE SLAIN.
YOU FORGET YOURSELF, LIZZY!
SHE MAY NOT BE A WARRIOR - BUT SHE IS CUNNING ENOUGH. DEAREST SISTER, I IMPLORE YOU -
- THIS UNHAPPINESS IS BEST REMEDIED BY THE HASTY APPLICATION OF A CUTLASS TO HER THROAT.
IF WE THOUGHT ALIKE, MY HONOR WOULD BE RESTORED -
- AT THE EXPENSE OF LOSING MISTER BINGLEY'S AFFECTIONS FOREVER.
YOU FORGET YOURSELF, JANE -
YOU HAVE ALLOWED YOUR FEELINGS FOR MISTER BINGLEY TO SOFTEN THE INSTINCTS BESTOWED BY OUR ORIENTAL MASTERS.
WE WILL NOT TELL MOTHER THE CONTENTS OF THE LETTER -
- WE WILL SIMPLY SAY THAT THE FAMILY HAS DEPARTED.
SHE'LL SOON BE TELLING US THAT MISTER BINGLEY WILL BE RETURNING TO DINE AT LONGBOURN! MARK MY WORDS!

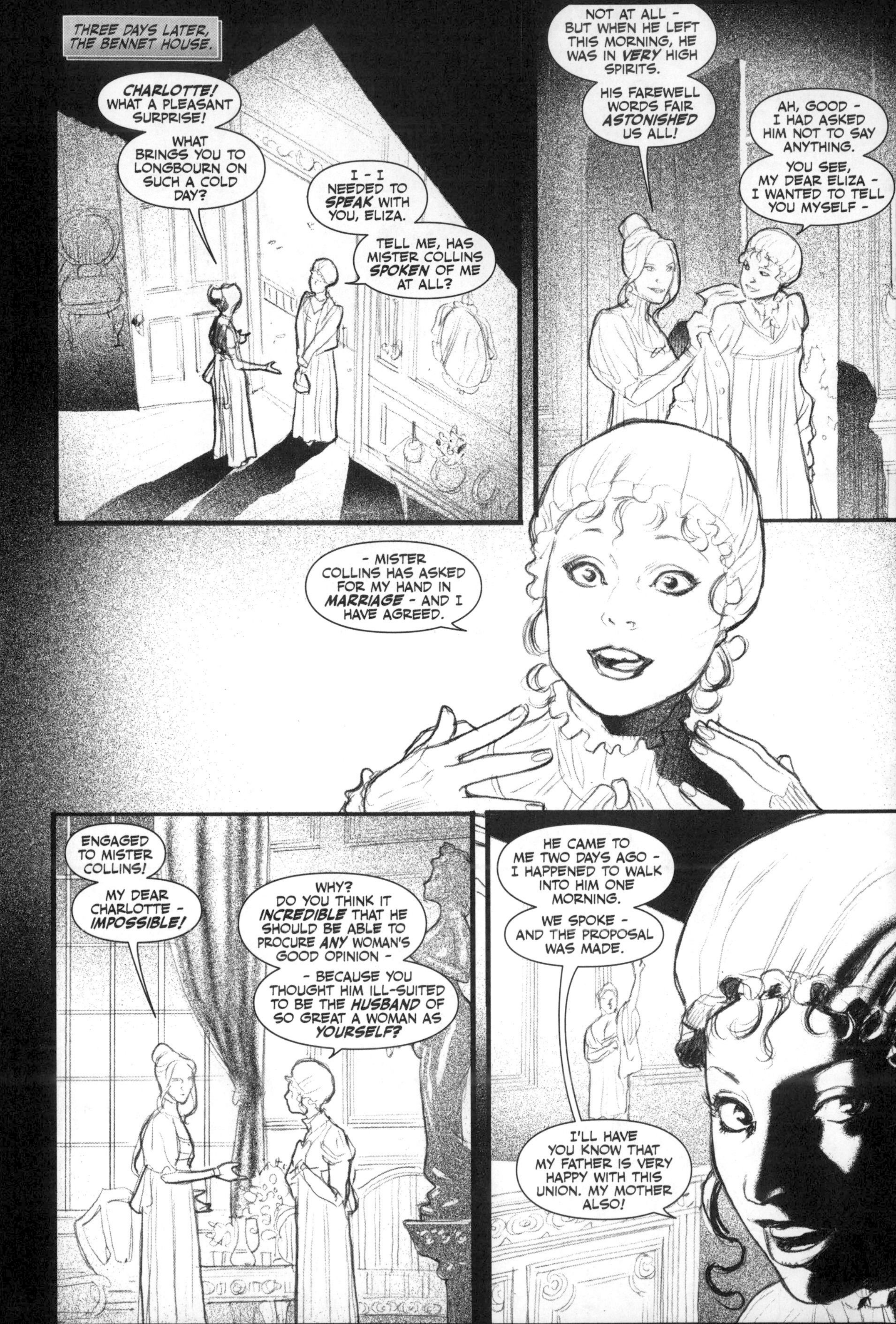
THREE DAYS LATER, THE BENNET HOUSE.
CHARLOTTE! WHAT A PLEASANT SURPRISE!
WHAT BRINGS YOU TO LONGBOURN ON SUCH A COLD DAY?
I - I NEEDED TO SPEAK WITH YOU, ELIZA.
TELL ME, HAS MISTER COLLINS SPOKEN OF ME AT ALL?
NOT AT ALL - BUT WHEN HE LEFT THIS MORNING, HE WAS IN VERY HIGH SPIRITS.
HIS FAREWELL WORDS FAIR ASTONISHED US ALL!
AH, GOOD - I HAD ASKED HIM NOT TO SAY ANYTHING.
YOU SEE, MY DEAR ELIZA - I WANTED TO TELL YOU MYSELF -
- MISTER COLLINS HAS ASKED FOR MY HAND IN MARRIAGE - AND I HAVE AGREED.
ENGAGED TO MISTER COLLINS!
MY DEAR CHARLOTTE - IMPOSSIBLE!
WHY? DO YOU THINK IT INCREDIBLE THAT HE SHOULD BE ABLE TO PROCURE ANY WOMAN'S GOOD OPINION -
- BECAUSE YOU THOUGHT HIM ILL-SUITED TO BE THE HUSBAND OF SO GREAT A WOMAN AS YOURSELF?
HE CAME TO ME TWO DAYS AGO - I HAPPENED TO WALK INTO HIM ONE MORNING.
WE SPOKE - AND THE PROPOSAL WAS MADE.
I'LL HAVE YOU KNOW THAT MY FATHER IS VERY HAPPY WITH THIS UNION. MY MOTHER ALSO!

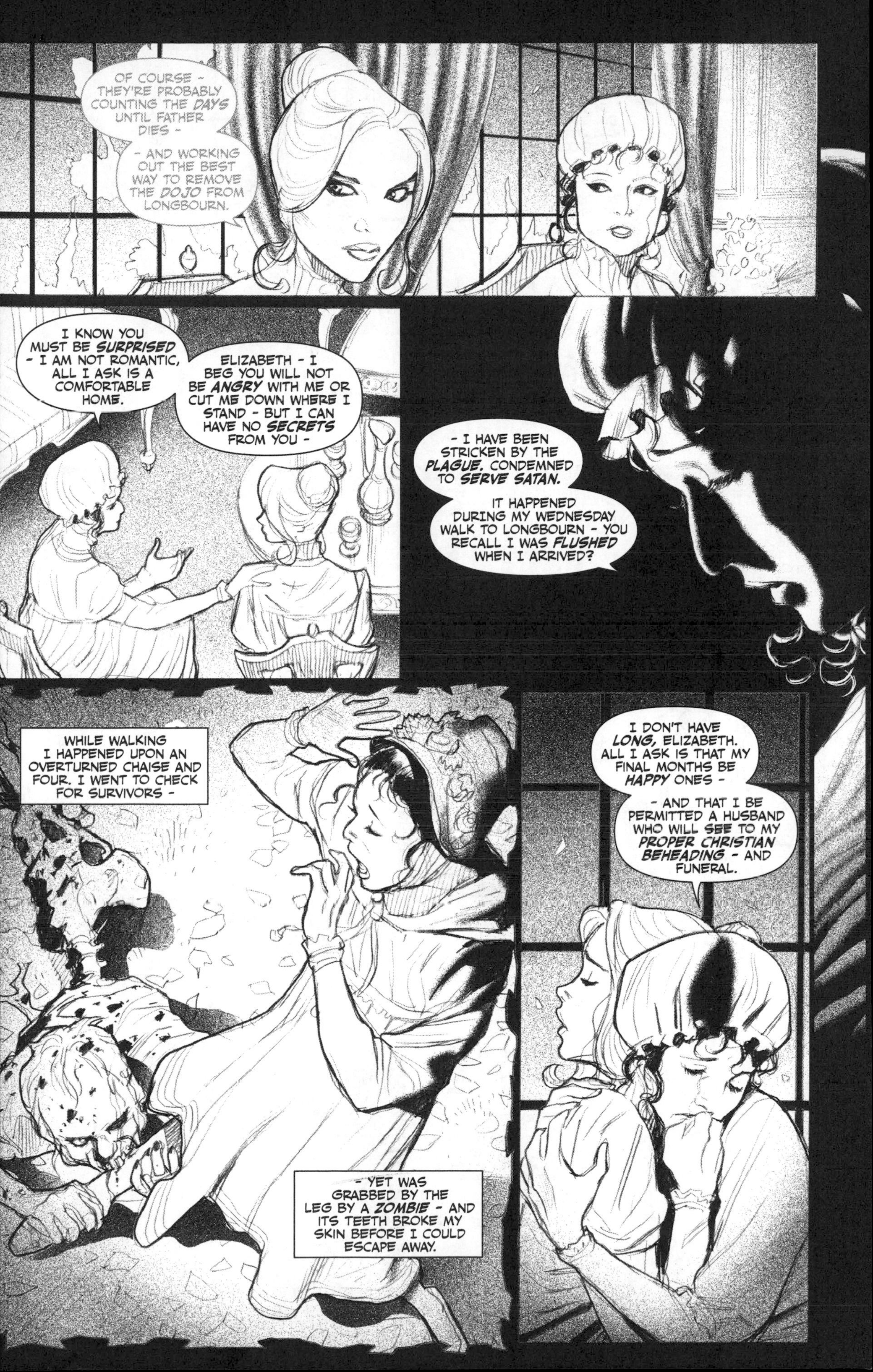
OF COURSE - THEY'RE PROBABLY COUNTING THE DAYS UNTIL FATHER DIES -
- AND WORKING OUT THE BEST WAY TO REMOVE THE DOJO FROM LONGBOURN.
I KNOW YOU MUST BE SURPRISED - I AM NOT ROMANTIC, ALL I ASK IS A COMFORTABLE HOME.
ELIZABETH - I BEG YOU WILL NOT BE ANGRY WITH ME OR CUT ME DOWN WHERE I STAND - BUT I CAN HAVE NO SECRETS FROM YOU -
- I HAVE BEEN STRICKEN BY THE PLAGUE. CONDEMNED TO SERVE SATAN.
IT HAPPENED DURING MY WEDNESDAY WALK TO LONGBOURN - YOU RECALL I WAS FLUSHED WHEN I ARRIVED?
WHILE WALKING I HAPPENED UPON AN OVERTURNED CHAISE AND FOUR. I WENT TO CHECK FOR SURVIVORS -
- YET WAS GRABBED BY THE LEG BY A ZOMBIE - AND ITS TEETH BROKE MY SKIN BEFORE I COULD ESCAPE AWAY.
I DON'T HAVE LONG, ELIZABETH. ALL I ASK IS THAT MY FINAL MONTHS BE HAPPY ONES -
- AND THAT I BE PERMITTED A HUSBAND WHO WILL SEE TO MY PROPER CHRISTIAN BEHEADING - AND FUNERAL.

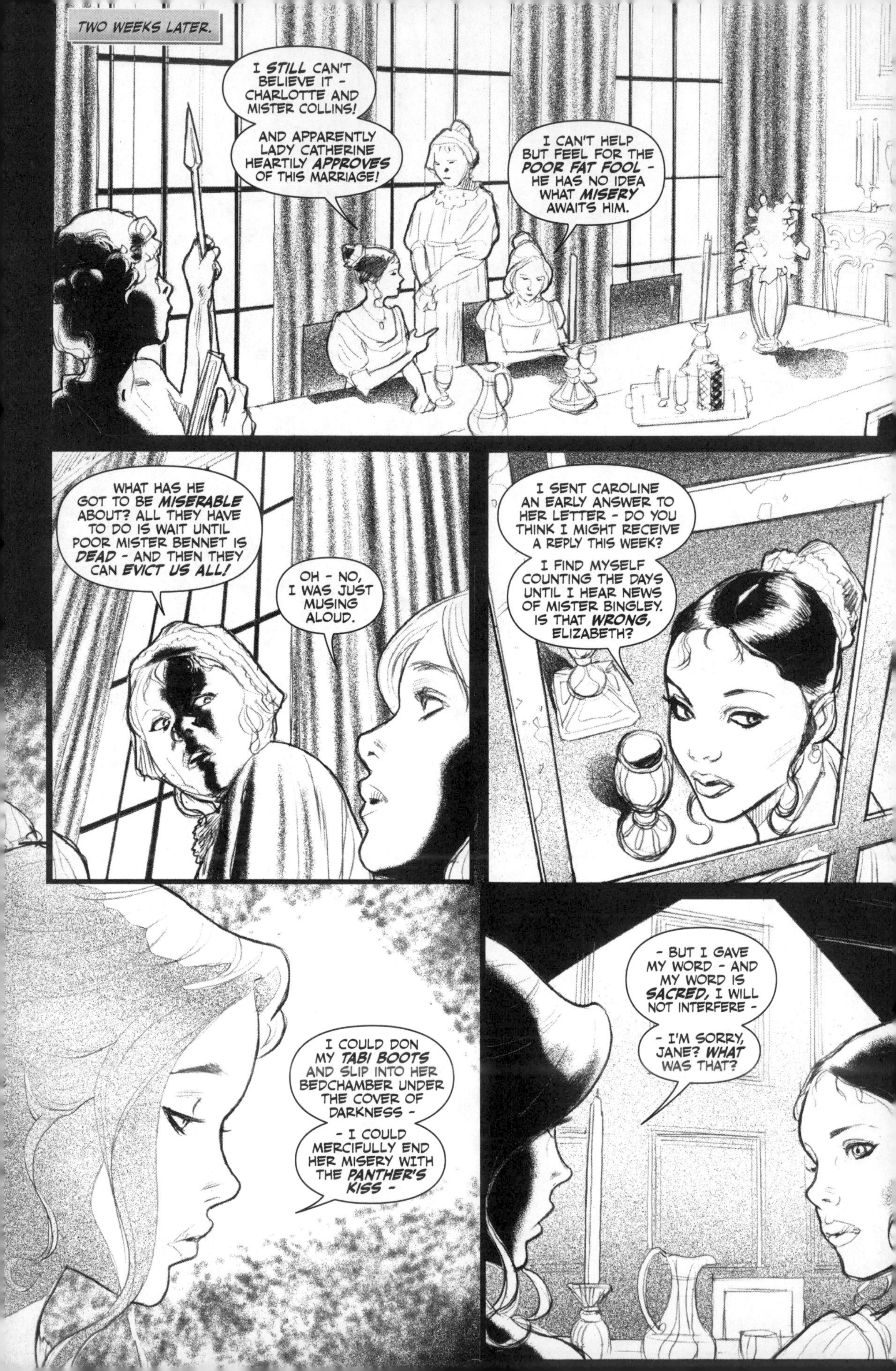
TWO WEEKS LATER.
I STILL CAN'T BELIEVE IT - CHARLOTTE AND MISTER COLLINS!
AND APPARENTLY LADY CATHERINE HEARTILY APPROVES OF THIS MARRIAGE!
I CAN'T HELP BUT FEEL FOR THE POOR FAT FOOL - HE HAS NO IDEA WHAT MISERY AWAITS HIM.
WHAT HAS HE GOT TO BE MISERABLE ABOUT? ALL THEY HAVE TO DO IS WAIT UNTIL POOR MISTER BENNET IS DEAD - AND THEN THEY CAN EVICT US ALL!
OH - NO, I WAS JUST MUSING ALOUD.
I SENT CAROLINE AN EARLY ANSWER TO HER LETTER - DO YOU THINK I MIGHT RECEIVE A REPLY THIS WEEK?
I FIND MYSELF COUNTING THE DAYS UNTIL I HEAR NEWS OF MISTER BINGLEY. IS THAT WRONG, ELIZABETH?
I COULD DON MY TABI BOOTS AND SLIP INTO HER BEDCHAMBER UNDER THE COVER OF DARKNESS -
- I COULD MERCIFULLY END HER MISERY WITH THE PANTHER'S KISS -
- BUT I GAVE MY WORD - AND MY WORD IS SACRED, I WILL NOT INTERFERE -
- I'M SORRY, JANE? WHAT WAS THAT?

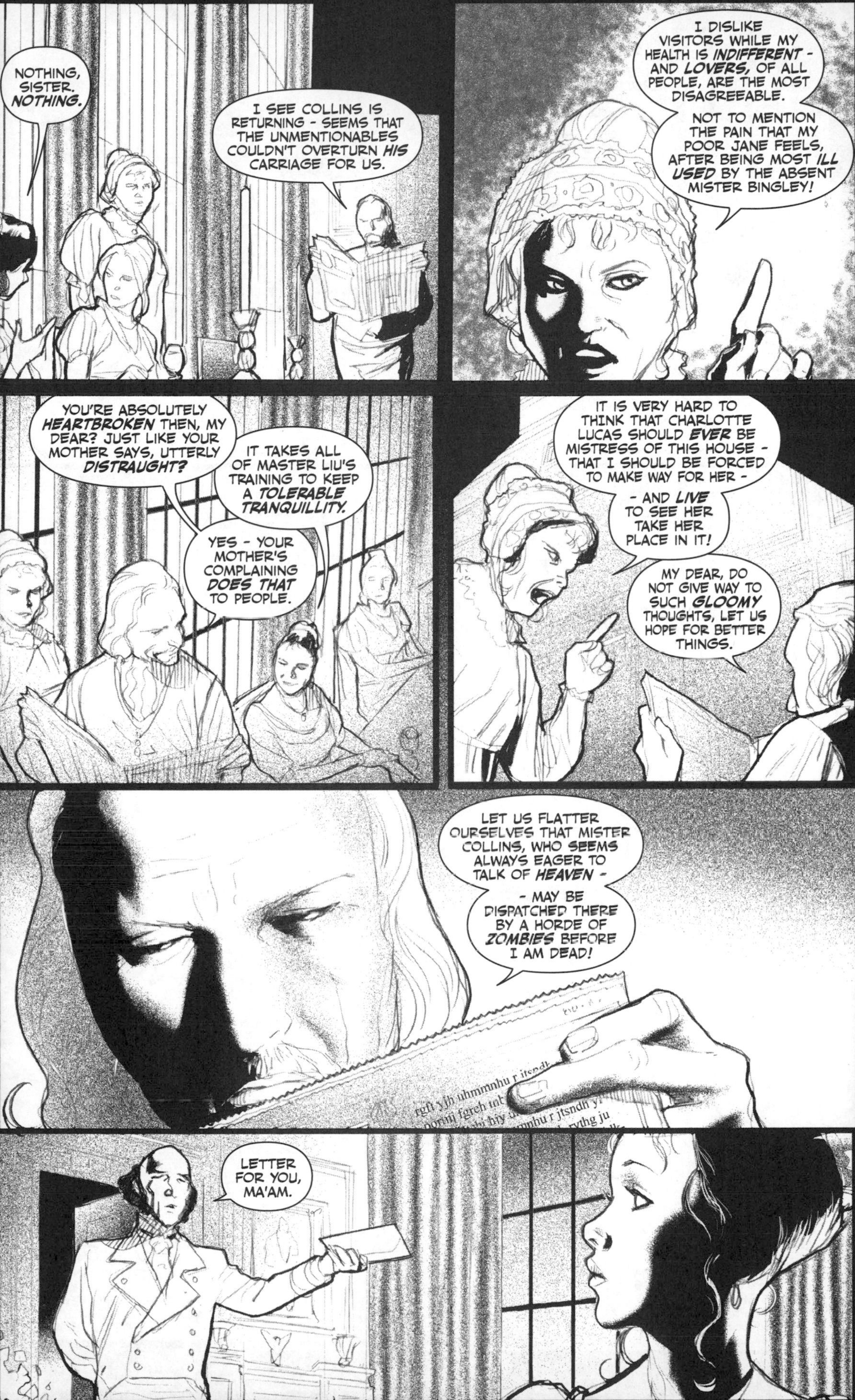

NOTHING, SISTER. *NOTHING.*
I SEE COLLINS IS RETURNING - SEEMS THAT THE UNMENTIONABLES COULDN'T OVERTURN *HIS* CARRIAGE FOR US.
I DISLIKE VISITORS WHILE MY HEALTH IS *INDIFFERENT* - AND *LOVERS,* OF ALL PEOPLE, ARE THE MOST DISAGREEABLE.
NOT TO MENTION THE PAIN THAT MY POOR JANE FEELS, AFTER BEING MOST *ILL USED* BY THE ABSENT MISTER BINGLEY!
YOU'RE ABSOLUTELY *HEARTBROKEN* THEN, MY DEAR? JUST LIKE YOUR MOTHER SAYS, UTTERLY *DISTRAUGHT?*
IT TAKES ALL OF MASTER LIU'S TRAINING TO KEEP A *TOLERABLE TRANQUILLITY.*
YES - YOUR MOTHER'S COMPLAINING *DOES THAT* TO PEOPLE.
IT IS VERY HARD TO THINK THAT CHARLOTTE LUCAS SHOULD *EVER* BE MISTRESS OF THIS HOUSE - THAT I SHOULD BE FORCED TO MAKE WAY FOR HER -
- AND *LIVE* TO SEE HER TAKE HER PLACE IN IT!
MY DEAR, DO NOT GIVE WAY TO SUCH *GLOOMY* THOUGHTS, LET US HOPE FOR BETTER THINGS.
LET US FLATTER OURSELVES THAT MISTER COLLINS, WHO *SEEMS* ALWAYS EAGER TO TALK OF *HEAVEN* -
- MAY BE DISPATCHED THERE BY A HORDE OF *ZOMBIES* BEFORE I AM DEAD!
LETTER FOR YOU, MA'AM.

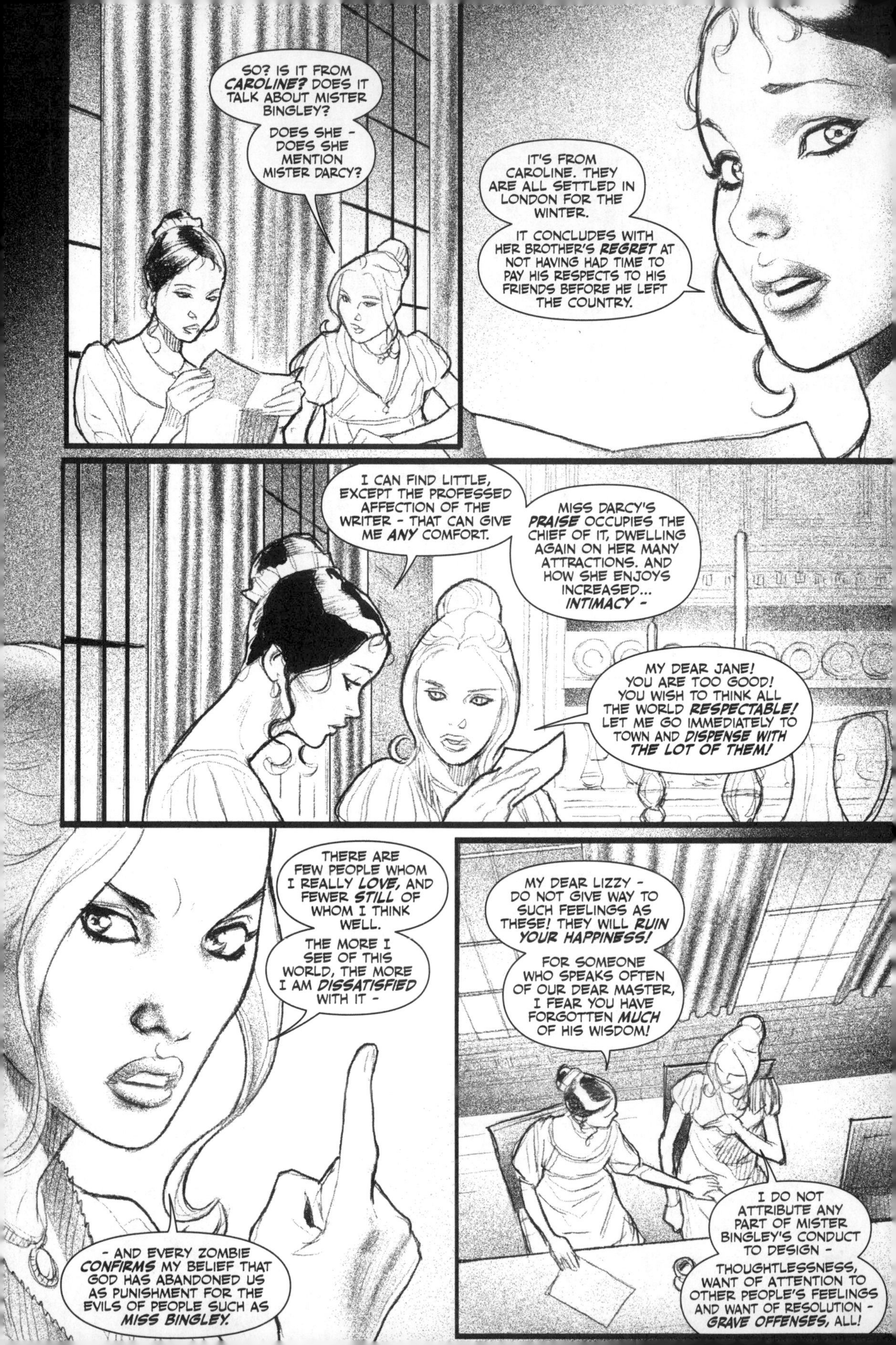
SO? IS IT FROM CAROLINE? DOES IT TALK ABOUT MISTER BINGLEY?
DOES SHE - DOES SHE MENTION MISTER DARCY?
IT'S FROM CAROLINE. THEY ARE ALL SETTLED IN LONDON FOR THE WINTER.
IT CONCLUDES WITH HER BROTHER'S REGRET AT NOT HAVING HAD TIME TO PAY HIS RESPECTS TO HIS FRIENDS BEFORE HE LEFT THE COUNTRY.
I CAN FIND LITTLE, EXCEPT THE PROFESSED AFFECTION OF THE WRITER - THAT CAN GIVE ME ANY COMFORT.
MISS DARCY'S PRAISE OCCUPIES THE CHIEF OF IT, DWELLING AGAIN ON HER MANY ATTRACTIONS. AND HOW SHE ENJOYS INCREASED... INTIMACY -
MY DEAR JANE! YOU ARE TOO GOOD! YOU WISH TO THINK ALL THE WORLD RESPECTABLE! LET ME GO IMMEDIATELY TO TOWN AND DISPENSE WITH THE LOT OF THEM!
THERE ARE FEW PEOPLE WHOM I REALLY LOVE, AND FEWER STILL OF WHOM I THINK WELL.
THE MORE I SEE OF THIS WORLD, THE MORE I AM DISSATISFIED WITH IT -
- AND EVERY ZOMBIE CONFIRMS MY BELIEF THAT GOD HAS ABANDONED US AS PUNISHMENT FOR THE EVILS OF PEOPLE SUCH AS MISS BINGLEY.
MY DEAR LIZZY - DO NOT GIVE WAY TO SUCH FEELINGS AS THESE! THEY WILL RUIN YOUR HAPPINESS!
FOR SOMEONE WHO SPEAKS OFTEN OF OUR DEAR MASTER, I FEAR YOU HAVE FORGOTTEN MUCH OF HIS WISDOM!
I DO NOT ATTRIBUTE ANY PART OF MISTER BINGLEY'S CONDUCT TO DESIGN -
THOUGHTLESSNESS, WANT OF ATTENTION TO OTHER PEOPLE'S FEELINGS AND WANT OF RESOLUTION - GRAVE OFFENSES, ALL!

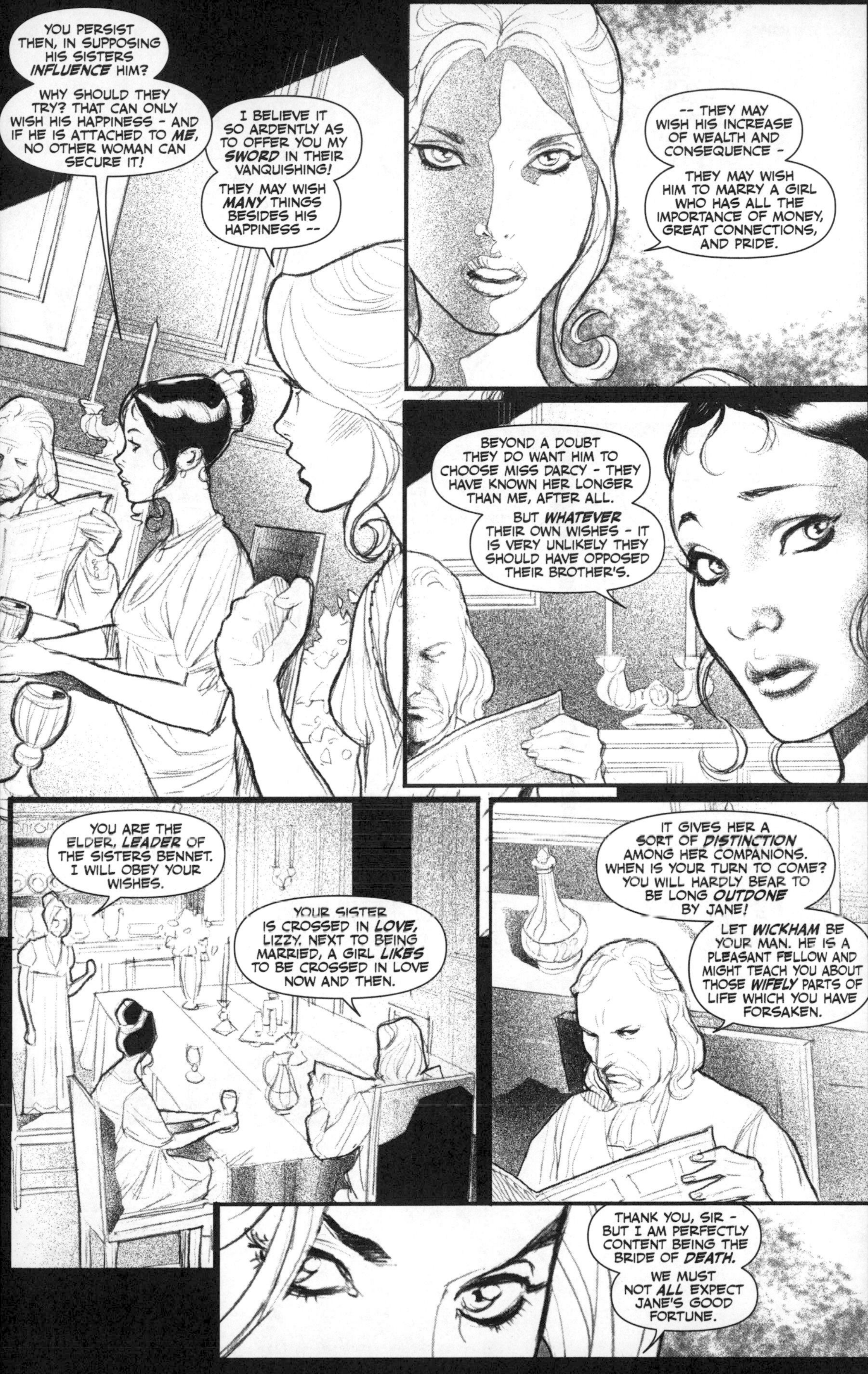
YOU PERSIST THEN, IN SUPPOSING HIS SISTERS INFLUENCE HIM?
WHY SHOULD THEY TRY? THAT CAN ONLY WISH HIS HAPPINESS - AND IF HE IS ATTACHED TO ME, NO OTHER WOMAN CAN SECURE IT!
I BELIEVE IT SO ARDENTLY AS TO OFFER YOU MY SWORD IN THEIR VANQUISHING!
THEY MAY WISH MANY THINGS BESIDES HIS HAPPINESS --
-- THEY MAY WISH HIS INCREASE OF WEALTH AND CONSEQUENCE -
THEY MAY WISH HIM TO MARRY A GIRL WHO HAS ALL THE IMPORTANCE OF MONEY, GREAT CONNECTIONS, AND PRIDE.
BEYOND A DOUBT THEY DO WANT HIM TO CHOOSE MISS DARCY - THEY HAVE KNOWN HER LONGER THAN ME, AFTER ALL.
BUT WHATEVER THEIR OWN WISHES - IT IS VERY UNLIKELY THEY SHOULD HAVE OPPOSED THEIR BROTHER'S.
YOU ARE THE ELDER, LEADER OF THE SISTERS BENNET. I WILL OBEY YOUR WISHES.
YOUR SISTER IS CROSSED IN LOVE, LIZZY. NEXT TO BEING MARRIED, A GIRL LIKES TO BE CROSSED IN LOVE NOW AND THEN.
IT GIVES HER A SORT OF DISTINCTION AMONG HER COMPANIONS. WHEN IS YOUR TURN TO COME? YOU WILL HARDLY BEAR TO BE LONG OUTDONE BY JANE!
LET WICKHAM BE YOUR MAN. HE IS A PLEASANT FELLOW AND MIGHT TEACH YOU ABOUT THOSE WIFELY PARTS OF LIFE WHICH YOU HAVE FORSAKEN.
THANK YOU, SIR - BUT I AM PERFECTLY CONTENT BEING THE BRIDE OF DEATH.
WE MUST NOT ALL EXPECT JANE'S GOOD FORTUNE.

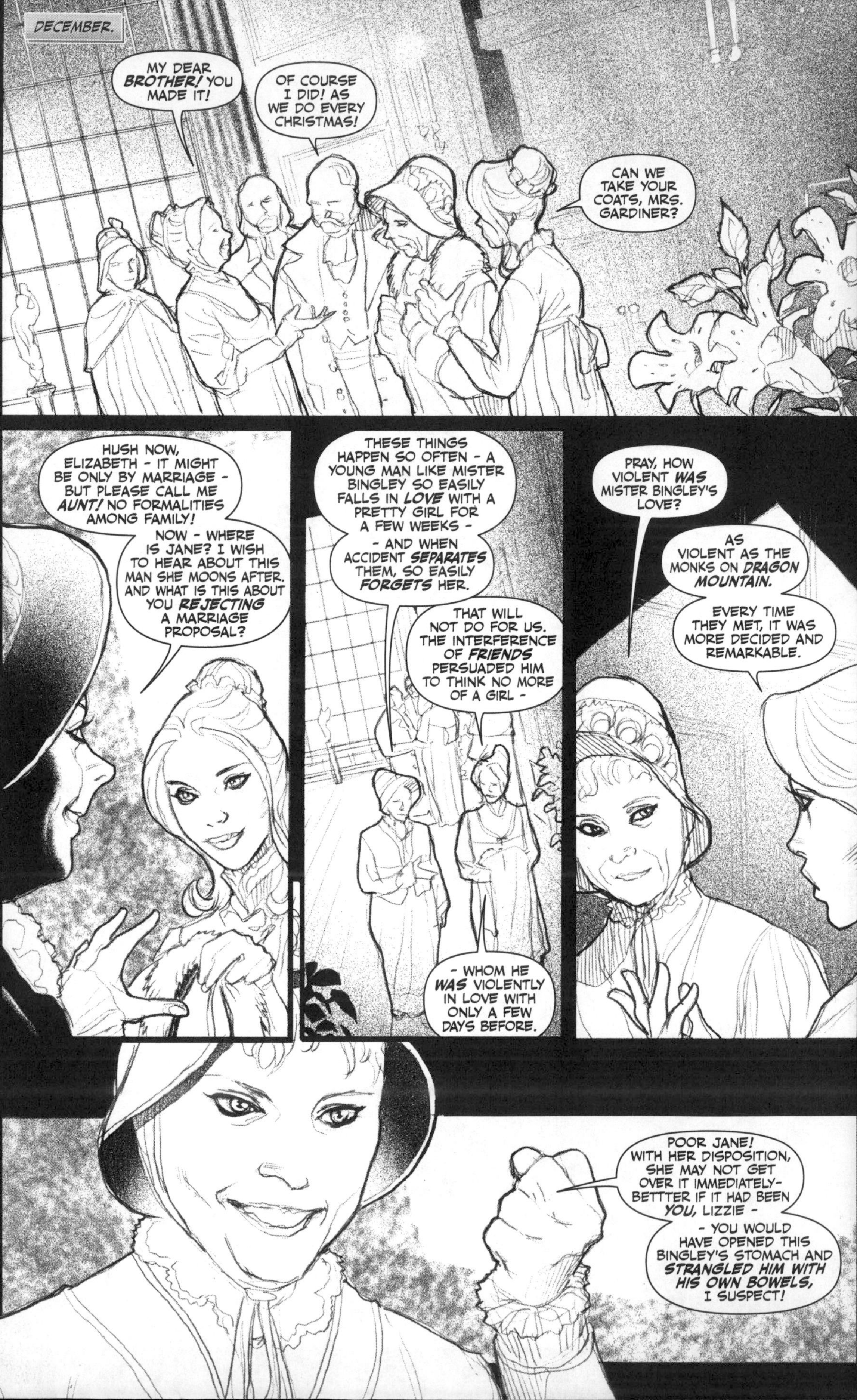
DECEMBER.
MY DEAR BROTHER! YOU MADE IT!
OF COURSE I DID! AS WE DO EVERY CHRISTMAS!
CAN WE TAKE YOUR COATS, MRS. GARDINER?
HUSH NOW, ELIZABETH - IT MIGHT BE ONLY BY MARRIAGE - BUT PLEASE CALL ME AUNT! NO FORMALITIES AMONG FAMILY!
NOW - WHERE IS JANE? I WISH TO HEAR ABOUT THIS MAN SHE MOONS AFTER. AND WHAT IS THIS ABOUT YOU REJECTING A MARRIAGE PROPOSAL?
THESE THINGS HAPPEN SO OFTEN - A YOUNG MAN LIKE MISTER BINGLEY SO EASILY FALLS IN LOVE WITH A PRETTY GIRL FOR A FEW WEEKS -
- AND WHEN ACCIDENT SEPARATES THEM, SO EASILY FORGETS HER.
THAT WILL NOT DO FOR US. THE INTERFERENCE OF FRIENDS PERSUADED HIM TO THINK NO MORE OF A GIRL -
- WHOM HE WAS VIOLENTLY IN LOVE WITH ONLY A FEW DAYS BEFORE.
PRAY, HOW VIOLENT WAS MISTER BINGLEY'S LOVE?
AS VIOLENT AS THE MONKS ON DRAGON MOUNTAIN.
EVERY TIME THEY MET, IT WAS MORE DECIDED AND REMARKABLE.
POOR JANE! WITH HER DISPOSITION, SHE MAY NOT GET OVER IT IMMEDIATELY-BETTTER IF IT HAD BEEN YOU, LIZZIE -
- YOU WOULD HAVE OPENED THIS BINGLEY'S STOMACH AND STRANGLED HIM WITH HIS OWN BOWELS, I SUSPECT!

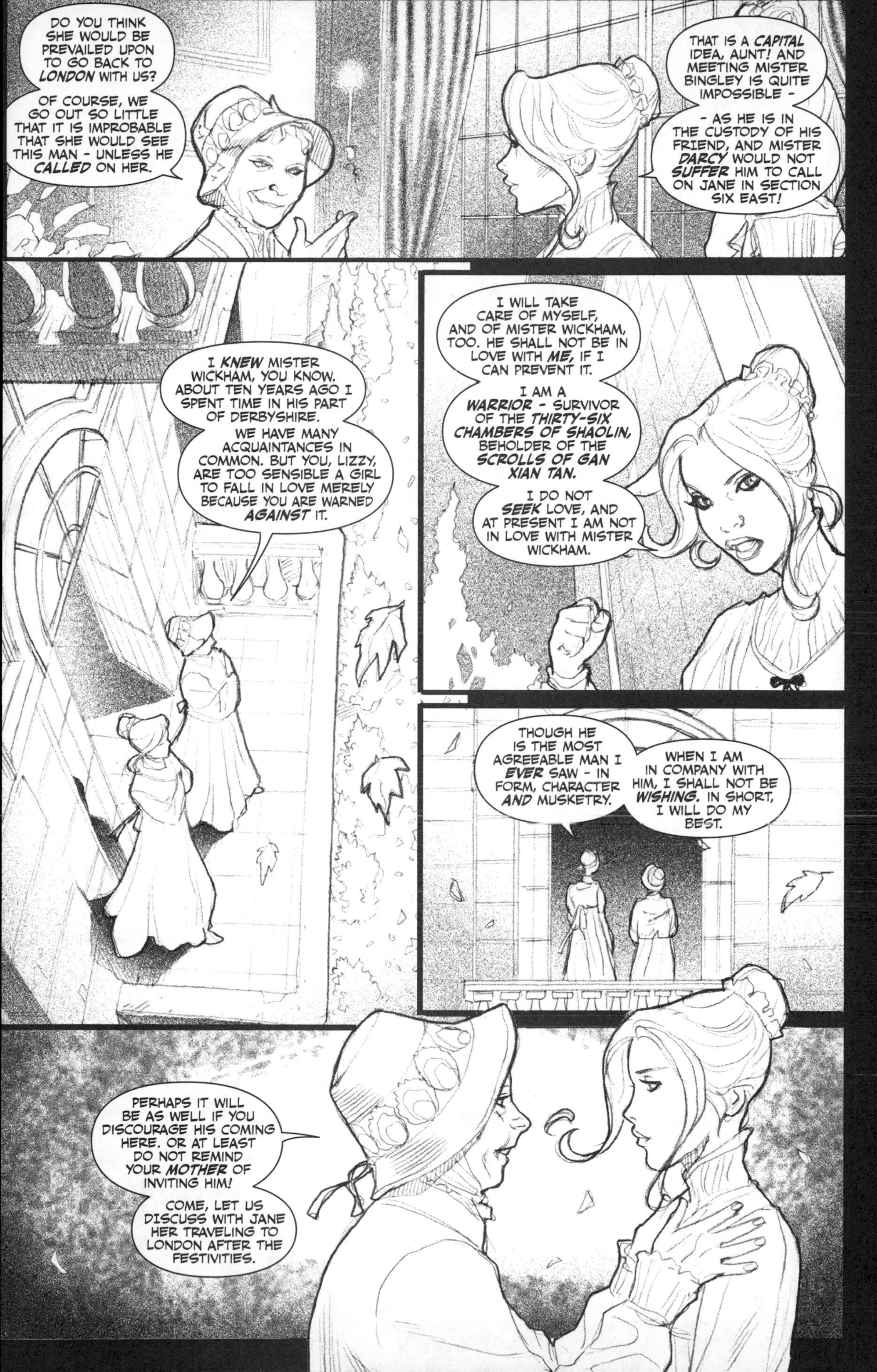
DO YOU THINK SHE WOULD BE PREVAILED UPON TO GO BACK TO LONDON WITH US?
OF COURSE, WE GO OUT SO LITTLE THAT IT IS IMPROBABLE THAT SHE WOULD SEE THIS MAN - UNLESS HE CALLED ON HER.
THAT IS A CAPITAL IDEA, AUNT! AND MEETING MISTER BINGLEY IS QUITE IMPOSSIBLE -
- AS HE IS IN THE CUSTODY OF HIS FRIEND, AND MISTER DARCY WOULD NOT SUFFER HIM TO CALL ON JANE IN SECTION SIX EAST!
I KNEW MISTER WICKHAM, YOU KNOW. ABOUT TEN YEARS AGO I SPENT TIME IN HIS PART OF DERBYSHIRE.
WE HAVE MANY ACQUAINTANCES IN COMMON. BUT YOU, LIZZY, ARE TOO SENSIBLE A GIRL TO FALL IN LOVE MERELY BECAUSE YOU ARE WARNED AGAINST IT.
I WILL TAKE CARE OF MYSELF, AND OF MISTER WICKHAM, TOO. HE SHALL NOT BE IN LOVE WITH ME, IF I CAN PREVENT IT.
I AM A WARRIOR - SURVIVOR OF THE THIRTY-SIX CHAMBERS OF SHAOLIN, BEHOLDER OF THE SCROLLS OF GAN XIAN TAN.
I DO NOT SEEK LOVE, AND AT PRESENT I AM NOT IN LOVE WITH MISTER WICKHAM.
THOUGH HE IS THE MOST AGREEABLE MAN I EVER SAW - IN FORM, CHARACTER AND MUSKETRY.
WHEN I AM IN COMPANY WITH HIM, I SHALL NOT BE WISHING. IN SHORT, I WILL DO MY BEST.
PERHAPS IT WILL BE AS WELL IF YOU DISCOURAGE HIS COMING HERE. OR AT LEAST DO NOT REMIND YOUR MOTHER OF INVITING HIM!
COME, LET US DISCUSS WITH JANE HER TRAVELING TO LONDON AFTER THE FESTIVITIES.

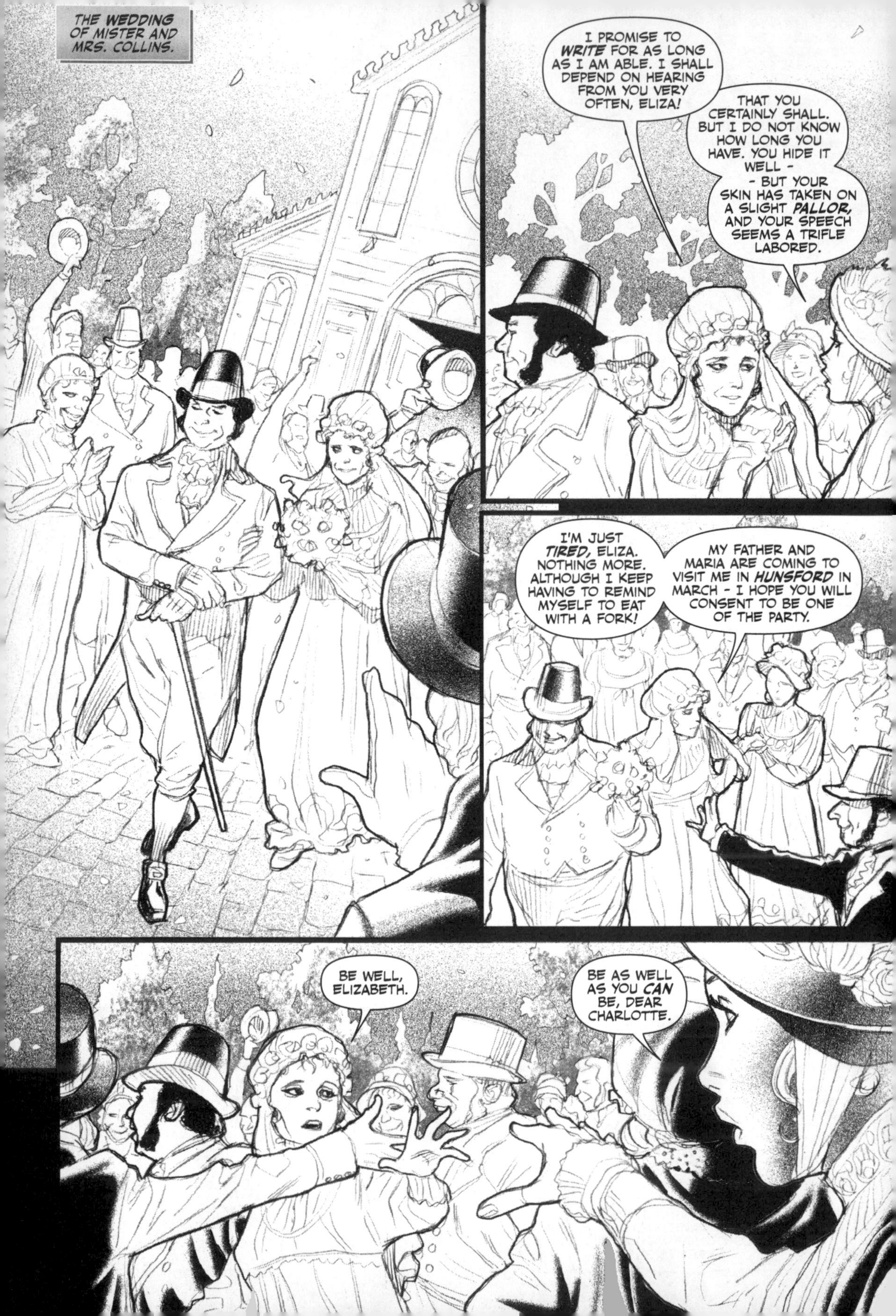
THE WEDDING OF MISTER AND MRS. COLLINS.
I PROMISE TO WRITE FOR AS LONG AS I AM ABLE. I SHALL DEPEND ON HEARING FROM YOU VERY OFTEN, ELIZA!
THAT YOU CERTAINLY SHALL. BUT I DO NOT KNOW HOW LONG YOU HAVE. YOU HIDE IT WELL -
- BUT YOUR SKIN HAS TAKEN ON A SLIGHT PALLOR, AND YOUR SPEECH SEEMS A TRIFLE LABORED.
I'M JUST TIRED, ELIZA. NOTHING MORE. ALTHOUGH I KEEP HAVING TO REMIND MYSELF TO EAT WITH A FORK!
MY FATHER AND MARIA ARE COMING TO VISIT ME IN HUNSFORD IN MARCH - I HOPE YOU WILL CONSENT TO BE ONE OF THE PARTY.
BE WELL, ELIZABETH.
BE AS WELL AS YOU CAN BE, DEAR CHARLOTTE.

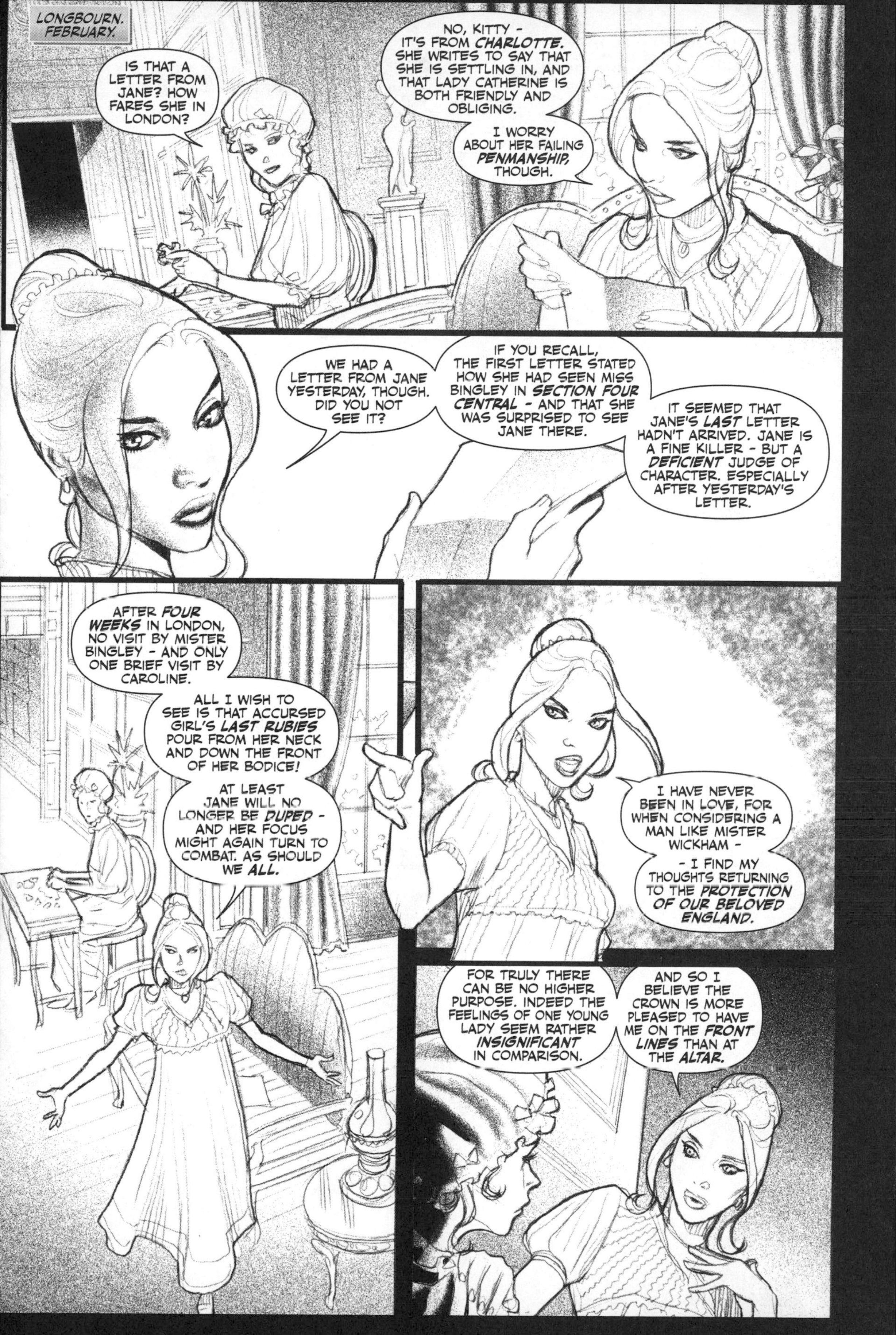
LONGBOURN. FEBRUARY.
IS THAT A LETTER FROM JANE? HOW FARES SHE IN LONDON?
NO, KITTY - IT'S FROM CHARLOTTE. SHE WRITES TO SAY THAT SHE IS SETTLING IN, AND THAT LADY CATHERINE IS BOTH FRIENDLY AND OBLIGING.
I WORRY ABOUT HER FAILING PENMANSHIP, THOUGH.
WE HAD A LETTER FROM JANE YESTERDAY, THOUGH. DID YOU NOT SEE IT?
IF YOU RECALL, THE FIRST LETTER STATED HOW SHE HAD SEEN MISS BINGLEY IN SECTION FOUR CENTRAL - AND THAT SHE WAS SURPRISED TO SEE JANE THERE.
IT SEEMED THAT JANE'S LAST LETTER HADN'T ARRIVED. JANE IS A FINE KILLER - BUT A DEFICIENT JUDGE OF CHARACTER. ESPECIALLY AFTER YESTERDAY'S LETTER.
AFTER FOUR WEEKS IN LONDON, NO VISIT BY MISTER BINGLEY - AND ONLY ONE BRIEF VISIT BY CAROLINE.
ALL I WISH TO SEE IS THAT ACCURSED GIRL'S LAST RUBIES POUR FROM HER NECK AND DOWN THE FRONT OF HER BODICE!
AT LEAST JANE WILL NO LONGER BE DUPED - AND HER FOCUS MIGHT AGAIN TURN TO COMBAT. AS SHOULD WE ALL.
I HAVE NEVER BEEN IN LOVE, FOR WHEN CONSIDERING A MAN LIKE MISTER WICKHAM -
- I FIND MY THOUGHTS RETURNING TO THE PROTECTION OF OUR BELOVED ENGLAND.
FOR TRULY THERE CAN BE NO HIGHER PURPOSE. INDEED THE FEELINGS OF ONE YOUNG LADY SEEM RATHER INSIGNIFICANT IN COMPARISON.
AND SO I BELIEVE THE CROWN IS MORE PLEASED TO HAVE ME ON THE FRONT LINES THAN AT THE ALTAR.

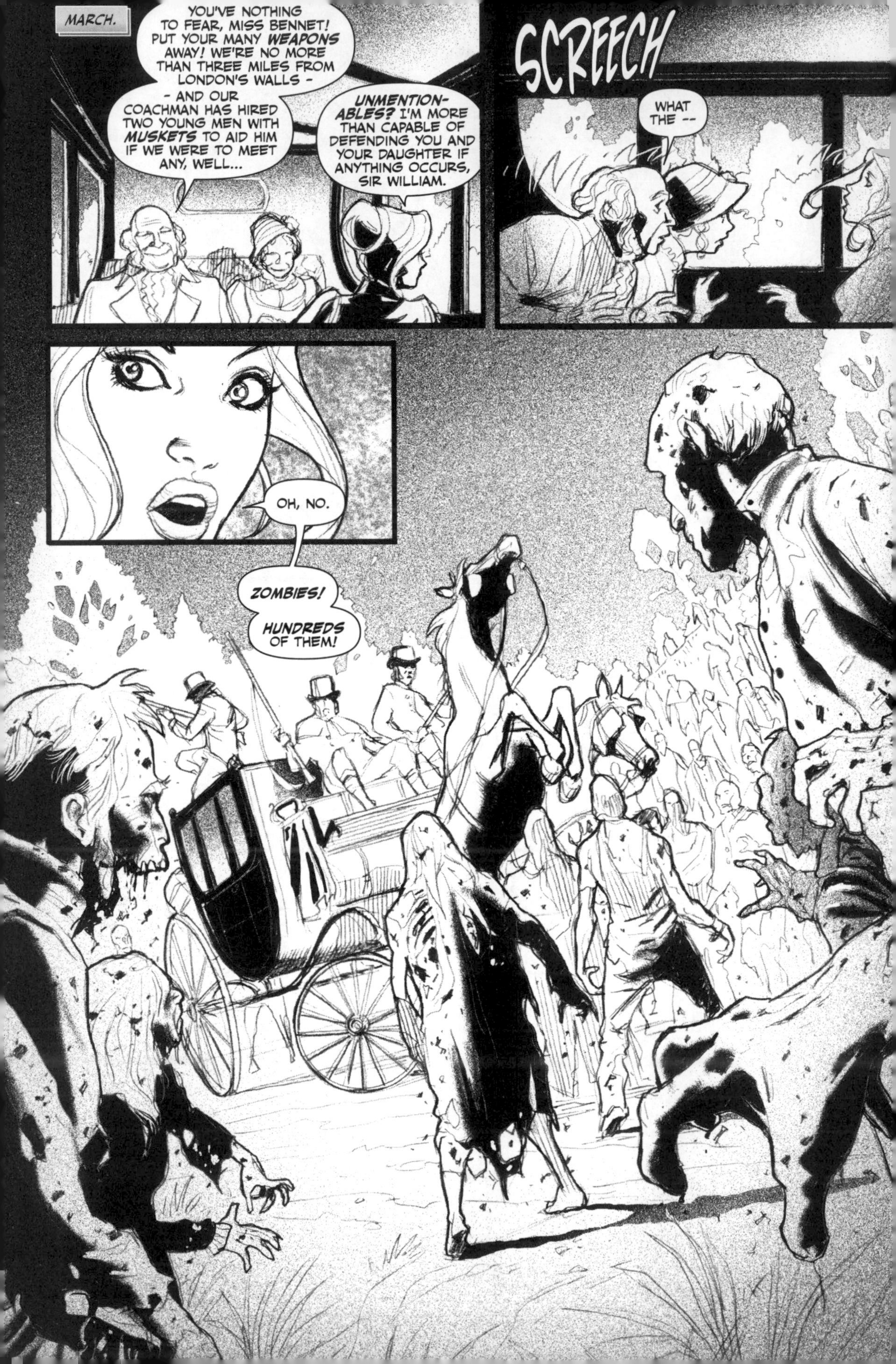
MARCH.
YOU'VE NOTHING TO FEAR, MISS BENNET! PUT YOUR MANY WEAPONS AWAY! WE'RE NO MORE THAN THREE MILES FROM LONDON'S WALLS -
- AND OUR COACHMAN HAS HIRED TWO YOUNG MEN WITH MUSKETS TO AID HIM IF WE WERE TO MEET ANY, WELL...
UNMENTION-ABLES? I'M MORE THAN CAPABLE OF DEFENDING YOU AND YOUR DAUGHTER IF ANYTHING OCCURS, SIR WILLIAM.
SCREECH
WHAT THE --
OH, NO.
ZOMBIES!
HUNDREDS OF THEM!

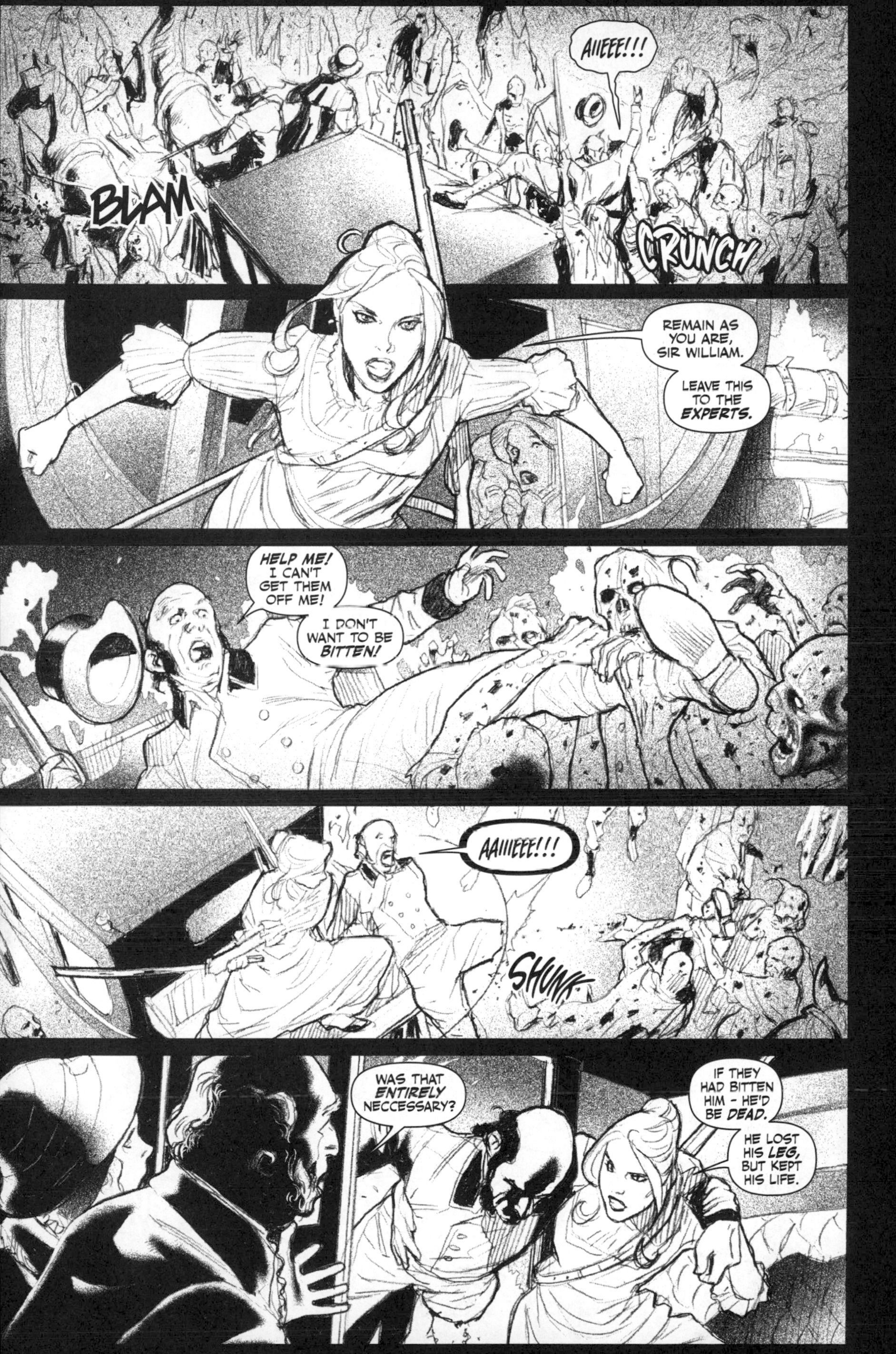
AIIEEE!!!
BLAM
CRUNCH
REMAIN AS YOU ARE, SIR WILLIAM.
LEAVE THIS TO THE EXPERTS.
HELP ME! I CAN'T GET THEM OFF ME!
I DON'T WANT TO BE BITTEN!
AAIIIEEE!!!
SHUNK
WAS THAT ENTIRELY NECCESSARY?
IF THEY HAD BITTEN HIM - HE'D BE DEAD.
HE LOST HIS LEG, BUT KEPT HIS LIFE.

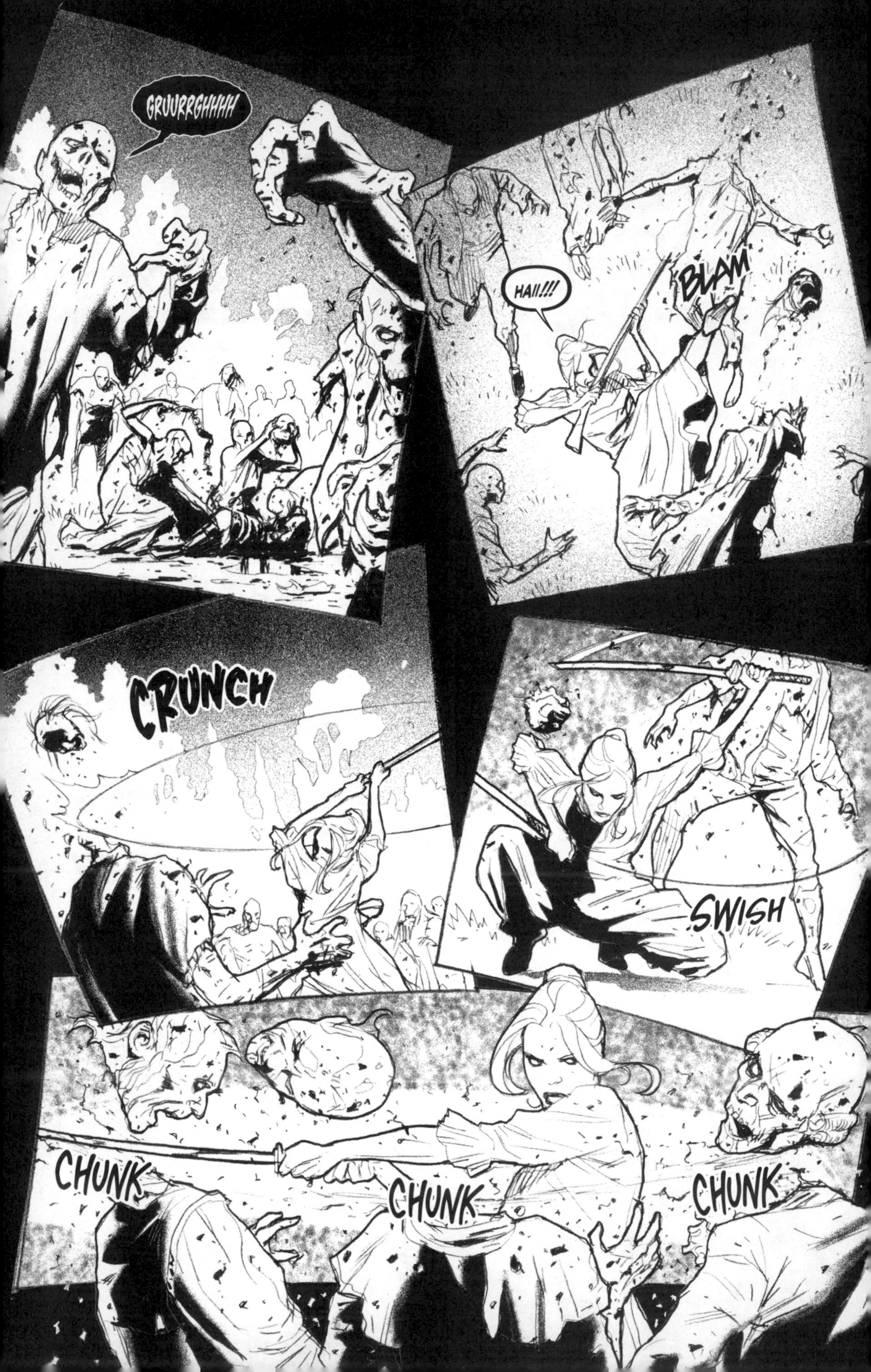
GRUURRGHHHH
HAI!!!
BLAM
CRUNCH
SWISH
CHUNK
CHUNK
CHUNK

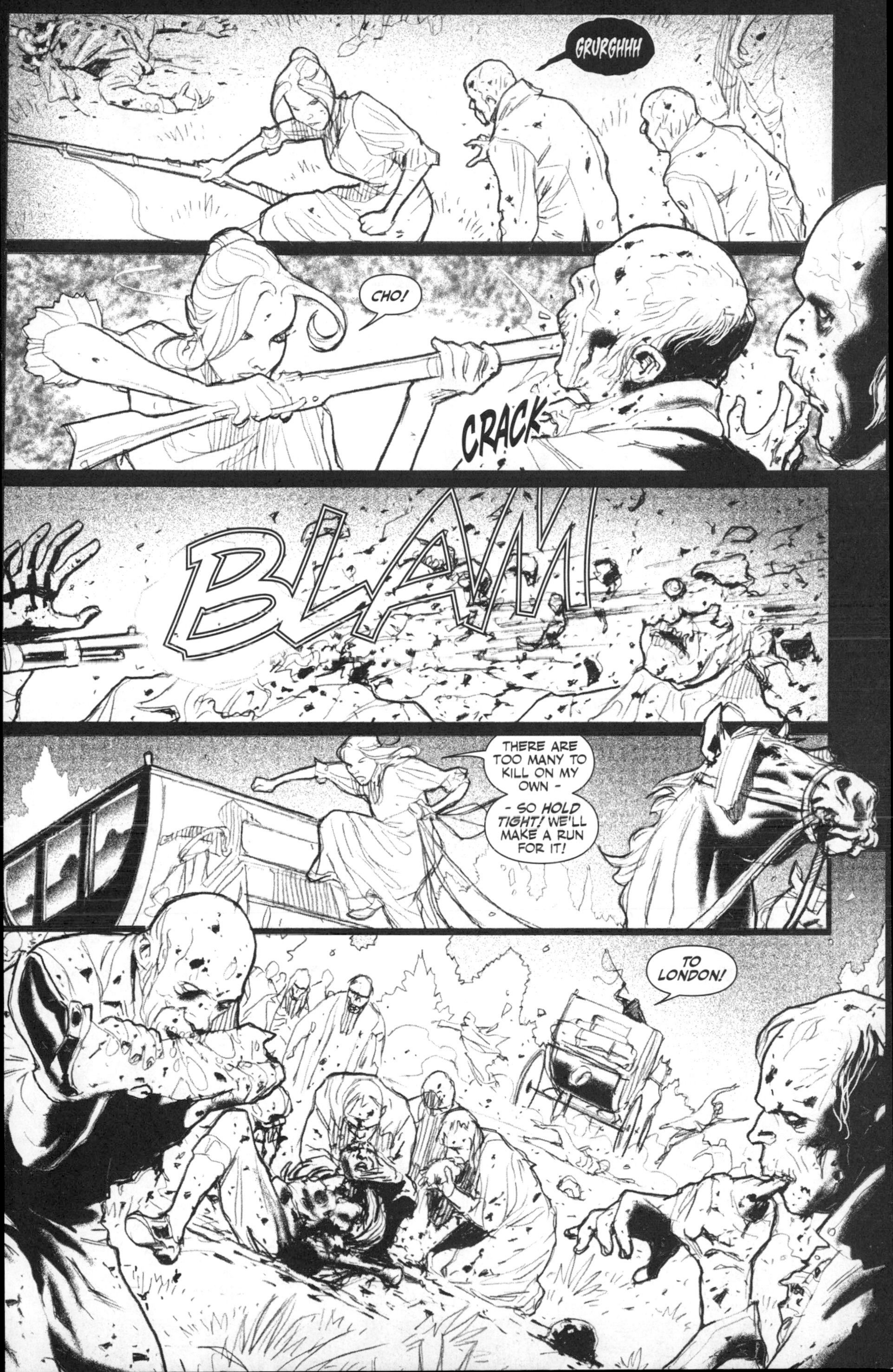
GRURGHHH
CHO!
CRACK
BLAM
THERE ARE TOO MANY TO KILL ON MY OWN -
- SO *HOLD TIGHT!* WE'LL MAKE A RUN FOR IT!
TO LONDON!

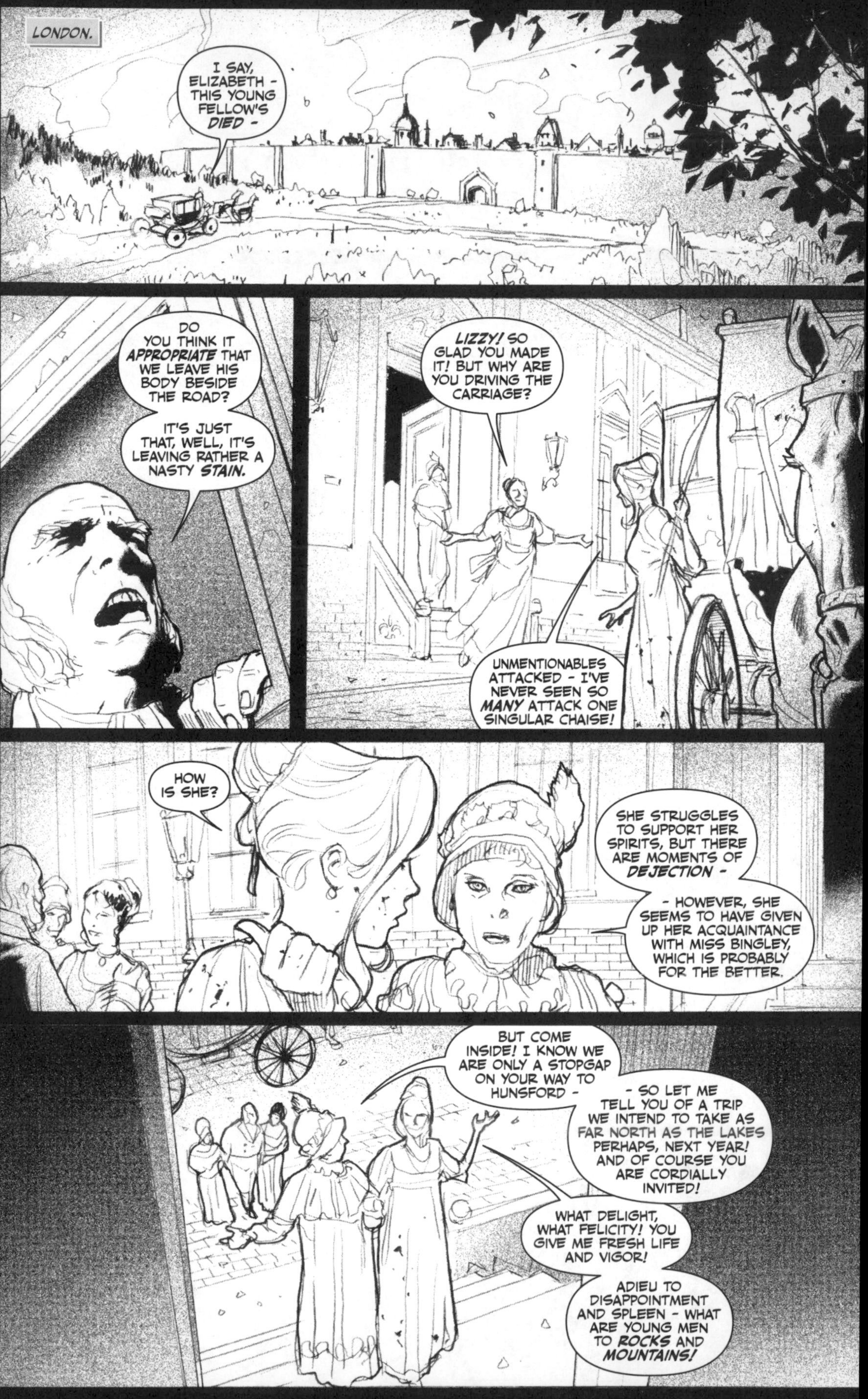
LONDON.
I SAY, ELIZABETH - THIS YOUNG FELLOW'S DIED -
DO YOU THINK IT APPROPRIATE THAT WE LEAVE HIS BODY BESIDE THE ROAD?
IT'S JUST THAT, WELL, IT'S LEAVING RATHER A NASTY STAIN.
LIZZY! SO GLAD YOU MADE IT! BUT WHY ARE YOU DRIVING THE CARRIAGE?
UNMENTIONABLES ATTACKED - I'VE NEVER SEEN SO MANY ATTACK ONE SINGULAR CHAISE!
HOW IS SHE?
SHE STRUGGLES TO SUPPORT HER SPIRITS, BUT THERE ARE MOMENTS OF DEJECTION -
- HOWEVER, SHE SEEMS TO HAVE GIVEN UP HER ACQUAINTANCE WITH MISS BINGLEY, WHICH IS PROBABLY FOR THE BETTER.
BUT COME INSIDE! I KNOW WE ARE ONLY A STOPGAP ON YOUR WAY TO HUNSFORD -
- SO LET ME TELL YOU OF A TRIP WE INTEND TO TAKE AS FAR NORTH AS THE LAKES PERHAPS, NEXT YEAR! AND OF COURSE YOU ARE CORDIALLY INVITED!
WHAT DELIGHT, WHAT FELICITY! YOU GIVE ME FRESH LIFE AND VIGOR!
ADIEU TO DISAPPOINTMENT AND SPLEEN - WHAT ARE YOUNG MEN TO ROCKS AND MOUNTAINS!

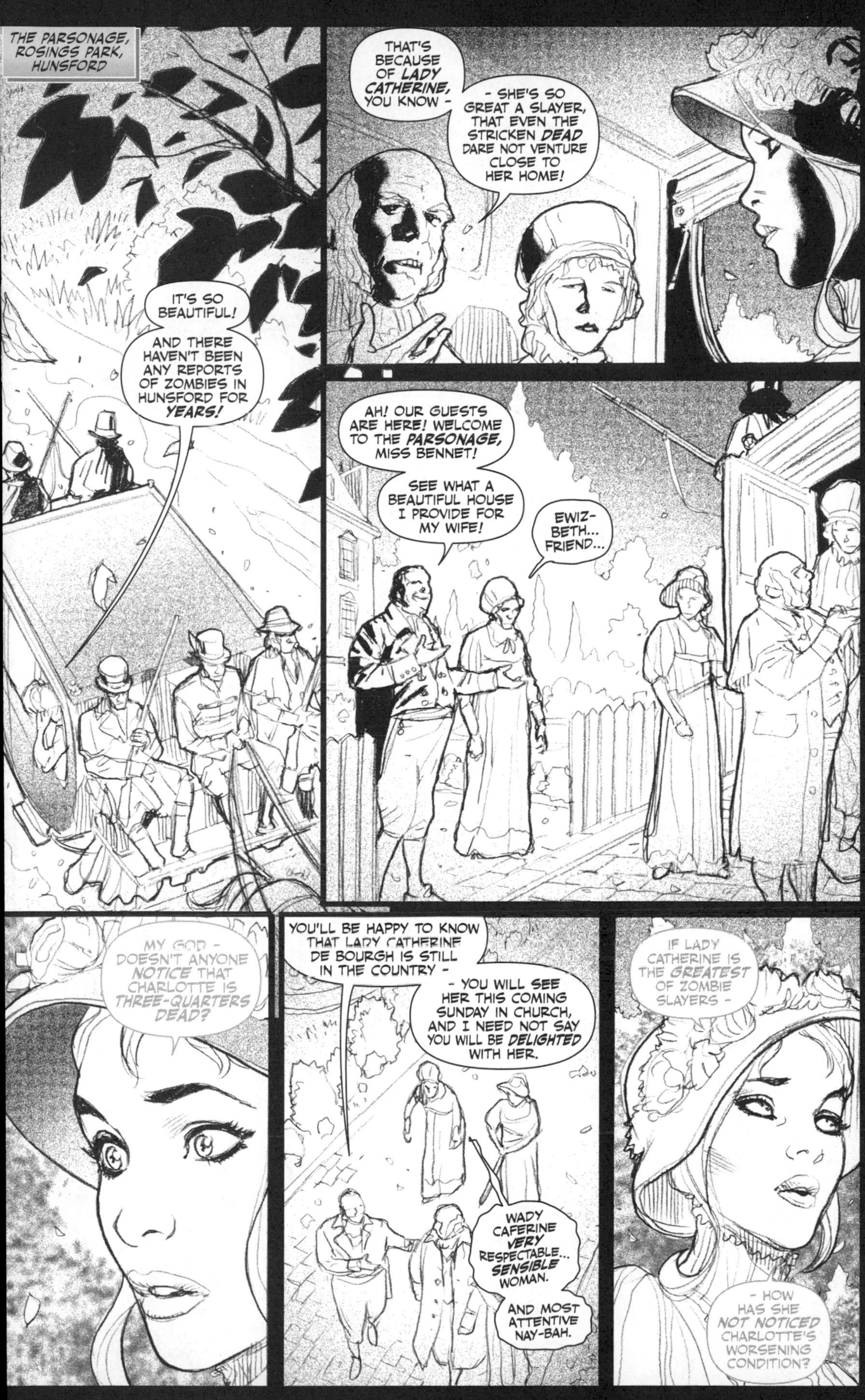
THE PARSONAGE, ROSINGS PARK, HUNSFORD
IT'S SO BEAUTIFUL!
AND THERE HAVEN'T BEEN ANY REPORTS OF ZOMBIES IN HUNSFORD FOR YEARS!
THAT'S BECAUSE OF LADY CATHERINE, YOU KNOW -
- SHE'S SO GREAT A SLAYER, THAT EVEN THE STRICKEN DEAD DARE NOT VENTURE CLOSE TO HER HOME!
AH! OUR GUESTS ARE HERE! WELCOME TO THE PARSONAGE, MISS BENNET!
SEE WHAT A BEAUTIFUL HOUSE I PROVIDE FOR MY WIFE!
EWIZ-BETH... FRIEND...
MY GOD - DOESN'T ANYONE NOTICE THAT CHARLOTTE IS THREE-QUARTERS DEAD?
YOU'LL BE HAPPY TO KNOW THAT LADY CATHERINE DE BOURGH IS STILL IN THE COUNTRY -
- YOU WILL SEE HER THIS COMING SUNDAY IN CHURCH, AND I NEED NOT SAY YOU WILL BE DELIGHTED WITH HER.
WADY CAFERINE VERY RESPECTABLE... SENSIBLE WOMAN.
AND MOST ATTENTIVE NAY-BAH.
IF LADY CATHERINE IS THE GREATEST OF ZOMBIE SLAYERS -
- HOW HAS SHE NOT NOTICED CHARLOTTE'S WORSENING CONDITION?

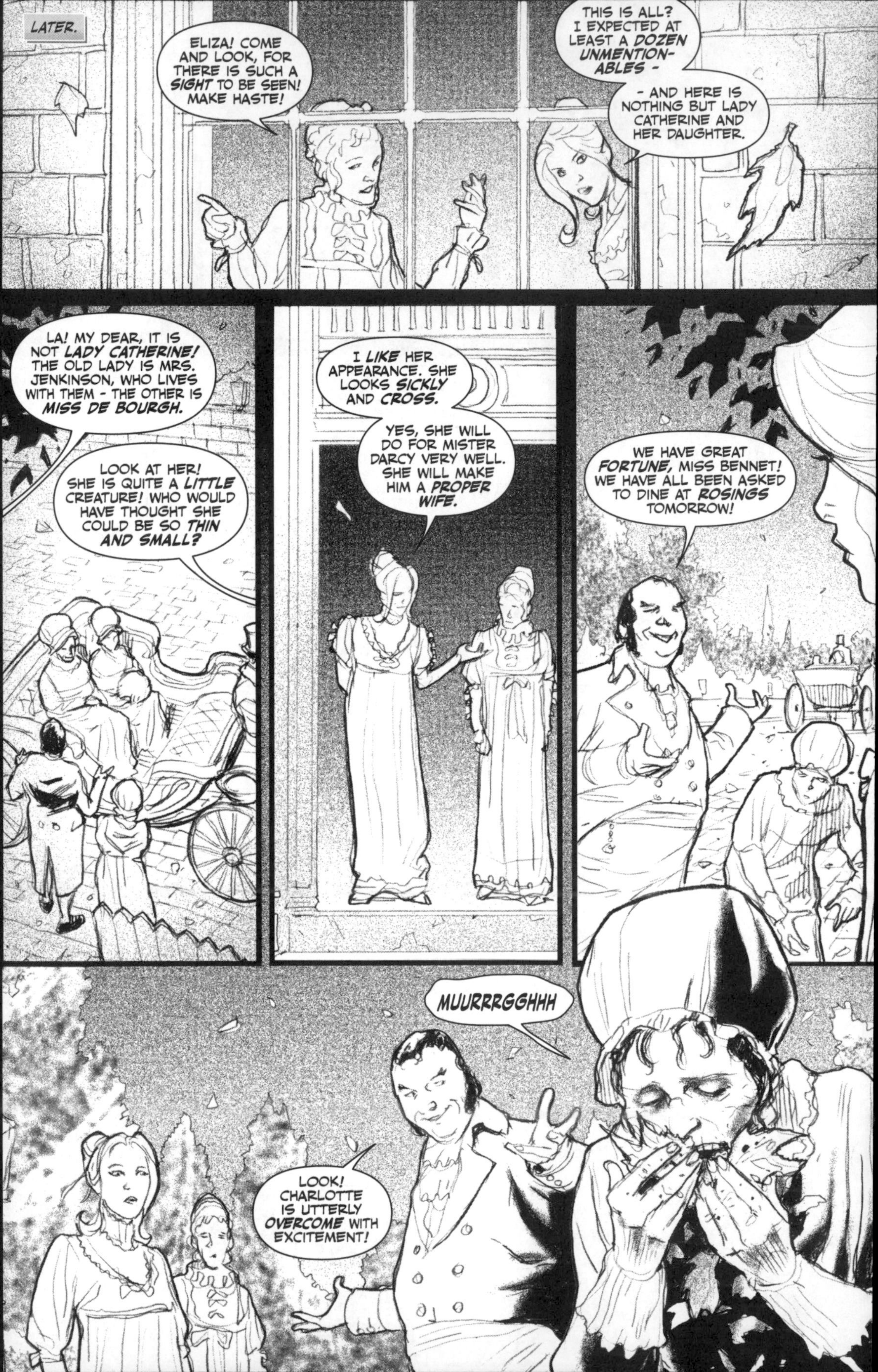
LATER.
ELIZA! COME AND LOOK, FOR THERE IS SUCH A SIGHT TO BE SEEN! MAKE HASTE!
THIS IS ALL? I EXPECTED AT LEAST A DOZEN UNMENTION-ABLES -
- AND HERE IS NOTHING BUT LADY CATHERINE AND HER DAUGHTER.
LA! MY DEAR, IT IS NOT LADY CATHERINE! THE OLD LADY IS MRS. JENKINSON, WHO LIVES WITH THEM - THE OTHER IS MISS DE BOURGH.
LOOK AT HER! SHE IS QUITE A LITTLE CREATURE! WHO WOULD HAVE THOUGHT SHE COULD BE SO THIN AND SMALL?
I LIKE HER APPEARANCE. SHE LOOKS SICKLY AND CROSS.
YES, SHE WILL DO FOR MISTER DARCY VERY WELL. SHE WILL MAKE HIM A PROPER WIFE.
WE HAVE GREAT FORTUNE, MISS BENNET! WE HAVE ALL BEEN ASKED TO DINE AT ROSINGS TOMORROW!
MUURRRGGHHH
LOOK! CHARLOTTE IS UTTERLY OVERCOME WITH EXCITEMENT!

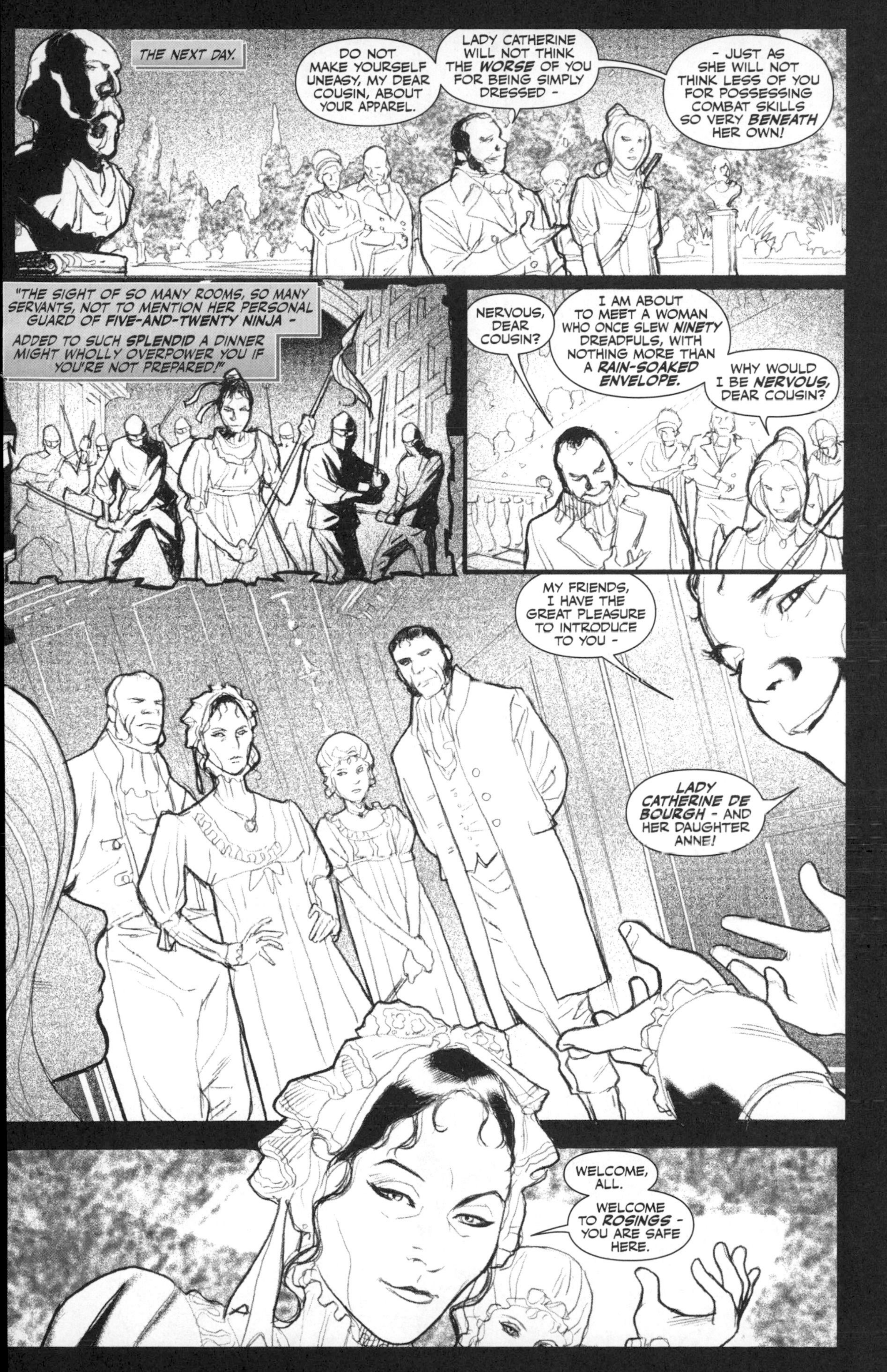
THE NEXT DAY.
DO NOT MAKE YOURSELF UNEASY, MY DEAR COUSIN, ABOUT YOUR APPAREL.
LADY CATHERINE WILL NOT THINK THE WORSE OF YOU FOR BEING SIMPLY DRESSED -
- JUST AS SHE WILL NOT THINK LESS OF YOU FOR POSSESSING COMBAT SKILLS SO VERY BENEATH HER OWN!
"THE SIGHT OF SO MANY ROOMS, SO MANY SERVANTS, NOT TO MENTION HER PERSONAL GUARD OF FIVE-AND-TWENTY NINJA -
ADDED TO SUCH SPLENDID A DINNER MIGHT WHOLLY OVERPOWER YOU IF YOU'RE NOT PREPARED!"
NERVOUS, DEAR COUSIN?
I AM ABOUT TO MEET A WOMAN WHO ONCE SLEW NINETY DREADFULS, WITH NOTHING MORE THAN A RAIN-SOAKED ENVELOPE.
WHY WOULD I BE NERVOUS, DEAR COUSIN?
MY FRIENDS, I HAVE THE GREAT PLEASURE TO INTRODUCE TO YOU -
LADY CATHERINE DE BOURGH - AND HER DAUGHTER ANNE!
WELCOME, ALL.
WELCOME TO ROSINGS - YOU ARE SAFE HERE.

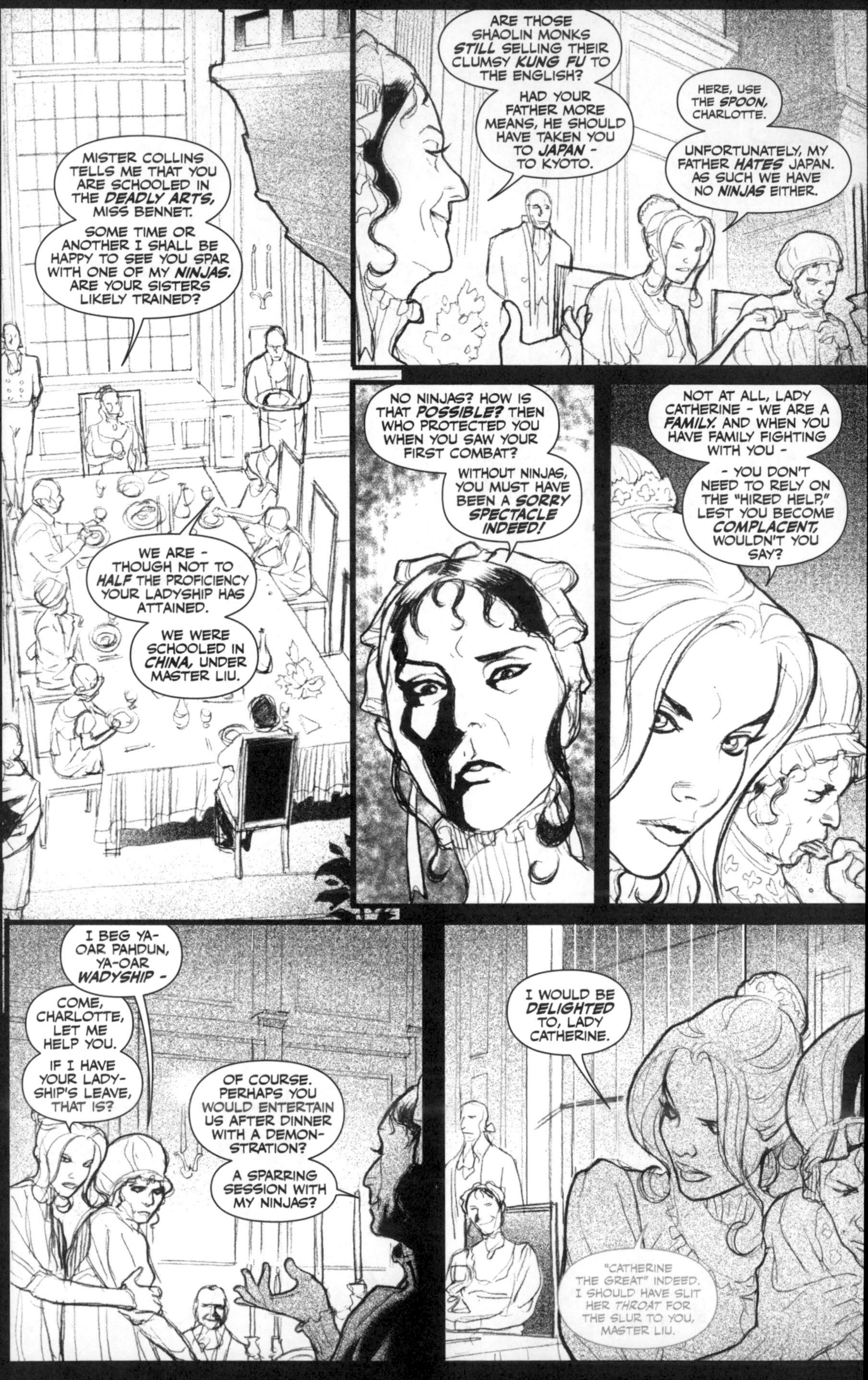
MISTER COLLINS TELLS ME THAT YOU ARE SCHOOLED IN THE *DEADLY ARTS,* MISS BENNET.
SOME TIME OR ANOTHER I SHALL BE HAPPY TO SEE YOU SPAR WITH ONE OF MY *NINJAS.* ARE YOUR SISTERS LIKELY TRAINED?
WE ARE - THOUGH NOT TO *HALF* THE PROFICIENCY YOUR LADYSHIP HAS ATTAINED.
WE WERE SCHOOLED IN *CHINA,* UNDER MASTER LIU.
ARE THOSE SHAOLIN MONKS *STILL* SELLING THEIR CLUMSY *KUNG FU* TO THE ENGLISH?
HAD YOUR FATHER MORE MEANS, HE SHOULD HAVE TAKEN YOU TO *JAPAN* - TO KYOTO.
HERE, USE THE *SPOON,* CHARLOTTE.
UNFORTUNATELY, MY FATHER *HATES* JAPAN. AS SUCH WE HAVE NO *NINJAS* EITHER.
NO NINJAS? HOW IS THAT *POSSIBLE?* THEN WHO PROTECTED YOU WHEN YOU SAW YOUR FIRST COMBAT?
WITHOUT NINJAS, YOU MUST HAVE BEEN A *SORRY SPECTACLE INDEED!*
NOT AT ALL, LADY CATHERINE - WE ARE A *FAMILY.* AND WHEN YOU HAVE FAMILY FIGHTING WITH YOU -
- YOU DON'T NEED TO RELY ON THE "HIRED HELP," LEST YOU BECOME *COMPLACENT,* WOULDN'T YOU SAY?
I BEG YA-OAR PAHDUN, YA-OAR *WADYSHIP* -
COME, CHARLOTTE, LET ME HELP YOU.
IF I HAVE YOUR LADYSHIP'S LEAVE, THAT IS?
OF COURSE. PERHAPS YOU WOULD ENTERTAIN US AFTER DINNER WITH A DEMONSTRATION?
A SPARRING SESSION WITH MY NINJAS?
I WOULD BE *DELIGHTED* TO, LADY CATHERINE.
"CATHERINE THE GREAT" INDEED. I SHOULD HAVE SLIT HER *THROAT* FOR THE SLUR TO YOU, MASTER LIU.

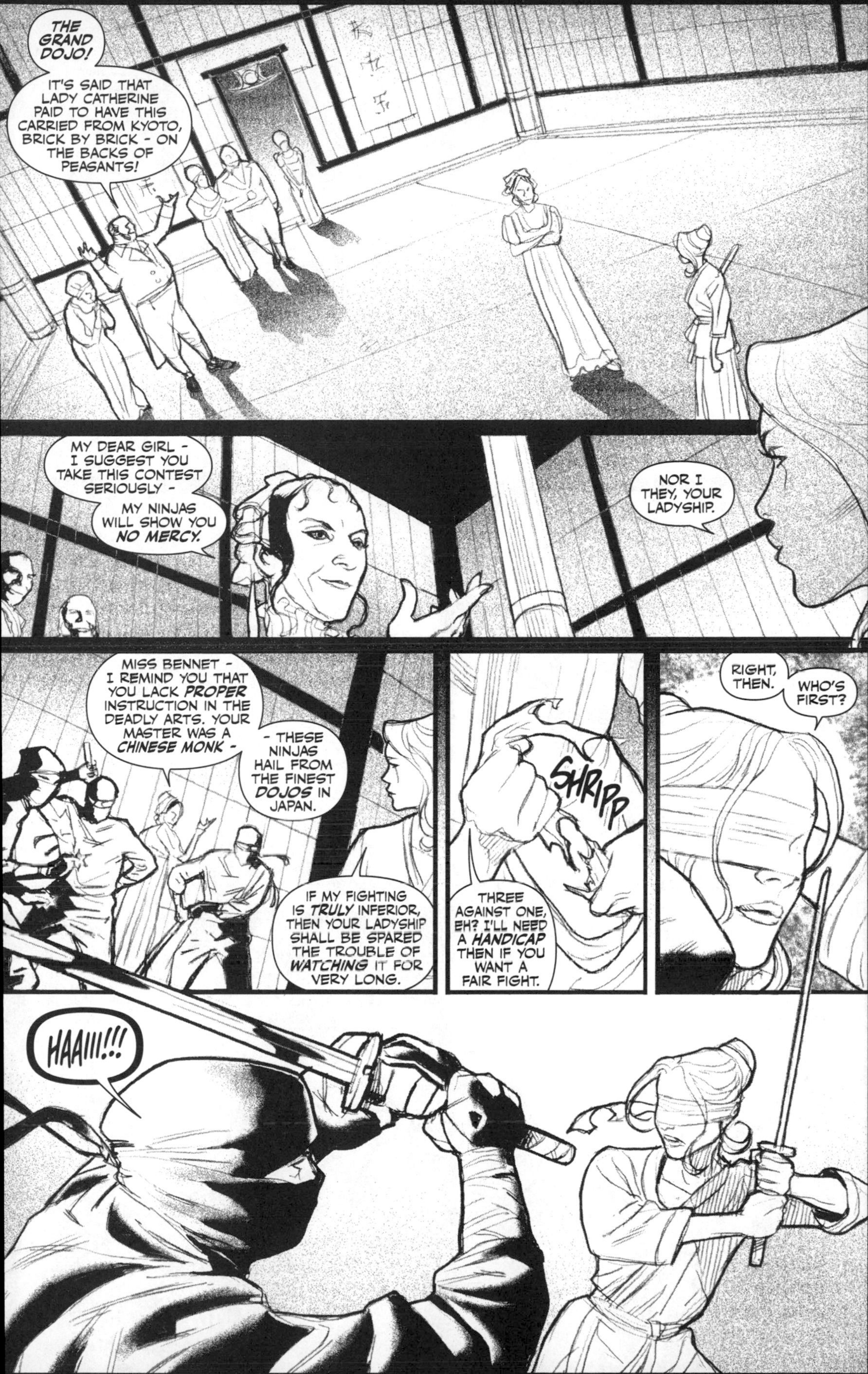

THE GRAND DOJO!
IT'S SAID THAT LADY CATHERINE PAID TO HAVE THIS CARRIED FROM KYOTO, BRICK BY BRICK - ON THE BACKS OF PEASANTS!
MY DEAR GIRL - I SUGGEST YOU TAKE THIS CONTEST SERIOUSLY -
MY NINJAS WILL SHOW YOU NO MERCY.
NOR I THEY, YOUR LADYSHIP.
MISS BENNET - I REMIND YOU THAT YOU LACK PROPER INSTRUCTION IN THE DEADLY ARTS. YOUR MASTER WAS A CHINESE MONK -
- THESE NINJAS HAIL FROM THE FINEST DOJOS IN JAPAN.
IF MY FIGHTING IS TRULY INFERIOR, THEN YOUR LADYSHIP SHALL BE SPARED THE TROUBLE OF WATCHING IT FOR VERY LONG.
SHRIPP
THREE AGAINST ONE, EH? I'LL NEED A HANDICAP THEN IF YOU WANT A FAIR FIGHT.
RIGHT, THEN.
WHO'S FIRST?
HAAIII!!!

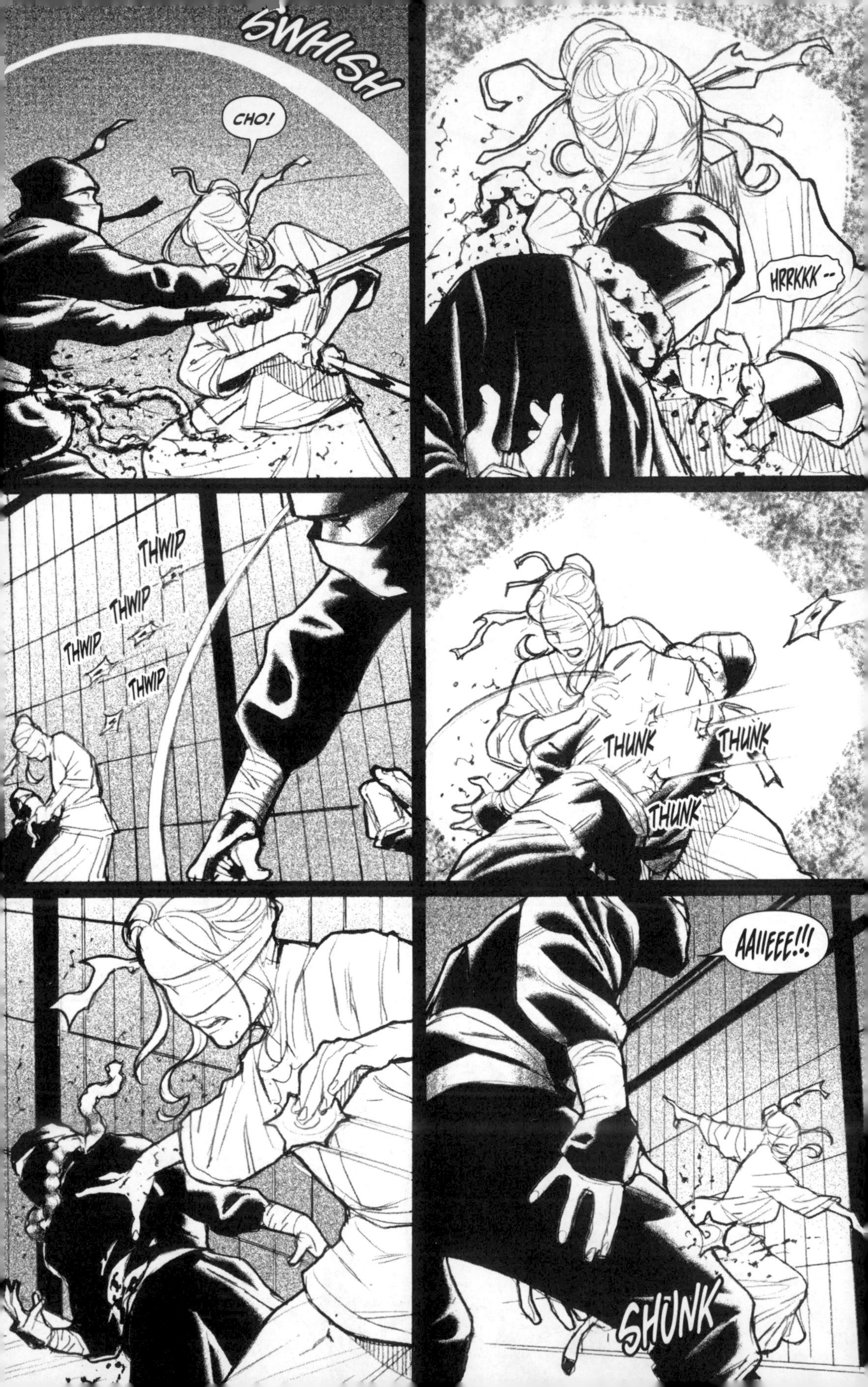
SWHISH
CHO!
HRRKKK --
THWIP
THWIP
THWIP
THWIP
THUNK
THUNK
THUNK
AAIIEEE!!!
SHUNK

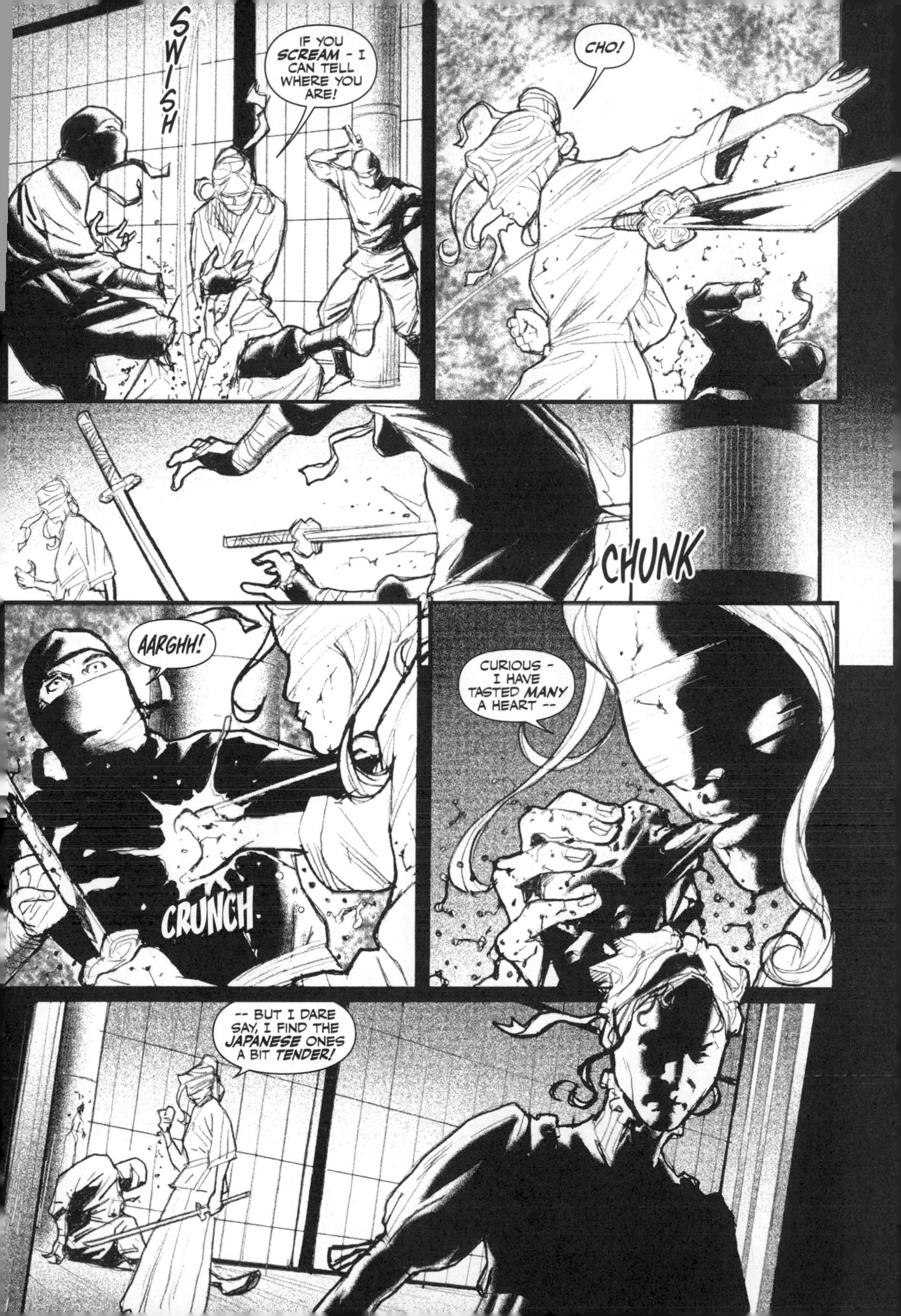
SWISH
IF YOU SCREAM - I CAN TELL WHERE YOU ARE!
CHO!
CHUNK
AARGHH!
CRUNCH
CURIOUS - I HAVE TASTED MANY A HEART --
-- BUT I DARE SAY, I FIND THE JAPANESE ONES A BIT TENDER!

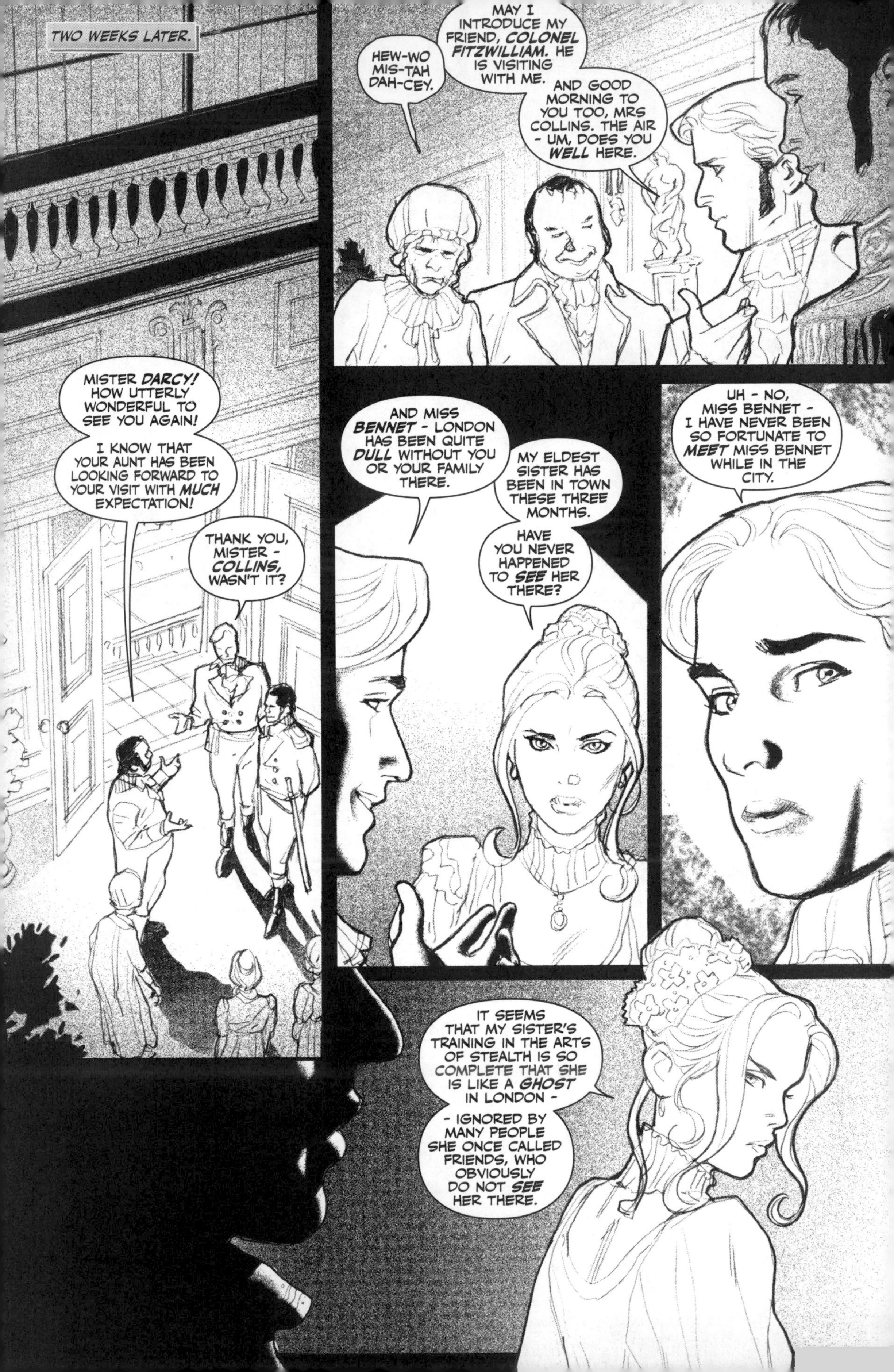
TWO WEEKS LATER.
MISTER DARCY! HOW UTTERLY WONDERFUL TO SEE YOU AGAIN!
I KNOW THAT YOUR AUNT HAS BEEN LOOKING FORWARD TO YOUR VISIT WITH MUCH EXPECTATION!
THANK YOU, MISTER - COLLINS, WASN'T IT?
MAY I INTRODUCE MY FRIEND, COLONEL FITZWILLIAM. HE IS VISITING WITH ME.
HEW-WO MIS-TAH DAH-CEY.
AND GOOD MORNING TO YOU TOO, MRS COLLINS. THE AIR - UM, DOES YOU WELL HERE.
AND MISS BENNET - LONDON HAS BEEN QUITE DULL WITHOUT YOU OR YOUR FAMILY THERE.
MY ELDEST SISTER HAS BEEN IN TOWN THESE THREE MONTHS.
HAVE YOU NEVER HAPPENED TO SEE HER THERE?
UH - NO, MISS BENNET - I HAVE NEVER BEEN SO FORTUNATE TO MEET MISS BENNET WHILE IN THE CITY.
IT SEEMS THAT MY SISTER'S TRAINING IN THE ARTS OF STEALTH IS SO COMPLETE THAT SHE IS LIKE A GHOST IN LONDON -
- IGNORED BY MANY PEOPLE SHE ONCE CALLED FRIENDS, WHO OBVIOUSLY DO NOT SEE HER THERE.

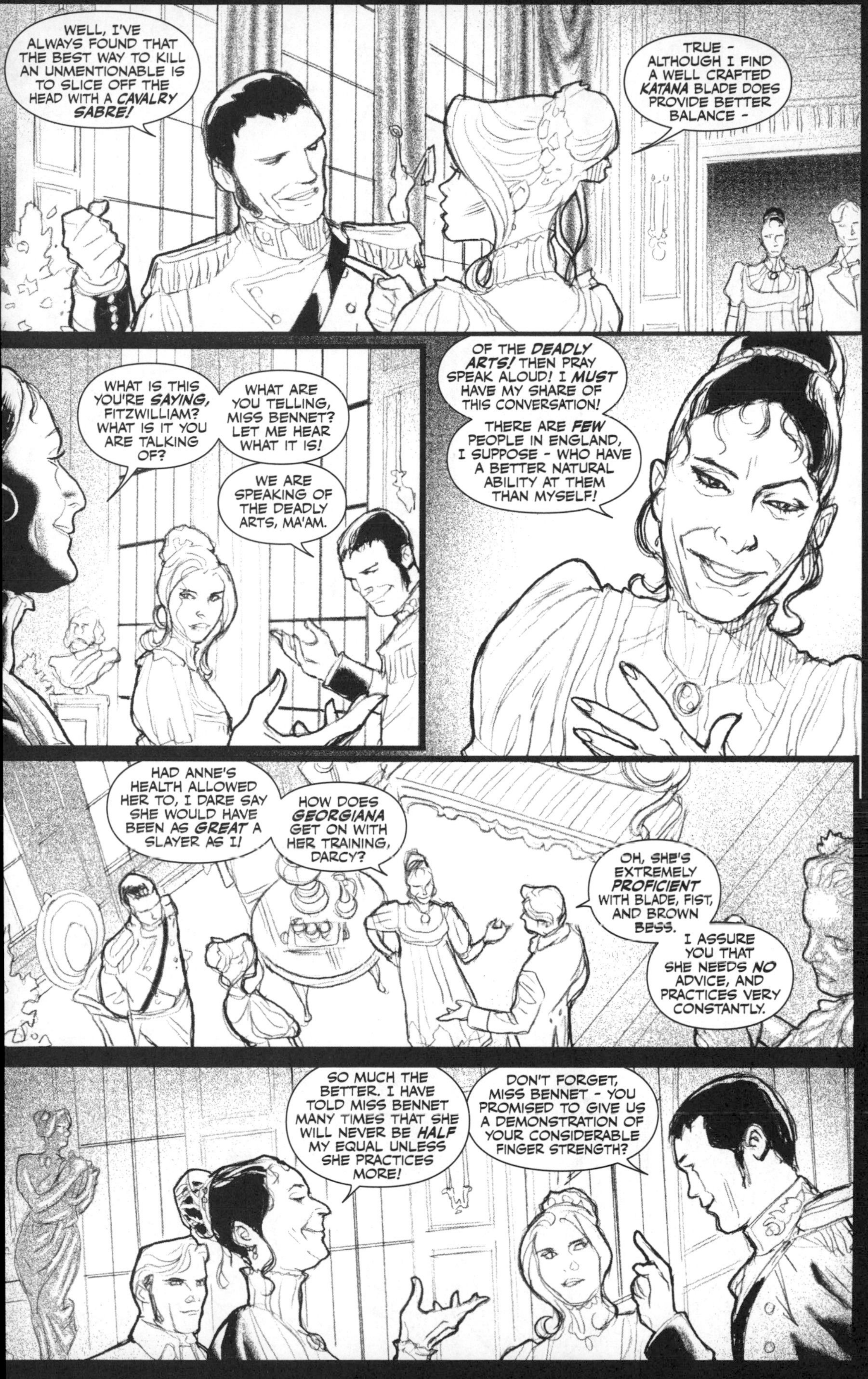
WELL, I'VE ALWAYS FOUND THAT THE BEST WAY TO KILL AN UNMENTIONABLE IS TO SLICE OFF THE HEAD WITH A *CAVALRY SABRE!*
TRUE - ALTHOUGH I FIND A WELL CRAFTED *KATANA* BLADE DOES PROVIDE BETTER BALANCE -
WHAT IS THIS YOU'RE *SAYING,* FITZWILLIAM? WHAT IS IT YOU ARE TALKING OF?
WHAT ARE YOU TELLING, MISS BENNET? LET ME HEAR WHAT IT IS!
WE ARE SPEAKING OF THE DEADLY ARTS, MA'AM.
OF THE *DEADLY ARTS!* THEN PRAY SPEAK ALOUD! I *MUST* HAVE MY SHARE OF THIS CONVERSATION!
THERE ARE *FEW* PEOPLE IN ENGLAND, I SUPPOSE - WHO HAVE A BETTER NATURAL ABILITY AT THEM THAN MYSELF!
HAD ANNE'S HEALTH ALLOWED HER TO, I DARE SAY SHE WOULD HAVE BEEN AS *GREAT* A SLAYER AS I!
HOW DOES *GEORGIANA* GET ON WITH HER TRAINING, DARCY?
OH, SHE'S EXTREMELY *PROFICIENT* WITH BLADE, FIST, AND BROWN BESS.
I ASSURE YOU THAT SHE NEEDS *NO* ADVICE, AND PRACTICES VERY CONSTANTLY.
SO MUCH THE BETTER. I HAVE TOLD MISS BENNET MANY TIMES THAT SHE WILL NEVER BE *HALF* MY EQUAL UNLESS SHE PRACTICES MORE!
DON'T FORGET, MISS BENNET - YOU PROMISED TO GIVE US A DEMONSTRATION OF YOUR CONSIDERABLE FINGER STRENGTH?

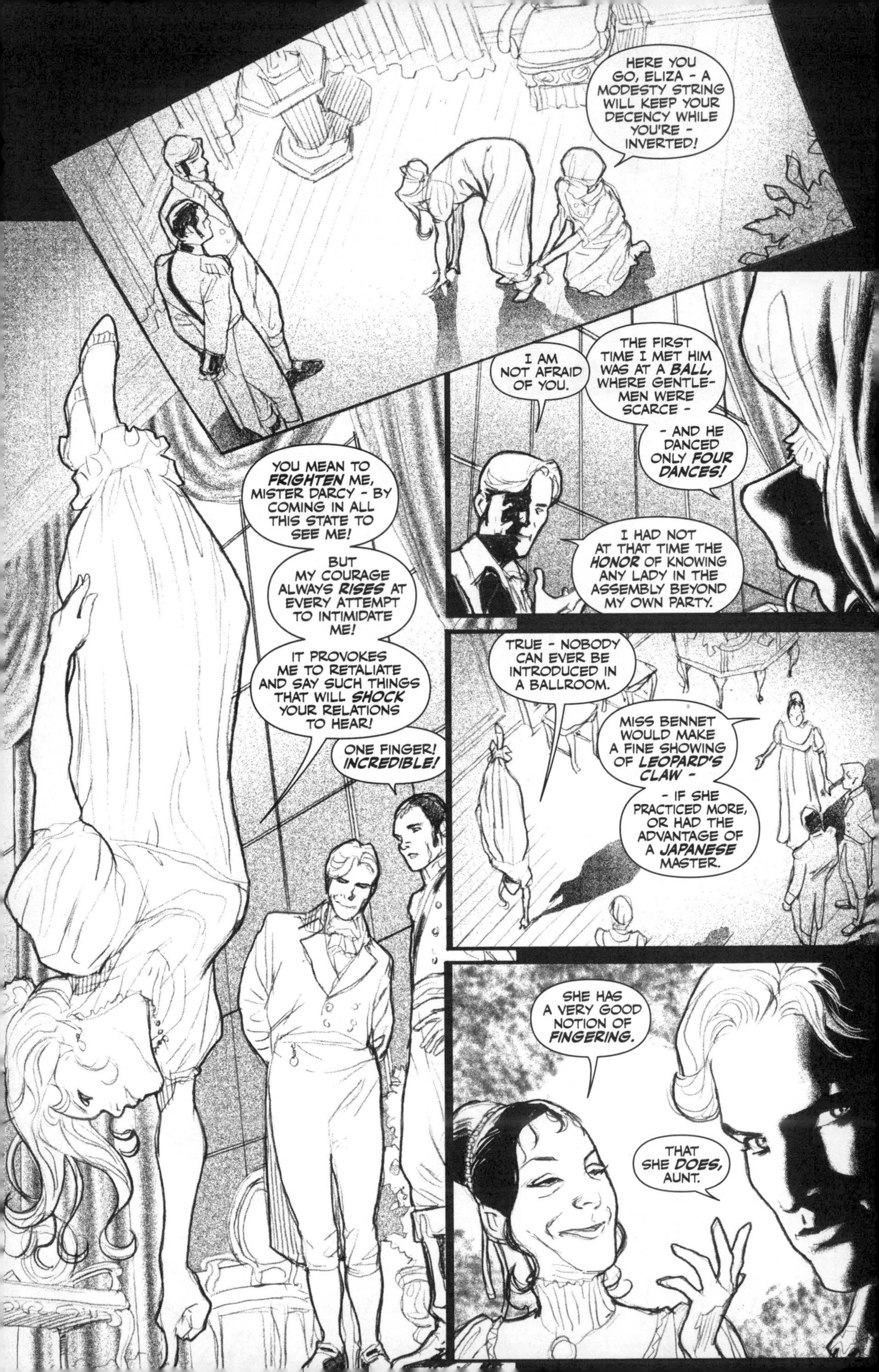
HERE YOU GO, ELIZA - A MODESTY STRING WILL KEEP YOUR DECENCY WHILE YOU'RE - INVERTED!
I AM NOT AFRAID OF YOU.
THE FIRST TIME I MET HIM WAS AT A BALL, WHERE GENTLEMEN WERE SCARCE -
- AND HE DANCED ONLY FOUR DANCES!
I HAD NOT AT THAT TIME THE HONOR OF KNOWING ANY LADY IN THE ASSEMBLY BEYOND MY OWN PARTY.
YOU MEAN TO FRIGHTEN ME, MISTER DARCY - BY COMING IN ALL THIS STATE TO SEE ME!
BUT MY COURAGE ALWAYS RISES AT EVERY ATTEMPT TO INTIMIDATE ME!
IT PROVOKES ME TO RETALIATE AND SAY SUCH THINGS THAT WILL SHOCK YOUR RELATIONS TO HEAR!
ONE FINGER! INCREDIBLE!
TRUE - NOBODY CAN EVER BE INTRODUCED IN A BALLROOM.
MISS BENNET WOULD MAKE A FINE SHOWING OF LEOPARD'S CLAW -
- IF SHE PRACTICED MORE, OR HAD THE ADVANTAGE OF A JAPANESE MASTER.
SHE HAS A VERY GOOD NOTION OF FINGERING.
THAT SHE DOES, AUNT.

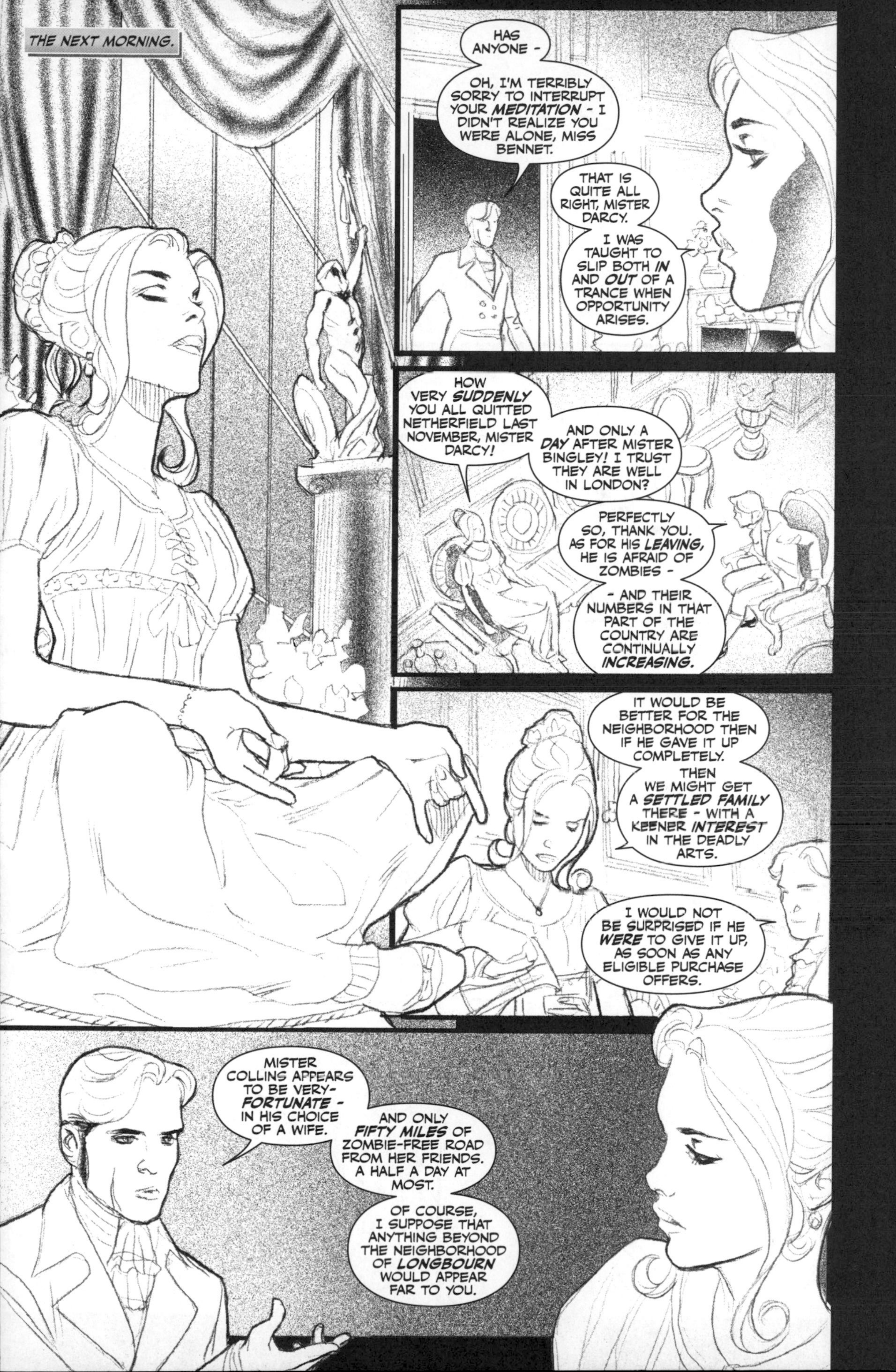
THE NEXT MORNING.
HAS ANYONE -
OH, I'M TERRIBLY SORRY TO INTERRUPT YOUR MEDITATION - I DIDN'T REALIZE YOU WERE ALONE, MISS BENNET.
THAT IS QUITE ALL RIGHT, MISTER DARCY.
I WAS TAUGHT TO SLIP BOTH IN AND OUT OF A TRANCE WHEN OPPORTUNITY ARISES.
HOW VERY SUDDENLY YOU ALL QUITTED NETHERFIELD LAST NOVEMBER, MISTER DARCY!
AND ONLY A DAY AFTER MISTER BINGLEY! I TRUST THEY ARE WELL IN LONDON?
PERFECTLY SO, THANK YOU. AS FOR HIS LEAVING, HE IS AFRAID OF ZOMBIES -
- AND THEIR NUMBERS IN THAT PART OF THE COUNTRY ARE CONTINUALLY INCREASING.
IT WOULD BE BETTER FOR THE NEIGHBORHOOD THEN IF HE GAVE IT UP COMPLETELY.
THEN WE MIGHT GET A SETTLED FAMILY THERE - WITH A KEENER INTEREST IN THE DEADLY ARTS.
I WOULD NOT BE SURPRISED IF HE WERE TO GIVE IT UP, AS SOON AS ANY ELIGIBLE PURCHASE OFFERS.
MISTER COLLINS APPEARS TO BE VERY- FORTUNATE - IN HIS CHOICE OF A WIFE.
AND ONLY FIFTY MILES OF ZOMBIE-FREE ROAD FROM HER FRIENDS. A HALF A DAY AT MOST.
OF COURSE, I SUPPOSE THAT ANYTHING BEYOND THE NEIGHBORHOOD OF LONGBOURN WOULD APPEAR FAR TO YOU.

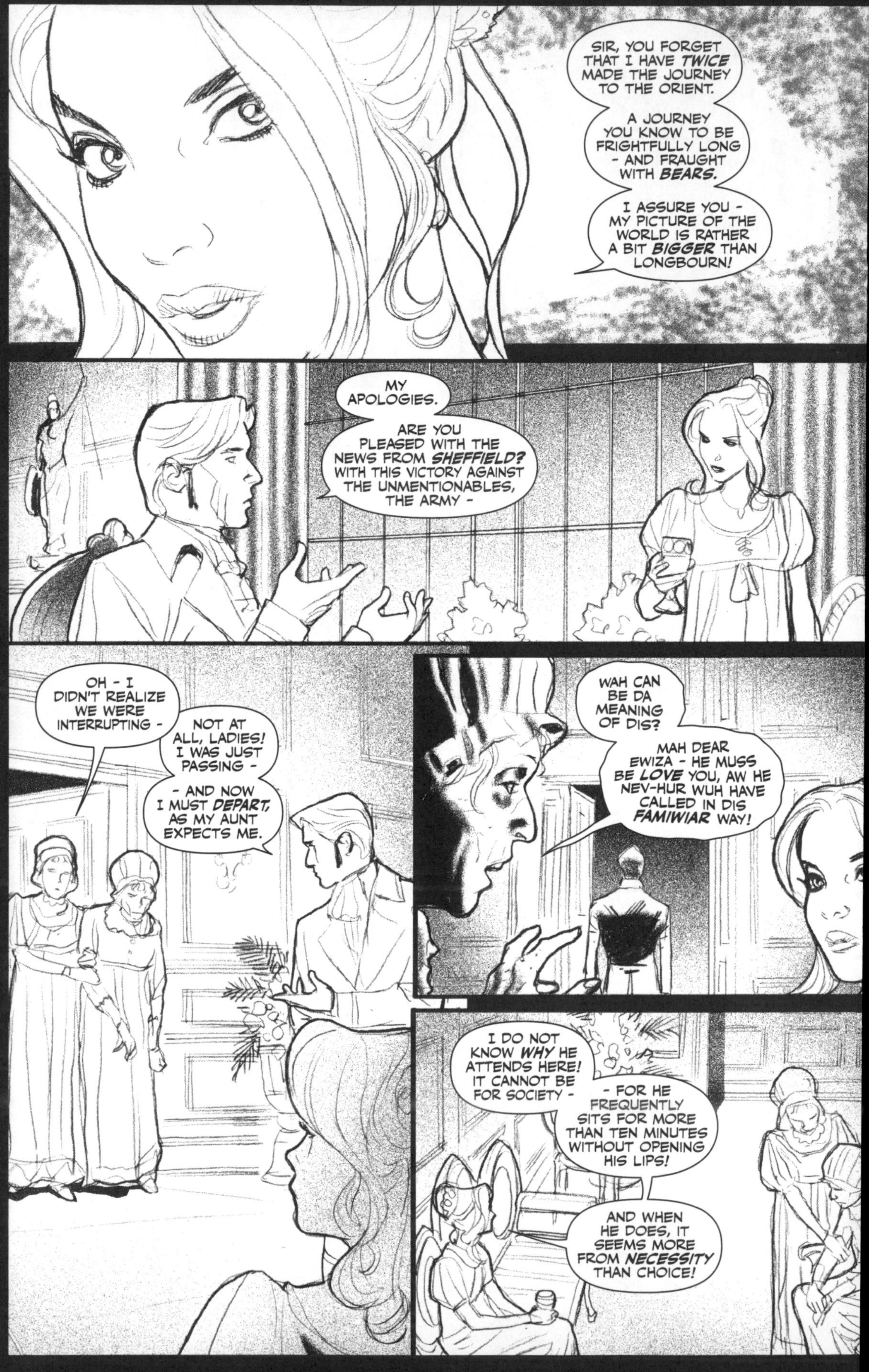
SIR, YOU FORGET THAT I HAVE TWICE MADE THE JOURNEY TO THE ORIENT.
A JOURNEY YOU KNOW TO BE FRIGHTFULLY LONG - AND FRAUGHT WITH BEARS.
I ASSURE YOU - MY PICTURE OF THE WORLD IS RATHER A BIT BIGGER THAN LONGBOURN!
MY APOLOGIES.
ARE YOU PLEASED WITH THE NEWS FROM SHEFFIELD? WITH THIS VICTORY AGAINST THE UNMENTIONABLES, THE ARMY -
OH - I DIDN'T REALIZE WE WERE INTERRUPTING -
NOT AT ALL, LADIES! I WAS JUST PASSING -
- AND NOW I MUST DEPART, AS MY AUNT EXPECTS ME.
WAH CAN BE DA MEANING OF DIS?
MAH DEAR EWIZA - HE MUSS BE LOVE YOU, AW HE NEV-HUR WUH HAVE CALLED IN DIS FAMIWIAR WAY!
I DO NOT KNOW WHY HE ATTENDS HERE! IT CANNOT BE FOR SOCIETY -
- FOR HE FREQUENTLY SITS FOR MORE THAN TEN MINUTES WITHOUT OPENING HIS LIPS!
AND WHEN HE DOES, IT SEEMS MORE FROM NECESSITY THAN CHOICE!

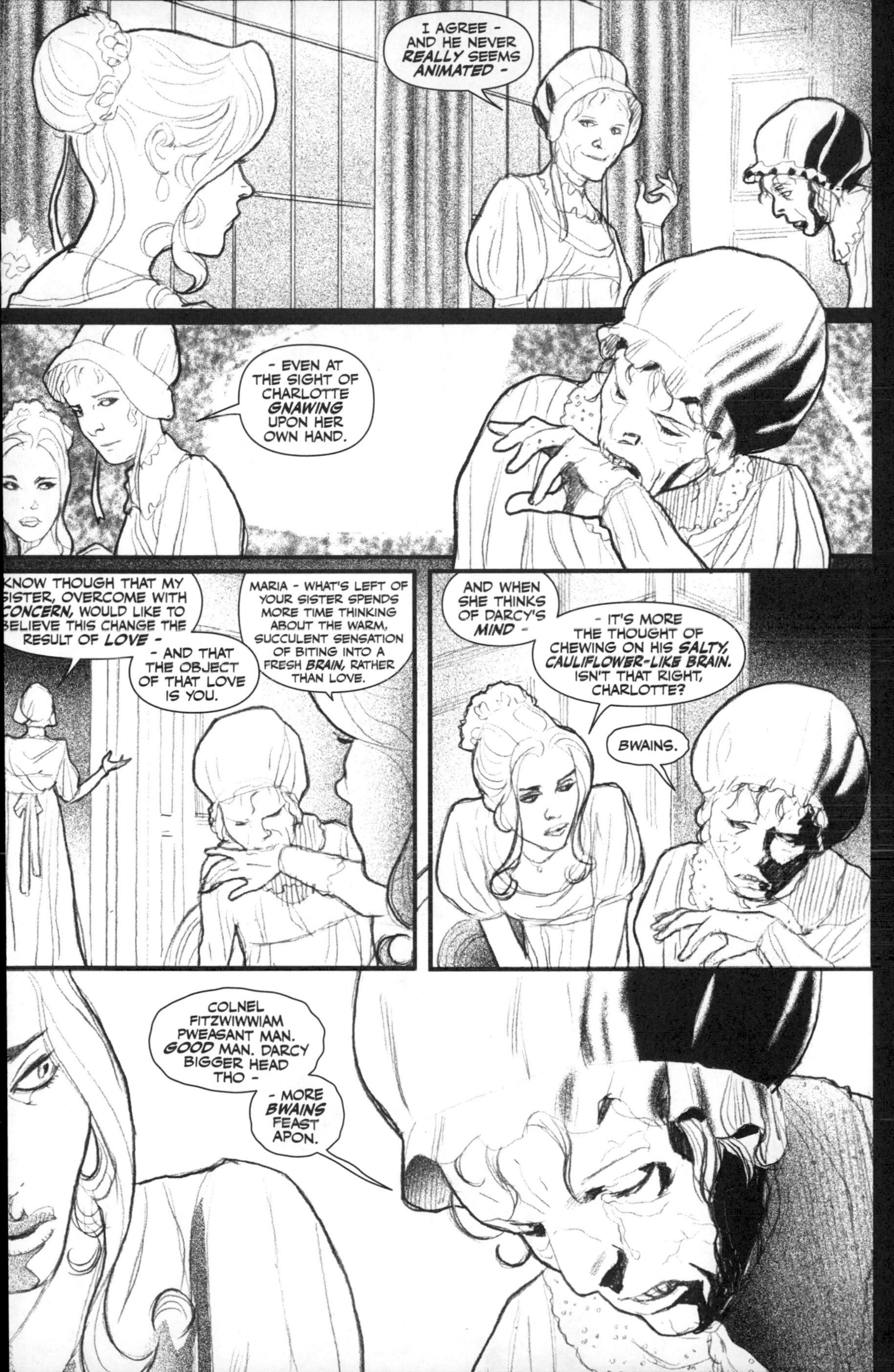
I AGREE - AND HE NEVER REALLY SEEMS ANIMATED -
- EVEN AT THE SIGHT OF CHARLOTTE GNAWING UPON HER OWN HAND.
KNOW THOUGH THAT MY SISTER, OVERCOME WITH CONCERN, WOULD LIKE TO BELIEVE THIS CHANGE THE RESULT OF LOVE -
- AND THAT THE OBJECT OF THAT LOVE IS YOU.
MARIA - WHAT'S LEFT OF YOUR SISTER SPENDS MORE TIME THINKING ABOUT THE WARM, SUCCULENT SENSATION OF BITING INTO A FRESH BRAIN, RATHER THAN LOVE.
AND WHEN SHE THINKS OF DARCY'S MIND -
- IT'S MORE THE THOUGHT OF CHEWING ON HIS SALTY, CAULIFLOWER-LIKE BRAIN. ISN'T THAT RIGHT, CHARLOTTE?
BWAINS.
COLNEL FITZWIWWIAM PWEASANT MAN. GOOD MAN. DARCY BIGGER HEAD THO -
- MORE BWAINS FEAST APON.

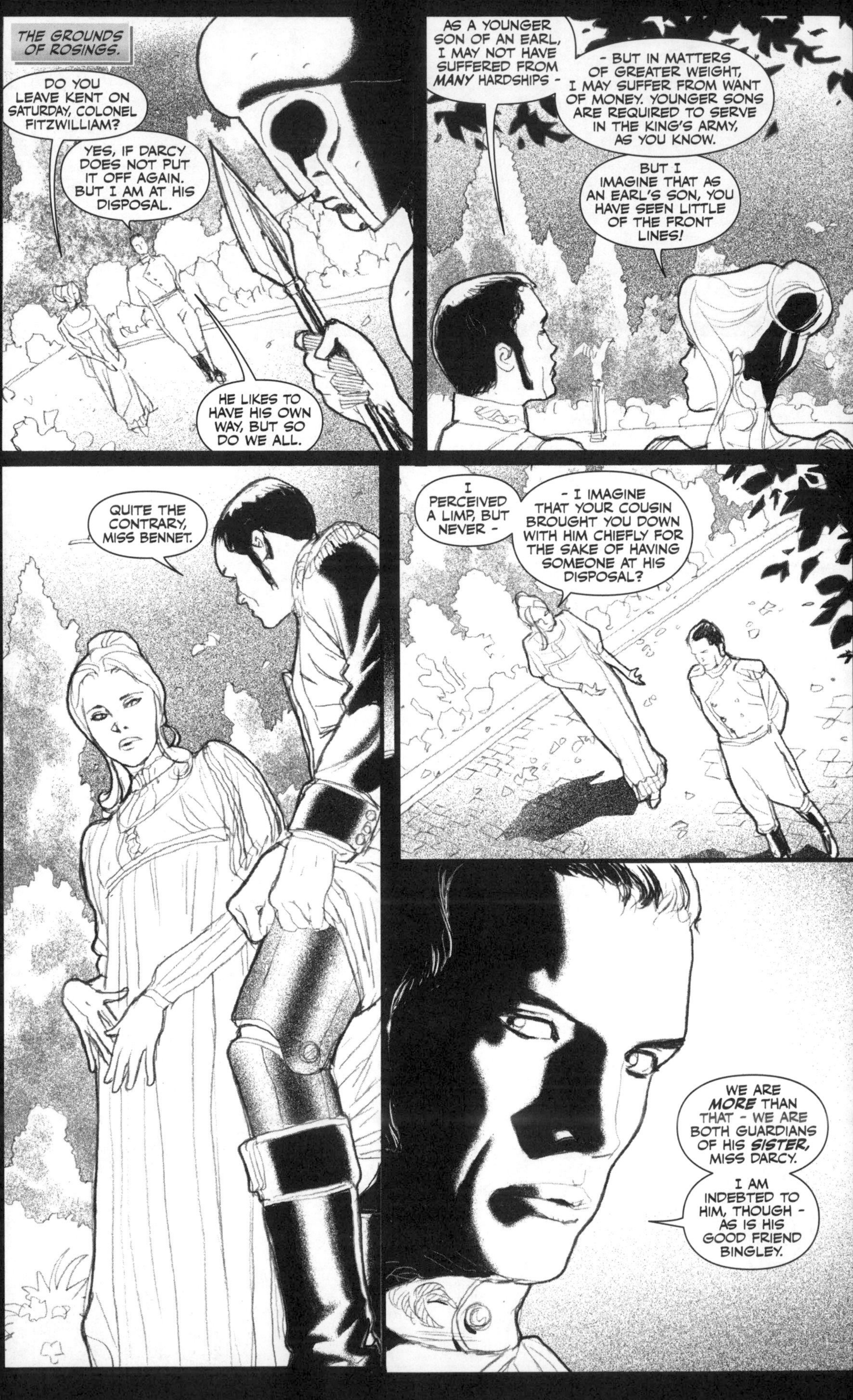
THE GROUNDS OF ROSINGS.
DO YOU LEAVE KENT ON SATURDAY, COLONEL FITZWILLIAM?
YES, IF DARCY DOES NOT PUT IT OFF AGAIN. BUT I AM AT HIS DISPOSAL.
HE LIKES TO HAVE HIS OWN WAY, BUT SO DO WE ALL.
AS A YOUNGER SON OF AN EARL, I MAY NOT HAVE SUFFERED FROM MANY HARDSHIPS -
- BUT IN MATTERS OF GREATER WEIGHT, I MAY SUFFER FROM WANT OF MONEY. YOUNGER SONS ARE REQUIRED TO SERVE IN THE KING'S ARMY, AS YOU KNOW.
BUT I IMAGINE THAT AS AN EARL'S SON, YOU HAVE SEEN LITTLE OF THE FRONT LINES!
QUITE THE CONTRARY, MISS BENNET.
I PERCEIVED A LIMP, BUT NEVER -
- I IMAGINE THAT YOUR COUSIN BROUGHT YOU DOWN WITH HIM CHIEFLY FOR THE SAKE OF HAVING SOMEONE AT HIS DISPOSAL?
WE ARE MORE THAN THAT - WE ARE BOTH GUARDIANS OF HIS SISTER, MISS DARCY.
I AM INDEBTED TO HIM, THOUGH - AS IS HIS GOOD FRIEND BINGLEY.

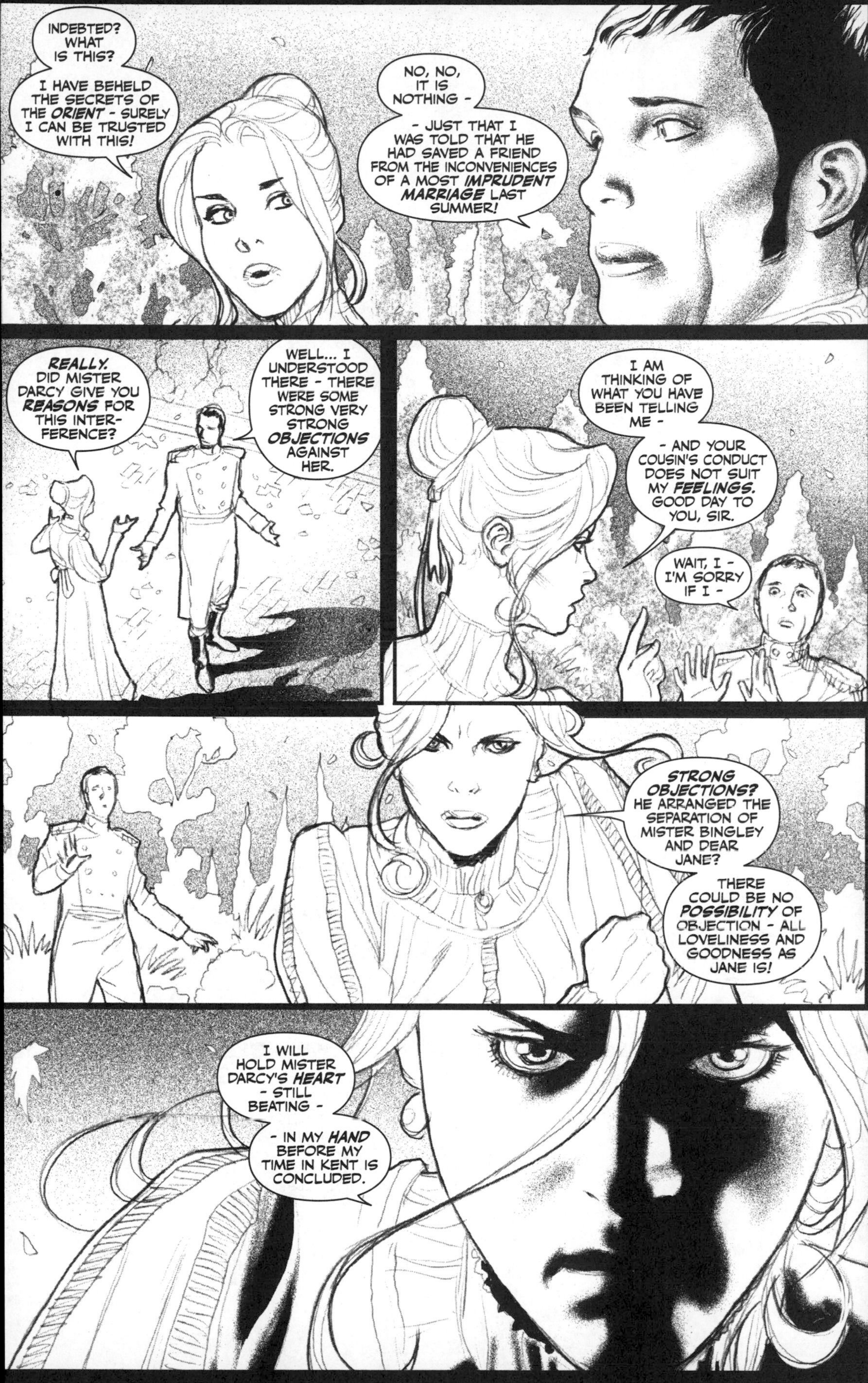
INDEBTED? WHAT IS THIS?
I HAVE BEHELD THE SECRETS OF THE *ORIENT* - SURELY I CAN BE TRUSTED WITH THIS!
NO, NO, IT IS NOTHING -
- JUST THAT I WAS TOLD THAT HE HAD SAVED A FRIEND FROM THE INCONVENIENCES OF A MOST *IMPRUDENT MARRIAGE* LAST SUMMER!
REALLY. DID MISTER DARCY GIVE YOU *REASONS* FOR THIS INTER-FERENCE?
WELL... I UNDERSTOOD THERE - THERE WERE SOME STRONG VERY STRONG *OBJECTIONS* AGAINST HER.
I AM THINKING OF WHAT YOU HAVE BEEN TELLING ME -
- AND YOUR COUSIN'S CONDUCT DOES NOT SUIT MY *FEELINGS.* GOOD DAY TO YOU, SIR.
WAIT, I - I'M SORRY IF I -
STRONG OBJECTIONS? HE ARRANGED THE SEPARATION OF MISTER BINGLEY AND DEAR JANE?
THERE COULD BE NO *POSSIBILITY* OF OBJECTION - ALL LOVELINESS AND GOODNESS AS JANE IS!
I WILL HOLD MISTER DARCY'S *HEART* - STILL BEATING -
- IN MY *HAND* BEFORE MY TIME IN KENT IS CONCLUDED.

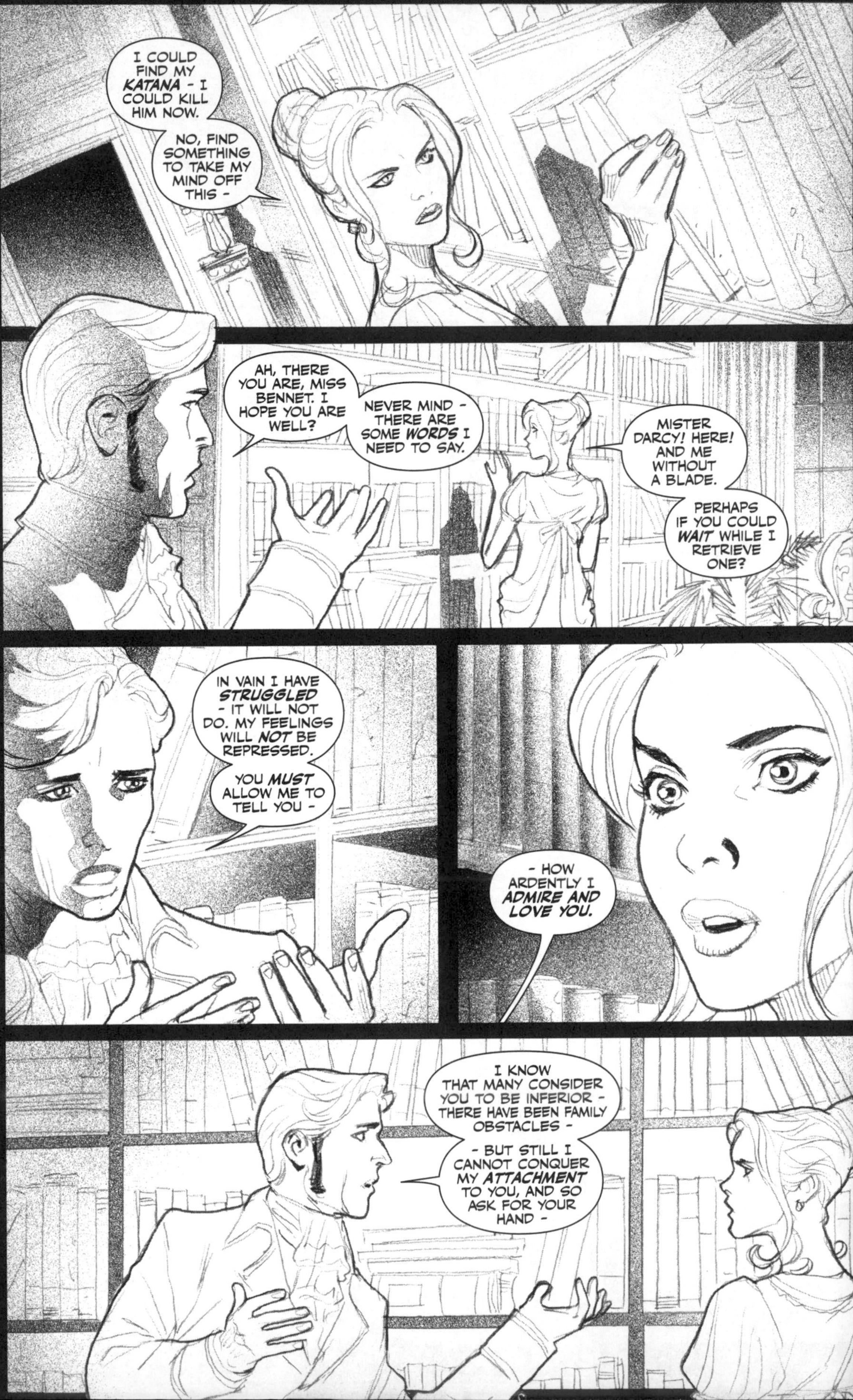
I COULD FIND MY KATANA - I COULD KILL HIM NOW.
NO, FIND SOMETHING TO TAKE MY MIND OFF THIS -
AH, THERE YOU ARE, MISS BENNET. I HOPE YOU ARE WELL?
NEVER MIND - THERE ARE SOME WORDS I NEED TO SAY.
MISTER DARCY! HERE! AND ME WITHOUT A BLADE.
PERHAPS IF YOU COULD WAIT WHILE I RETRIEVE ONE?
IN VAIN I HAVE STRUGGLED - IT WILL NOT DO. MY FEELINGS WILL NOT BE REPRESSED.
YOU MUST ALLOW ME TO TELL YOU -
- HOW ARDENTLY I ADMIRE AND LOVE YOU.
I KNOW THAT MANY CONSIDER YOU TO BE INFERIOR - THERE HAVE BEEN FAMILY OBSTACLES -
- BUT STILL I CANNOT CONQUER MY ATTACHMENT TO YOU, AND SO ASK FOR YOUR HAND -

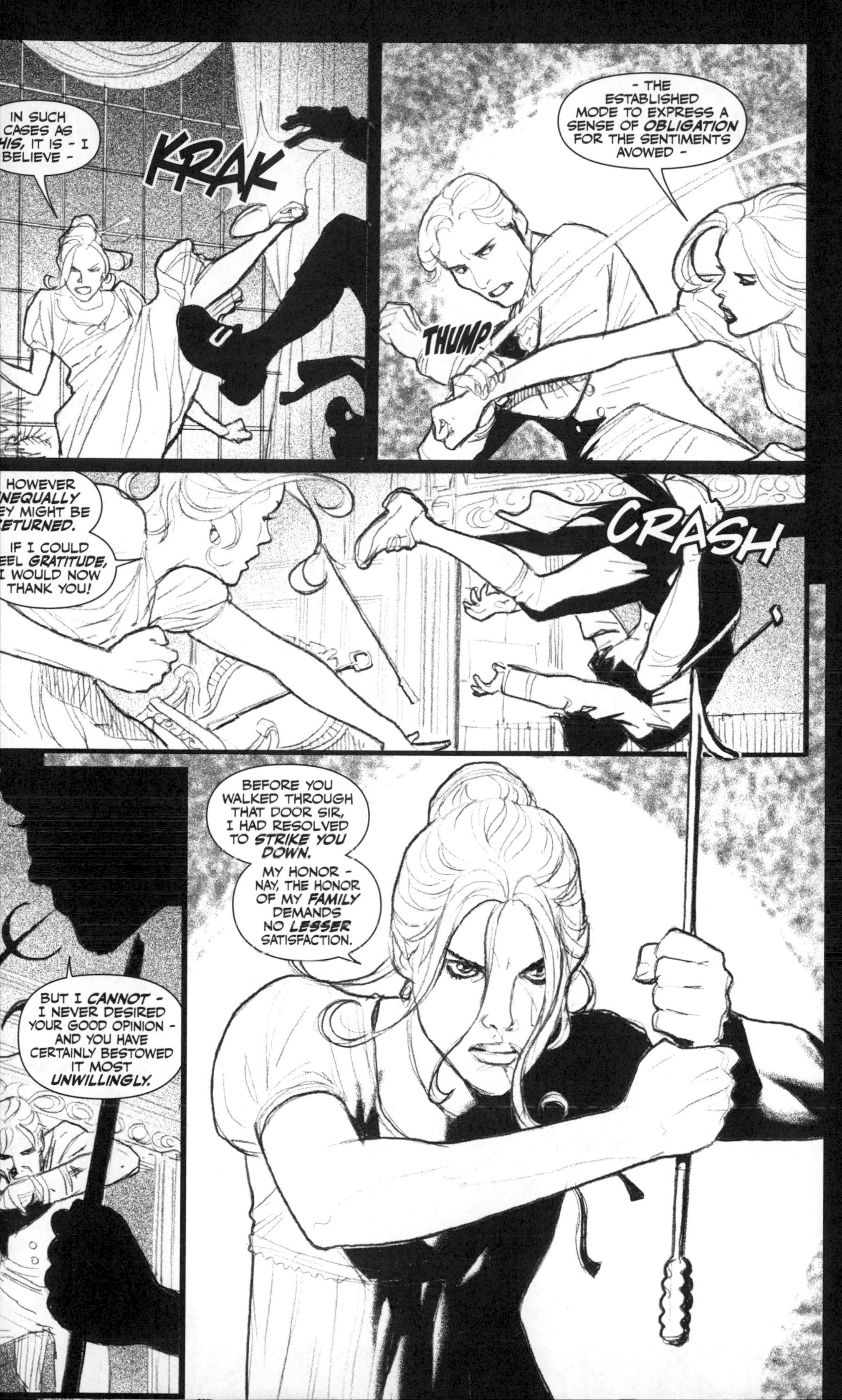

IN SUCH CASES AS THIS, IT IS - I BELIEVE -
KRAK
- THE ESTABLISHED MODE TO EXPRESS A SENSE OF OBLIGATION FOR THE SENTIMENTS AVOWED -
THUMP
HOWEVER UNEQUALLY THEY MIGHT BE RETURNED.
IF I COULD FEEL GRATITUDE, I WOULD NOW THANK YOU!
CRASH
BEFORE YOU WALKED THROUGH THAT DOOR SIR, I HAD RESOLVED TO STRIKE YOU DOWN.
MY HONOR - NAY, THE HONOR OF MY FAMILY DEMANDS NO LESSER SATISFACTION.
BUT I CANNOT - I NEVER DESIRED YOUR GOOD OPINION - AND YOU HAVE CERTAINLY BESTOWED IT MOST UNWILLINGLY.

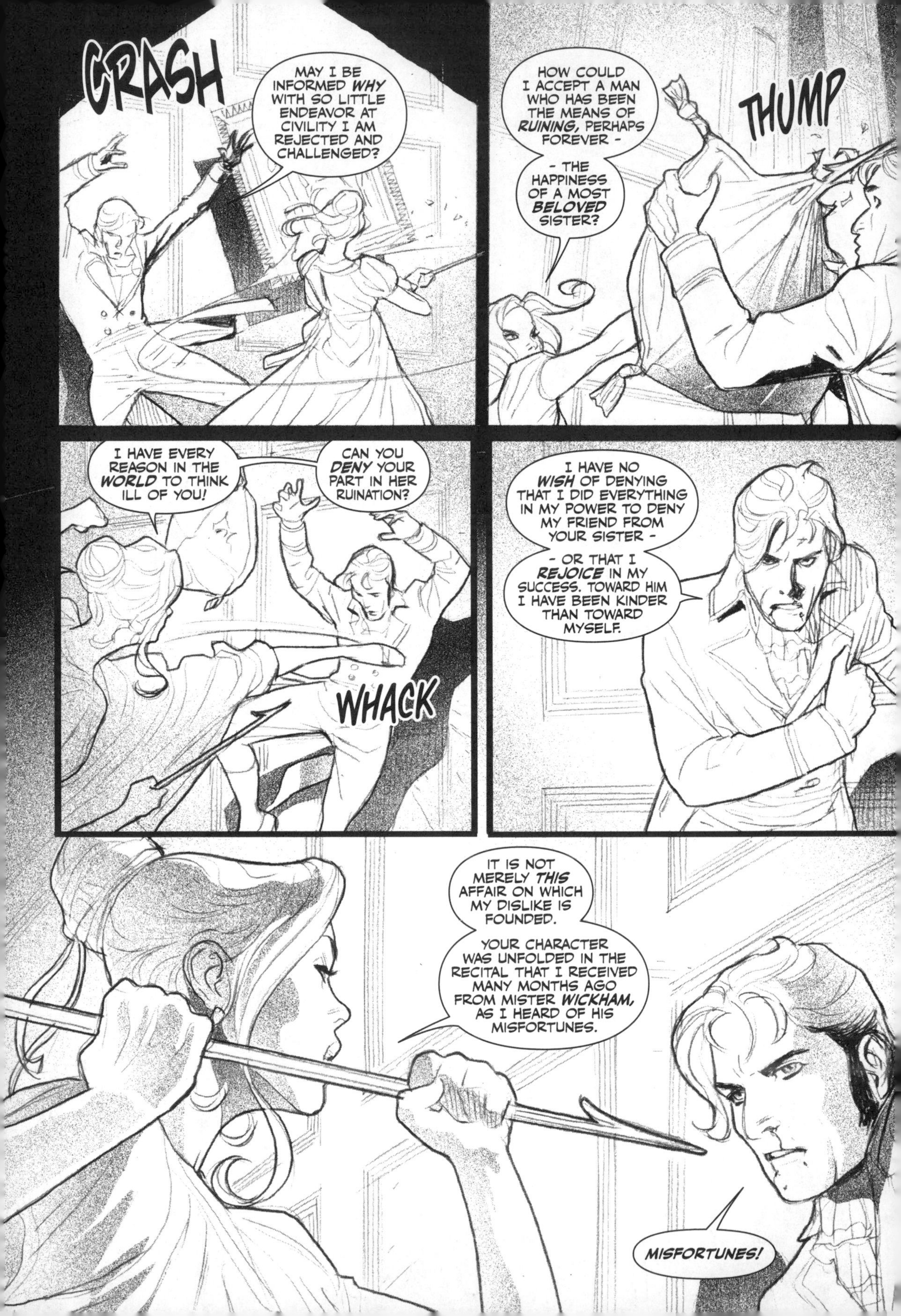
CRASH
MAY I BE INFORMED WHY WITH SO LITTLE ENDEAVOR AT CIVILITY I AM REJECTED AND CHALLENGED?
HOW COULD I ACCEPT A MAN WHO HAS BEEN THE MEANS OF RUINING, PERHAPS FOREVER -
- THE HAPPINESS OF A MOST BELOVED SISTER?
THUMP
I HAVE EVERY REASON IN THE WORLD TO THINK ILL OF YOU!
CAN YOU DENY YOUR PART IN HER RUINATION?
WHACK
I HAVE NO WISH OF DENYING THAT I DID EVERYTHING IN MY POWER TO DENY MY FRIEND FROM YOUR SISTER -
- OR THAT I REJOICE IN MY SUCCESS. TOWARD HIM I HAVE BEEN KINDER THAN TOWARD MYSELF.
IT IS NOT MERELY THIS AFFAIR ON WHICH MY DISLIKE IS FOUNDED.
YOUR CHARACTER WAS UNFOLDED IN THE RECITAL THAT I RECEIVED MANY MONTHS AGO FROM MISTER WICKHAM, AS I HEARD OF HIS MISFORTUNES.
MISFORTUNES!

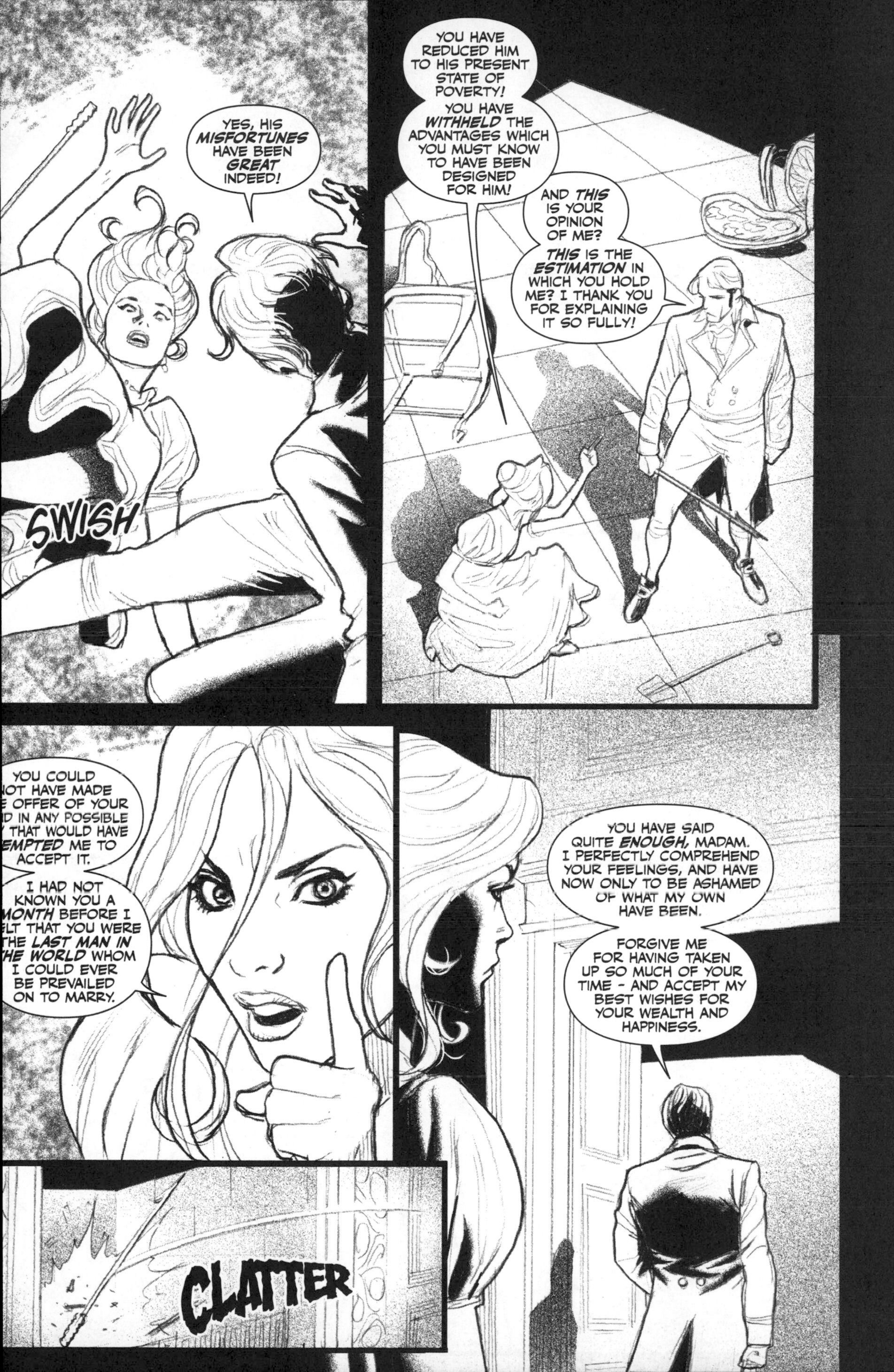
YES, HIS MISFORTUNES HAVE BEEN GREAT INDEED!
YOU HAVE REDUCED HIM TO HIS PRESENT STATE OF POVERTY!
YOU HAVE WITHHELD THE ADVANTAGES WHICH YOU MUST KNOW TO HAVE BEEN DESIGNED FOR HIM!
SWISH
AND THIS IS YOUR OPINION OF ME?
THIS IS THE ESTIMATION IN WHICH YOU HOLD ME? I THANK YOU FOR EXPLAINING IT SO FULLY!
YOU COULD NOT HAVE MADE E OFFER OF YOUR D IN ANY POSSIBLE Y THAT WOULD HAVE EMPTED ME TO ACCEPT IT.
I HAD NOT KNOWN YOU A MONTH BEFORE I LT THAT YOU WERE THE LAST MAN IN THE WORLD WHOM I COULD EVER BE PREVAILED ON TO MARRY.
YOU HAVE SAID QUITE ENOUGH, MADAM. I PERFECTLY COMPREHEND YOUR FEELINGS, AND HAVE NOW ONLY TO BE ASHAMED OF WHAT MY OWN HAVE BEEN.
FORGIVE ME FOR HAVING TAKEN UP SO MUCH OF YOUR TIME - AND ACCEPT MY BEST WISHES FOR YOUR WEALTH AND HAPPINESS.
CLATTER

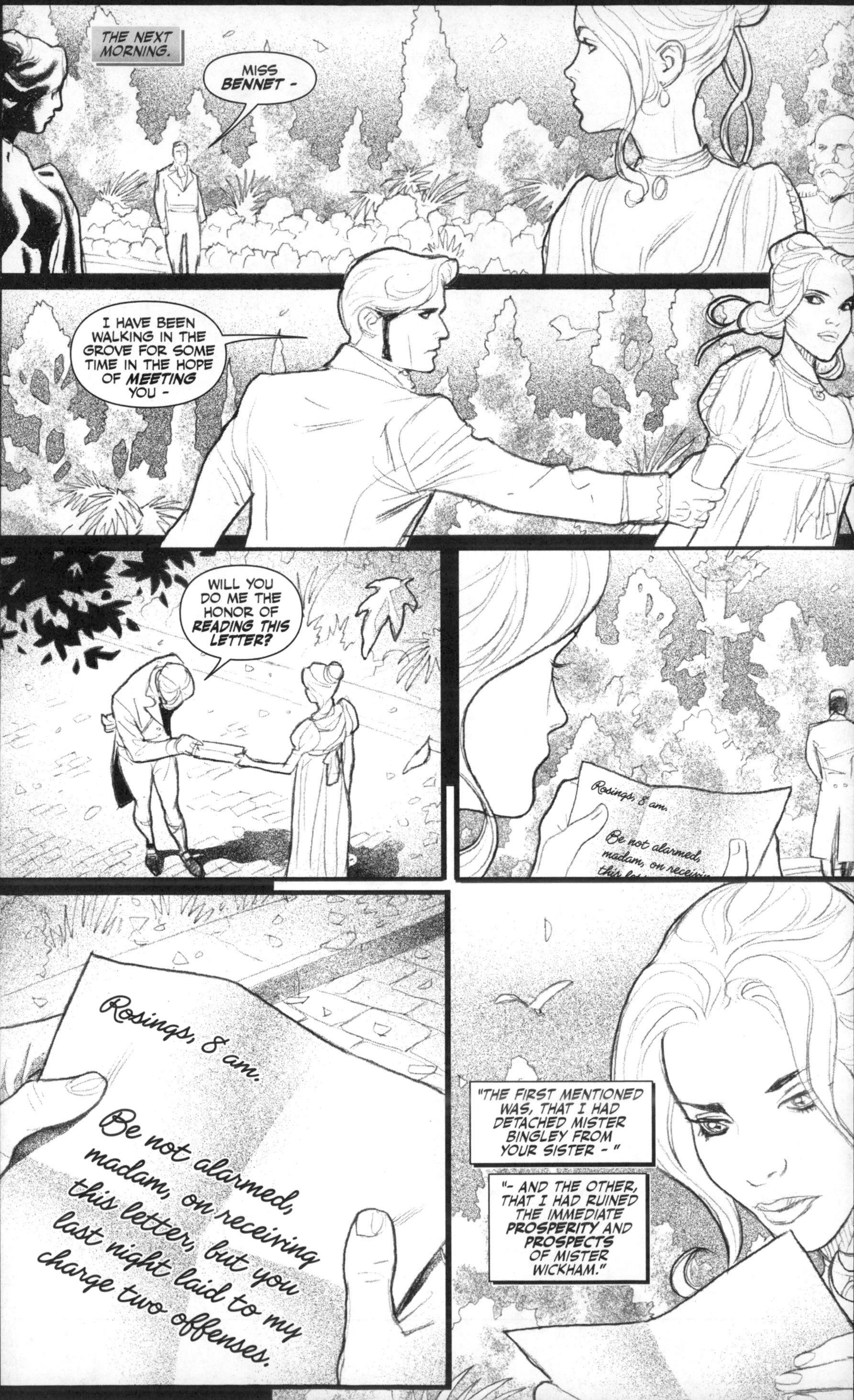
THE NEXT MORNING.
MISS BENNET -
I HAVE BEEN WALKING IN THE GROVE FOR SOME TIME IN THE HOPE OF MEETING YOU -
WILL YOU DO ME THE HONOR OF READING THIS LETTER?
Rosings, 8 am.
Be not alarmed, madam, on receiving this letter, but you last night laid to my charge two offenses.
"THE FIRST MENTIONED WAS, THAT I HAD DETACHED MISTER BINGLEY FROM YOUR SISTER - "
"- AND THE OTHER, THAT I HAD RUINED THE IMMEDIATE PROSPERITY AND PROSPECTS OF MISTER WICKHAM."

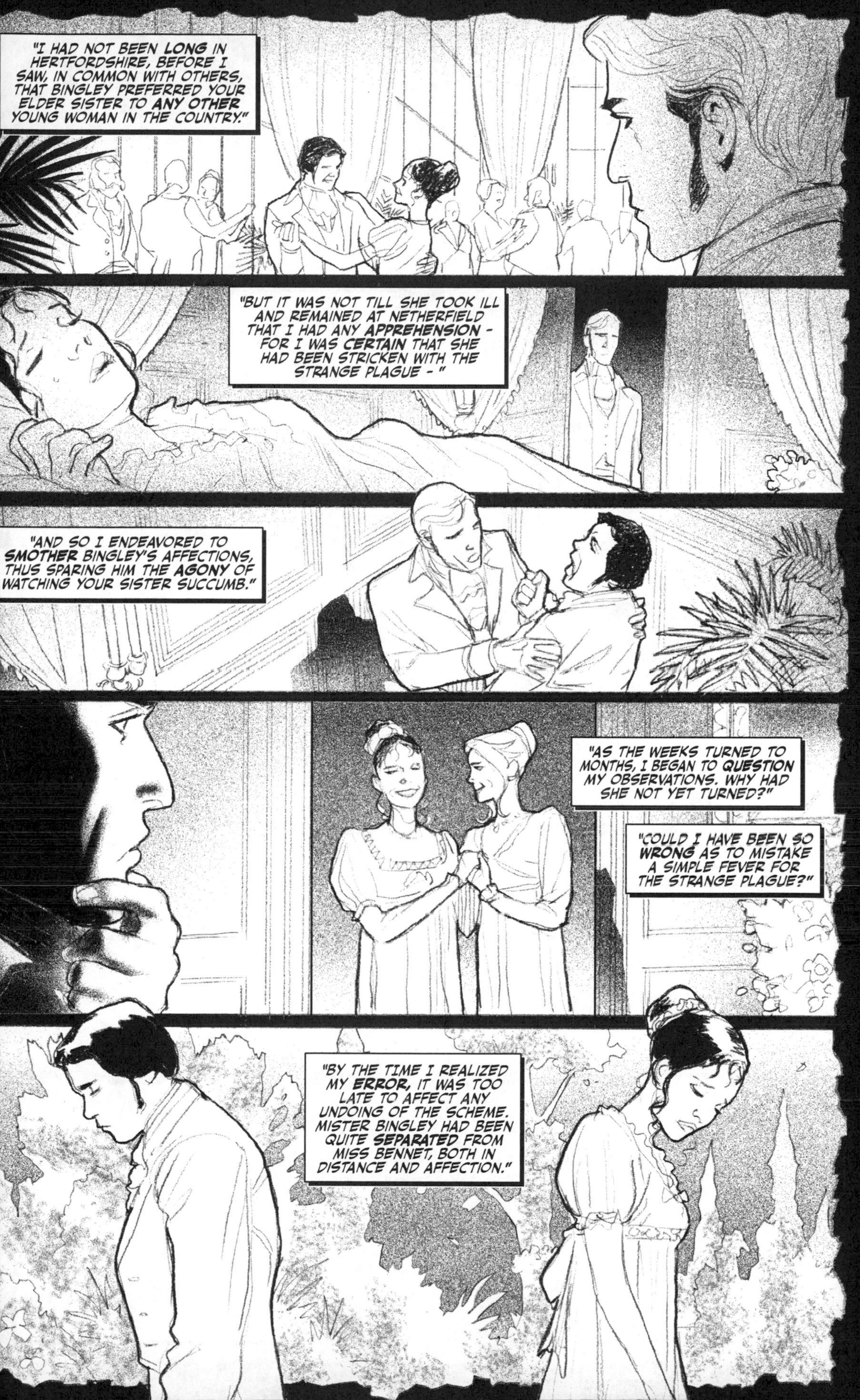
"I HAD NOT BEEN LONG IN HERTFORDSHIRE, BEFORE I SAW, IN COMMON WITH OTHERS, THAT BINGLEY PREFERRED YOUR ELDER SISTER TO ANY OTHER YOUNG WOMAN IN THE COUNTRY."
"BUT IT WAS NOT TILL SHE TOOK ILL AND REMAINED AT NETHERFIELD THAT I HAD ANY APPREHENSION - FOR I WAS CERTAIN THAT SHE HAD BEEN STRICKEN WITH THE STRANGE PLAGUE - "
"AND SO I ENDEAVORED TO SMOTHER BINGLEY'S AFFECTIONS, THUS SPARING HIM THE AGONY OF WATCHING YOUR SISTER SUCCUMB."
"AS THE WEEKS TURNED TO MONTHS, I BEGAN TO QUESTION MY OBSERVATIONS. WHY HAD SHE NOT YET TURNED?"
"COULD I HAVE BEEN SO WRONG AS TO MISTAKE A SIMPLE FEVER FOR THE STRANGE PLAGUE?"
"BY THE TIME I REALIZED MY ERROR, IT WAS TOO LATE TO AFFECT ANY UNDOING OF THE SCHEME. MISTER BINGLEY HAD BEEN QUITE SEPARATED FROM MISS BENNET, BOTH IN DISTANCE AND AFFECTION."

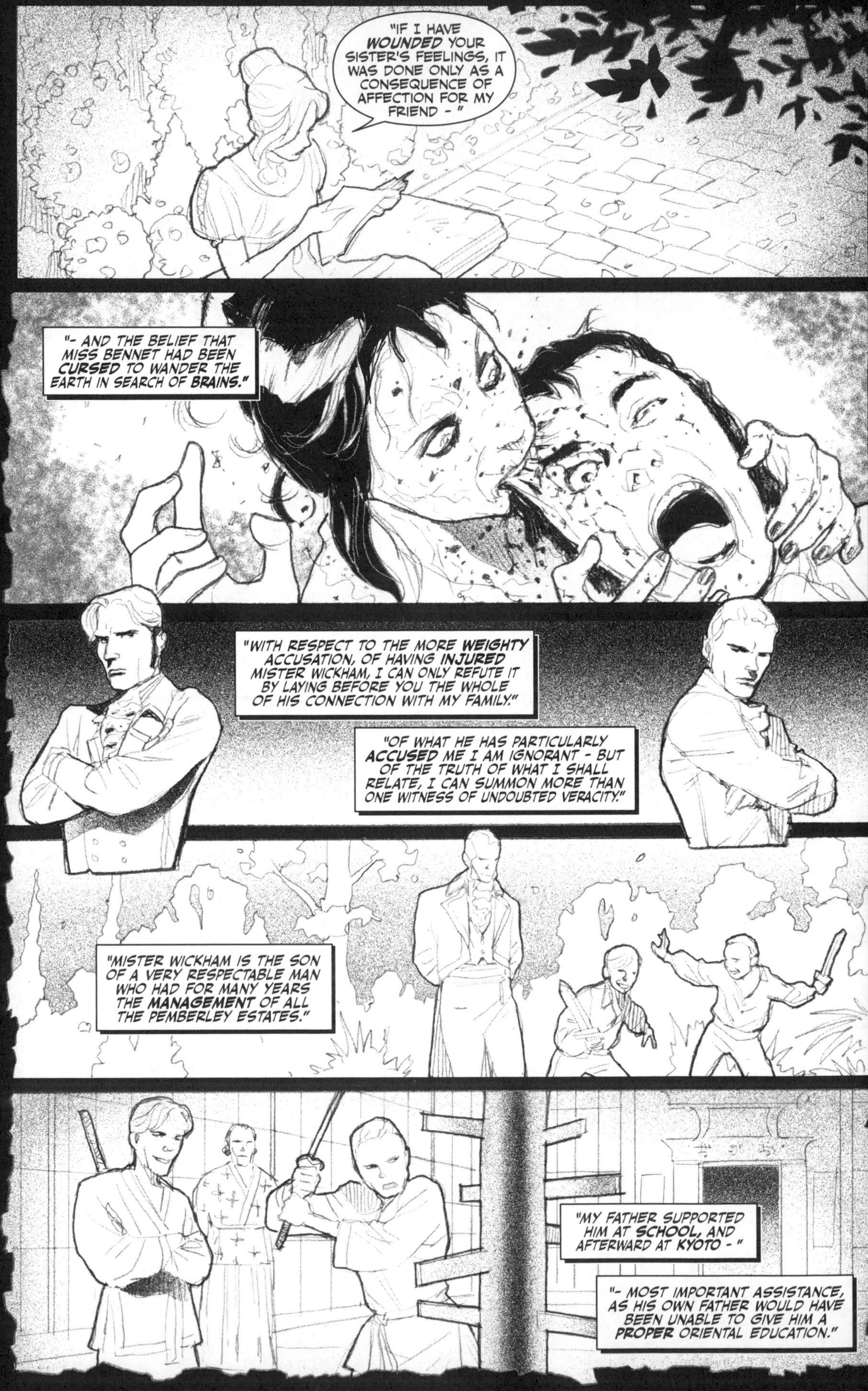

"IF I HAVE WOUNDED YOUR SISTER'S FEELINGS, IT WAS DONE ONLY AS A CONSEQUENCE OF AFFECTION FOR MY FRIEND - "
"- AND THE BELIEF THAT MISS BENNET HAD BEEN CURSED TO WANDER THE EARTH IN SEARCH OF BRAINS."
"WITH RESPECT TO THE MORE WEIGHTY ACCUSATION, OF HAVING INJURED MISTER WICKHAM, I CAN ONLY REFUTE IT BY LAYING BEFORE YOU THE WHOLE OF HIS CONNECTION WITH MY FAMILY."
"OF WHAT HE HAS PARTICULARLY ACCUSED ME I AM IGNORANT - BUT OF THE TRUTH OF WHAT I SHALL RELATE, I CAN SUMMON MORE THAN ONE WITNESS OF UNDOUBTED VERACITY."
"MISTER WICKHAM IS THE SON OF A VERY RESPECTABLE MAN WHO HAD FOR MANY YEARS THE MANAGEMENT OF ALL THE PEMBERLEY ESTATES."
"MY FATHER SUPPORTED HIM AT SCHOOL, AND AFTERWARD AT KYOTO - "
"- MOST IMPORTANT ASSISTANCE, AS HIS OWN FATHER WOULD HAVE BEEN UNABLE TO GIVE HIM A PROPER ORIENTAL EDUCATION."

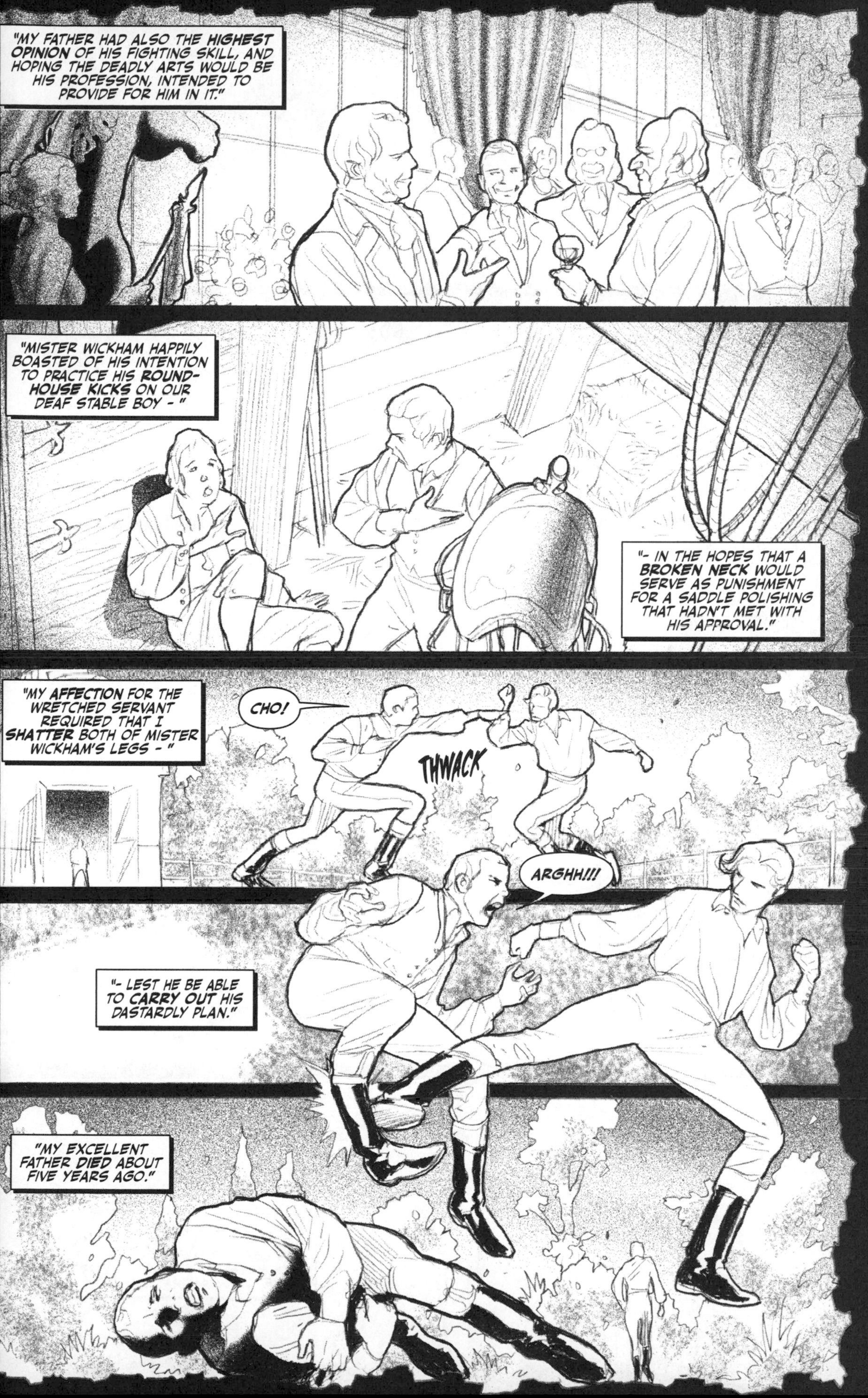
"MY FATHER HAD ALSO THE HIGHEST OPINION OF HIS FIGHTING SKILL, AND HOPING THE DEADLY ARTS WOULD BE HIS PROFESSION, INTENDED TO PROVIDE FOR HIM IN IT."
"MISTER WICKHAM HAPPILY BOASTED OF HIS INTENTION TO PRACTICE HIS ROUND-HOUSE KICKS ON OUR DEAF STABLE BOY - "
"- IN THE HOPES THAT A BROKEN NECK WOULD SERVE AS PUNISHMENT FOR A SADDLE POLISHING THAT HADN'T MET WITH HIS APPROVAL."
"MY AFFECTION FOR THE WRETCHED SERVANT REQUIRED THAT I SHATTER BOTH OF MISTER WICKHAM'S LEGS - "
CHO!
THWACK
ARGHH!!!
"- LEST HE BE ABLE TO CARRY OUT HIS DASTARDLY PLAN."
"MY EXCELLENT FATHER DIED ABOUT FIVE YEARS AGO."

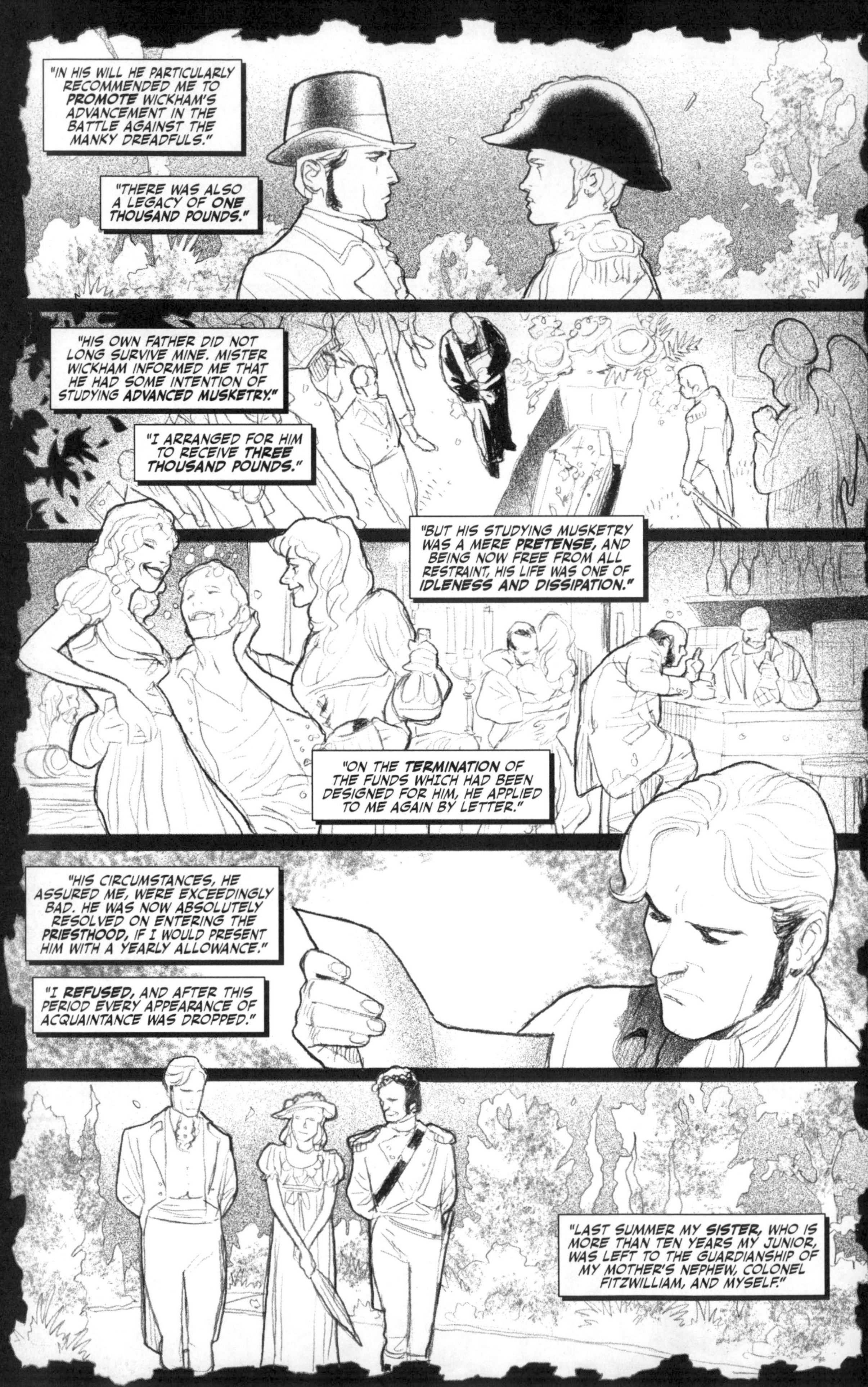
"IN HIS WILL HE PARTICULARLY RECOMMENDED ME TO PROMOTE WICKHAM'S ADVANCEMENT IN THE BATTLE AGAINST THE MANKY DREADFULS."
"THERE WAS ALSO A LEGACY OF ONE THOUSAND POUNDS."
"HIS OWN FATHER DID NOT LONG SURVIVE MINE. MISTER WICKHAM INFORMED ME THAT HE HAD SOME INTENTION OF STUDYING ADVANCED MUSKETRY."
"I ARRANGED FOR HIM TO RECEIVE THREE THOUSAND POUNDS."
"BUT HIS STUDYING MUSKETRY WAS A MERE PRETENSE, AND BEING NOW FREE FROM ALL RESTRAINT, HIS LIFE WAS ONE OF IDLENESS AND DISSIPATION."
"ON THE TERMINATION OF THE FUNDS WHICH HAD BEEN DESIGNED FOR HIM, HE APPLIED TO ME AGAIN BY LETTER."
"HIS CIRCUMSTANCES, HE ASSURED ME, WERE EXCEEDINGLY BAD. HE WAS NOW ABSOLUTELY RESOLVED ON ENTERING THE PRIESTHOOD, IF I WOULD PRESENT HIM WITH A YEARLY ALLOWANCE."
"I REFUSED, AND AFTER THIS PERIOD EVERY APPEARANCE OF ACQUAINTANCE WAS DROPPED."
"LAST SUMMER MY SISTER, WHO IS MORE THAN TEN YEARS MY JUNIOR, WAS LEFT TO THE GUARDIANSHIP OF MY MOTHER'S NEPHEW, COLONEL FITZWILLIAM, AND MYSELF."

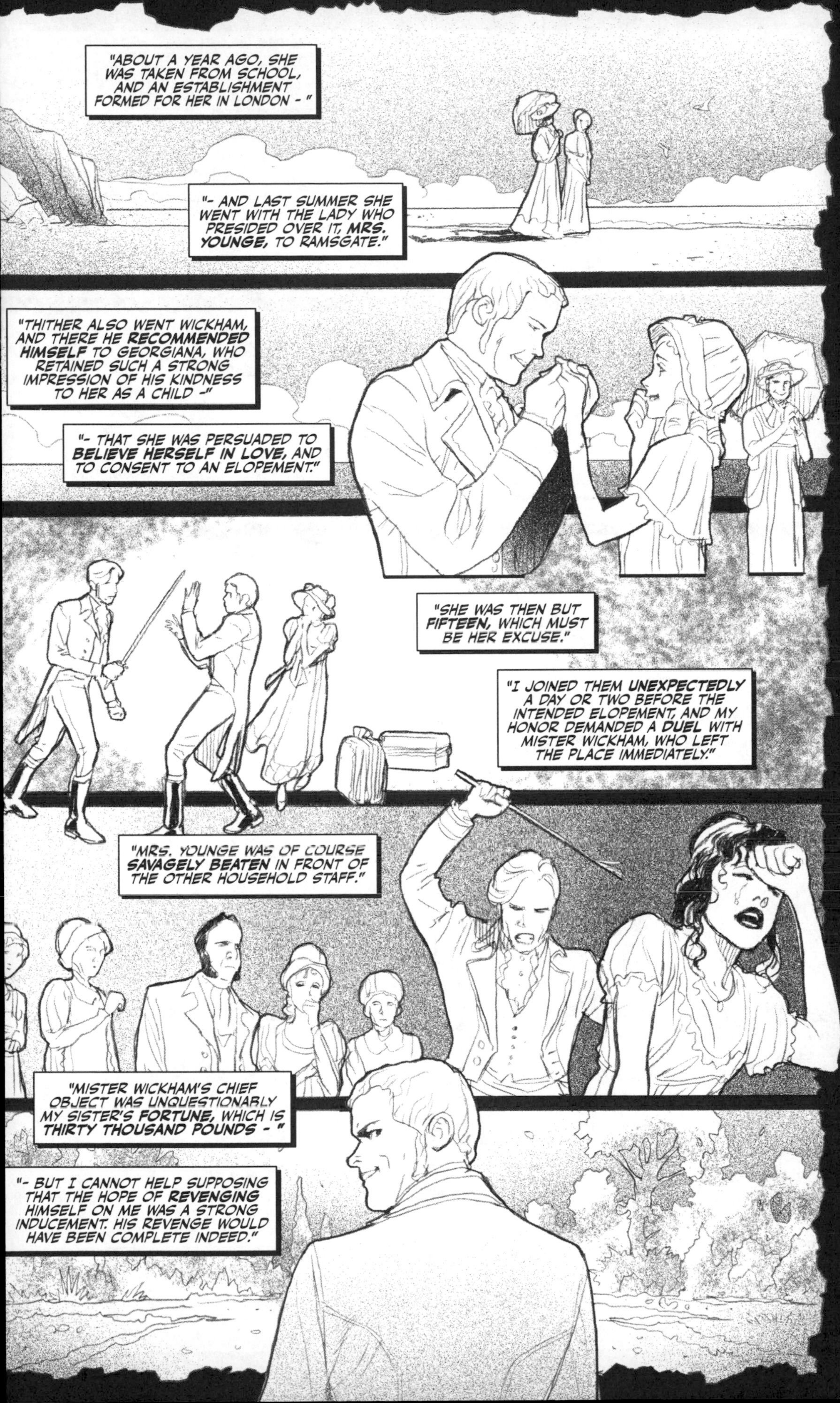
"ABOUT A YEAR AGO, SHE WAS TAKEN FROM SCHOOL, AND AN ESTABLISHMENT FORMED FOR HER IN LONDON -"
"- AND LAST SUMMER SHE WENT WITH THE LADY WHO PRESIDED OVER IT, MRS. YOUNGE, TO RAMSGATE."
"THITHER ALSO WENT WICKHAM, AND THERE HE RECOMMENDED HIMSELF TO GEORGIANA, WHO RETAINED SUCH A STRONG IMPRESSION OF HIS KINDNESS TO HER AS A CHILD -"
"- THAT SHE WAS PERSUADED TO BELIEVE HERSELF IN LOVE, AND TO CONSENT TO AN ELOPEMENT."
"SHE WAS THEN BUT FIFTEEN, WHICH MUST BE HER EXCUSE."
"I JOINED THEM UNEXPECTEDLY A DAY OR TWO BEFORE THE INTENDED ELOPEMENT, AND MY HONOR DEMANDED A DUEL WITH MISTER WICKHAM, WHO LEFT THE PLACE IMMEDIATELY."
"MRS. YOUNGE WAS OF COURSE SAVAGELY BEATEN IN FRONT OF THE OTHER HOUSEHOLD STAFF."
"MISTER WICKHAM'S CHIEF OBJECT WAS UNQUESTIONABLY MY SISTER'S FORTUNE, WHICH IS THIRTY THOUSAND POUNDS -"
"- BUT I CANNOT HELP SUPPOSING THAT THE HOPE OF REVENGING HIMSELF ON ME WAS A STRONG INDUCEMENT. HIS REVENGE WOULD HAVE BEEN COMPLETE INDEED."

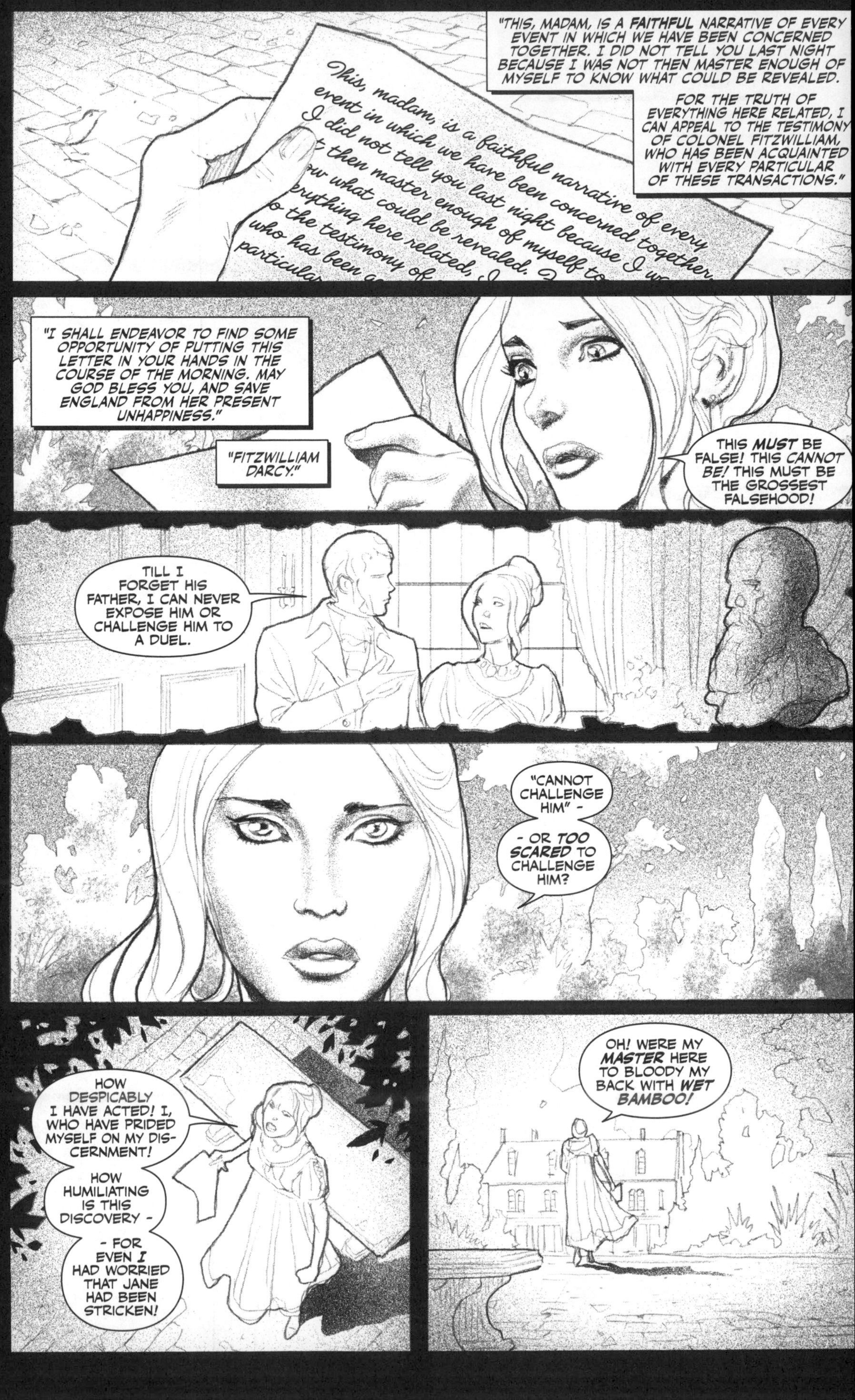
"THIS, MADAM, IS A FAITHFUL NARRATIVE OF EVERY EVENT IN WHICH WE HAVE BEEN CONCERNED TOGETHER. I DID NOT TELL YOU LAST NIGHT BECAUSE I WAS NOT THEN MASTER ENOUGH OF MYSELF TO KNOW WHAT COULD BE REVEALED.
FOR THE TRUTH OF EVERYTHING HERE RELATED, I CAN APPEAL TO THE TESTIMONY OF COLONEL FITZWILLIAM, WHO HAS BEEN ACQUAINTED WITH EVERY PARTICULAR OF THESE TRANSACTIONS."
"I SHALL ENDEAVOR TO FIND SOME OPPORTUNITY OF PUTTING THIS LETTER IN YOUR HANDS IN THE COURSE OF THE MORNING. MAY GOD BLESS YOU, AND SAVE ENGLAND FROM HER PRESENT UNHAPPINESS."
"FITZWILLIAM DARCY."
THIS MUST BE FALSE! THIS CANNOT BE! THIS MUST BE THE GROSSEST FALSEHOOD!
TILL I FORGET HIS FATHER, I CAN NEVER EXPOSE HIM OR CHALLENGE HIM TO A DUEL.
"CANNOT CHALLENGE HIM" -
- OR TOO SCARED TO CHALLENGE HIM?
HOW DESPICABLY I HAVE ACTED! I, WHO HAVE PRIDED MYSELF ON MY DISCERNMENT!
HOW HUMILIATING IS THIS DISCOVERY -
- FOR EVEN I HAD WORRIED THAT JANE HAD BEEN STRICKEN!
OH! WERE MY MASTER HERE TO BLOODY MY BACK WITH WET BAMBOO!

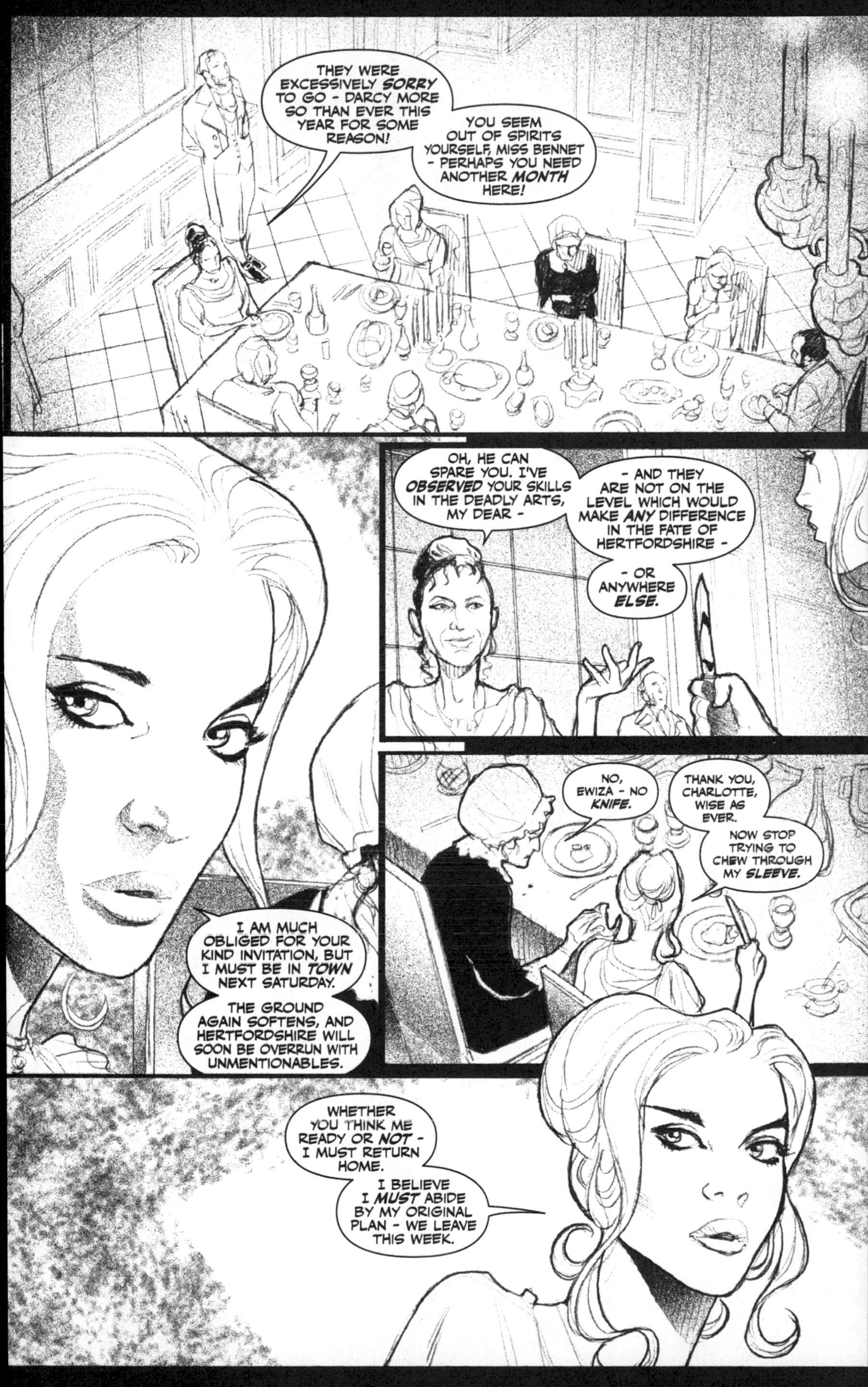
THEY WERE EXCESSIVELY SORRY TO GO - DARCY MORE SO THAN EVER THIS YEAR FOR SOME REASON!
YOU SEEM OUT OF SPIRITS YOURSELF, MISS BENNET - PERHAPS YOU NEED ANOTHER MONTH HERE!
OH, HE CAN SPARE YOU. I'VE OBSERVED YOUR SKILLS IN THE DEADLY ARTS, MY DEAR -
- AND THEY ARE NOT ON THE LEVEL WHICH WOULD MAKE ANY DIFFERENCE IN THE FATE OF HERTFORDSHIRE -
- OR ANYWHERE ELSE.
NO, EWIZA - NO KNIFE.
THANK YOU, CHARLOTTE, WISE AS EVER.
NOW STOP TRYING TO CHEW THROUGH MY SLEEVE.
I AM MUCH OBLIGED FOR YOUR KIND INVITATION, BUT I MUST BE IN TOWN NEXT SATURDAY.
THE GROUND AGAIN SOFTENS, AND HERTFORDSHIRE WILL SOON BE OVERRUN WITH UNMENTIONABLES.
WHETHER YOU THINK ME READY OR NOT - I MUST RETURN HOME.
I BELIEVE I MUST ABIDE BY MY ORIGINAL PLAN - WE LEAVE THIS WEEK.

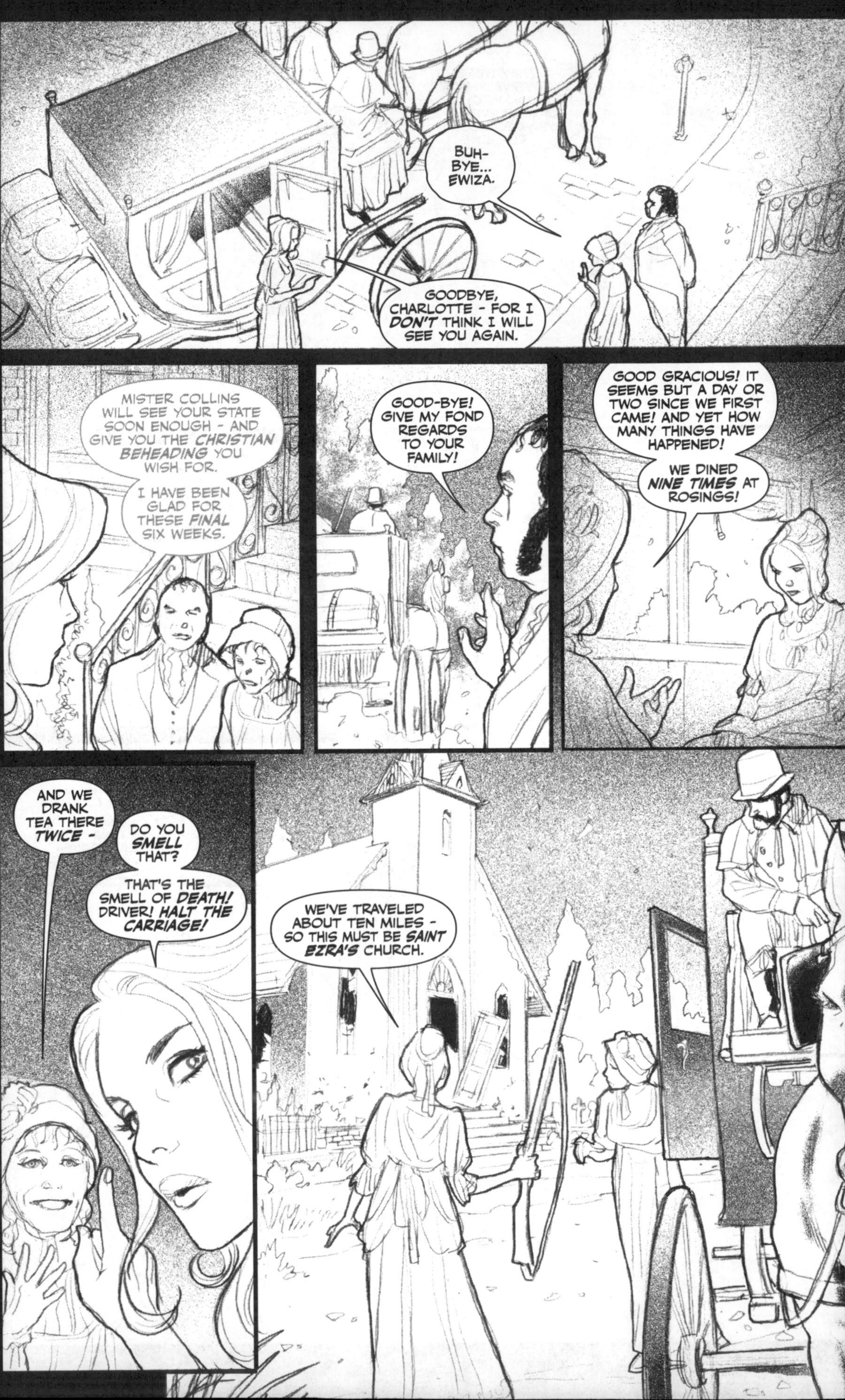
BUH-BYE... EWIZA.
GOODBYE, CHARLOTTE - FOR I *DON'T* THINK I WILL SEE YOU AGAIN.
MISTER COLLINS WILL SEE YOUR STATE SOON ENOUGH - AND GIVE YOU THE *CHRISTIAN BEHEADING* YOU WISH FOR.
I HAVE BEEN GLAD FOR THESE *FINAL* SIX WEEKS.
GOOD-BYE! GIVE MY FOND REGARDS TO YOUR FAMILY!
GOOD GRACIOUS! IT SEEMS BUT A DAY OR TWO SINCE WE FIRST CAME! AND YET HOW MANY THINGS HAVE HAPPENED!
WE DINED *NINE TIMES* AT ROSINGS!
AND WE DRANK TEA THERE *TWICE* -
DO YOU *SMELL* THAT?
THAT'S THE SMELL OF *DEATH!* DRIVER! *HALT THE CARRIAGE!*
WE'VE TRAVELED ABOUT TEN MILES - SO THIS MUST BE *SAINT EZRA'S* CHURCH.

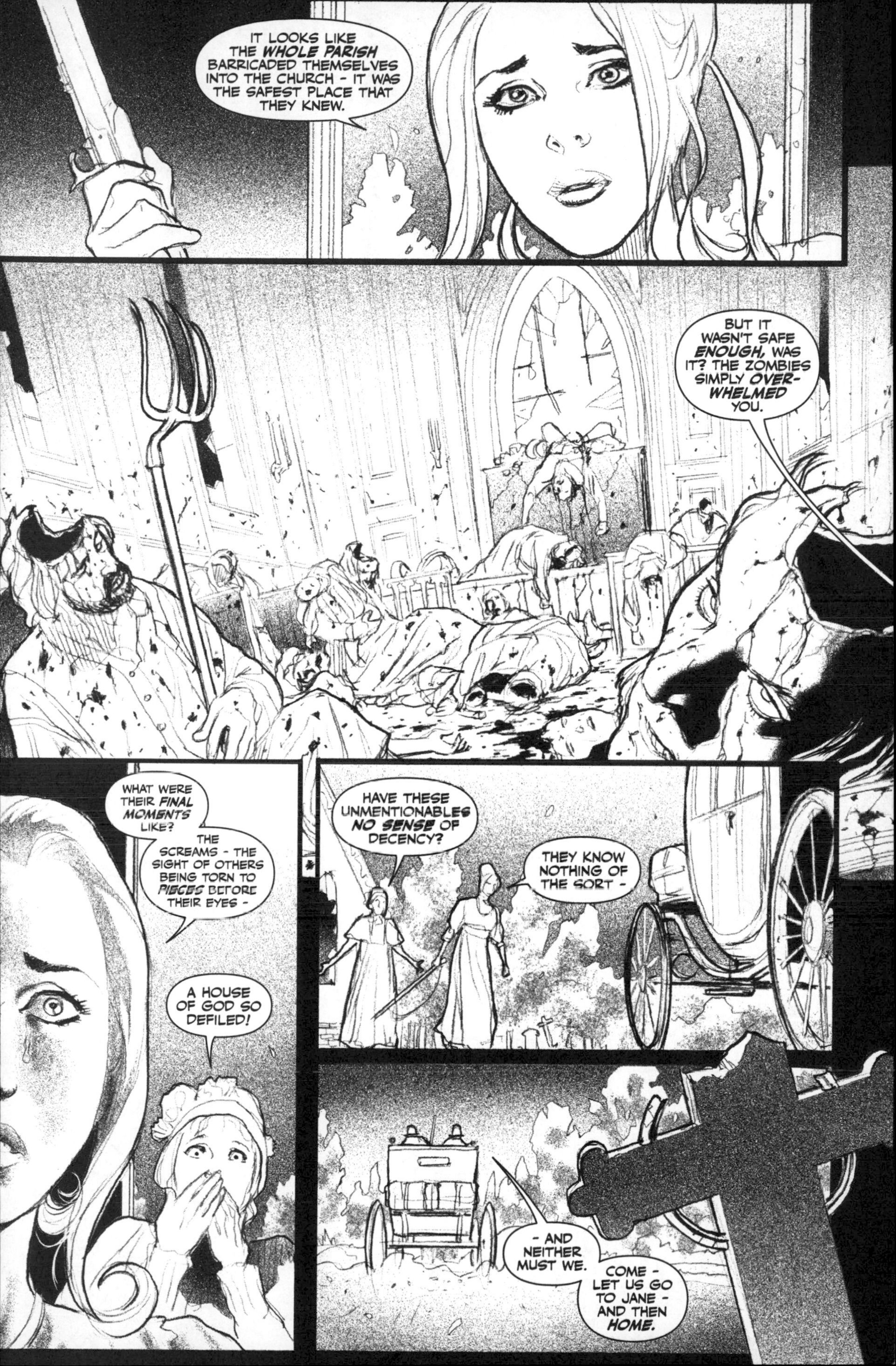
IT LOOKS LIKE THE WHOLE PARISH BARRICADED THEMSELVES INTO THE CHURCH - IT WAS THE SAFEST PLACE THAT THEY KNEW.
BUT IT WASN'T SAFE ENOUGH, WAS IT? THE ZOMBIES SIMPLY OVER-WHELMED YOU.
WHAT WERE THEIR FINAL MOMENTS LIKE?
THE SCREAMS - THE SIGHT OF OTHERS BEING TORN TO PIECES BEFORE THEIR EYES -
A HOUSE OF GOD SO DEFILED!
HAVE THESE UNMENTIONABLES NO SENSE OF DECENCY?
THEY KNOW NOTHING OF THE SORT -
- AND NEITHER MUST WE.
COME - LET US GO TO JANE - AND THEN HOME.

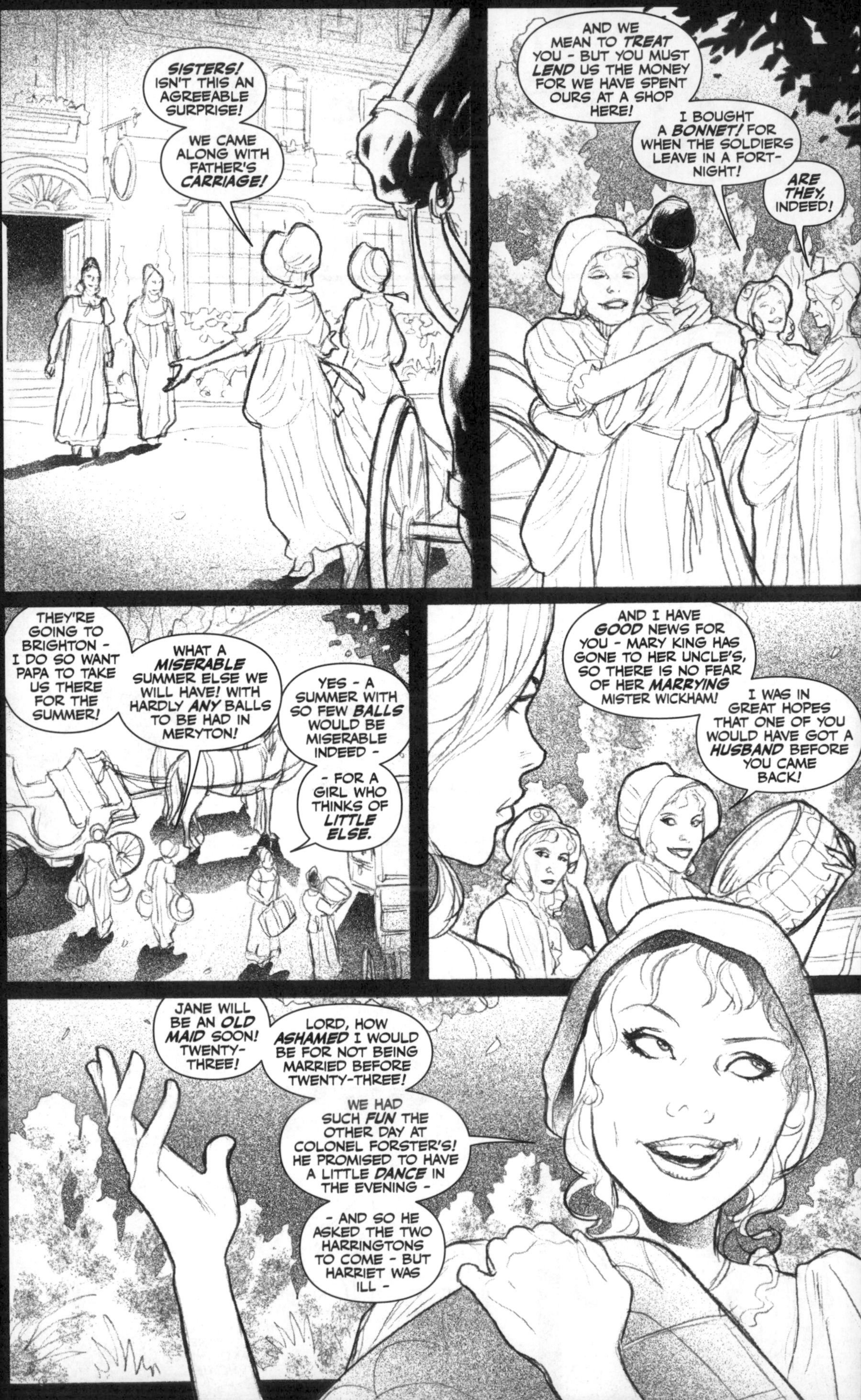
SISTERS! ISN'T THIS AN AGREEABLE SURPRISE!
WE CAME ALONG WITH FATHER'S CARRIAGE!
AND WE MEAN TO TREAT YOU - BUT YOU MUST LEND US THE MONEY FOR WE HAVE SPENT OURS AT A SHOP HERE!
I BOUGHT A BONNET! FOR WHEN THE SOLDIERS LEAVE IN A FORT-NIGHT!
ARE THEY, INDEED!
THEY'RE GOING TO BRIGHTON - I DO SO WANT PAPA TO TAKE US THERE FOR THE SUMMER!
WHAT A MISERABLE SUMMER ELSE WE WILL HAVE! WITH HARDLY ANY BALLS TO BE HAD IN MERYTON!
YES - A SUMMER WITH SO FEW BALLS WOULD BE MISERABLE INDEED -
- FOR A GIRL WHO THINKS OF LITTLE ELSE.
AND I HAVE GOOD NEWS FOR YOU - MARY KING HAS GONE TO HER UNCLE'S, SO THERE IS NO FEAR OF HER MARRYING MISTER WICKHAM!
I WAS IN GREAT HOPES THAT ONE OF YOU WOULD HAVE GOT A HUSBAND BEFORE YOU CAME BACK!
JANE WILL BE AN OLD MAID SOON! TWENTY-THREE!
LORD, HOW ASHAMED I WOULD BE FOR NOT BEING MARRIED BEFORE TWENTY-THREE!
WE HAD SUCH FUN THE OTHER DAY AT COLONEL FORSTER'S! HE PROMISED TO HAVE A LITTLE DANCE IN THE EVENING -
- AND SO HE ASKED THE TWO HARRINGTONS TO COME - BUT HARRIET WAS ILL -

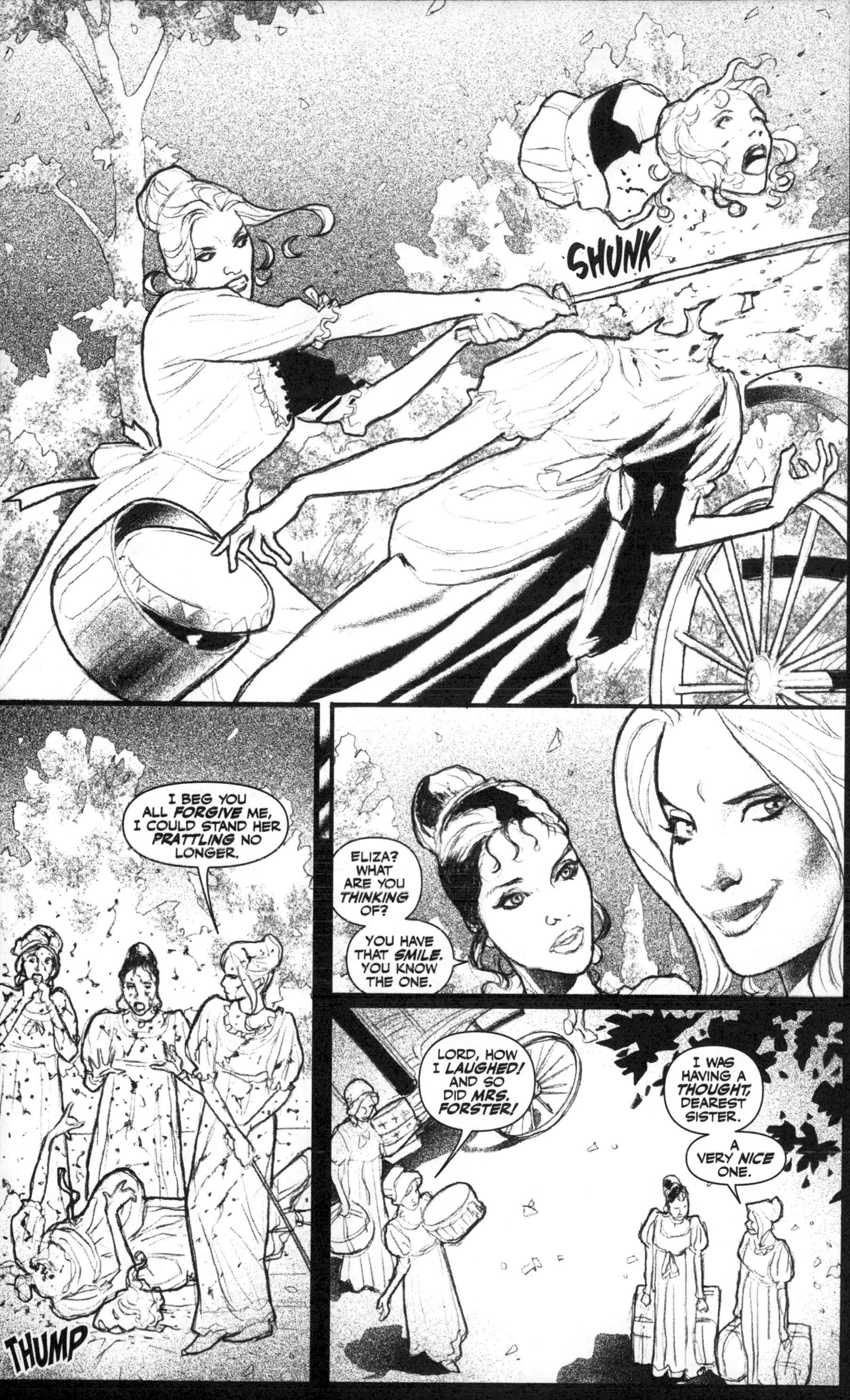
SHUNK
I BEG YOU ALL FORGIVE ME, I COULD STAND HER PRATTLING NO LONGER.
THUMP
ELIZA? WHAT ARE YOU THINKING OF?
YOU HAVE THAT SMILE. YOU KNOW THE ONE.
LORD, HOW I LAUGHED! AND SO DID MRS. FORSTER!
I WAS HAVING A THOUGHT, DEAREST SISTER.
A VERY NICE ONE.

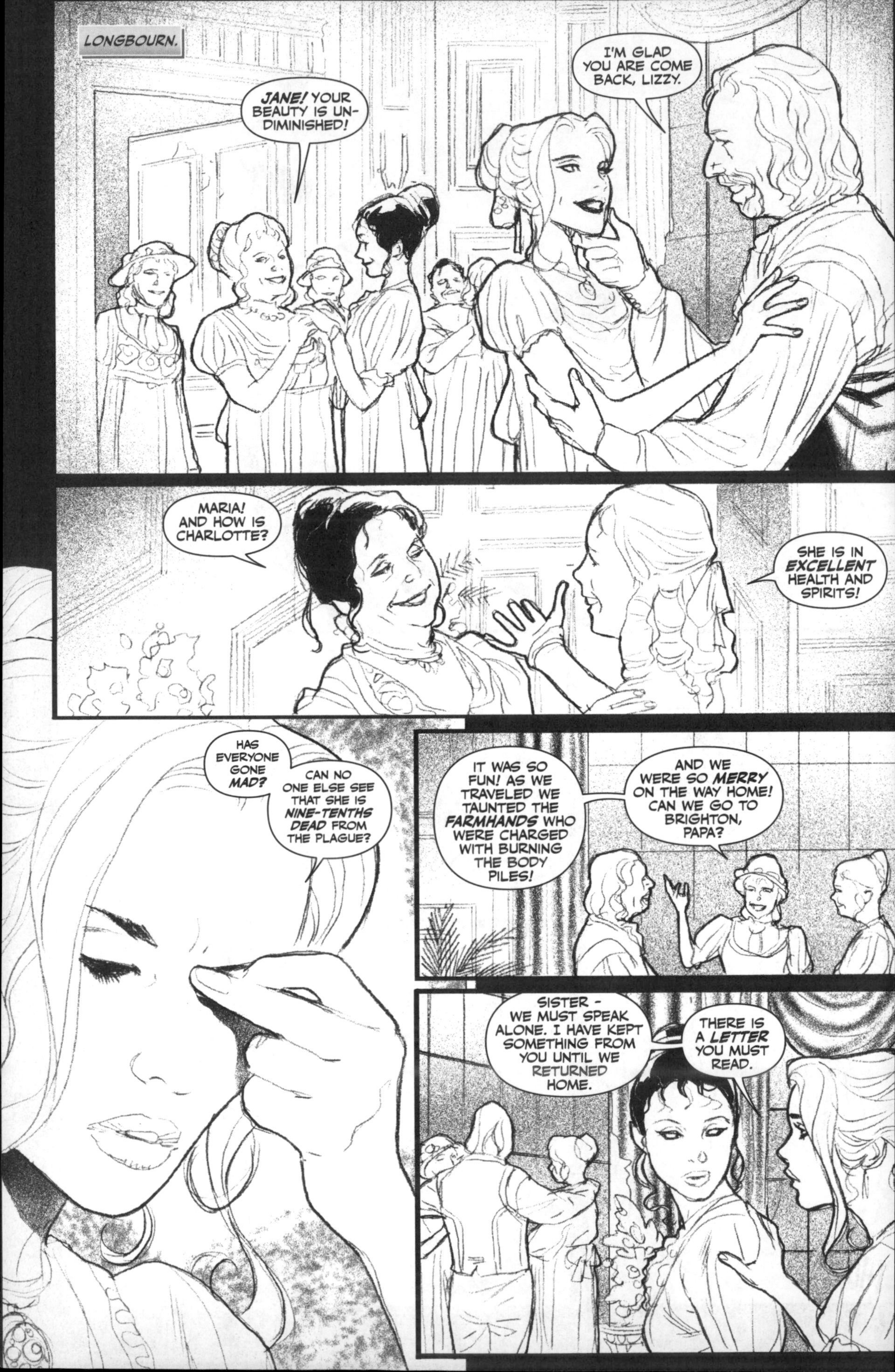
LONGBOURN.
JANE! YOUR BEAUTY IS UN-DIMINISHED!
I'M GLAD YOU ARE COME BACK, LIZZY.
MARIA! AND HOW IS CHARLOTTE?
SHE IS IN EXCELLENT HEALTH AND SPIRITS!
HAS EVERYONE GONE MAD?
CAN NO ONE ELSE SEE THAT SHE IS NINE-TENTHS DEAD FROM THE PLAGUE?
IT WAS SO FUN! AS WE TRAVELED WE TAUNTED THE FARMHANDS WHO WERE CHARGED WITH BURNING THE BODY PILES!
AND WE WERE SO MERRY ON THE WAY HOME! CAN WE GO TO BRIGHTON, PAPA?
SISTER - WE MUST SPEAK ALONE. I HAVE KEPT SOMETHING FROM YOU UNTIL WE RETURNED HOME.
THERE IS A LETTER YOU MUST READ.

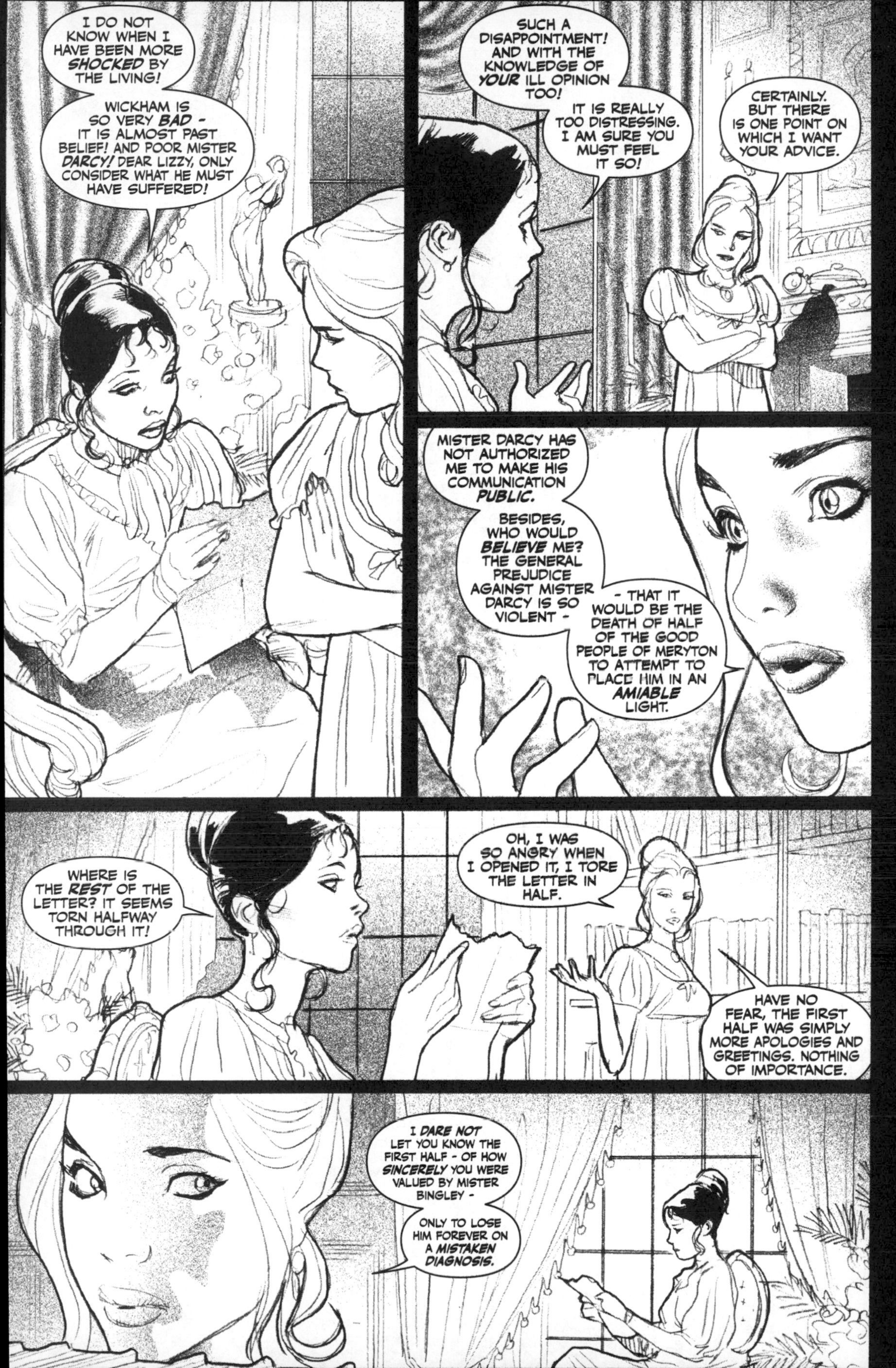

I DO NOT KNOW WHEN I HAVE BEEN MORE SHOCKED BY THE LIVING!
WICKHAM IS SO VERY BAD - IT IS ALMOST PAST BELIEF! AND POOR MISTER DARCY! DEAR LIZZY, ONLY CONSIDER WHAT HE MUST HAVE SUFFERED!
SUCH A DISAPPOINTMENT! AND WITH THE KNOWLEDGE OF YOUR ILL OPINION TOO!
IT IS REALLY TOO DISTRESSING. I AM SURE YOU MUST FEEL IT SO!
CERTAINLY. BUT THERE IS ONE POINT ON WHICH I WANT YOUR ADVICE.
MISTER DARCY HAS NOT AUTHORIZED ME TO MAKE HIS COMMUNICATION PUBLIC.
BESIDES, WHO WOULD BELIEVE ME? THE GENERAL PREJUDICE AGAINST MISTER DARCY IS SO VIOLENT -
- THAT IT WOULD BE THE DEATH OF HALF OF THE GOOD PEOPLE OF MERYTON TO ATTEMPT TO PLACE HIM IN AN AMIABLE LIGHT.
WHERE IS THE REST OF THE LETTER? IT SEEMS TORN HALFWAY THROUGH IT!
OH, I WAS SO ANGRY WHEN I OPENED IT, I TORE THE LETTER IN HALF.
HAVE NO FEAR, THE FIRST HALF WAS SIMPLY MORE APOLOGIES AND GREETINGS. NOTHING OF IMPORTANCE.
I DARE NOT LET YOU KNOW THE FIRST HALF - OF HOW SINCERELY YOU WERE VALUED BY MISTER BINGLEY -
ONLY TO LOSE HIM FOREVER ON A MISTAKEN DIAGNOSIS.

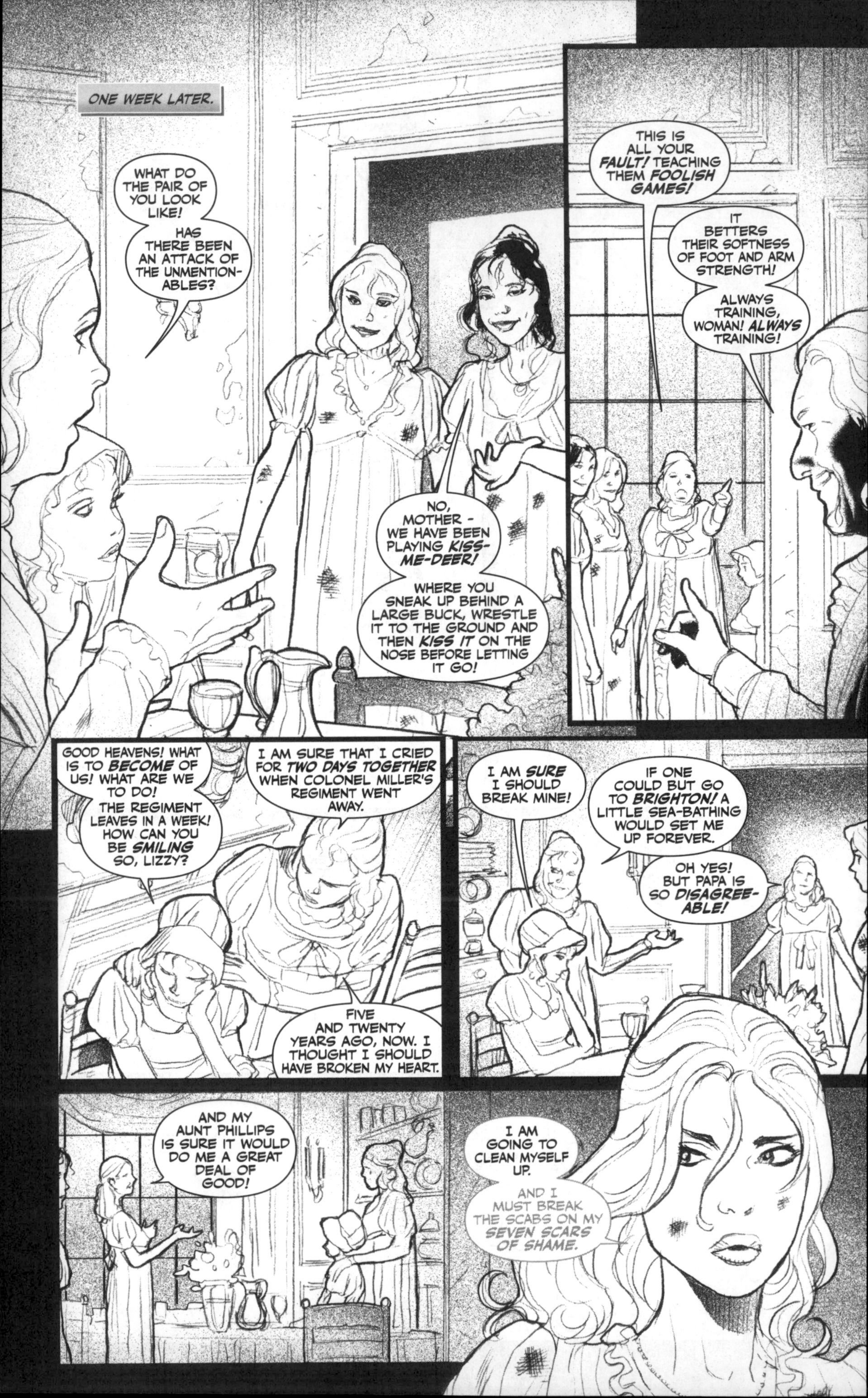
ONE WEEK LATER.
WHAT DO THE PAIR OF YOU LOOK LIKE!
HAS THERE BEEN AN ATTACK OF THE UNMENTION-ABLES?
NO, MOTHER - WE HAVE BEEN PLAYING *KISS-ME-DEER!*
WHERE YOU SNEAK UP BEHIND A LARGE BUCK, WRESTLE IT TO THE GROUND AND THEN *KISS IT* ON THE NOSE BEFORE LETTING IT GO!
THIS IS ALL YOUR *FAULT!* TEACHING THEM *FOOLISH GAMES!*
IT BETTERS THEIR SOFTNESS OF FOOT AND ARM STRENGTH!
ALWAYS TRAINING, WOMAN! *ALWAYS* TRAINING!
GOOD HEAVENS! WHAT IS TO *BECOME* OF US! WHAT ARE WE TO DO!
THE REGIMENT LEAVES IN A WEEK! HOW CAN YOU BE *SMILING* SO, LIZZY?
I AM SURE THAT I CRIED FOR *TWO DAYS TOGETHER* WHEN COLONEL MILLER'S REGIMENT WENT AWAY.
FIVE AND TWENTY YEARS AGO, NOW. I THOUGHT I SHOULD HAVE BROKEN MY HEART.
I AM *SURE* I SHOULD BREAK MINE!
IF ONE COULD BUT GO TO *BRIGHTON!* A LITTLE SEA-BATHING WOULD SET ME UP FOREVER.
OH YES! BUT PAPA IS SO *DISAGREE-ABLE!*
AND MY AUNT PHILLIPS IS SURE IT WOULD DO ME A GREAT DEAL OF GOOD!
I AM GOING TO CLEAN MYSELF UP.
AND I MUST BREAK THE SCABS ON MY *SEVEN SCARS OF SHAME.*

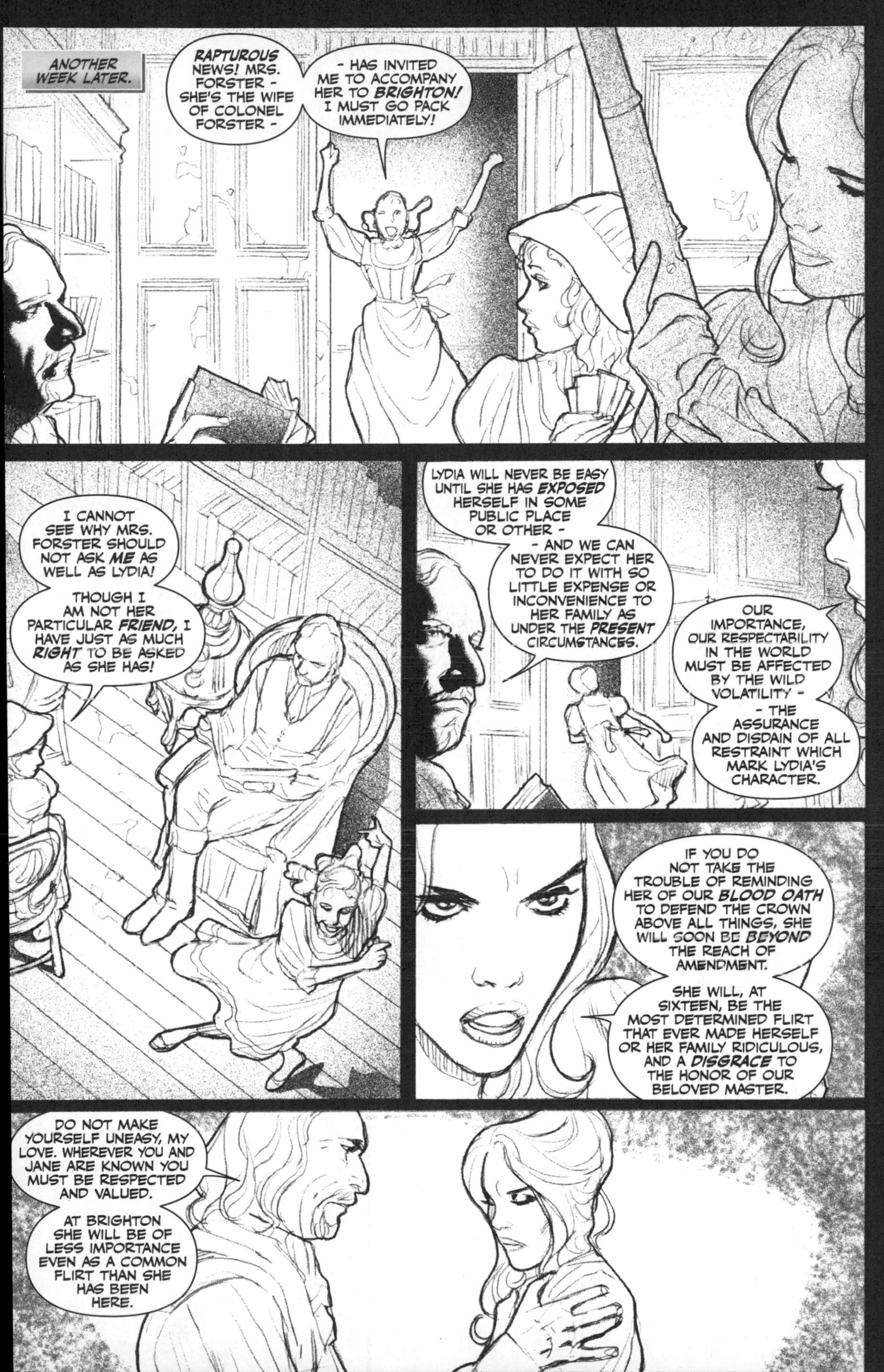

ANOTHER WEEK LATER.
RAPTUROUS NEWS! MRS. FORSTER - SHE'S THE WIFE OF COLONEL FORSTER -
- HAS INVITED ME TO ACCOMPANY HER TO BRIGHTON! I MUST GO PACK IMMEDIATELY!
I CANNOT SEE WHY MRS. FORSTER SHOULD NOT ASK ME AS WELL AS LYDIA!
THOUGH I AM NOT HER PARTICULAR FRIEND, I HAVE JUST AS MUCH RIGHT TO BE ASKED AS SHE HAS!
LYDIA WILL NEVER BE EASY UNTIL SHE HAS EXPOSED HERSELF IN SOME PUBLIC PLACE OR OTHER -
- AND WE CAN NEVER EXPECT HER TO DO IT WITH SO LITTLE EXPENSE OR INCONVENIENCE TO HER FAMILY AS UNDER THE PRESENT CIRCUMSTANCES.
OUR IMPORTANCE, OUR RESPECTABILITY IN THE WORLD MUST BE AFFECTED BY THE WILD VOLATILITY -
- THE ASSURANCE AND DISDAIN OF ALL RESTRAINT WHICH MARK LYDIA'S CHARACTER.
IF YOU DO NOT TAKE THE TROUBLE OF REMINDING HER OF OUR BLOOD OATH TO DEFEND THE CROWN ABOVE ALL THINGS, SHE WILL SOON BE BEYOND THE REACH OF AMENDMENT.
SHE WILL, AT SIXTEEN, BE THE MOST DETERMINED FLIRT THAT EVER MADE HERSELF OR HER FAMILY RIDICULOUS, AND A DISGRACE TO THE HONOR OF OUR BELOVED MASTER.
DO NOT MAKE YOURSELF UNEASY, MY LOVE. WHEREVER YOU AND JANE ARE KNOWN YOU MUST BE RESPECTED AND VALUED.
AT BRIGHTON SHE WILL BE OF LESS IMPORTANCE EVEN AS A COMMON FLIRT THAN SHE HAS BEEN HERE.

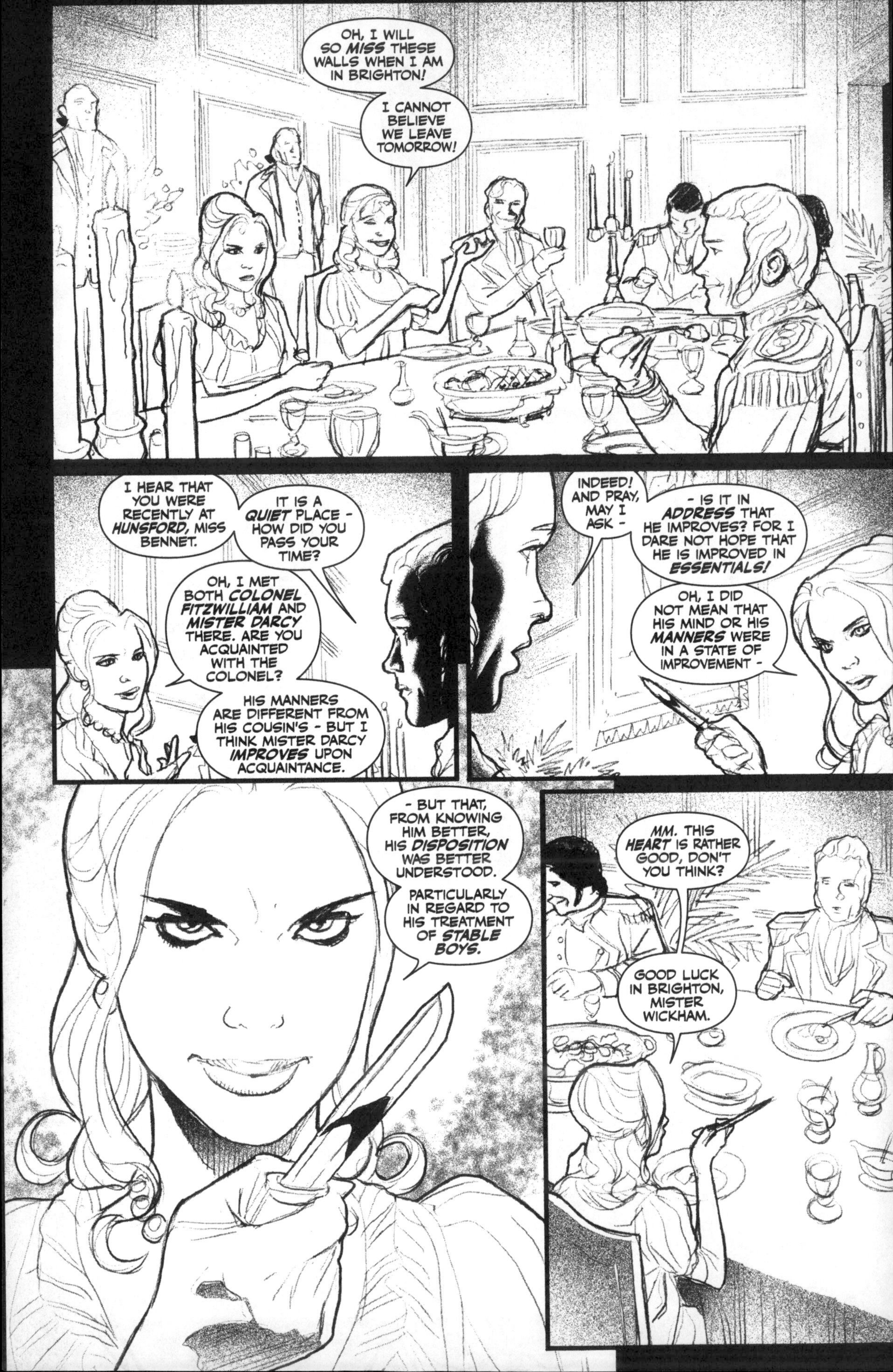
OH, I WILL SO MISS THESE WALLS WHEN I AM IN BRIGHTON!
I CANNOT BELIEVE WE LEAVE TOMORROW!
I HEAR THAT YOU WERE RECENTLY AT HUNSFORD, MISS BENNET.
IT IS A QUIET PLACE - HOW DID YOU PASS YOUR TIME?
OH, I MET BOTH COLONEL FITZWILLIAM AND MISTER DARCY THERE. ARE YOU ACQUAINTED WITH THE COLONEL?
HIS MANNERS ARE DIFFERENT FROM HIS COUSIN'S - BUT I THINK MISTER DARCY IMPROVES UPON ACQUAINTANCE.
INDEED! AND PRAY, MAY I ASK -
- IS IT IN ADDRESS THAT HE IMPROVES? FOR I DARE NOT HOPE THAT HE IS IMPROVED IN ESSENTIALS!
OH, I DID NOT MEAN THAT HIS MIND OR HIS MANNERS WERE IN A STATE OF IMPROVEMENT -
- BUT THAT, FROM KNOWING HIM BETTER, HIS DISPOSITION WAS BETTER UNDERSTOOD.
PARTICULARLY IN REGARD TO HIS TREATMENT OF STABLE BOYS.
MM. THIS HEART IS RATHER GOOD, DON'T YOU THINK?
GOOD LUCK IN BRIGHTON, MISTER WICKHAM.

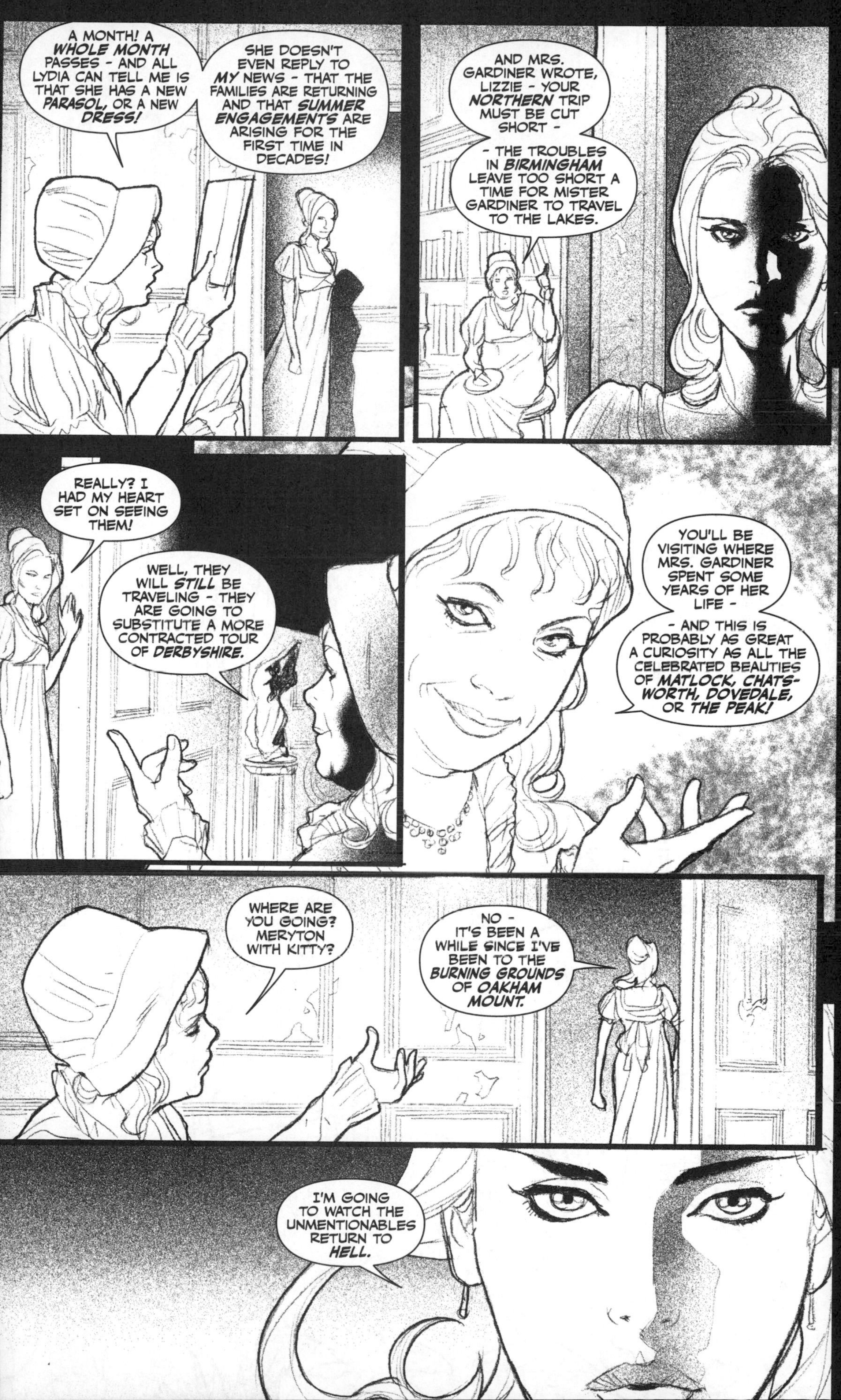
A MONTH! A WHOLE MONTH PASSES - AND ALL LYDIA CAN TELL ME IS THAT SHE HAS A NEW PARASOL, OR A NEW DRESS!
SHE DOESN'T EVEN REPLY TO MY NEWS - THAT THE FAMILIES ARE RETURNING AND THAT SUMMER ENGAGEMENTS ARE ARISING FOR THE FIRST TIME IN DECADES!
AND MRS. GARDINER WROTE, LIZZIE - YOUR NORTHERN TRIP MUST BE CUT SHORT -
- THE TROUBLES IN BIRMINGHAM LEAVE TOO SHORT A TIME FOR MISTER GARDINER TO TRAVEL TO THE LAKES.
REALLY? I HAD MY HEART SET ON SEEING THEM!
WELL, THEY WILL STILL BE TRAVELING - THEY ARE GOING TO SUBSTITUTE A MORE CONTRACTED TOUR OF DERBYSHIRE.
YOU'LL BE VISITING WHERE MRS. GARDINER SPENT SOME YEARS OF HER LIFE -
- AND THIS IS PROBABLY AS GREAT A CURIOSITY AS ALL THE CELEBRATED BEAUTIES OF MATLOCK, CHATSWORTH, DOVEDALE, OR THE PEAK!
WHERE ARE YOU GOING? MERYTON WITH KITTY?
NO - IT'S BEEN A WHILE SINCE I'VE BEEN TO THE BURNING GROUNDS OF OAKHAM MOUNT.
I'M GOING TO WATCH THE UNMENTIONABLES RETURN TO HELL.

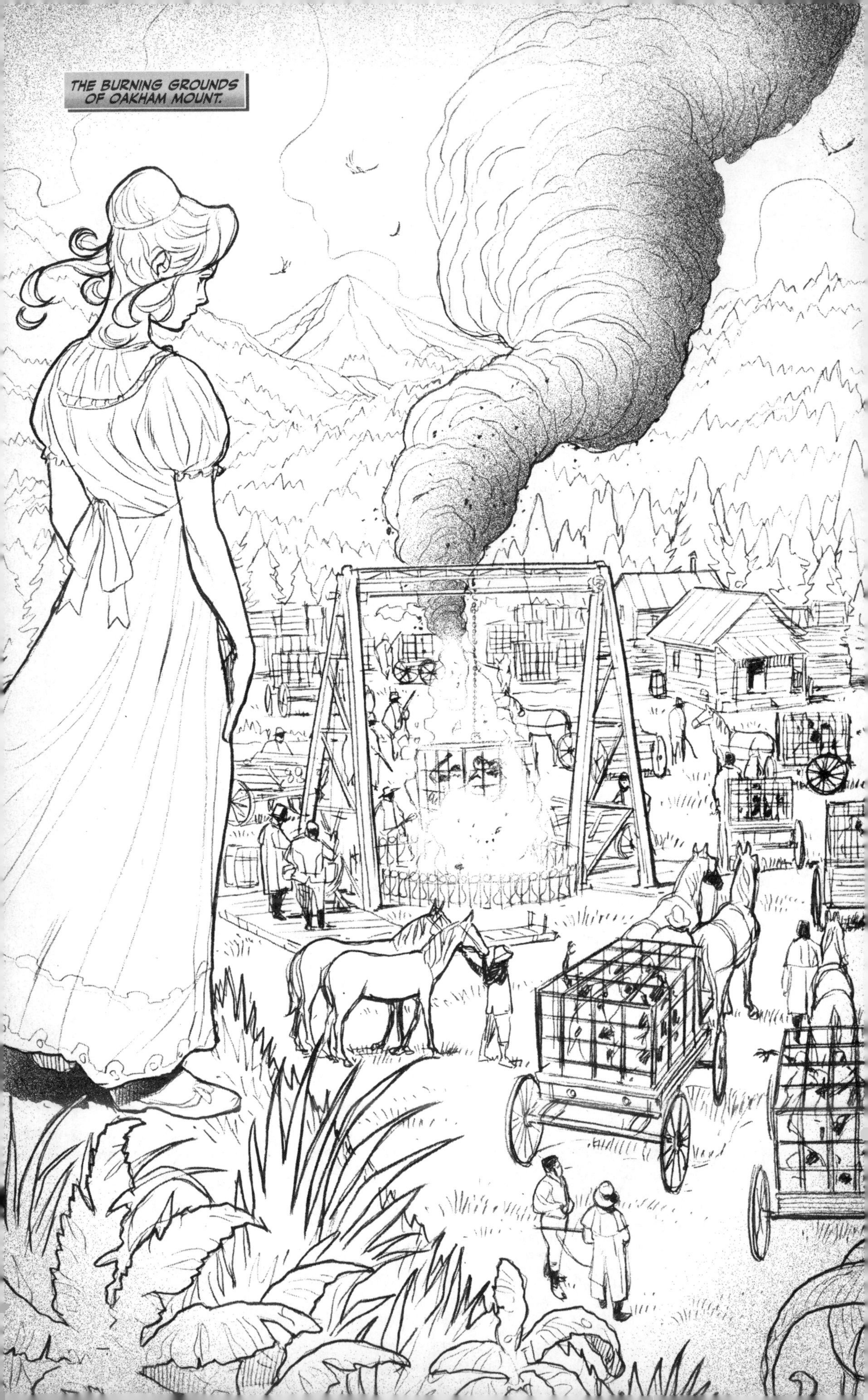
THE BURNING GROUNDS OF OAKHAM MOUNT.

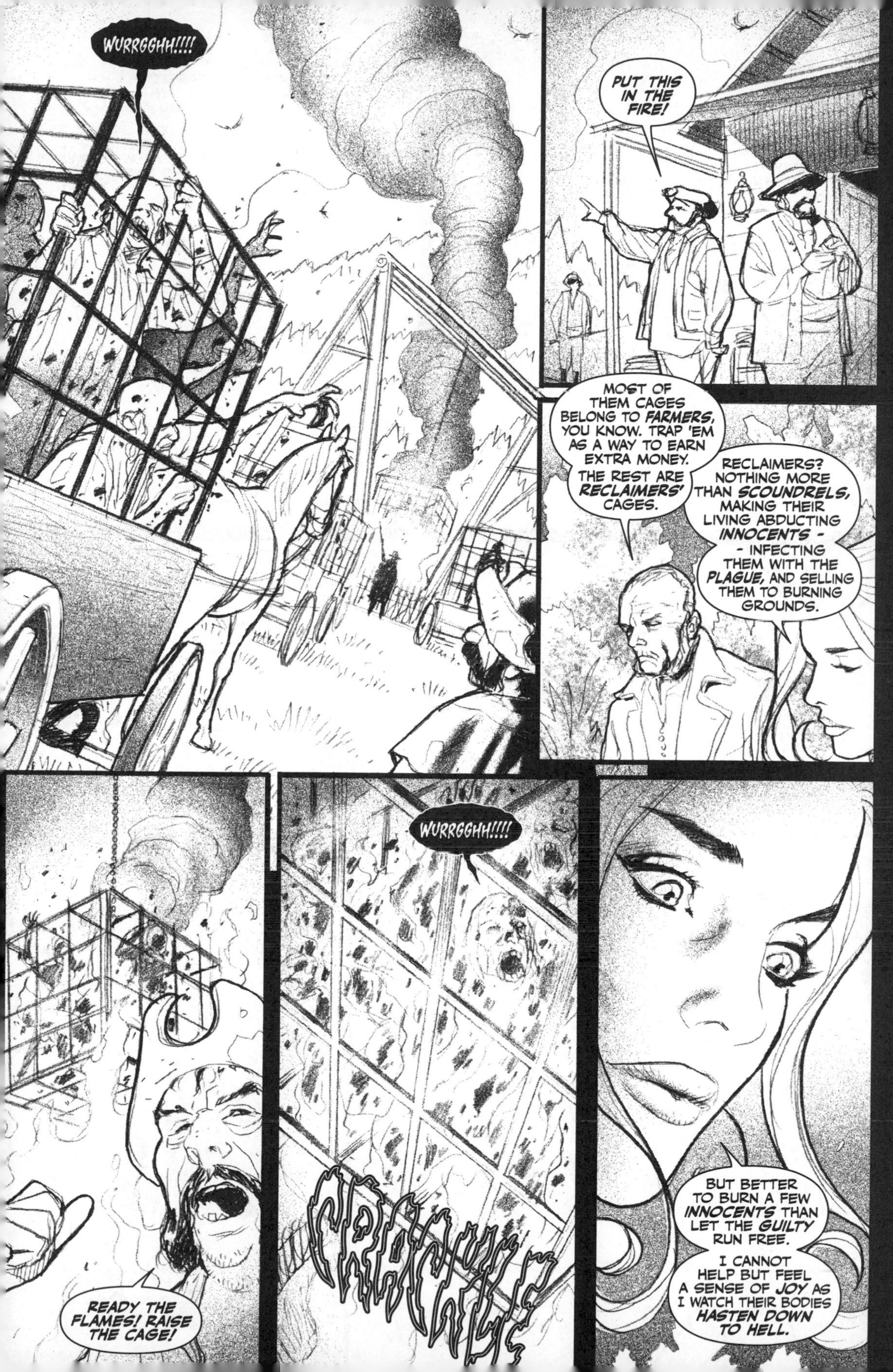
WURRGGHH!!!!
PUT THIS IN THE FIRE!
MOST OF THEM CAGES BELONG TO FARMERS, YOU KNOW. TRAP 'EM AS A WAY TO EARN EXTRA MONEY.
THE REST ARE RECLAIMERS' CAGES.
RECLAIMERS? NOTHING MORE THAN SCOUNDRELS, MAKING THEIR LIVING ABDUCTING INNOCENTS -
- INFECTING THEM WITH THE PLAGUE, AND SELLING THEM TO BURNING GROUNDS.
READY THE FLAMES! RAISE THE CAGE!
WURRGGHH!!!!
BUT BETTER TO BURN A FEW INNOCENTS THAN LET THE GUILTY RUN FREE.
I CANNOT HELP BUT FEEL A SENSE OF JOY AS I WATCH THEIR BODIES HASTEN DOWN TO HELL.

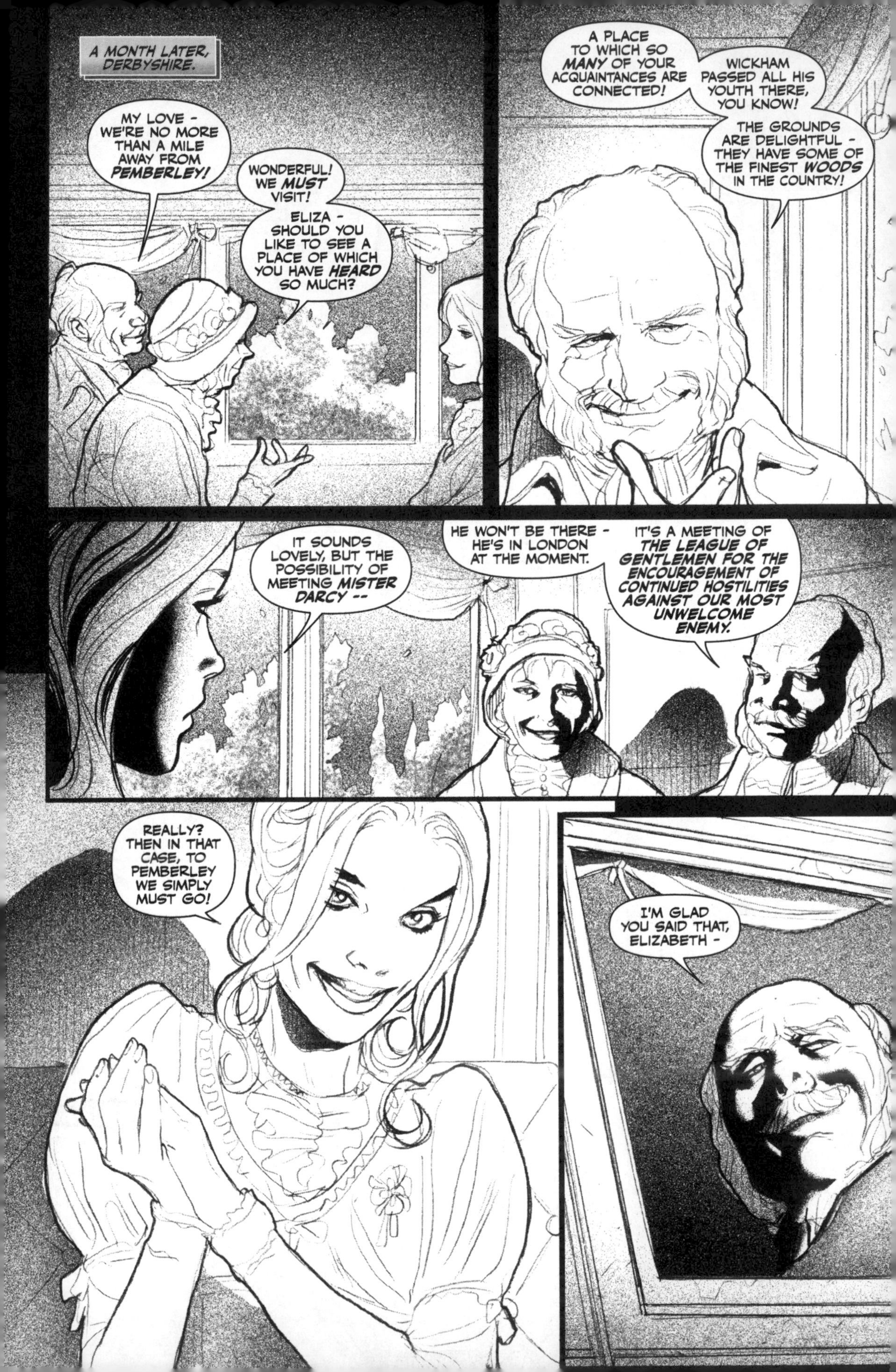

A MONTH LATER, DERBYSHIRE.
MY LOVE - WE'RE NO MORE THAN A MILE AWAY FROM PEMBERLEY!
WONDERFUL! WE MUST VISIT!
ELIZA - SHOULD YOU LIKE TO SEE A PLACE OF WHICH YOU HAVE HEARD SO MUCH?
A PLACE TO WHICH SO MANY OF YOUR ACQUAINTANCES ARE CONNECTED!
WICKHAM PASSED ALL HIS YOUTH THERE, YOU KNOW!
THE GROUNDS ARE DELIGHTFUL - THEY HAVE SOME OF THE FINEST WOODS IN THE COUNTRY!
IT SOUNDS LOVELY, BUT THE POSSIBILITY OF MEETING MISTER DARCY --
HE WON'T BE THERE - HE'S IN LONDON AT THE MOMENT.
IT'S A MEETING OF THE LEAGUE OF GENTLEMEN FOR THE ENCOURAGEMENT OF CONTINUED HOSTILITIES AGAINST OUR MOST UNWELCOME ENEMY.
REALLY? THEN IN THAT CASE, TO PEMBERLEY WE SIMPLY MUST GO!
I'M GLAD YOU SAID THAT, ELIZABETH -

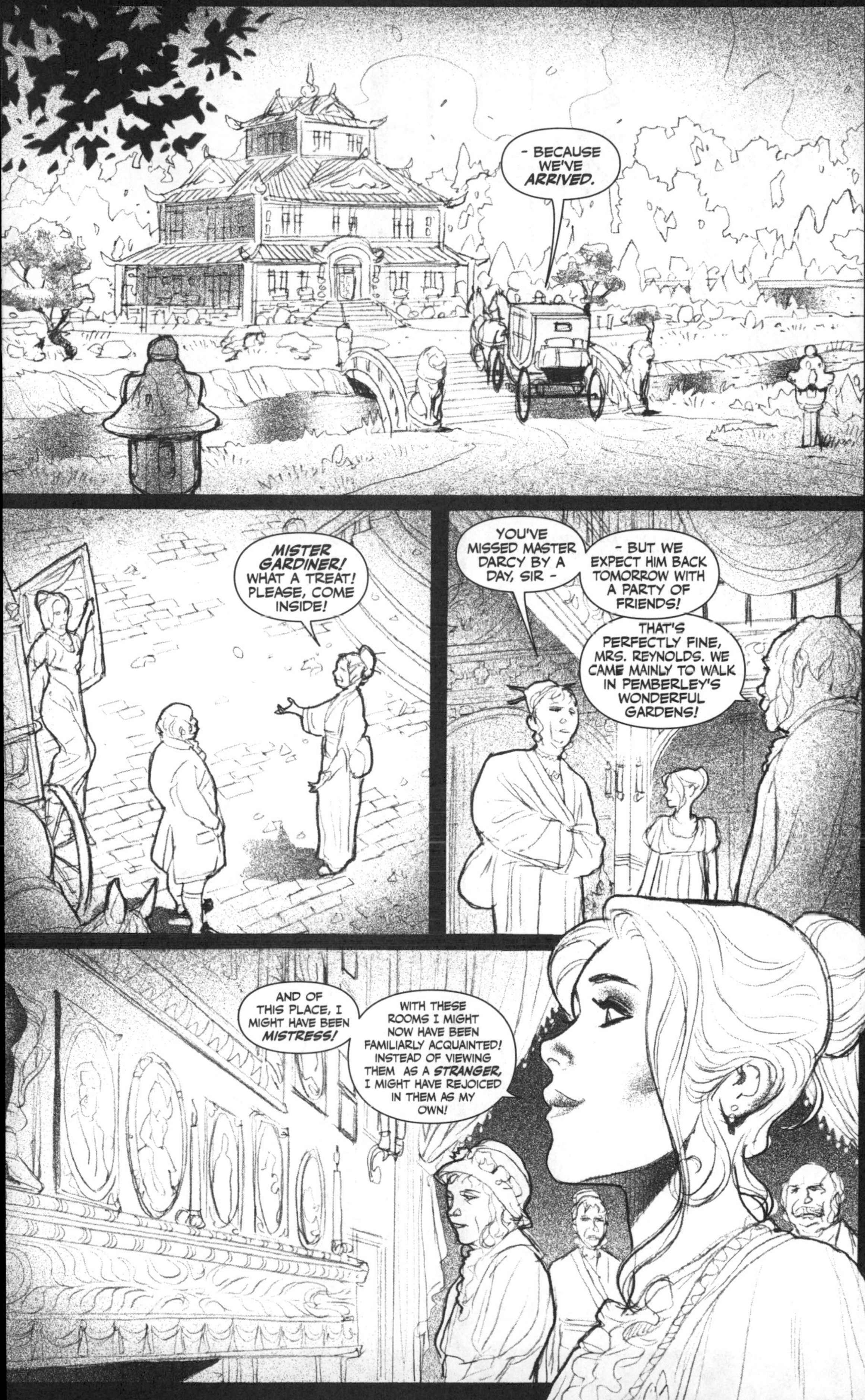
- BECAUSE WE'VE *ARRIVED.*
MISTER GARDINER! WHAT A TREAT! PLEASE, COME INSIDE!
YOU'VE MISSED MASTER DARCY BY A DAY, SIR -
- BUT WE EXPECT HIM BACK TOMORROW WITH A PARTY OF FRIENDS!
THAT'S PERFECTLY FINE, MRS. REYNOLDS. WE CAME MAINLY TO WALK IN PEMBERLEY'S WONDERFUL GARDENS!
AND OF THIS PLACE, I MIGHT HAVE BEEN *MISTRESS!*
WITH THESE ROOMS I MIGHT NOW HAVE BEEN FAMILIARLY ACQUAINTED! INSTEAD OF VIEWING THEM AS A *STRANGER,* I MIGHT HAVE REJOICED IN THEM AS MY OWN!

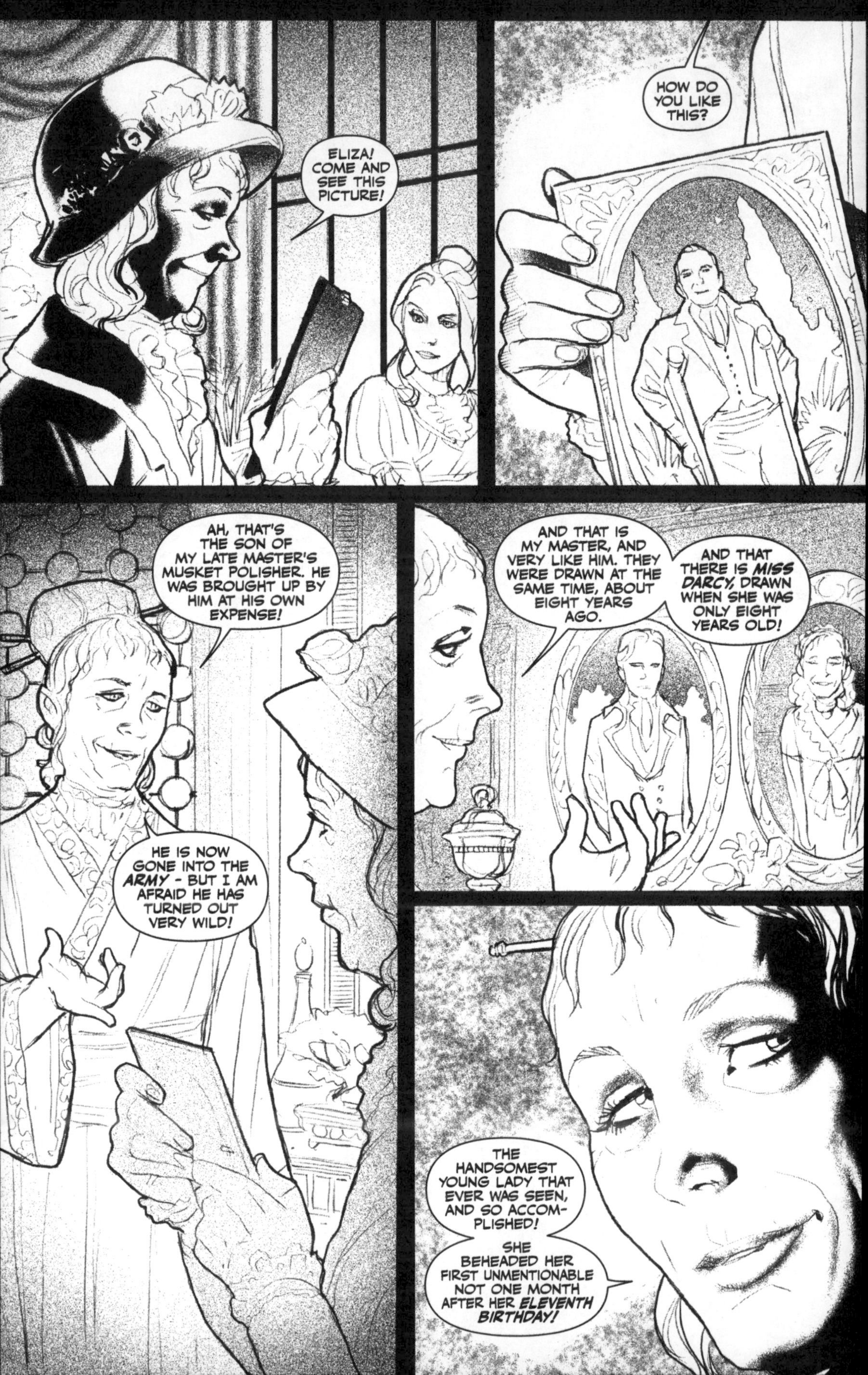
ELIZA! COME AND SEE THIS PICTURE!
HOW DO YOU LIKE THIS?
AH, THAT'S THE SON OF MY LATE MASTER'S MUSKET POLISHER. HE WAS BROUGHT UP BY HIM AT HIS OWN EXPENSE!
HE IS NOW GONE INTO THE ARMY - BUT I AM AFRAID HE HAS TURNED OUT VERY WILD!
AND THAT IS MY MASTER, AND VERY LIKE HIM. THEY WERE DRAWN AT THE SAME TIME, ABOUT EIGHT YEARS AGO.
AND THAT THERE IS MISS DARCY, DRAWN WHEN SHE WAS ONLY EIGHT YEARS OLD!
THE HANDSOMEST YOUNG LADY THAT EVER WAS SEEN, AND SO ACCOMPLISHED!
SHE BEHEADED HER FIRST UNMENTIONABLE NOT ONE MONTH AFTER HER ELEVENTH BIRTHDAY!

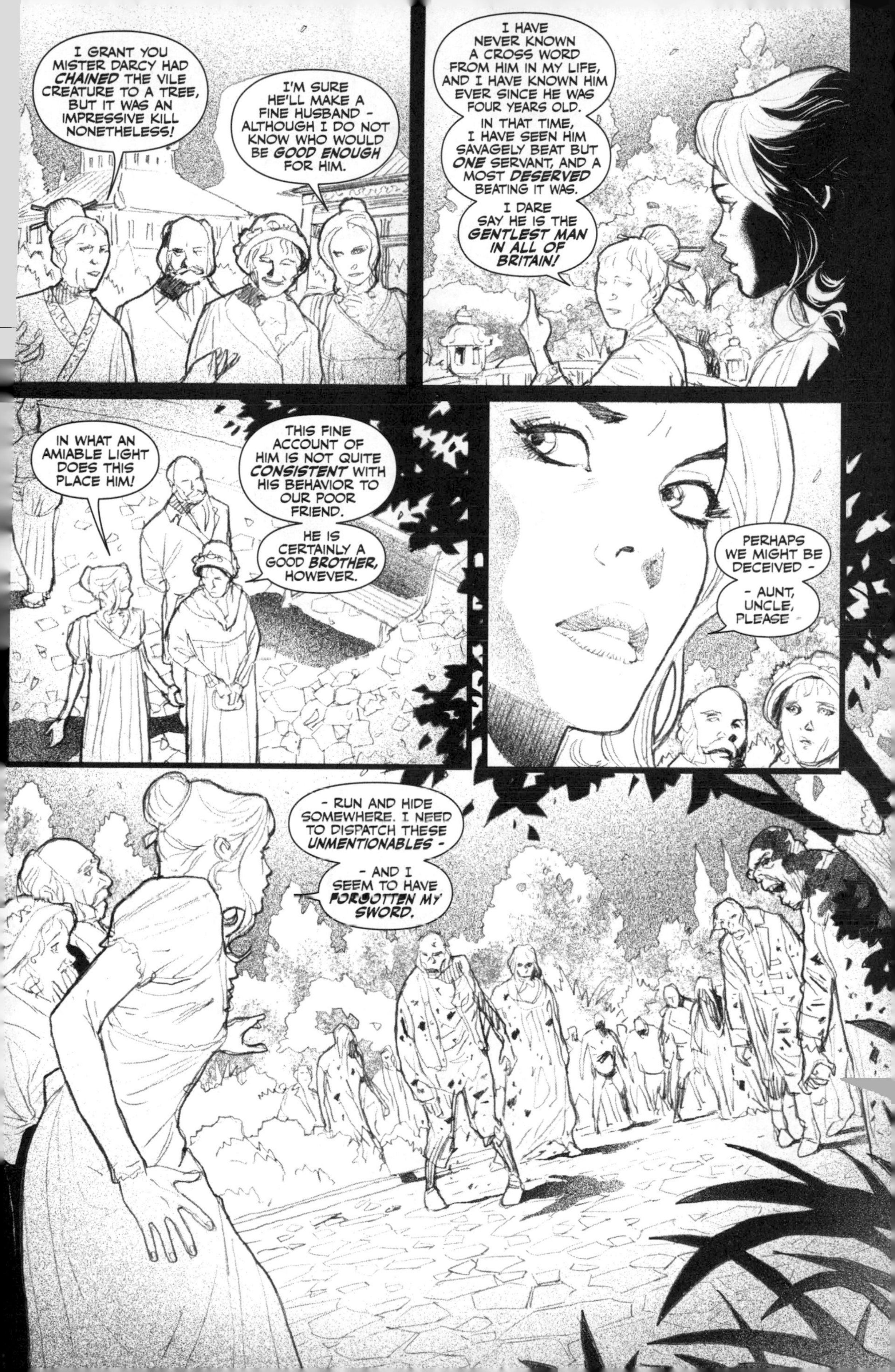
I GRANT YOU MISTER DARCY HAD CHAINED THE VILE CREATURE TO A TREE, BUT IT WAS AN IMPRESSIVE KILL NONETHELESS!
I'M SURE HE'LL MAKE A FINE HUSBAND - ALTHOUGH I DO NOT KNOW WHO WOULD BE GOOD ENOUGH FOR HIM.
I HAVE NEVER KNOWN A CROSS WORD FROM HIM IN MY LIFE, AND I HAVE KNOWN HIM EVER SINCE HE WAS FOUR YEARS OLD.
IN THAT TIME, I HAVE SEEN HIM SAVAGELY BEAT BUT ONE SERVANT, AND A MOST DESERVED BEATING IT WAS.
I DARE SAY HE IS THE GENTLEST MAN IN ALL OF BRITAIN!
IN WHAT AN AMIABLE LIGHT DOES THIS PLACE HIM!
THIS FINE ACCOUNT OF HIM IS NOT QUITE CONSISTENT WITH HIS BEHAVIOR TO OUR POOR FRIEND.
HE IS CERTAINLY A GOOD BROTHER, HOWEVER.
PERHAPS WE MIGHT BE DECEIVED -
- AUNT, UNCLE, PLEASE
- RUN AND HIDE SOMEWHERE. I NEED TO DISPATCH THESE UNMENTIONABLES -
- AND I SEEM TO HAVE FORGOTTEN MY SWORD.

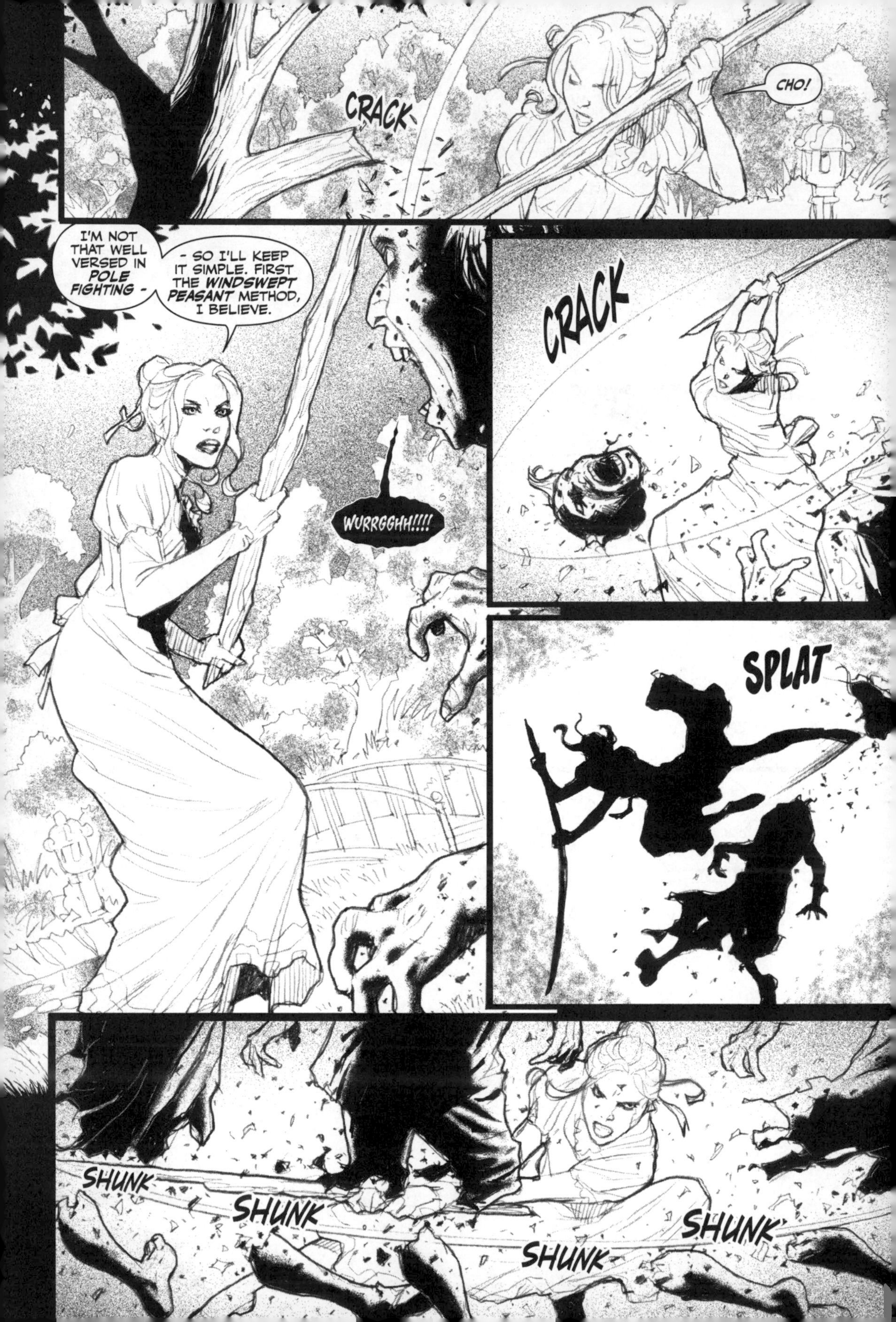

CRACK
CHO!
I'M NOT THAT WELL VERSED IN POLE FIGHTING -
- SO I'LL KEEP IT SIMPLE. FIRST THE WINDSWEPT PEASANT METHOD, I BELIEVE.
WURRGGHH!!!!
CRACK
SPLAT
SHUNK
SHUNK
SHUNK
SHUNK

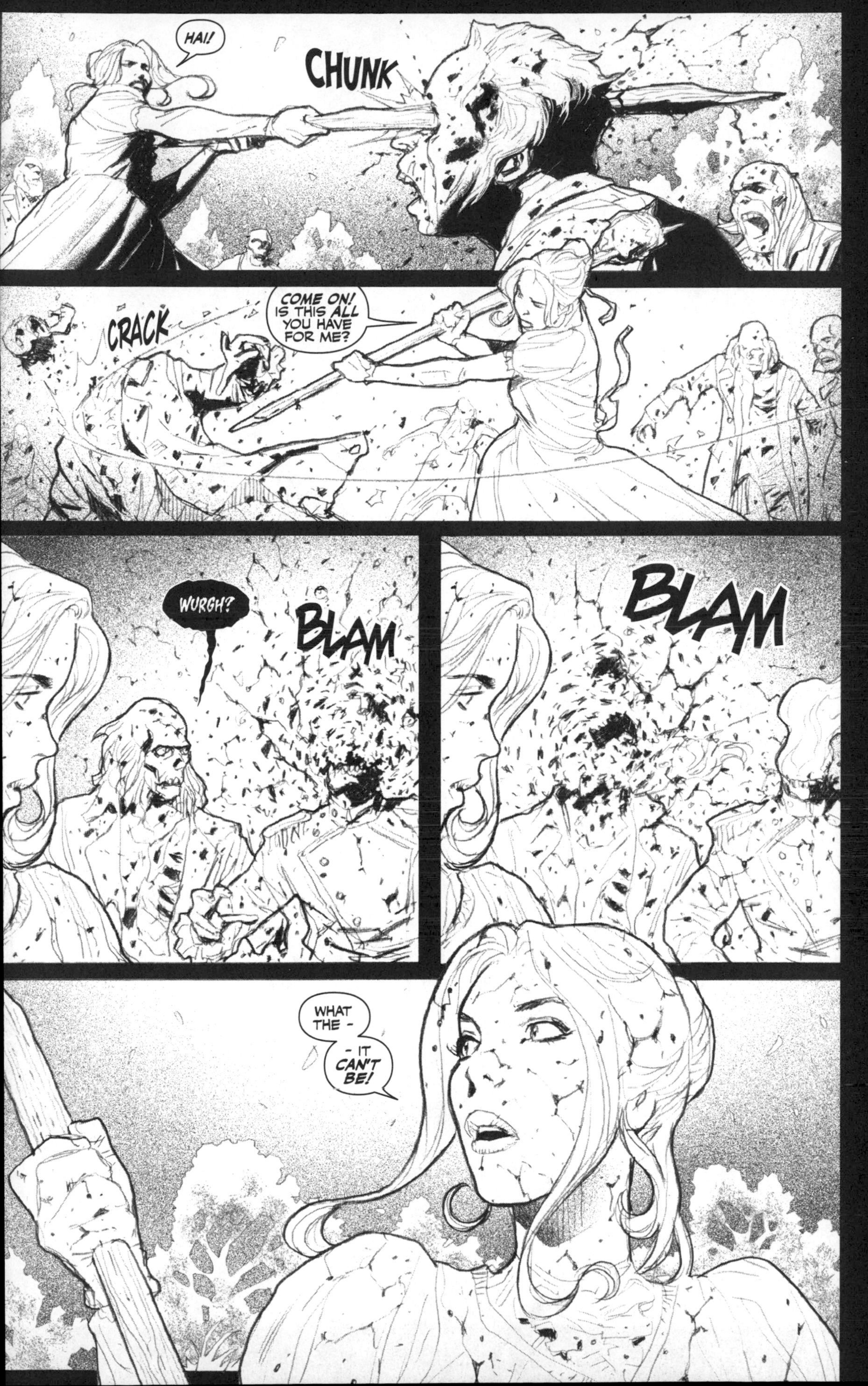
HAI!
CHUNK
CRACK
COME ON! IS THIS ALL YOU HAVE FOR ME?
WURGH?
BLAM
BLAM
WHAT THE -
- IT CAN'T BE!

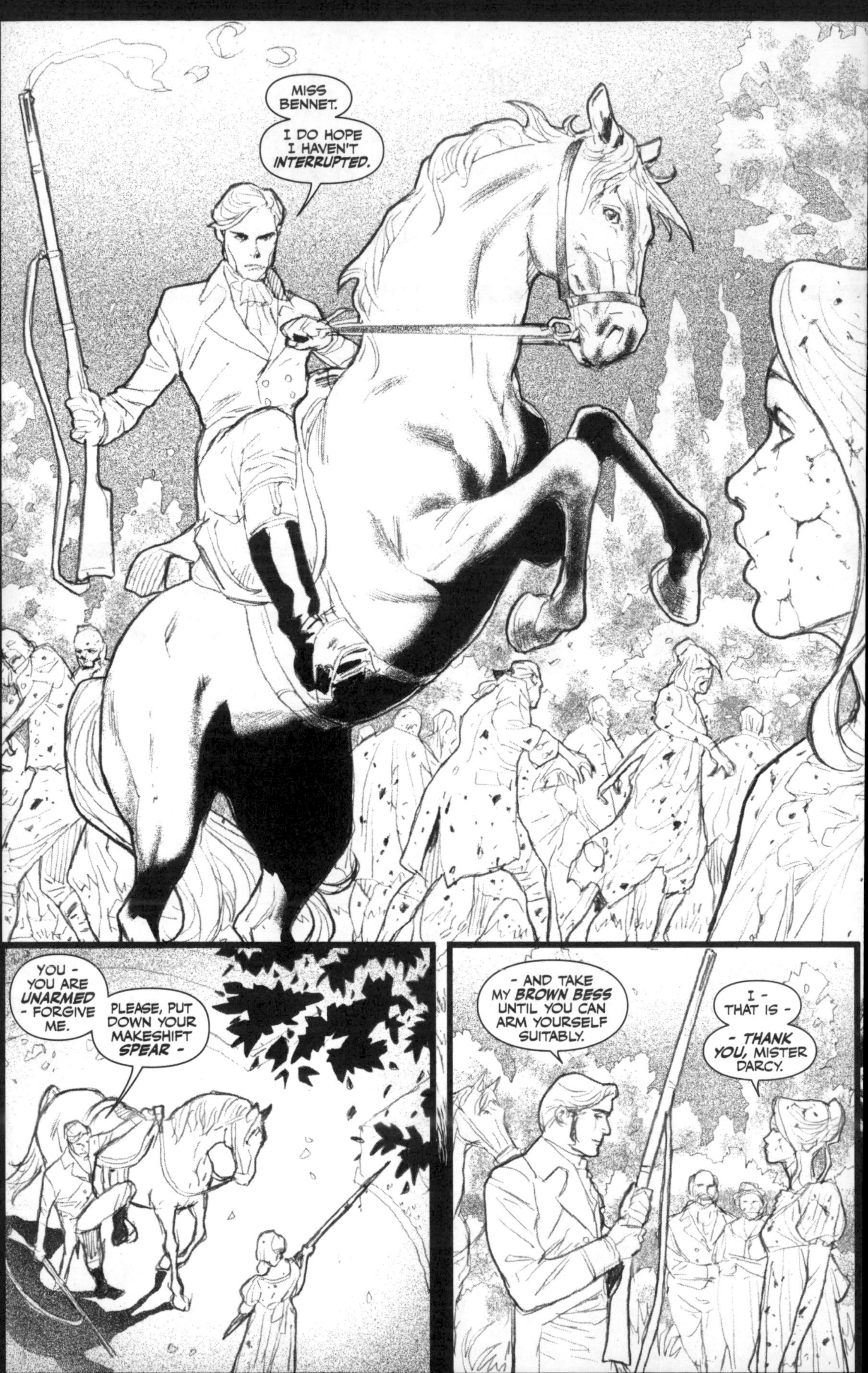
MISS BENNET.
I DO HOPE I HAVEN'T *INTERRUPTED.*
YOU - YOU ARE *UNARMED* - FORGIVE ME.
PLEASE, PUT DOWN YOUR MAKESHIFT *SPEAR* -
- AND TAKE MY *BROWN BESS* UNTIL YOU CAN ARM YOURSELF SUITABLY.
I - THAT IS -
- THANK YOU, MISTER DARCY.

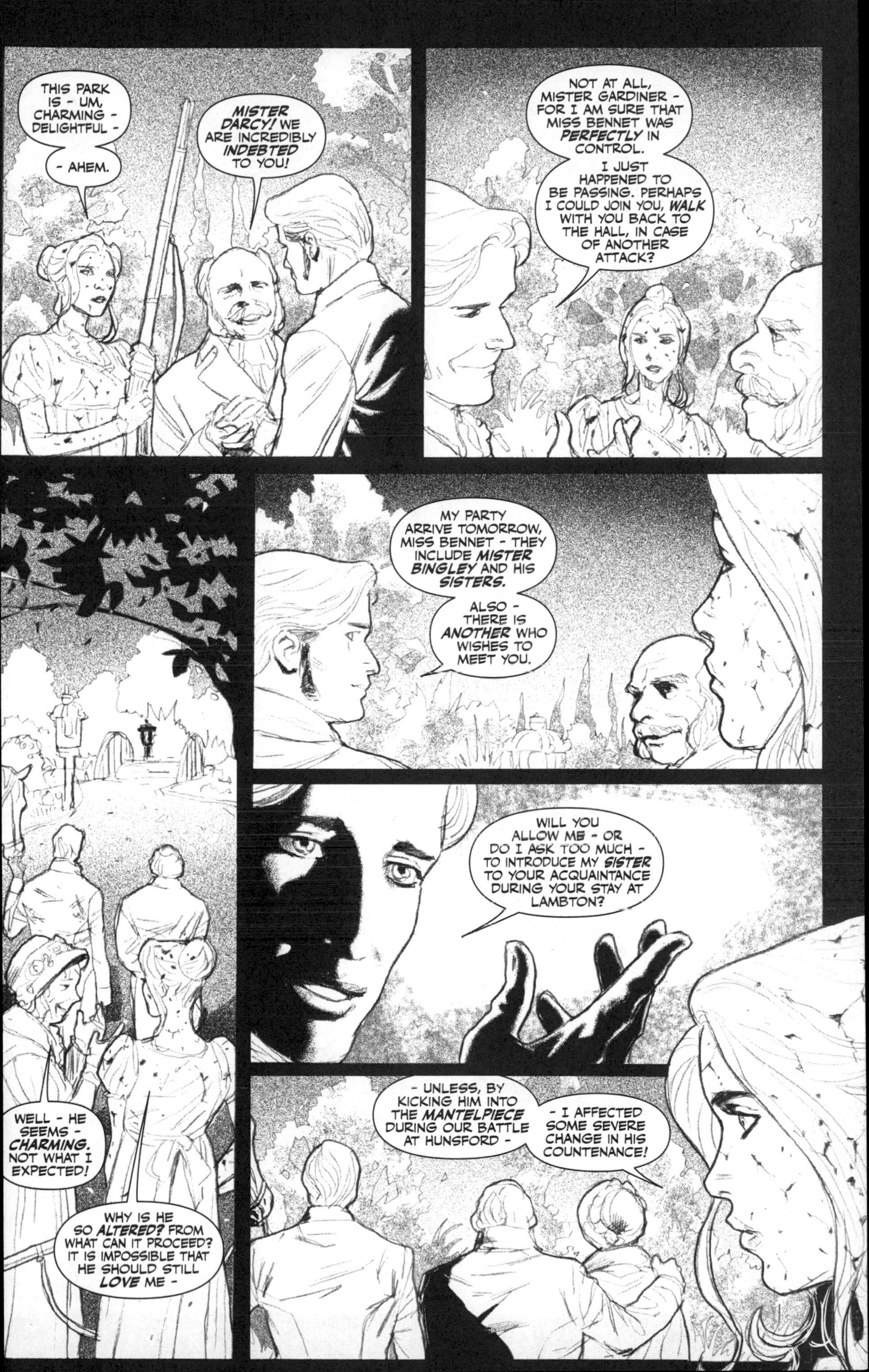
THIS PARK IS - UM, CHARMING - DELIGHTFUL -
- AHEM.
MISTER DARCY! WE ARE INCREDIBLY *INDEBTED* TO YOU!
NOT AT ALL, MISTER GARDINER - FOR I AM SURE THAT MISS BENNET WAS *PERFECTLY* IN CONTROL.
I JUST HAPPENED TO BE PASSING. PERHAPS I COULD JOIN YOU, *WALK* WITH YOU BACK TO THE HALL, IN CASE OF ANOTHER ATTACK?
MY PARTY ARRIVE TOMORROW, MISS BENNET - THEY INCLUDE *MISTER BINGLEY* AND HIS *SISTERS.*
ALSO - THERE IS *ANOTHER* WHO WISHES TO MEET YOU.
WILL YOU ALLOW ME - OR DO I ASK TOO MUCH - TO INTRODUCE MY *SISTER* TO YOUR ACQUAINTANCE DURING YOUR STAY AT LAMBTON?
WELL - HE SEEMS - *CHARMING.* NOT WHAT I EXPECTED!
WHY IS HE SO *ALTERED?* FROM WHAT CAN IT PROCEED? IT IS IMPOSSIBLE THAT HE SHOULD STILL *LOVE* ME -
- UNLESS, BY KICKING HIM INTO THE *MANTELPIECE* DURING OUR BATTLE AT HUNSFORD -
- I AFFECTED SOME SEVERE CHANGE IN HIS COUNTENANCE!

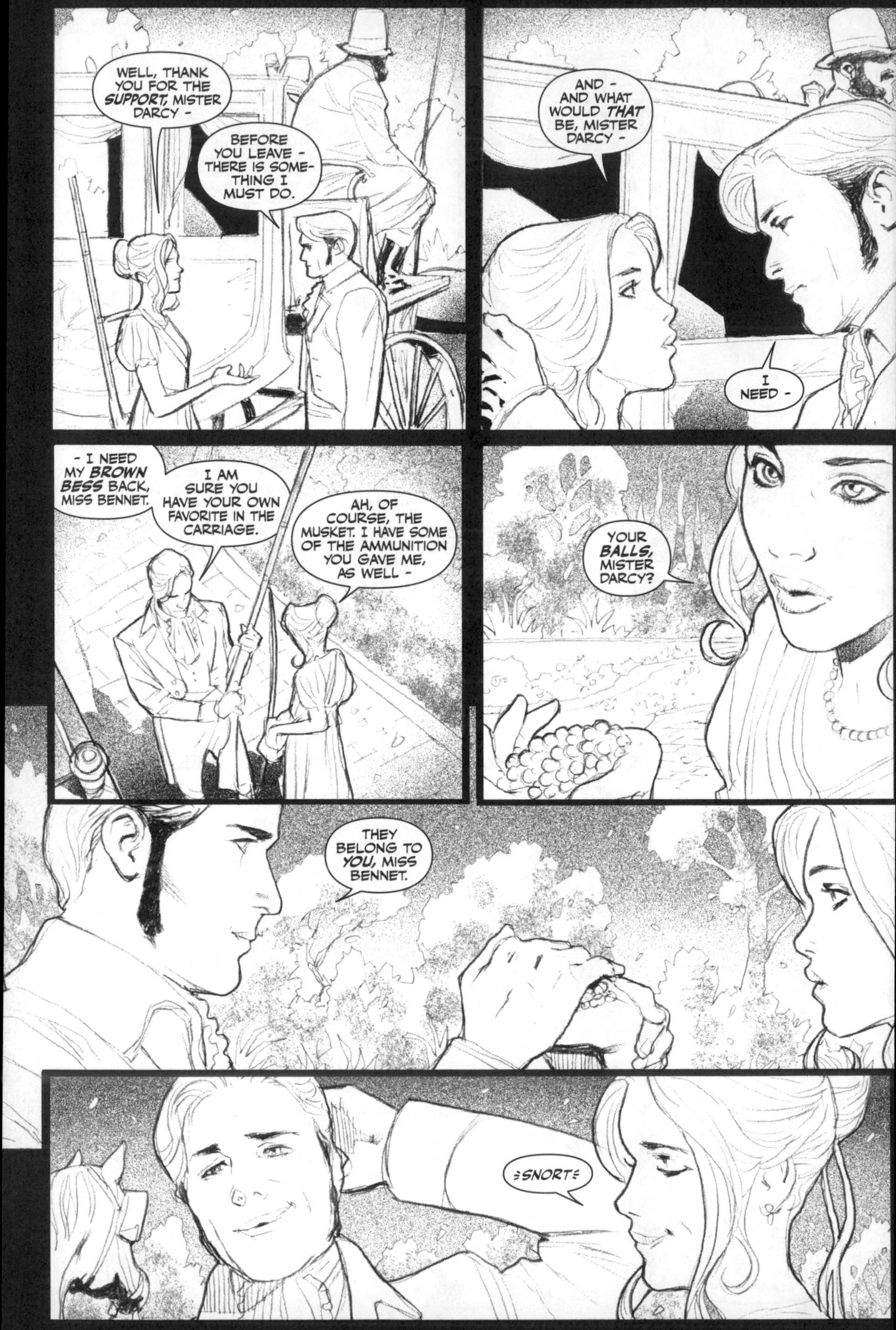
WELL, THANK YOU FOR THE SUPPORT, MISTER DARCY -
BEFORE YOU LEAVE - THERE IS SOMETHING I MUST DO.
AND - AND WHAT WOULD THAT BE, MISTER DARCY -
I NEED -
- I NEED MY BROWN BESS BACK, MISS BENNET.
I AM SURE YOU HAVE YOUR OWN FAVORITE IN THE CARRIAGE.
AH, OF COURSE, THE MUSKET. I HAVE SOME OF THE AMMUNITION YOU GAVE ME, AS WELL -
YOUR BALLS, MISTER DARCY?
THEY BELONG TO YOU, MISS BENNET.
SNORT

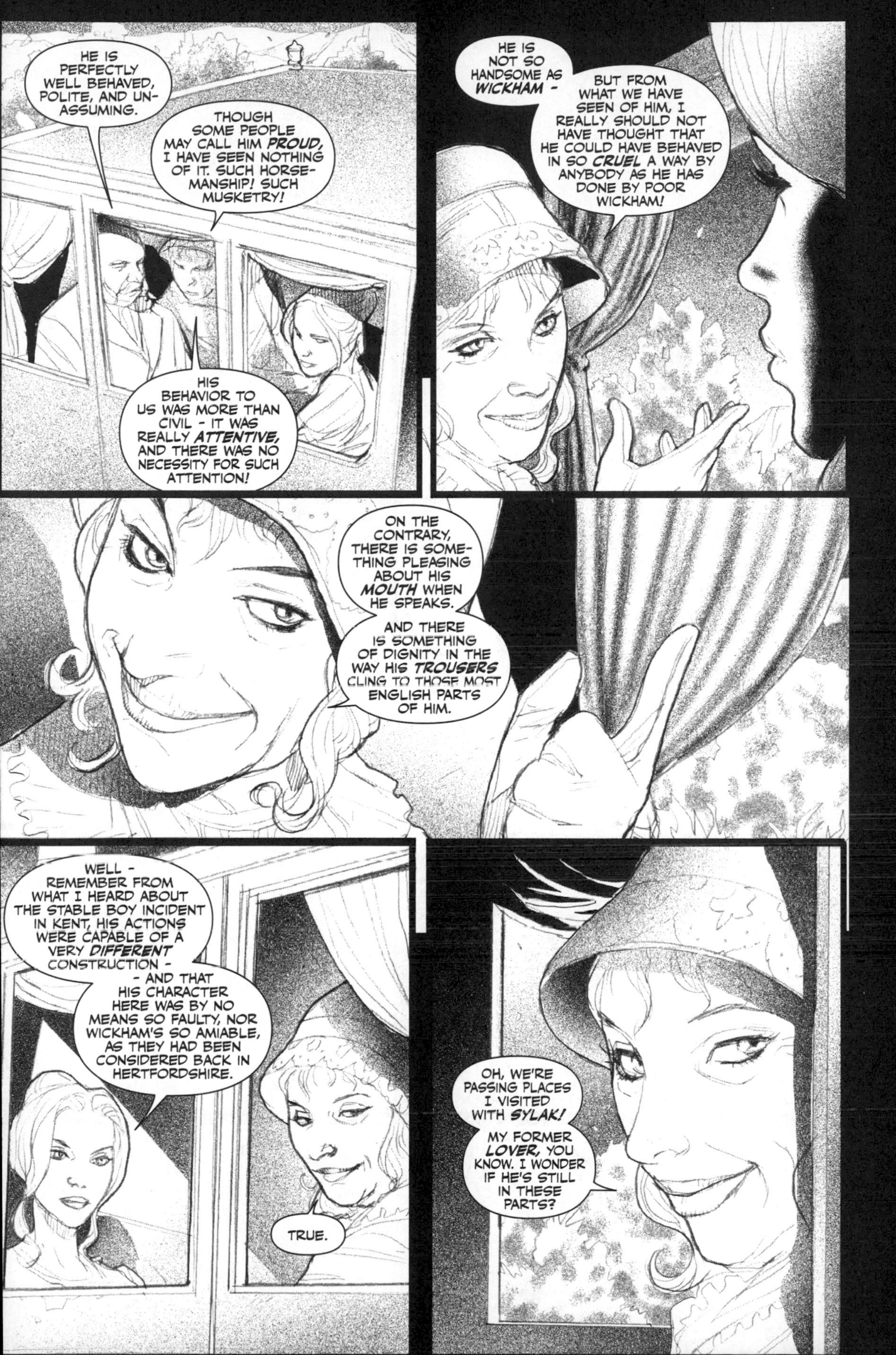

HE IS PERFECTLY WELL BEHAVED, POLITE, AND UN-ASSUMING.
THOUGH SOME PEOPLE MAY CALL HIM PROUD, I HAVE SEEN NOTHING OF IT. SUCH HORSE-MANSHIP! SUCH MUSKETRY!
HIS BEHAVIOR TO US WAS MORE THAN CIVIL - IT WAS REALLY ATTENTIVE, AND THERE WAS NO NECESSITY FOR SUCH ATTENTION!
HE IS NOT SO HANDSOME AS WICKHAM -
BUT FROM WHAT WE HAVE SEEN OF HIM, I REALLY SHOULD NOT HAVE THOUGHT THAT HE COULD HAVE BEHAVED IN SO CRUEL A WAY BY ANYBODY AS HE HAS DONE BY POOR WICKHAM!
ON THE CONTRARY, THERE IS SOME-THING PLEASING ABOUT HIS MOUTH WHEN HE SPEAKS.
AND THERE IS SOMETHING OF DIGNITY IN THE WAY HIS TROUSERS CLING TO THOSE MOST ENGLISH PARTS OF HIM.
WELL - REMEMBER FROM WHAT I HEARD ABOUT THE STABLE BOY INCIDENT IN KENT, HIS ACTIONS WERE CAPABLE OF A VERY DIFFERENT CONSTRUCTION -
- AND THAT HIS CHARACTER HERE WAS BY NO MEANS SO FAULTY, NOR WICKHAM'S SO AMIABLE, AS THEY HAD BEEN CONSIDERED BACK IN HERTFORDSHIRE.
TRUE.
OH, WE'RE PASSING PLACES I VISITED WITH SYLAK!
MY FORMER LOVER, YOU KNOW. I WONDER IF HE'S STILL IN THESE PARTS?

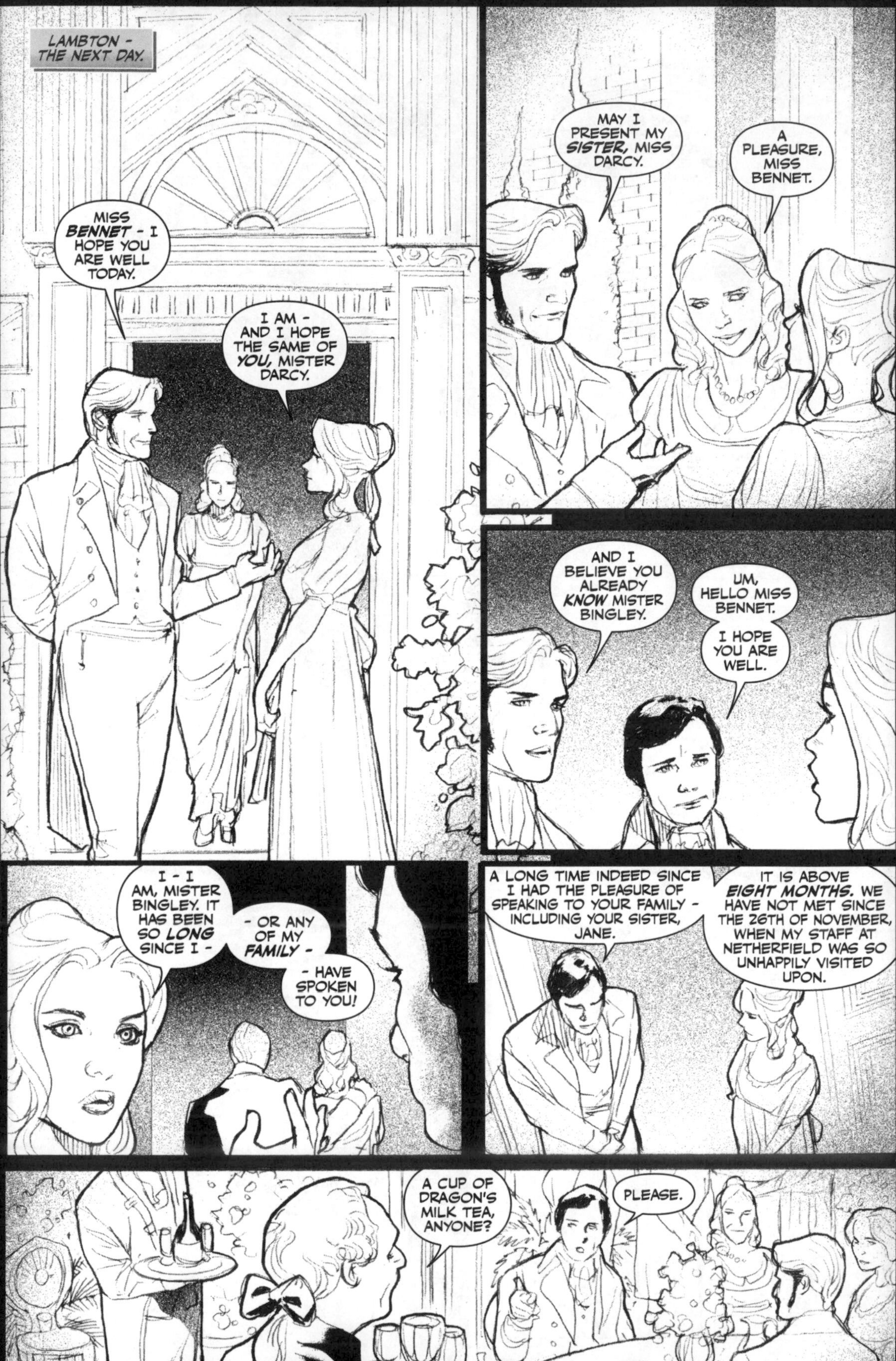
LAMBTON - THE NEXT DAY.
MISS BENNET - I HOPE YOU ARE WELL TODAY.
I AM - AND I HOPE THE SAME OF YOU, MISTER DARCY.
MAY I PRESENT MY SISTER, MISS DARCY.
A PLEASURE, MISS BENNET.
AND I BELIEVE YOU ALREADY KNOW MISTER BINGLEY.
UM, HELLO MISS BENNET.
I HOPE YOU ARE WELL.
I - I AM, MISTER BINGLEY. IT HAS BEEN SO LONG SINCE I -
- OR ANY OF MY FAMILY -
- HAVE SPOKEN TO YOU!
A LONG TIME INDEED SINCE I HAD THE PLEASURE OF SPEAKING TO YOUR FAMILY - INCLUDING YOUR SISTER, JANE.
IT IS ABOVE EIGHT MONTHS. WE HAVE NOT MET SINCE THE 26TH OF NOVEMBER, WHEN MY STAFF AT NETHERFIELD WAS SO UNHAPPILY VISITED UPON.
A CUP OF DRAGON'S MILK TEA, ANYONE?
PLEASE.

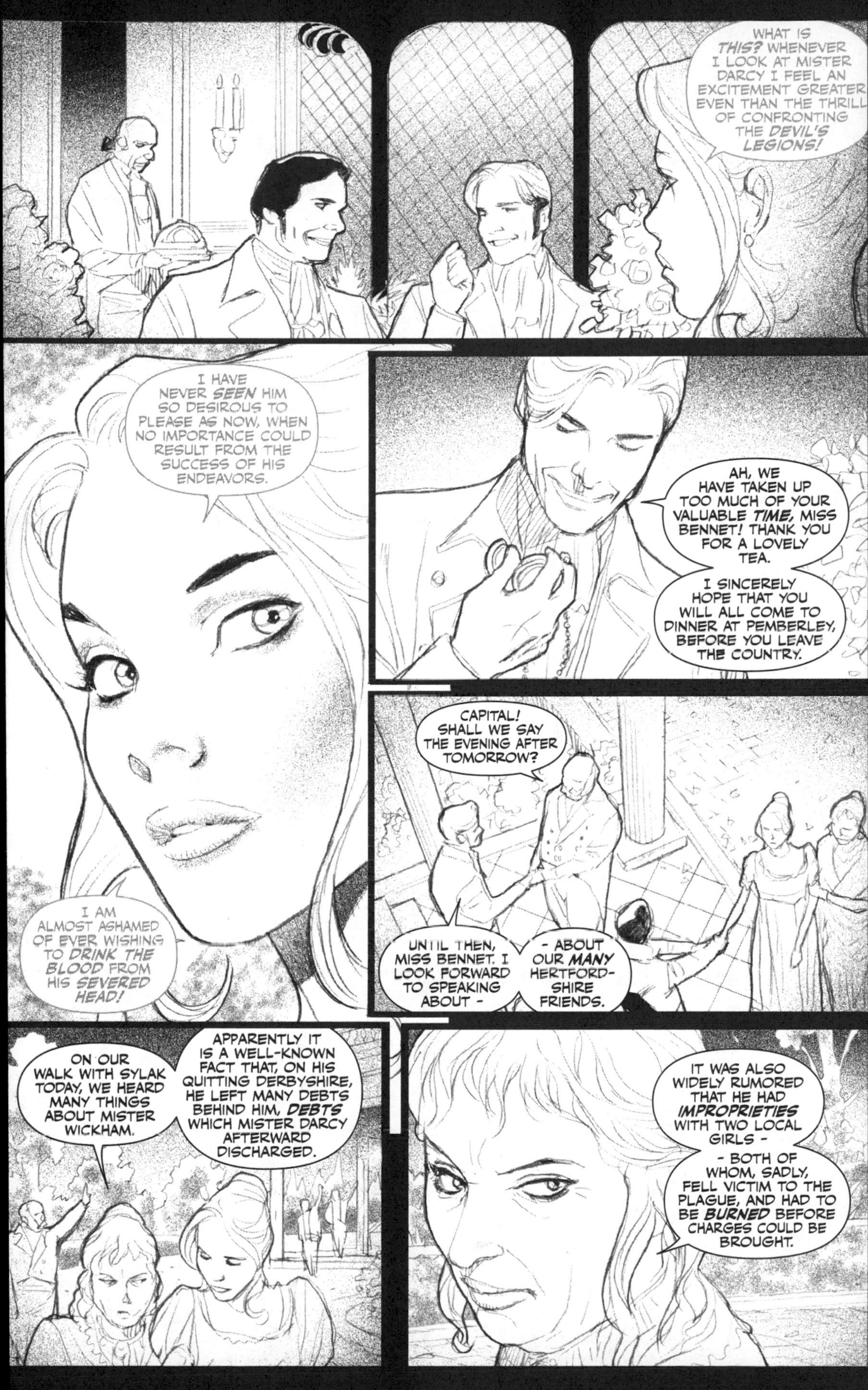
WHAT IS THIS? WHENEVER I LOOK AT MISTER DARCY I FEEL AN EXCITEMENT GREATER EVEN THAN THE THRILL OF CONFRONTING THE DEVIL'S LEGIONS!
I HAVE NEVER SEEN HIM SO DESIROUS TO PLEASE AS NOW, WHEN NO IMPORTANCE COULD RESULT FROM THE SUCCESS OF HIS ENDEAVORS.
I AM ALMOST ASHAMED OF EVER WISHING TO DRINK THE BLOOD FROM HIS SEVERED HEAD!
AH, WE HAVE TAKEN UP TOO MUCH OF YOUR VALUABLE TIME, MISS BENNET! THANK YOU FOR A LOVELY TEA.
I SINCERELY HOPE THAT YOU WILL ALL COME TO DINNER AT PEMBERLEY, BEFORE YOU LEAVE THE COUNTRY.
CAPITAL! SHALL WE SAY THE EVENING AFTER TOMORROW?
UNTIL THEN, MISS BENNET. I LOOK FORWARD TO SPEAKING ABOUT -
- ABOUT OUR MANY HERTFORD-SHIRE FRIENDS.
ON OUR WALK WITH SYLAK TODAY, WE HEARD MANY THINGS ABOUT MISTER WICKHAM.
APPARENTLY IT IS A WELL-KNOWN FACT THAT, ON HIS QUITTING DERBYSHIRE, HE LEFT MANY DEBTS BEHIND HIM, DEBTS WHICH MISTER DARCY AFTERWARD DISCHARGED.
IT WAS ALSO WIDELY RUMORED THAT HE HAD IMPROPRIETIES WITH TWO LOCAL GIRLS -
- BOTH OF WHOM, SADLY, FELL VICTIM TO THE PLAGUE, AND HAD TO BE BURNED BEFORE CHARGES COULD BE BROUGHT.

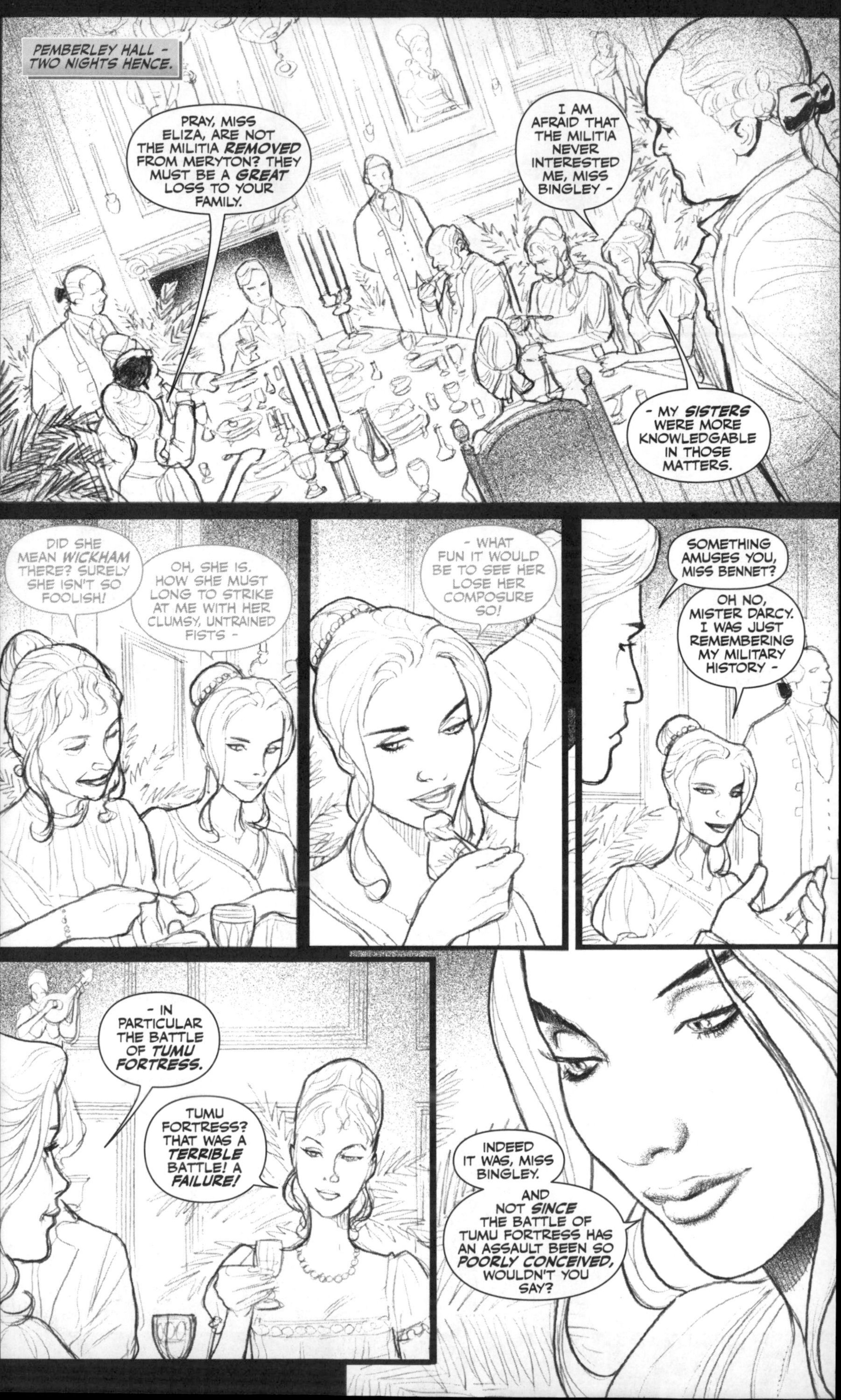
PEMBERLEY HALL - TWO NIGHTS HENCE.
PRAY, MISS ELIZA, ARE NOT THE MILITIA REMOVED FROM MERYTON? THEY MUST BE A GREAT LOSS TO YOUR FAMILY.
I AM AFRAID THAT THE MILITIA NEVER INTERESTED ME, MISS BINGLEY -
- MY SISTERS WERE MORE KNOWLEDGABLE IN THOSE MATTERS.
DID SHE MEAN WICKHAM THERE? SURELY SHE ISN'T SO FOOLISH!
OH, SHE IS. HOW SHE MUST LONG TO STRIKE AT ME WITH HER CLUMSY, UNTRAINED FISTS -
- WHAT FUN IT WOULD BE TO SEE HER LOSE HER COMPOSURE SO!
SOMETHING AMUSES YOU, MISS BENNET?
OH NO, MISTER DARCY. I WAS JUST REMEMBERING MY MILITARY HISTORY -
- IN PARTICULAR THE BATTLE OF TUMU FORTRESS.
TUMU FORTRESS? THAT WAS A TERRIBLE BATTLE! A FAILURE!
INDEED IT WAS, MISS BINGLEY.
AND NOT SINCE THE BATTLE OF TUMU FORTRESS HAS AN ASSAULT BEEN SO POORLY CONCEIVED, WOULDN'T YOU SAY?

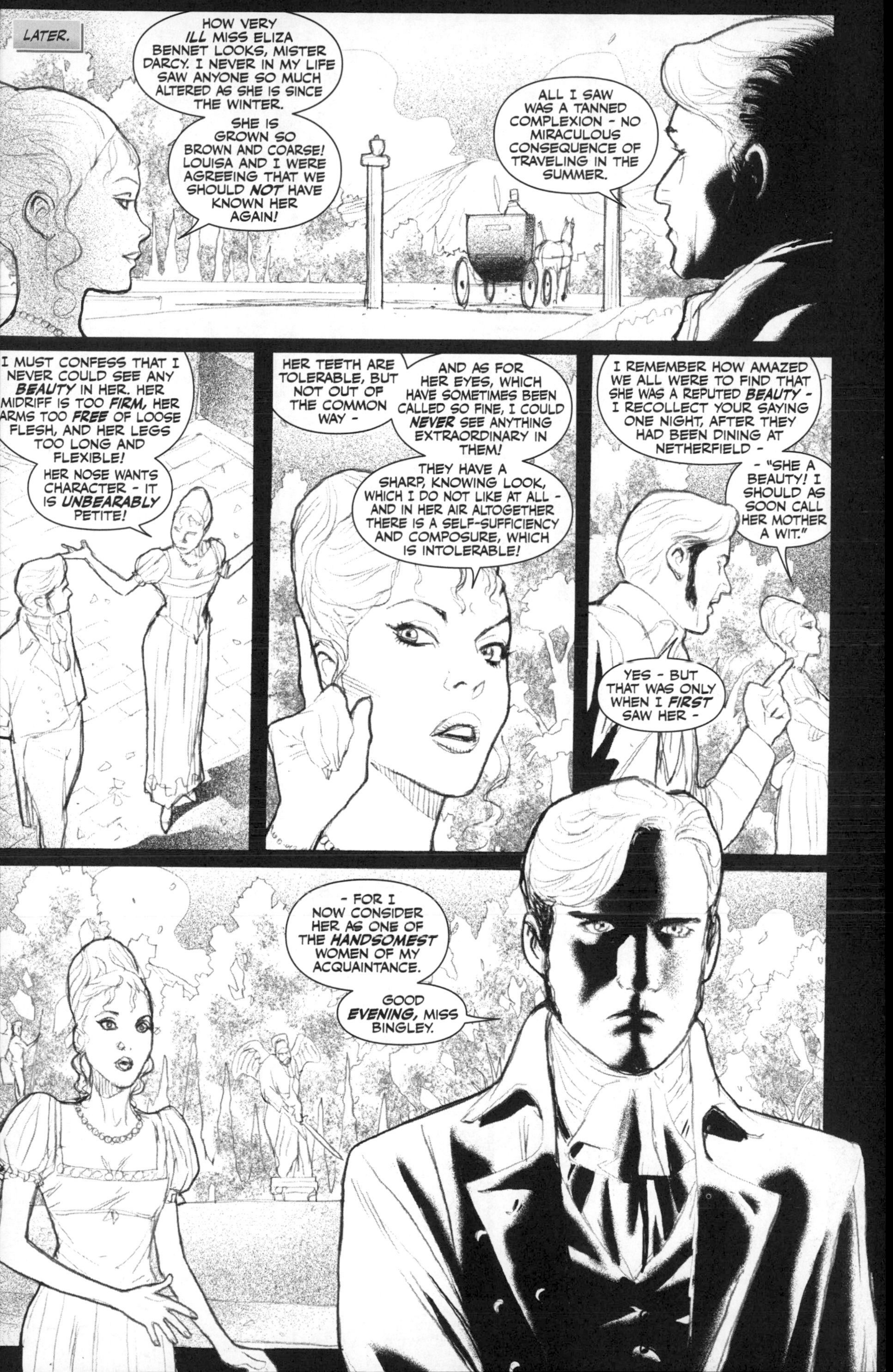
LATER.
HOW VERY ILL MISS ELIZA BENNET LOOKS, MISTER DARCY. I NEVER IN MY LIFE SAW ANYONE SO MUCH ALTERED AS SHE IS SINCE THE WINTER.
SHE IS GROWN SO BROWN AND COARSE! LOUISA AND I WERE AGREEING THAT WE SHOULD NOT HAVE KNOWN HER AGAIN!
ALL I SAW WAS A TANNED COMPLEXION - NO MIRACULOUS CONSEQUENCE OF TRAVELING IN THE SUMMER.
I MUST CONFESS THAT I NEVER COULD SEE ANY BEAUTY IN HER. HER MIDRIFF IS TOO FIRM, HER ARMS TOO FREE OF LOOSE FLESH, AND HER LEGS TOO LONG AND FLEXIBLE!
HER NOSE WANTS CHARACTER - IT IS UNBEARABLY PETITE!
HER TEETH ARE TOLERABLE, BUT NOT OUT OF THE COMMON WAY -
AND AS FOR HER EYES, WHICH HAVE SOMETIMES BEEN CALLED SO FINE, I COULD NEVER SEE ANYTHING EXTRAORDINARY IN THEM!
THEY HAVE A SHARP, KNOWING LOOK, WHICH I DO NOT LIKE AT ALL - AND IN HER AIR ALTOGETHER THERE IS A SELF-SUFFICIENCY AND COMPOSURE, WHICH IS INTOLERABLE!
I REMEMBER HOW AMAZED WE ALL WERE TO FIND THAT SHE WAS A REPUTED BEAUTY - I RECOLLECT YOUR SAYING ONE NIGHT, AFTER THEY HAD BEEN DINING AT NETHERFIELD -
- "SHE A BEAUTY! I SHOULD AS SOON CALL HER MOTHER A WIT."
YES - BUT THAT WAS ONLY WHEN I FIRST SAW HER -
- FOR I NOW CONSIDER HER AS ONE OF THE HANDSOMEST WOMEN OF MY ACQUAINTANCE.
GOOD EVENING, MISS BINGLEY.

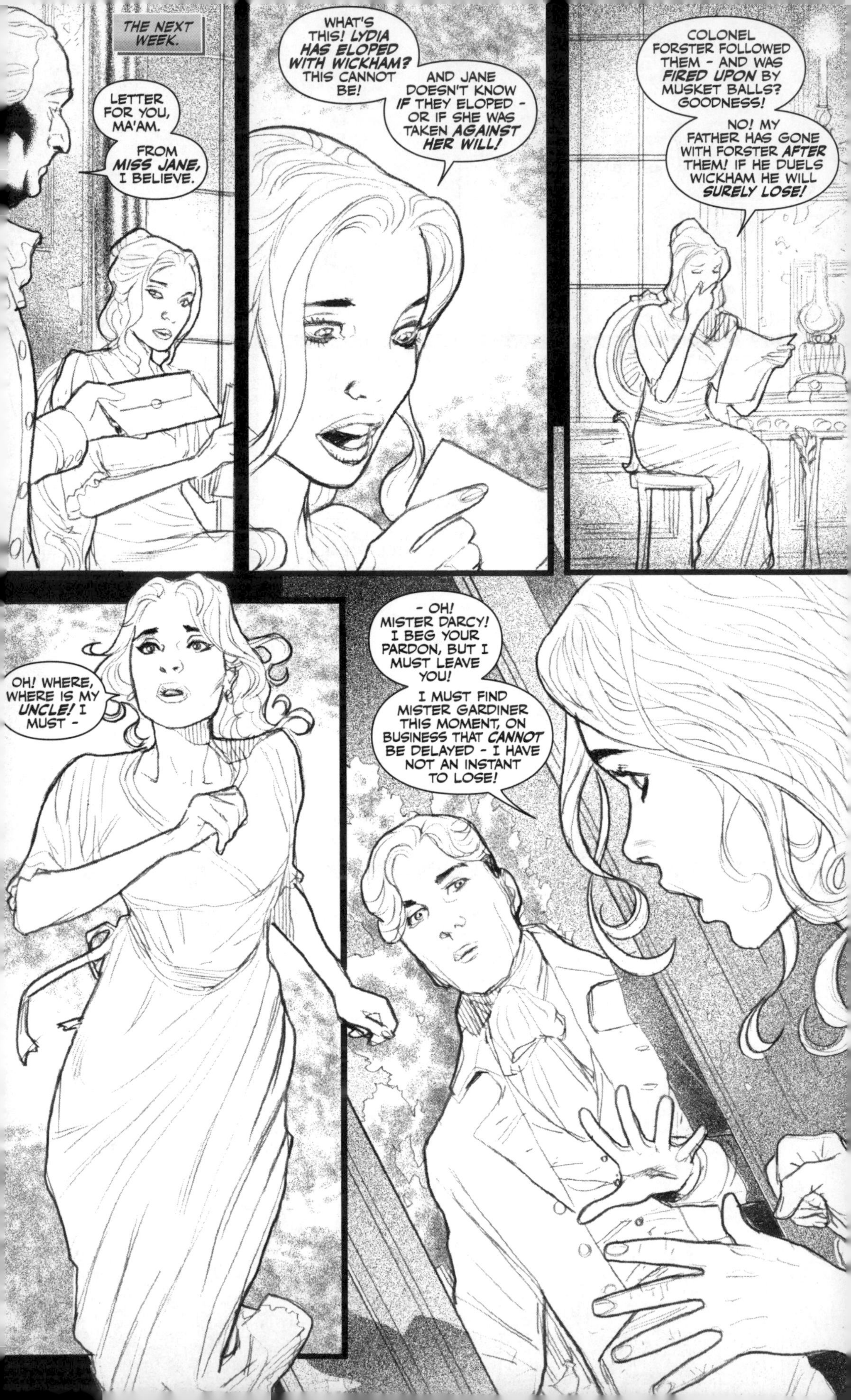
THE NEXT WEEK.
LETTER FOR YOU, MA'AM.
FROM MISS JANE, I BELIEVE.
WHAT'S THIS! LYDIA HAS ELOPED WITH WICKHAM? THIS CANNOT BE!
AND JANE DOESN'T KNOW IF THEY ELOPED - OR IF SHE WAS TAKEN AGAINST HER WILL!
COLONEL FORSTER FOLLOWED THEM - AND WAS FIRED UPON BY MUSKET BALLS? GOODNESS!
NO! MY FATHER HAS GONE WITH FORSTER AFTER THEM! IF HE DUELS WICKHAM HE WILL SURELY LOSE!
OH! WHERE, WHERE IS MY UNCLE! I MUST -
- OH! MISTER DARCY! I BEG YOUR PARDON, BUT I MUST LEAVE YOU!
I MUST FIND MISTER GARDINER THIS MOMENT, ON BUSINESS THAT CANNOT BE DELAYED - I HAVE NOT AN INSTANT TO LOSE!

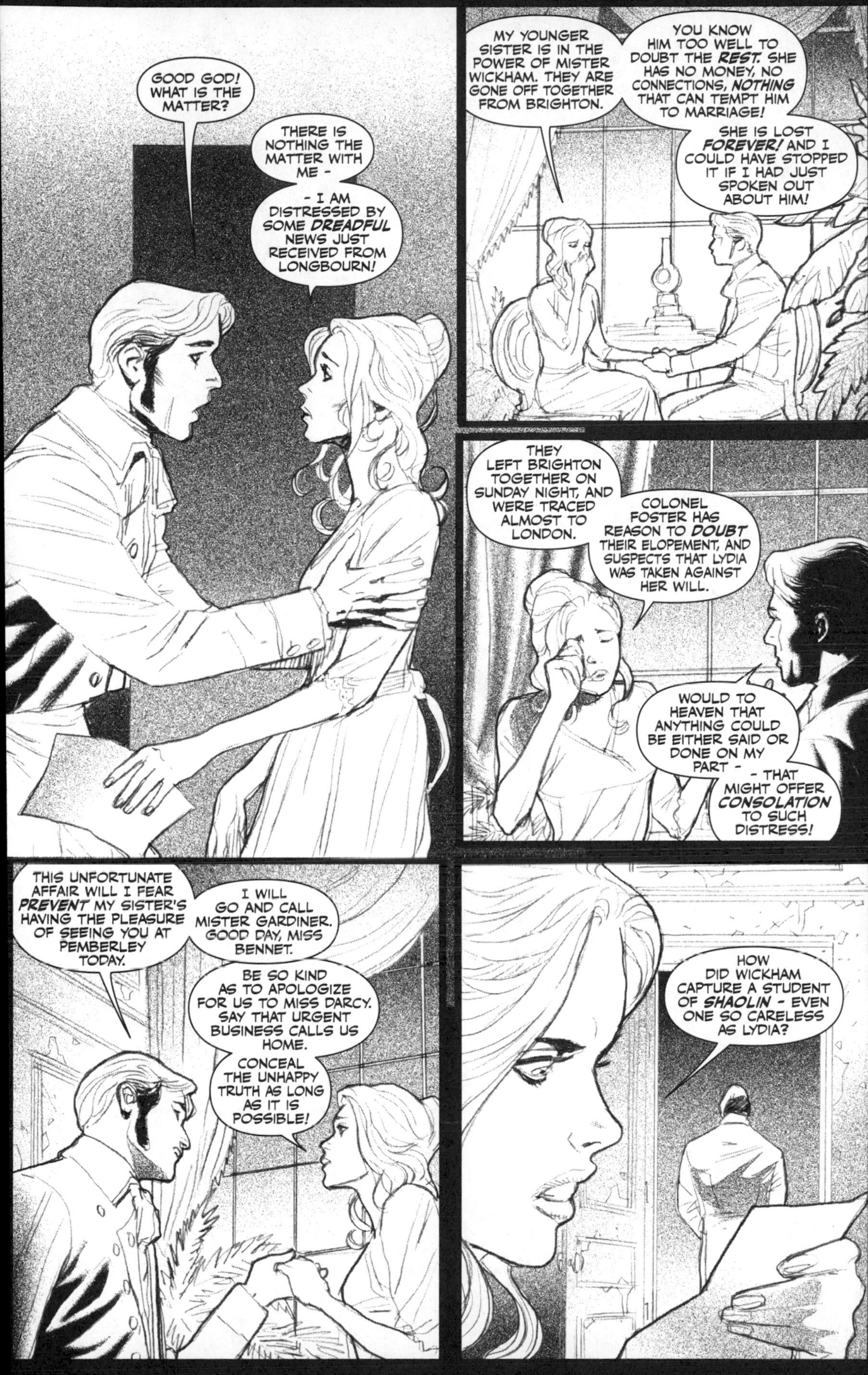
GOOD GOD! WHAT IS THE MATTER?
THERE IS NOTHING THE MATTER WITH ME -
- I AM DISTRESSED BY SOME DREADFUL NEWS JUST RECEIVED FROM LONGBOURN!
MY YOUNGER SISTER IS IN THE POWER OF MISTER WICKHAM. THEY ARE GONE OFF TOGETHER FROM BRIGHTON.
YOU KNOW HIM TOO WELL TO DOUBT THE REST. SHE HAS NO MONEY, NO CONNECTIONS, NOTHING THAT CAN TEMPT HIM TO MARRIAGE!
SHE IS LOST FOREVER! AND I COULD HAVE STOPPED IT IF I HAD JUST SPOKEN OUT ABOUT HIM!
THEY LEFT BRIGHTON TOGETHER ON SUNDAY NIGHT, AND WERE TRACED ALMOST TO LONDON.
COLONEL FOSTER HAS REASON TO DOUBT THEIR ELOPEMENT, AND SUSPECTS THAT LYDIA WAS TAKEN AGAINST HER WILL.
WOULD TO HEAVEN THAT ANYTHING COULD BE EITHER SAID OR DONE ON MY PART -
- THAT MIGHT OFFER CONSOLATION TO SUCH DISTRESS!
THIS UNFORTUNATE AFFAIR WILL I FEAR PREVENT MY SISTER'S HAVING THE PLEASURE OF SEEING YOU AT PEMBERLEY TODAY.
I WILL GO AND CALL MISTER GARDINER. GOOD DAY, MISS BENNET.
BE SO KIND AS TO APOLOGIZE FOR US TO MISS DARCY. SAY THAT URGENT BUSINESS CALLS US HOME.
CONCEAL THE UNHAPPY TRUTH AS LONG AS IT IS POSSIBLE!
HOW DID WICKHAM CAPTURE A STUDENT OF SHAOLIN - EVEN ONE SO CARELESS AS LYDIA?

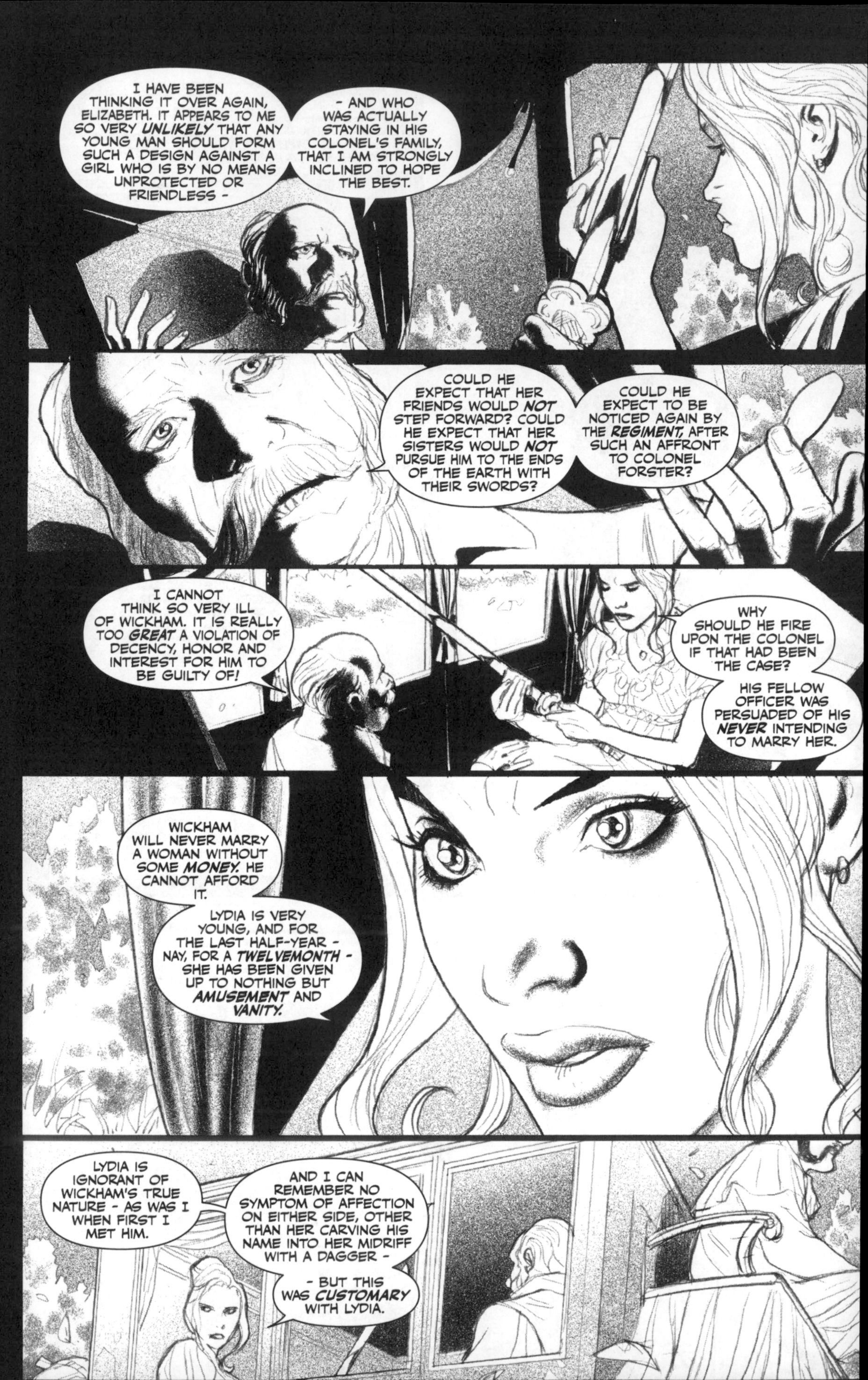
I HAVE BEEN THINKING IT OVER AGAIN, ELIZABETH. IT APPEARS TO ME SO VERY UNLIKELY THAT ANY YOUNG MAN SHOULD FORM SUCH A DESIGN AGAINST A GIRL WHO IS BY NO MEANS UNPROTECTED OR FRIENDLESS -
- AND WHO WAS ACTUALLY STAYING IN HIS COLONEL'S FAMILY, THAT I AM STRONGLY INCLINED TO HOPE THE BEST.
COULD HE EXPECT THAT HER FRIENDS WOULD NOT STEP FORWARD? COULD HE EXPECT THAT HER SISTERS WOULD NOT PURSUE HIM TO THE ENDS OF THE EARTH WITH THEIR SWORDS?
COULD HE EXPECT TO BE NOTICED AGAIN BY THE REGIMENT, AFTER SUCH AN AFFRONT TO COLONEL FORSTER?
I CANNOT THINK SO VERY ILL OF WICKHAM. IT IS REALLY TOO GREAT A VIOLATION OF DECENCY, HONOR AND INTEREST FOR HIM TO BE GUILTY OF!
WHY SHOULD HE FIRE UPON THE COLONEL IF THAT HAD BEEN THE CASE?
HIS FELLOW OFFICER WAS PERSUADED OF HIS NEVER INTENDING TO MARRY HER.
WICKHAM WILL NEVER MARRY A WOMAN WITHOUT SOME MONEY. HE CANNOT AFFORD IT.
LYDIA IS VERY YOUNG, AND FOR THE LAST HALF-YEAR - NAY, FOR A TWELVEMONTH - SHE HAS BEEN GIVEN UP TO NOTHING BUT AMUSEMENT AND VANITY.
LYDIA IS IGNORANT OF WICKHAM'S TRUE NATURE - AS WAS I WHEN FIRST I MET HIM.
AND I CAN REMEMBER NO SYMPTOM OF AFFECTION ON EITHER SIDE, OTHER THAN HER CARVING HIS NAME INTO HER MIDRIFF WITH A DAGGER -
- BUT THIS WAS CUSTOMARY WITH LYDIA.

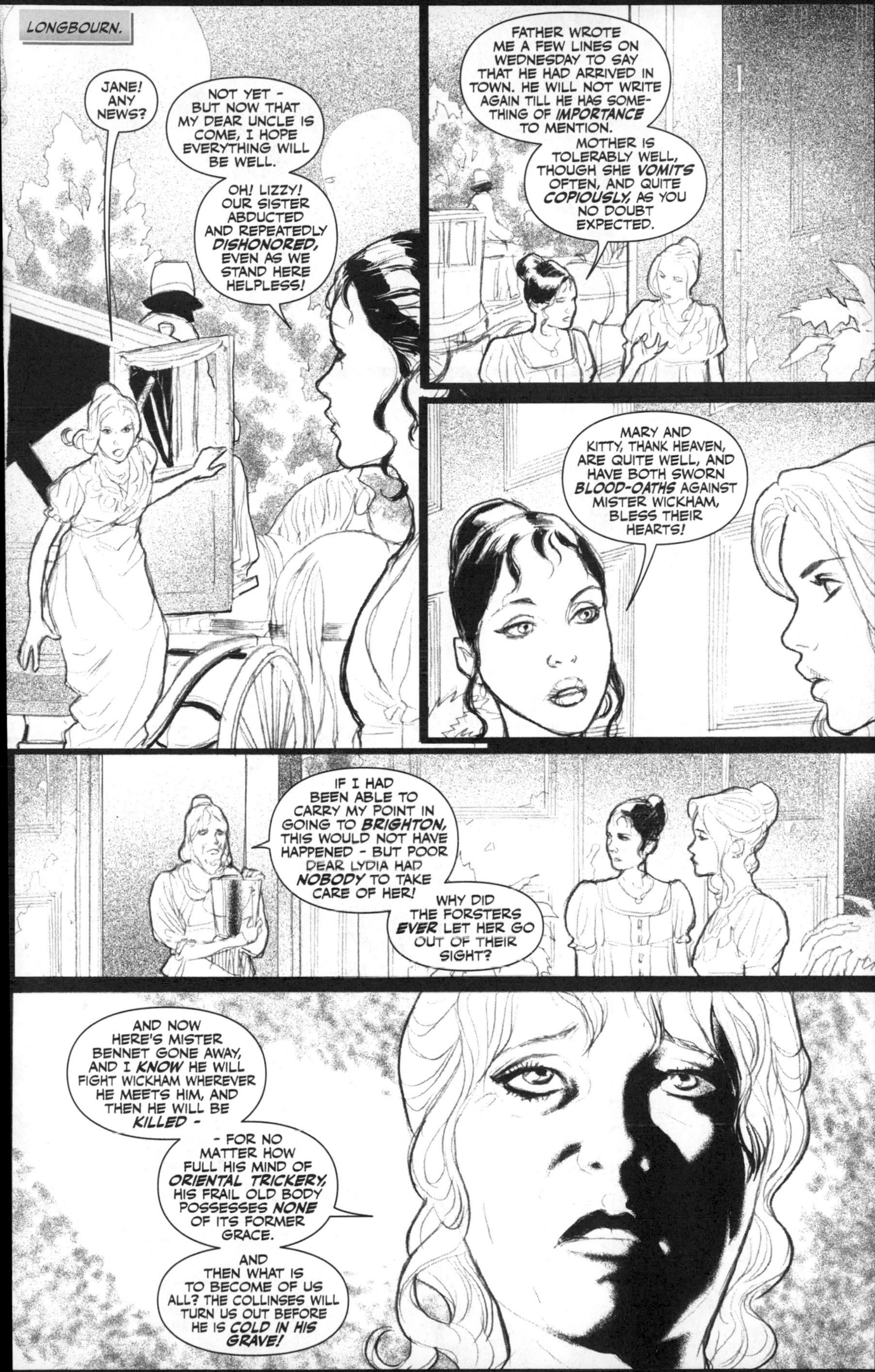
LONGBOURN.
JANE! ANY NEWS?
NOT YET - BUT NOW THAT MY DEAR UNCLE IS COME, I HOPE EVERYTHING WILL BE WELL.
OH! LIZZY! OUR SISTER ABDUCTED AND REPEATEDLY DISHONORED, EVEN AS WE STAND HERE HELPLESS!
FATHER WROTE ME A FEW LINES ON WEDNESDAY TO SAY THAT HE HAD ARRIVED IN TOWN. HE WILL NOT WRITE AGAIN TILL HE HAS SOMETHING OF IMPORTANCE TO MENTION.
MOTHER IS TOLERABLY WELL, THOUGH SHE VOMITS OFTEN, AND QUITE COPIOUSLY, AS YOU NO DOUBT EXPECTED.
MARY AND KITTY, THANK HEAVEN, ARE QUITE WELL, AND HAVE BOTH SWORN BLOOD-OATHS AGAINST MISTER WICKHAM, BLESS THEIR HEARTS!
IF I HAD BEEN ABLE TO CARRY MY POINT IN GOING TO BRIGHTON, THIS WOULD NOT HAVE HAPPENED - BUT POOR DEAR LYDIA HAD NOBODY TO TAKE CARE OF HER!
WHY DID THE FORSTERS EVER LET HER GO OUT OF THEIR SIGHT?
AND NOW HERE'S MISTER BENNET GONE AWAY, AND I KNOW HE WILL FIGHT WICKHAM WHEREVER HE MEETS HIM, AND THEN HE WILL BE KILLED -
- FOR NO MATTER HOW FULL HIS MIND OF ORIENTAL TRICKERY, HIS FRAIL OLD BODY POSSESSES NONE OF ITS FORMER GRACE.
AND THEN WHAT IS TO BECOME OF US ALL? THE COLLINSES WILL TURN US OUT BEFORE HE IS COLD IN HIS GRAVE!

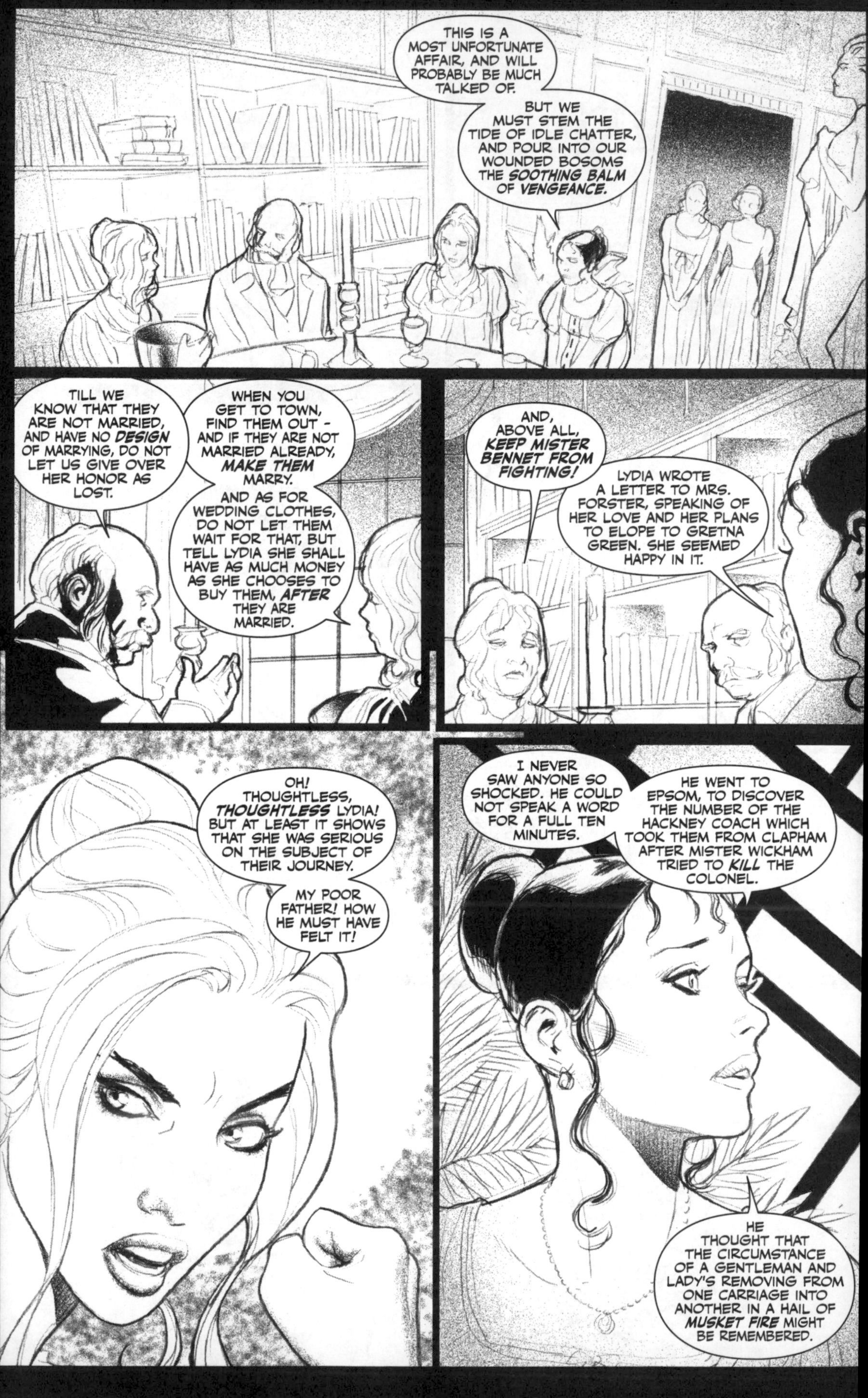
THIS IS A MOST UNFORTUNATE AFFAIR, AND WILL PROBABLY BE MUCH TALKED OF.
BUT WE MUST STEM THE TIDE OF IDLE CHATTER, AND POUR INTO OUR WOUNDED BOSOMS THE *SOOTHING BALM* OF *VENGEANCE*.
TILL WE KNOW THAT THEY ARE NOT MARRIED, AND HAVE NO *DESIGN* OF MARRYING, DO NOT LET US GIVE OVER HER HONOR AS LOST.
WHEN YOU GET TO TOWN, FIND THEM OUT - AND IF THEY ARE NOT MARRIED ALREADY, *MAKE THEM* MARRY.
AND AS FOR WEDDING CLOTHES, DO NOT LET THEM WAIT FOR THAT, BUT TELL LYDIA SHE SHALL HAVE AS MUCH MONEY AS SHE CHOOSES TO BUY THEM, *AFTER* THEY ARE MARRIED.
AND, ABOVE ALL, *KEEP MISTER BENNET FROM FIGHTING!*
LYDIA WROTE A LETTER TO MRS. FORSTER, SPEAKING OF HER LOVE AND HER PLANS TO ELOPE TO GRETNA GREEN. SHE SEEMED HAPPY IN IT.
OH! THOUGHTLESS, *THOUGHTLESS* LYDIA! BUT AT LEAST IT SHOWS THAT SHE WAS SERIOUS ON THE SUBJECT OF THEIR JOURNEY.
MY POOR FATHER! HOW HE MUST HAVE FELT IT!
I NEVER SAW ANYONE SO SHOCKED. HE COULD NOT SPEAK A WORD FOR A FULL TEN MINUTES.
HE WENT TO EPSOM, TO DISCOVER THE NUMBER OF THE HACKNEY COACH WHICH TOOK THEM FROM CLAPHAM AFTER MISTER WICKHAM TRIED TO *KILL* THE COLONEL.
HE THOUGHT THAT THE CIRCUMSTANCE OF A GENTLEMAN AND LADY'S REMOVING FROM ONE CARRIAGE INTO ANOTHER IN A HAIL OF *MUSKET FIRE* MIGHT BE REMEMBERED.

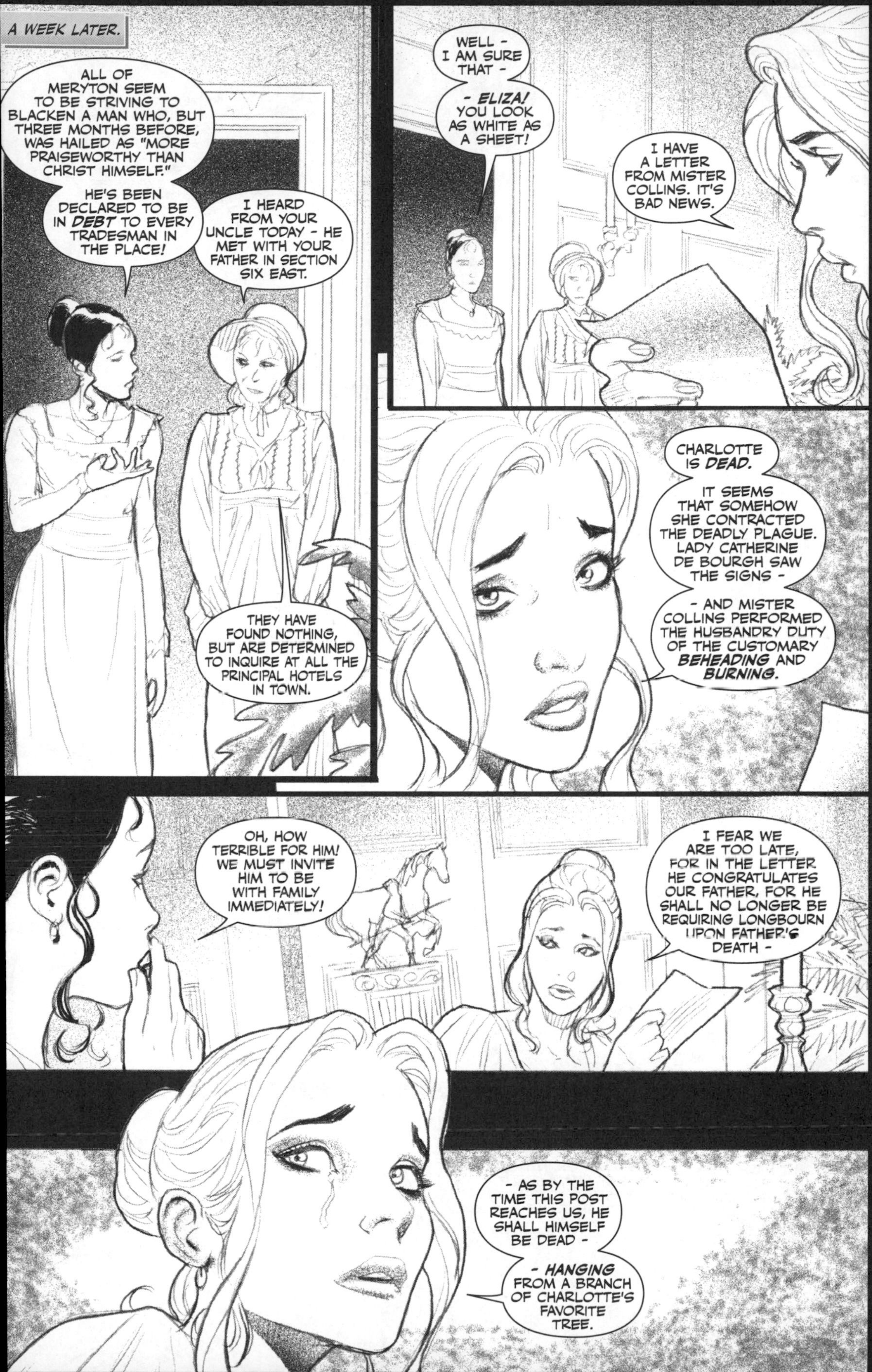
A WEEK LATER.
ALL OF MERYTON SEEM TO BE STRIVING TO BLACKEN A MAN WHO, BUT THREE MONTHS BEFORE, WAS HAILED AS "MORE PRAISEWORTHY THAN CHRIST HIMSELF."
HE'S BEEN DECLARED TO BE IN DEBT TO EVERY TRADESMAN IN THE PLACE!
I HEARD FROM YOUR UNCLE TODAY - HE MET WITH YOUR FATHER IN SECTION SIX EAST.
THEY HAVE FOUND NOTHING, BUT ARE DETERMINED TO INQUIRE AT ALL THE PRINCIPAL HOTELS IN TOWN.
WELL - I AM SURE THAT -
- ELIZA! YOU LOOK AS WHITE AS A SHEET!
I HAVE A LETTER FROM MISTER COLLINS. IT'S BAD NEWS.
CHARLOTTE IS DEAD.
IT SEEMS THAT SOMEHOW SHE CONTRACTED THE DEADLY PLAGUE. LADY CATHERINE DE BOURGH SAW THE SIGNS -
- AND MISTER COLLINS PERFORMED THE HUSBANDRY DUTY OF THE CUSTOMARY BEHEADING AND BURNING.
OH, HOW TERRIBLE FOR HIM! WE MUST INVITE HIM TO BE WITH FAMILY IMMEDIATELY!
I FEAR WE ARE TOO LATE, FOR IN THE LETTER HE CONGRATULATES OUR FATHER, FOR HE SHALL NO LONGER BE REQUIRING LONGBOURN UPON FATHER'S DEATH -
- AS BY THE TIME THIS POST REACHES US, HE SHALL HIMSELF BE DEAD -
- HANGING FROM A BRANCH OF CHARLOTTE'S FAVORITE TREE.

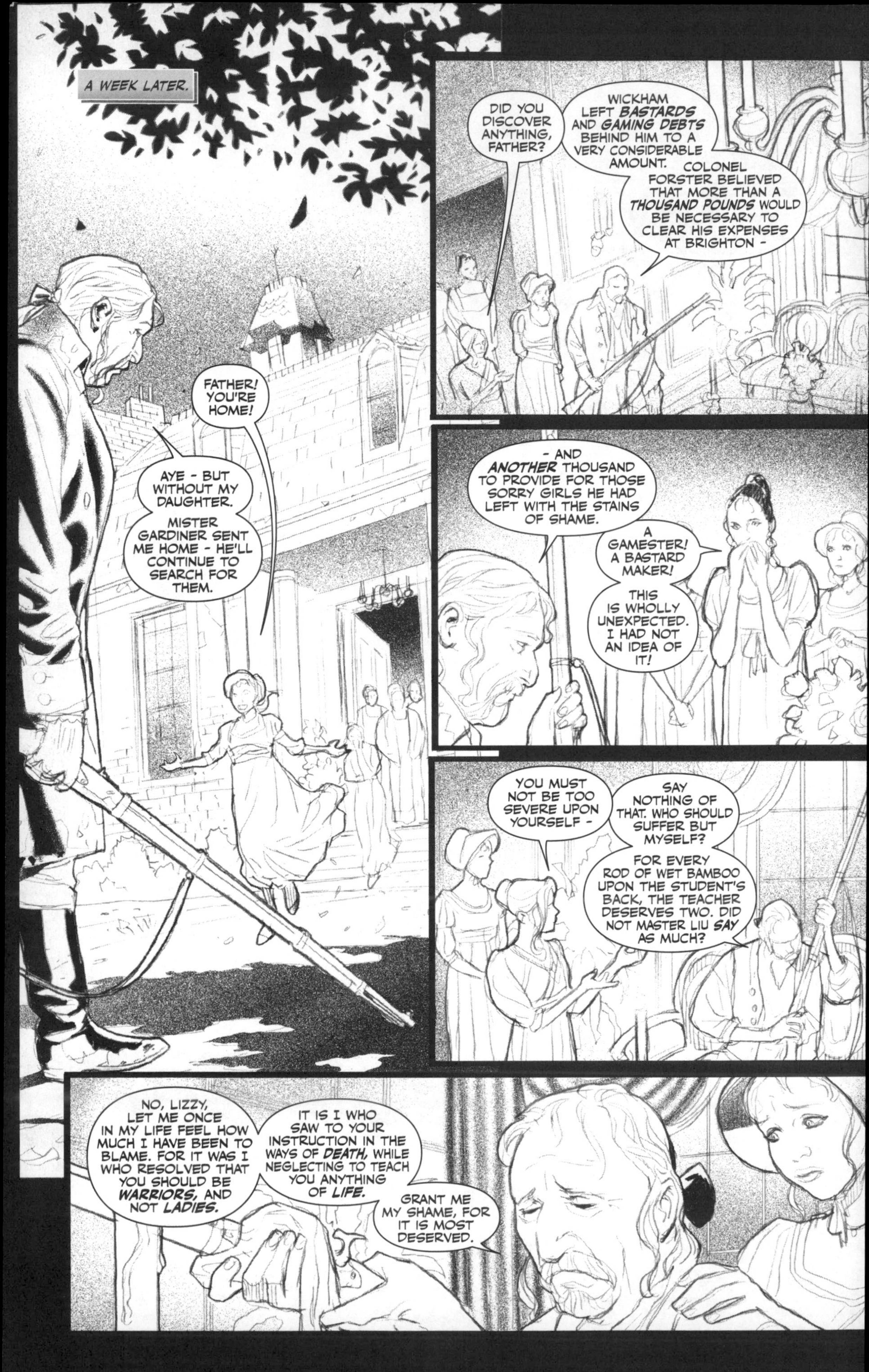
A WEEK LATER.
FATHER! YOU'RE HOME!
AYE - BUT WITHOUT MY DAUGHTER.
MISTER GARDINER SENT ME HOME - HE'LL CONTINUE TO SEARCH FOR THEM.
DID YOU DISCOVER ANYTHING, FATHER?
WICKHAM LEFT BASTARDS AND GAMING DEBTS BEHIND HIM TO A VERY CONSIDERABLE AMOUNT.
COLONEL FORSTER BELIEVED THAT MORE THAN A THOUSAND POUNDS WOULD BE NECESSARY TO CLEAR HIS EXPENSES AT BRIGHTON -
- AND ANOTHER THOUSAND TO PROVIDE FOR THOSE SORRY GIRLS HE HAD LEFT WITH THE STAINS OF SHAME.
A GAMESTER! A BASTARD MAKER!
THIS IS WHOLLY UNEXPECTED. I HAD NOT AN IDEA OF IT!
YOU MUST NOT BE TOO SEVERE UPON YOURSELF -
SAY NOTHING OF THAT. WHO SHOULD SUFFER BUT MYSELF?
FOR EVERY ROD OF WET BAMBOO UPON THE STUDENT'S BACK, THE TEACHER DESERVES TWO. DID NOT MASTER LIU SAY AS MUCH?
NO, LIZZY, LET ME ONCE IN MY LIFE FEEL HOW MUCH I HAVE BEEN TO BLAME. FOR IT WAS I WHO RESOLVED THAT YOU SHOULD BE WARRIORS, AND NOT LADIES.
IT IS I WHO SAW TO YOUR INSTRUCTION IN THE WAYS OF DEATH, WHILE NEGLECTING TO TEACH YOU ANYTHING OF LIFE.
GRANT ME MY SHAME, FOR IT IS MOST DESERVED.

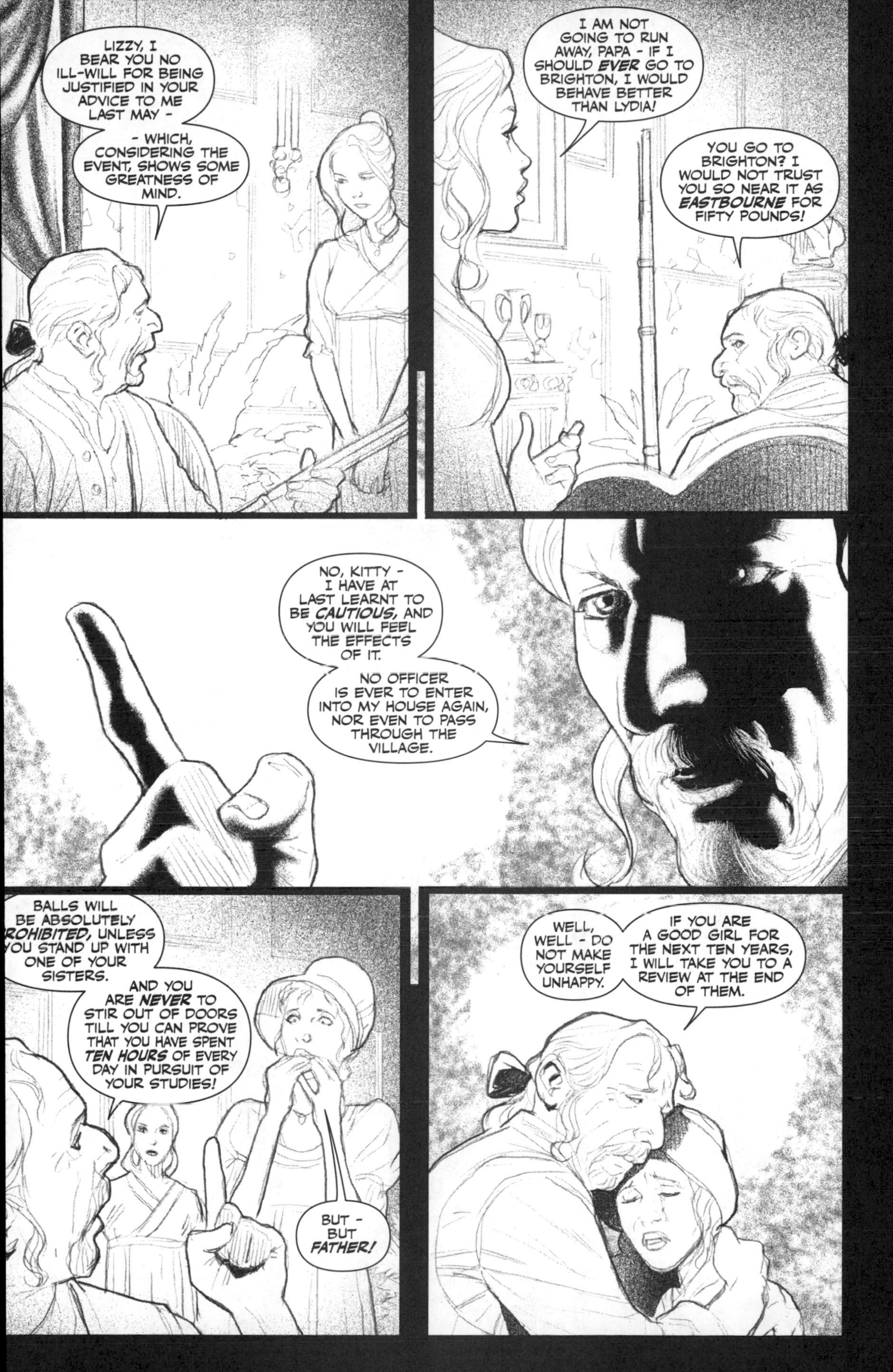
LIZZY, I BEAR YOU NO ILL-WILL FOR BEING JUSTIFIED IN YOUR ADVICE TO ME LAST MAY -
- WHICH, CONSIDERING THE EVENT, SHOWS SOME GREATNESS OF MIND.
I AM NOT GOING TO RUN AWAY, PAPA - IF I SHOULD EVER GO TO BRIGHTON, I WOULD BEHAVE BETTER THAN LYDIA!
YOU GO TO BRIGHTON? I WOULD NOT TRUST YOU SO NEAR IT AS EASTBOURNE FOR FIFTY POUNDS!
NO, KITTY - I HAVE AT LAST LEARNT TO BE CAUTIOUS, AND YOU WILL FEEL THE EFFECTS OF IT.
NO OFFICER IS EVER TO ENTER INTO MY HOUSE AGAIN, NOR EVEN TO PASS THROUGH THE VILLAGE.
BALLS WILL BE ABSOLUTELY ROHIBITED, UNLESS YOU STAND UP WITH ONE OF YOUR SISTERS.
AND YOU ARE NEVER TO STIR OUT OF DOORS TILL YOU CAN PROVE THAT YOU HAVE SPENT TEN HOURS OF EVERY DAY IN PURSUIT OF YOUR STUDIES!
BUT - BUT FATHER!
WELL, WELL - DO NOT MAKE YOURSELF UNHAPPY.
IF YOU ARE A GOOD GIRL FOR THE NEXT TEN YEARS, I WILL TAKE YOU TO A REVIEW AT THE END OF THEM.

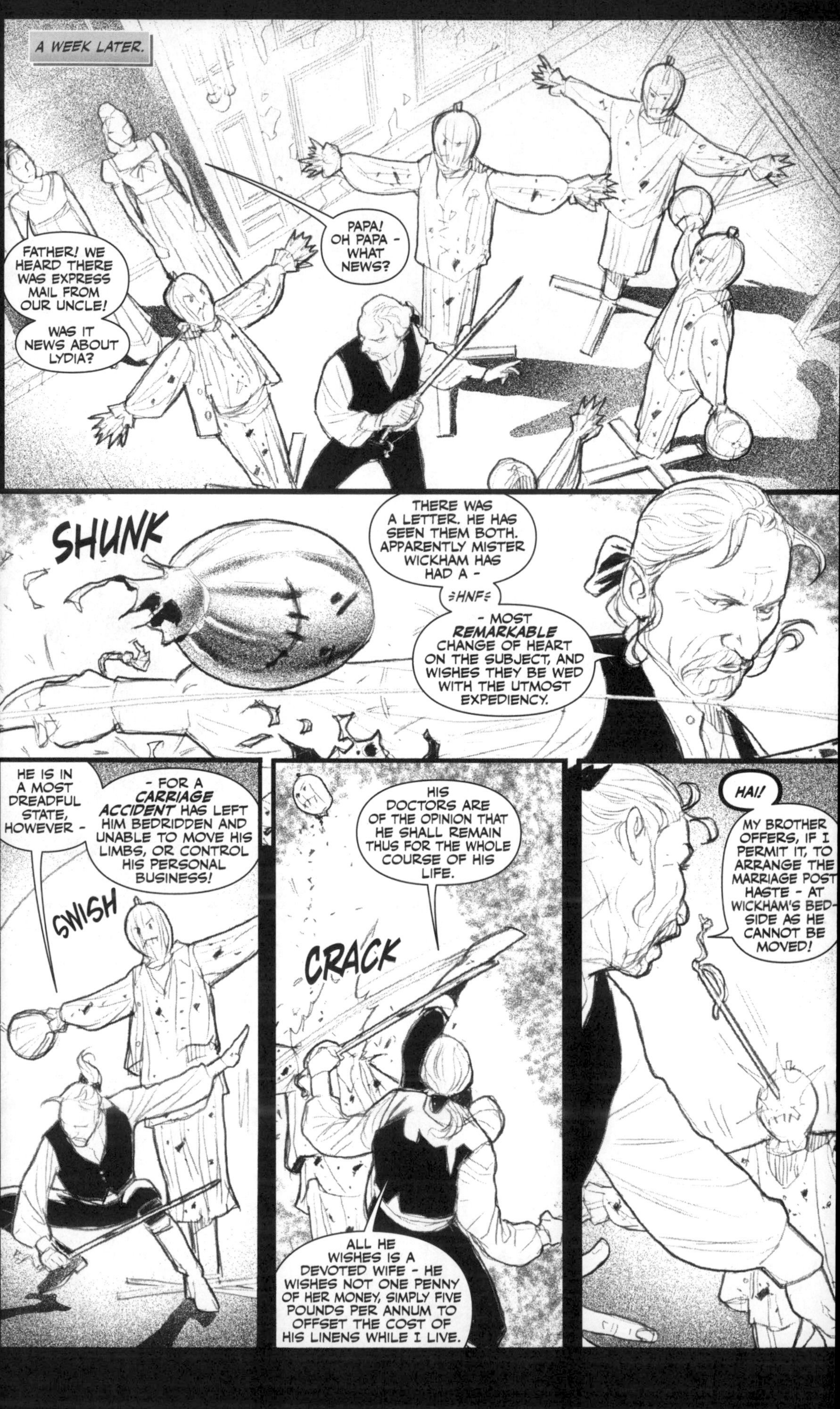
A WEEK LATER.
FATHER! WE HEARD THERE WAS EXPRESS MAIL FROM OUR UNCLE!
WAS IT NEWS ABOUT LYDIA?
PAPA! OH PAPA - WHAT NEWS?
SHUNK
THERE WAS A LETTER. HE HAS SEEN THEM BOTH. APPARENTLY MISTER WICKHAM HAS HAD A -
HNF
- MOST REMARKABLE CHANGE OF HEART ON THE SUBJECT, AND WISHES THEY BE WED WITH THE UTMOST EXPEDIENCY.
HE IS IN A MOST DREADFUL STATE, HOWEVER -
- FOR A CARRIAGE ACCIDENT HAS LEFT HIM BEDRIDDEN AND UNABLE TO MOVE HIS LIMBS, OR CONTROL HIS PERSONAL BUSINESS!
SWISH
HIS DOCTORS ARE OF THE OPINION THAT HE SHALL REMAIN THUS FOR THE WHOLE COURSE OF HIS LIFE.
CRACK
ALL HE WISHES IS A DEVOTED WIFE - HE WISHES NOT ONE PENNY OF HER MONEY, SIMPLY FIVE POUNDS PER ANNUM TO OFFSET THE COST OF HIS LINENS WHILE I LIVE.
HAI!
MY BROTHER OFFERS, IF I PERMIT IT, TO ARRANGE THE MARRIAGE POST HASTE - AT WICKHAM'S BED-SIDE AS HE CANNOT BE MOVED!

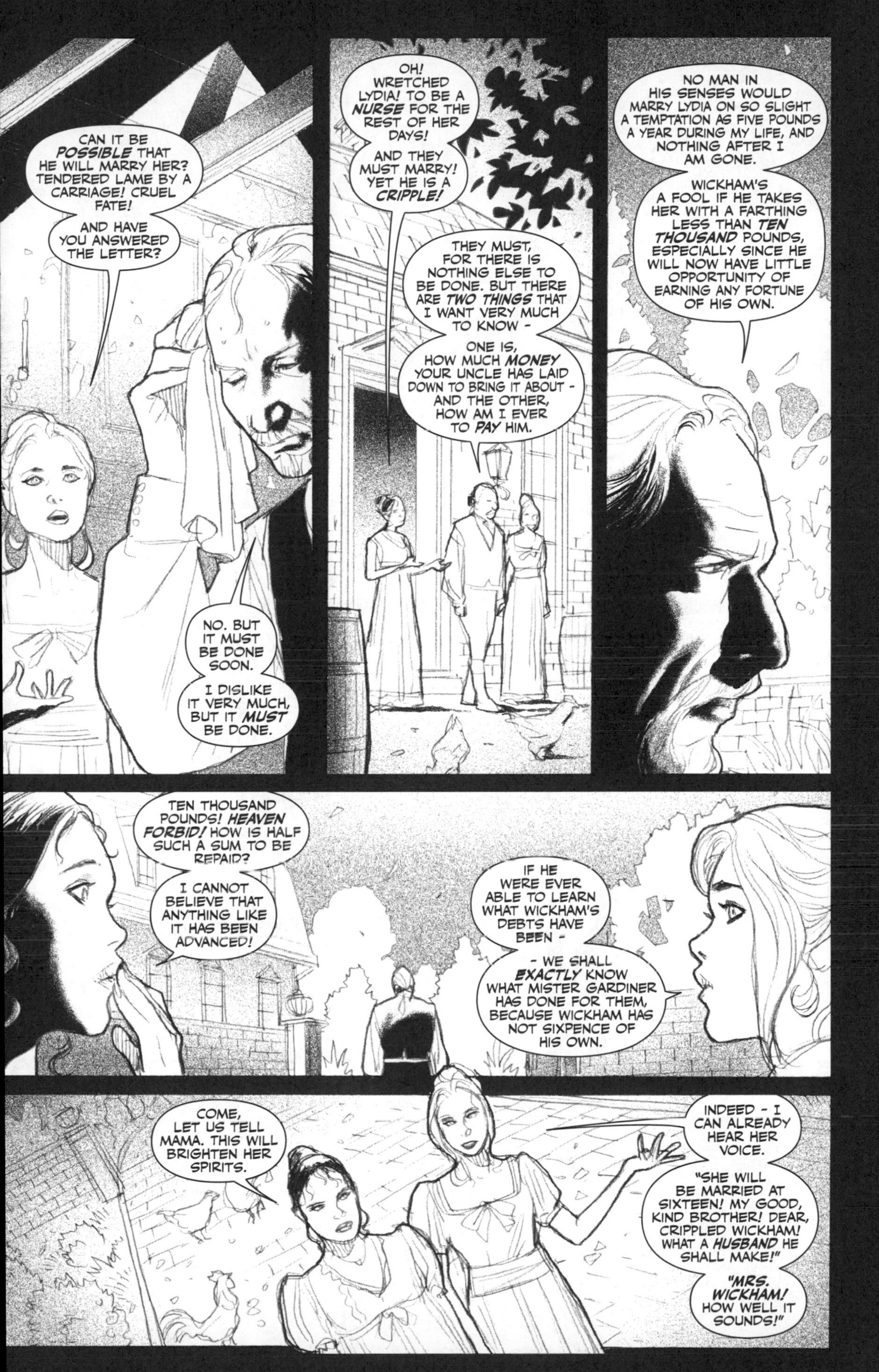
CAN IT BE POSSIBLE THAT HE WILL MARRY HER? TENDERED LAME BY A CARRIAGE! CRUEL FATE!
AND HAVE YOU ANSWERED THE LETTER?
NO. BUT IT MUST BE DONE SOON.
I DISLIKE IT VERY MUCH, BUT IT MUST BE DONE.
OH! WRETCHED LYDIA! TO BE A NURSE FOR THE REST OF HER DAYS!
AND THEY MUST MARRY! YET HE IS A CRIPPLE!
THEY MUST, FOR THERE IS NOTHING ELSE TO BE DONE. BUT THERE ARE TWO THINGS THAT I WANT VERY MUCH TO KNOW -
ONE IS, HOW MUCH MONEY YOUR UNCLE HAS LAID DOWN TO BRING IT ABOUT - AND THE OTHER, HOW AM I EVER TO PAY HIM.
NO MAN IN HIS SENSES WOULD MARRY LYDIA ON SO SLIGHT A TEMPTATION AS FIVE POUNDS A YEAR DURING MY LIFE, AND NOTHING AFTER I AM GONE.
WICKHAM'S A FOOL IF HE TAKES HER WITH A FARTHING LESS THAN TEN THOUSAND POUNDS, ESPECIALLY SINCE HE WILL NOW HAVE LITTLE OPPORTUNITY OF EARNING ANY FORTUNE OF HIS OWN.
TEN THOUSAND POUNDS! HEAVEN FORBID! HOW IS HALF SUCH A SUM TO BE REPAID?
I CANNOT BELIEVE THAT ANYTHING LIKE IT HAS BEEN ADVANCED!
IF HE WERE EVER ABLE TO LEARN WHAT WICKHAM'S DEBTS HAVE BEEN -
- WE SHALL EXACTLY KNOW WHAT MISTER GARDINER HAS DONE FOR THEM, BECAUSE WICKHAM HAS NOT SIXPENCE OF HIS OWN.
COME, LET US TELL MAMA. THIS WILL BRIGHTEN HER SPIRITS.
INDEED - I CAN ALREADY HEAR HER VOICE.
"SHE WILL BE MARRIED AT SIXTEEN! MY GOOD, KIND BROTHER! DEAR, CRIPPLED WICKHAM! WHAT A HUSBAND HE SHALL MAKE!"
"MRS. WICKHAM! HOW WELL IT SOUNDS!"

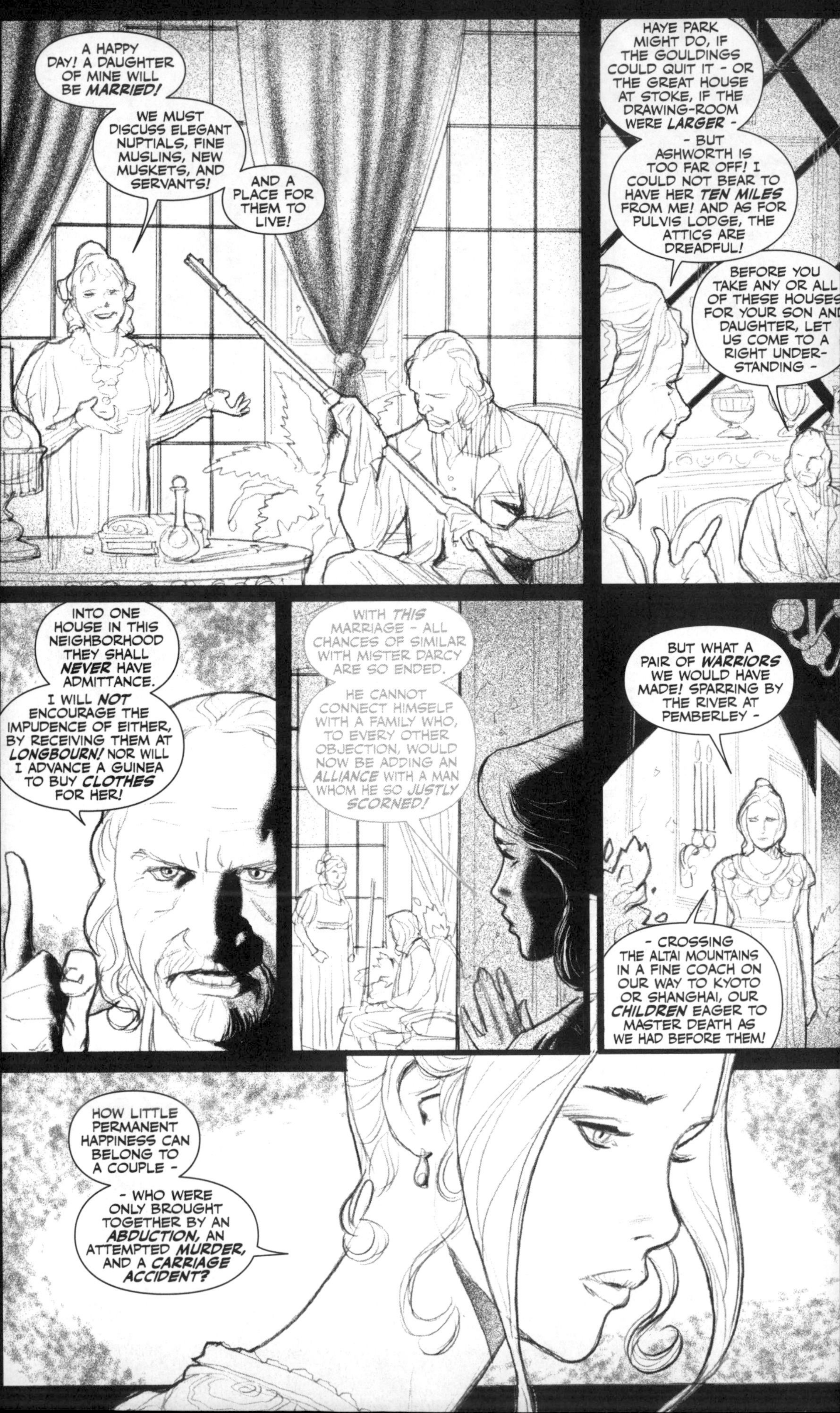
A HAPPY DAY! A DAUGHTER OF MINE WILL BE MARRIED!
WE MUST DISCUSS ELEGANT NUPTIALS, FINE MUSLINS, NEW MUSKETS, AND SERVANTS!
AND A PLACE FOR THEM TO LIVE!
HAYE PARK MIGHT DO, IF THE GOULDINGS COULD QUIT IT - OR THE GREAT HOUSE AT STOKE, IF THE DRAWING-ROOM WERE LARGER -
- BUT ASHWORTH IS TOO FAR OFF! I COULD NOT BEAR TO HAVE HER TEN MILES FROM ME! AND AS FOR PULVIS LODGE, THE ATTICS ARE DREADFUL!
BEFORE YOU TAKE ANY OR ALL OF THESE HOUSES FOR YOUR SON AND DAUGHTER, LET US COME TO A RIGHT UNDER-STANDING -
INTO ONE HOUSE IN THIS NEIGHBORHOOD THEY SHALL NEVER HAVE ADMITTANCE.
I WILL NOT ENCOURAGE THE IMPUDENCE OF EITHER, BY RECEIVING THEM AT LONGBOURN! NOR WILL I ADVANCE A GUINEA TO BUY CLOTHES FOR HER!
WITH THIS MARRIAGE - ALL CHANCES OF SIMILAR WITH MISTER DARCY ARE SO ENDED.
HE CANNOT CONNECT HIMSELF WITH A FAMILY WHO, TO EVERY OTHER OBJECTION, WOULD NOW BE ADDING AN ALLIANCE WITH A MAN WHOM HE SO JUSTLY SCORNED!
BUT WHAT A PAIR OF WARRIORS WE WOULD HAVE MADE! SPARRING BY THE RIVER AT PEMBERLEY -
- CROSSING THE ALTAI MOUNTAINS IN A FINE COACH ON OUR WAY TO KYOTO OR SHANGHAI, OUR CHILDREN EAGER TO MASTER DEATH AS WE HAD BEFORE THEM!
HOW LITTLE PERMANENT HAPPINESS CAN BELONG TO A COUPLE -
- WHO WERE ONLY BROUGHT TOGETHER BY AN ABDUCTION, AN ATTEMPTED MURDER, AND A CARRIAGE ACCIDENT?

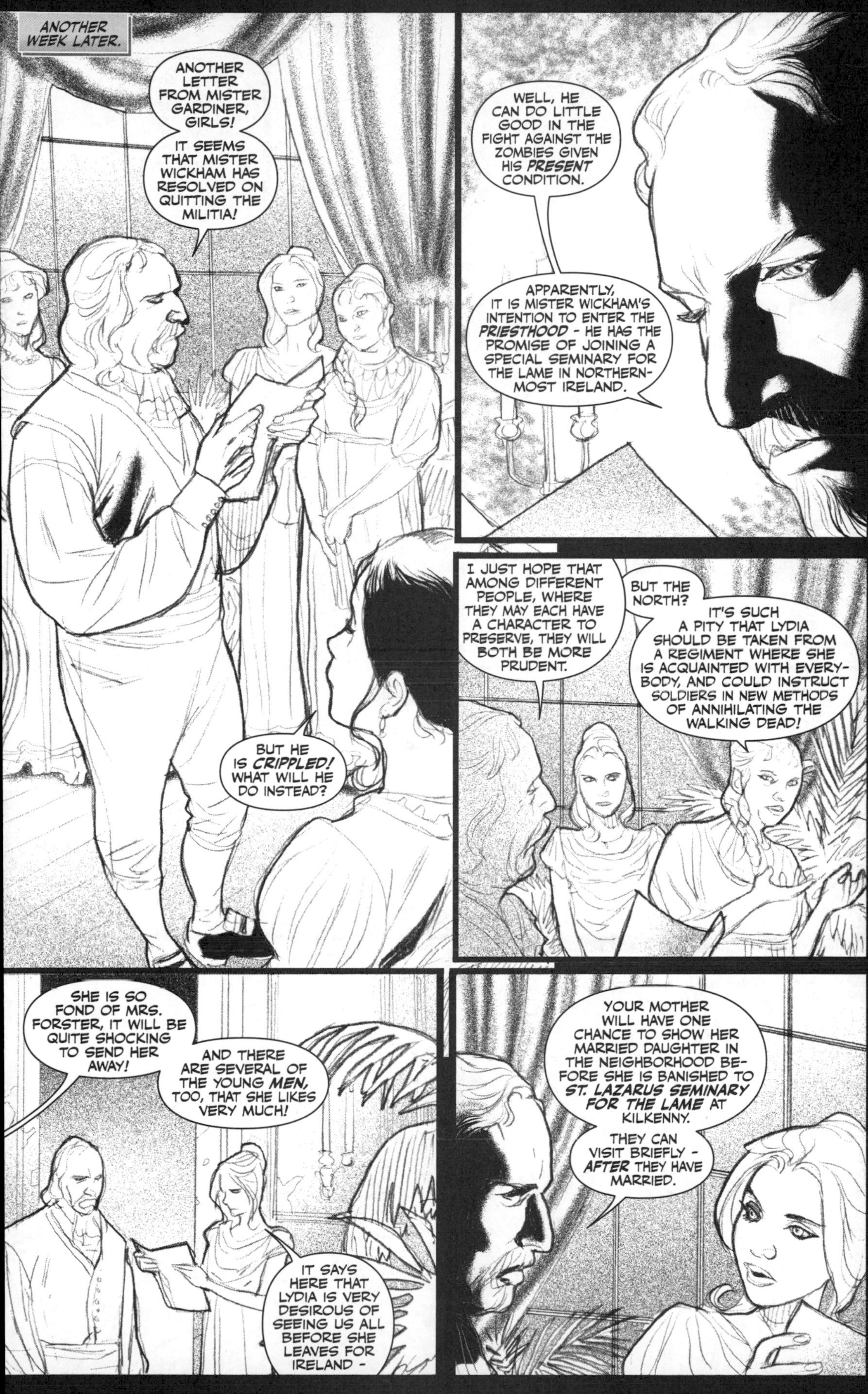
ANOTHER WEEK LATER.
ANOTHER LETTER FROM MISTER GARDINER, GIRLS!
IT SEEMS THAT MISTER WICKHAM HAS RESOLVED ON QUITTING THE MILITIA!
WELL, HE CAN DO LITTLE GOOD IN THE FIGHT AGAINST THE ZOMBIES GIVEN HIS PRESENT CONDITION.
APPARENTLY, IT IS MISTER WICKHAM'S INTENTION TO ENTER THE PRIESTHOOD - HE HAS THE PROMISE OF JOINING A SPECIAL SEMINARY FOR THE LAME IN NORTHERN-MOST IRELAND.
BUT HE IS CRIPPLED! WHAT WILL HE DO INSTEAD?
I JUST HOPE THAT AMONG DIFFERENT PEOPLE, WHERE THEY MAY EACH HAVE A CHARACTER TO PRESERVE, THEY WILL BOTH BE MORE PRUDENT.
BUT THE NORTH?
IT'S SUCH A PITY THAT LYDIA SHOULD BE TAKEN FROM A REGIMENT WHERE SHE IS ACQUAINTED WITH EVERY-BODY, AND COULD INSTRUCT SOLDIERS IN NEW METHODS OF ANNIHILATING THE WALKING DEAD!
SHE IS SO FOND OF MRS. FORSTER, IT WILL BE QUITE SHOCKING TO SEND HER AWAY!
AND THERE ARE SEVERAL OF THE YOUNG MEN, TOO, THAT SHE LIKES VERY MUCH!
IT SAYS HERE THAT LYDIA IS VERY DESIROUS OF SEEING US ALL BEFORE SHE LEAVES FOR IRELAND -
YOUR MOTHER WILL HAVE ONE CHANCE TO SHOW HER MARRIED DAUGHTER IN THE NEIGHBORHOOD BE-FORE SHE IS BANISHED TO ST. LAZARUS SEMINARY FOR THE LAME AT KILKENNY.
THEY CAN VISIT BRIEFLY - AFTER THEY HAVE MARRIED.

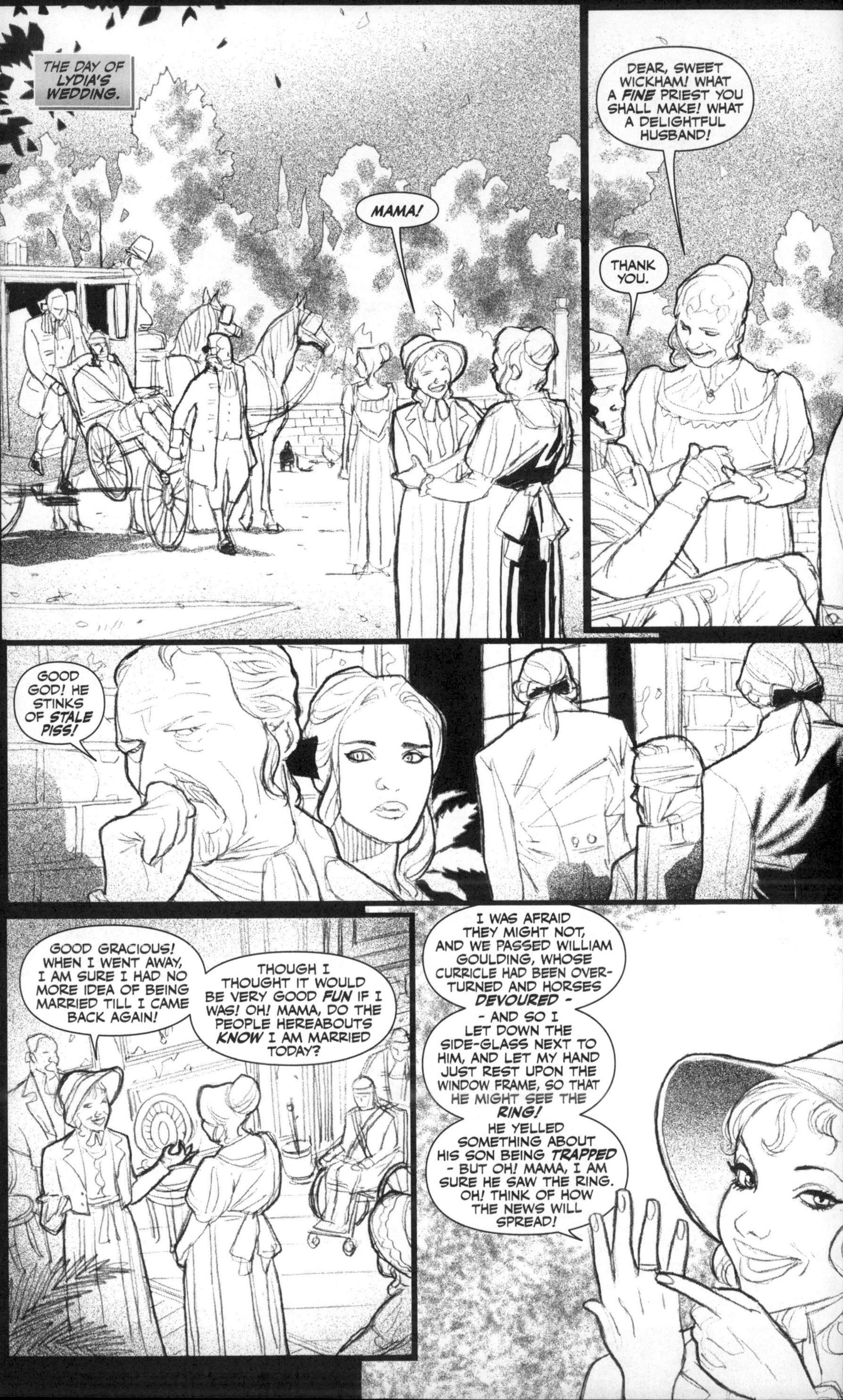
THE DAY OF LYDIA'S WEDDING.
MAMA!
DEAR, SWEET WICKHAM! WHAT A FINE PRIEST YOU SHALL MAKE! WHAT A DELIGHTFUL HUSBAND!
THANK YOU.
GOOD GOD! HE STINKS OF STALE PISS!
GOOD GRACIOUS! WHEN I WENT AWAY, I AM SURE I HAD NO MORE IDEA OF BEING MARRIED TILL I CAME BACK AGAIN!
THOUGH I THOUGHT IT WOULD BE VERY GOOD FUN IF I WAS! OH! MAMA, DO THE PEOPLE HEREABOUTS KNOW I AM MARRIED TODAY?
I WAS AFRAID THEY MIGHT NOT, AND WE PASSED WILLIAM GOULDING, WHOSE CURRICLE HAD BEEN OVER-TURNED AND HORSES DEVOURED -
- AND SO I LET DOWN THE SIDE-GLASS NEXT TO HIM, AND LET MY HAND JUST REST UPON THE WINDOW FRAME, SO THAT HE MIGHT SEE THE RING!
HE YELLED SOMETHING ABOUT HIS SON BEING TRAPPED - BUT OH! MAMA, I AM SURE HE SAW THE RING. OH! THINK OF HOW THE NEWS WILL SPREAD!

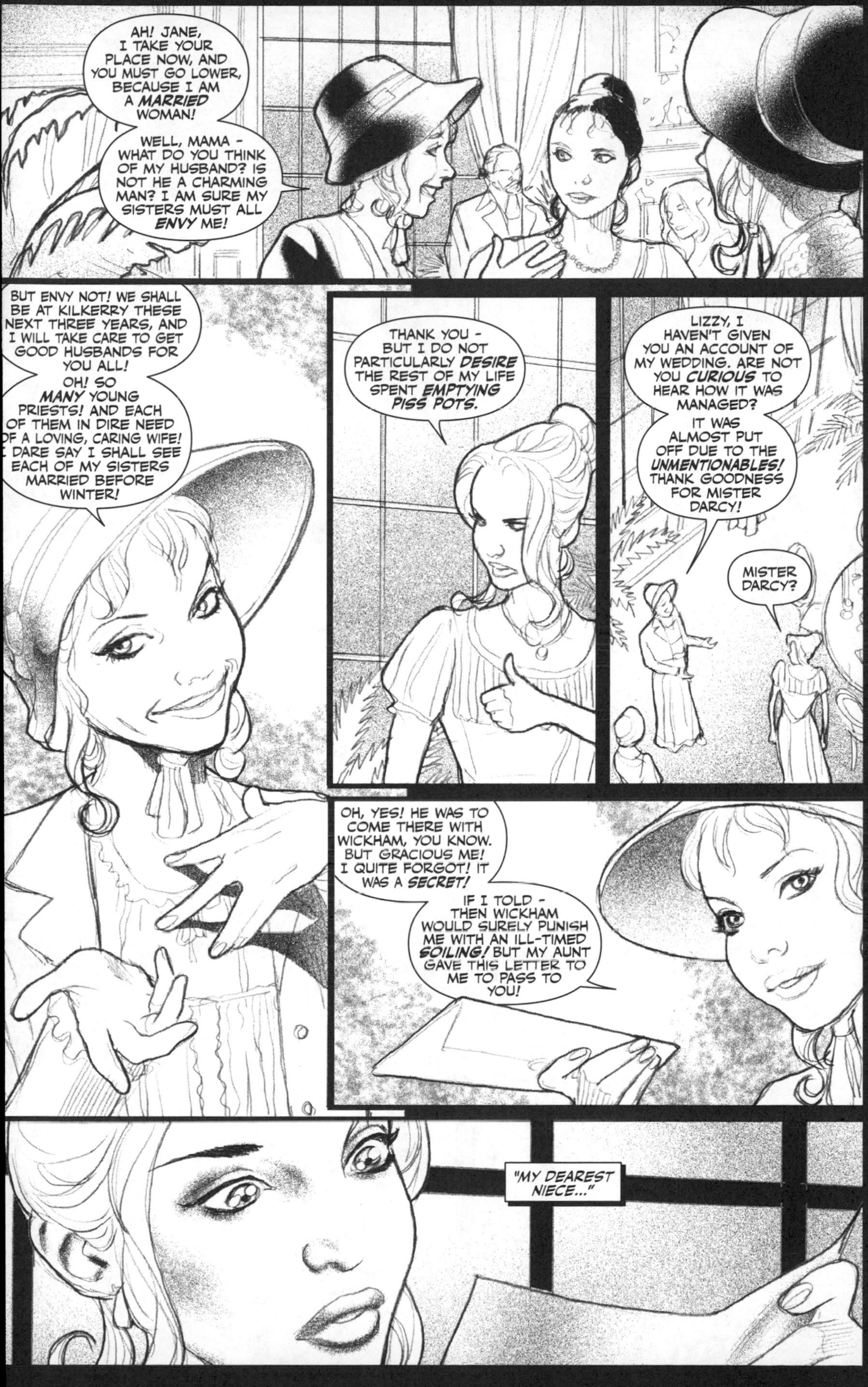
AH! JANE, I TAKE YOUR PLACE NOW, AND YOU MUST GO LOWER, BECAUSE I AM A MARRIED WOMAN!
WELL, MAMA - WHAT DO YOU THINK OF MY HUSBAND? IS NOT HE A CHARMING MAN? I AM SURE MY SISTERS MUST ALL ENVY ME!
BUT ENVY NOT! WE SHALL BE AT KILKERRY THESE NEXT THREE YEARS, AND I WILL TAKE CARE TO GET GOOD HUSBANDS FOR YOU ALL!
OH! SO MANY YOUNG PRIESTS! AND EACH OF THEM IN DIRE NEED OF A LOVING, CARING WIFE! I DARE SAY I SHALL SEE EACH OF MY SISTERS MARRIED BEFORE WINTER!
THANK YOU - BUT I DO NOT PARTICULARLY DESIRE THE REST OF MY LIFE SPENT EMPTYING PISS POTS.
LIZZY, I HAVEN'T GIVEN YOU AN ACCOUNT OF MY WEDDING. ARE NOT YOU CURIOUS TO HEAR HOW IT WAS MANAGED?
IT WAS ALMOST PUT OFF DUE TO THE UNMENTIONABLES! THANK GOODNESS FOR MISTER DARCY!
MISTER DARCY?
OH, YES! HE WAS TO COME THERE WITH WICKHAM, YOU KNOW. BUT GRACIOUS ME! I QUITE FORGOT! IT WAS A SECRET!
IF I TOLD - THEN WICKHAM WOULD SURELY PUNISH ME WITH AN ILL-TIMED SOILING! BUT MY AUNT GAVE THIS LETTER TO ME TO PASS TO YOU!
"MY DEAREST NIECE..."

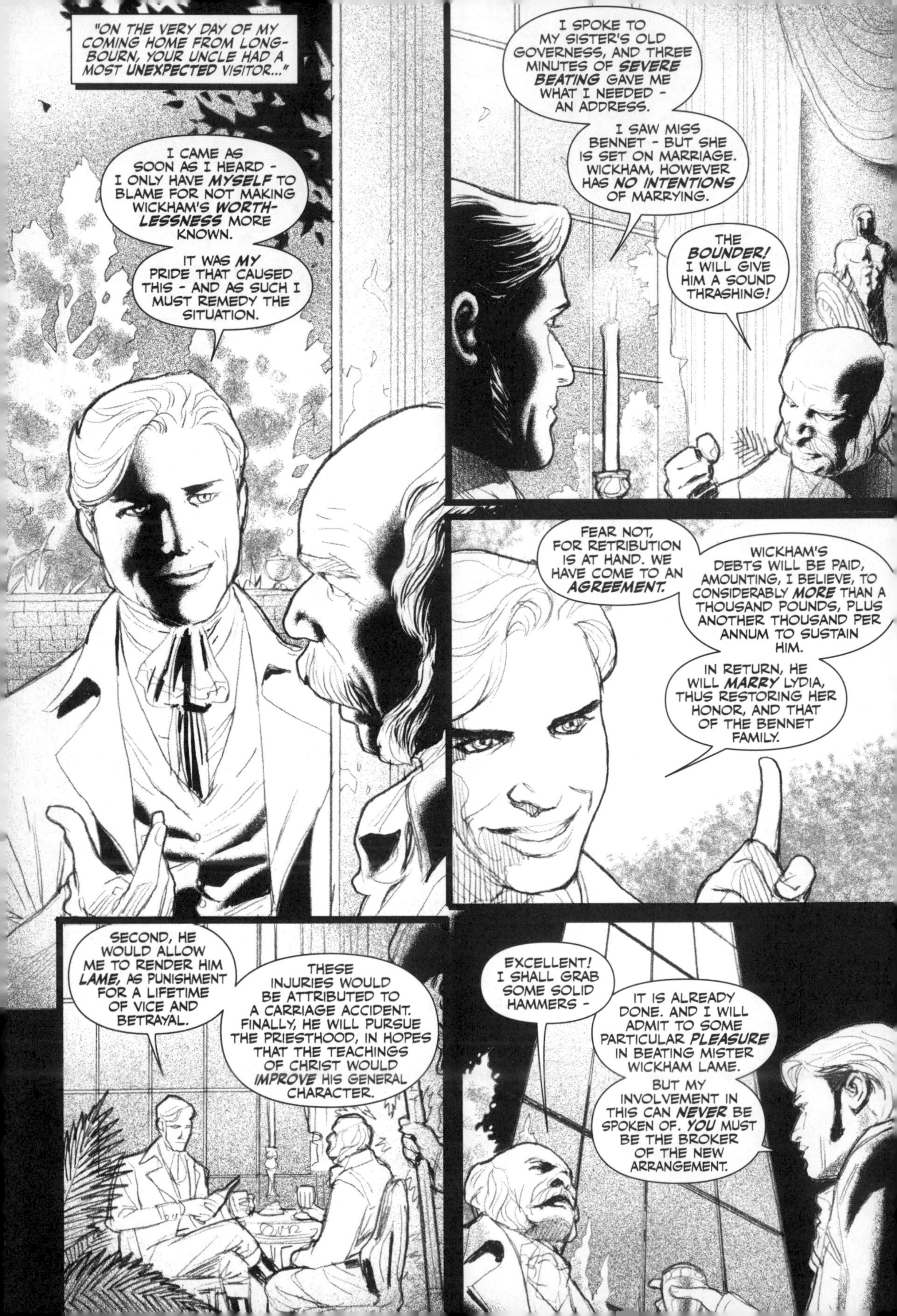
"ON THE VERY DAY OF MY COMING HOME FROM LONG-BOURN, YOUR UNCLE HAD A MOST *UNEXPECTED* VISITOR..."
I CAME AS SOON AS I HEARD - I ONLY HAVE *MYSELF* TO BLAME FOR NOT MAKING WICKHAM'S *WORTH-LESSNESS* MORE KNOWN.
IT WAS *MY* PRIDE THAT CAUSED THIS - AND AS SUCH I MUST REMEDY THE SITUATION.
I SPOKE TO MY SISTER'S OLD GOVERNESS, AND THREE MINUTES OF *SEVERE BEATING* GAVE ME WHAT I NEEDED - AN ADDRESS.
I SAW MISS BENNET - BUT SHE IS SET ON MARRIAGE. WICKHAM, HOWEVER HAS *NO INTENTIONS* OF MARRYING.
THE *BOUNDER!* I WILL GIVE HIM A SOUND THRASHING!
FEAR NOT, FOR RETRIBUTION IS AT HAND. WE HAVE COME TO AN *AGREEMENT.*
WICKHAM'S DEBTS WILL BE PAID, AMOUNTING, I BELIEVE, TO CONSIDERABLY *MORE* THAN A THOUSAND POUNDS, PLUS ANOTHER THOUSAND PER ANNUM TO SUSTAIN HIM.
IN RETURN, HE WILL *MARRY* LYDIA, THUS RESTORING HER HONOR, AND THAT OF THE BENNET FAMILY.
SECOND, HE WOULD ALLOW ME TO RENDER HIM *LAME,* AS PUNISHMENT FOR A LIFETIME OF VICE AND BETRAYAL.
THESE INJURIES WOULD BE ATTRIBUTED TO A CARRIAGE ACCIDENT. FINALLY, HE WILL PURSUE THE PRIESTHOOD, IN HOPES THAT THE TEACHINGS OF CHRIST WOULD *IMPROVE* HIS GENERAL CHARACTER.
EXCELLENT! I SHALL GRAB SOME SOLID HAMMERS -
IT IS ALREADY DONE. AND I WILL ADMIT TO SOME PARTICULAR *PLEASURE* IN BEATING MISTER WICKHAM LAME.
BUT MY INVOLVEMENT IN THIS CAN *NEVER* BE SPOKEN OF. *YOU* MUST BE THE BROKER OF THE NEW ARRANGEMENT.

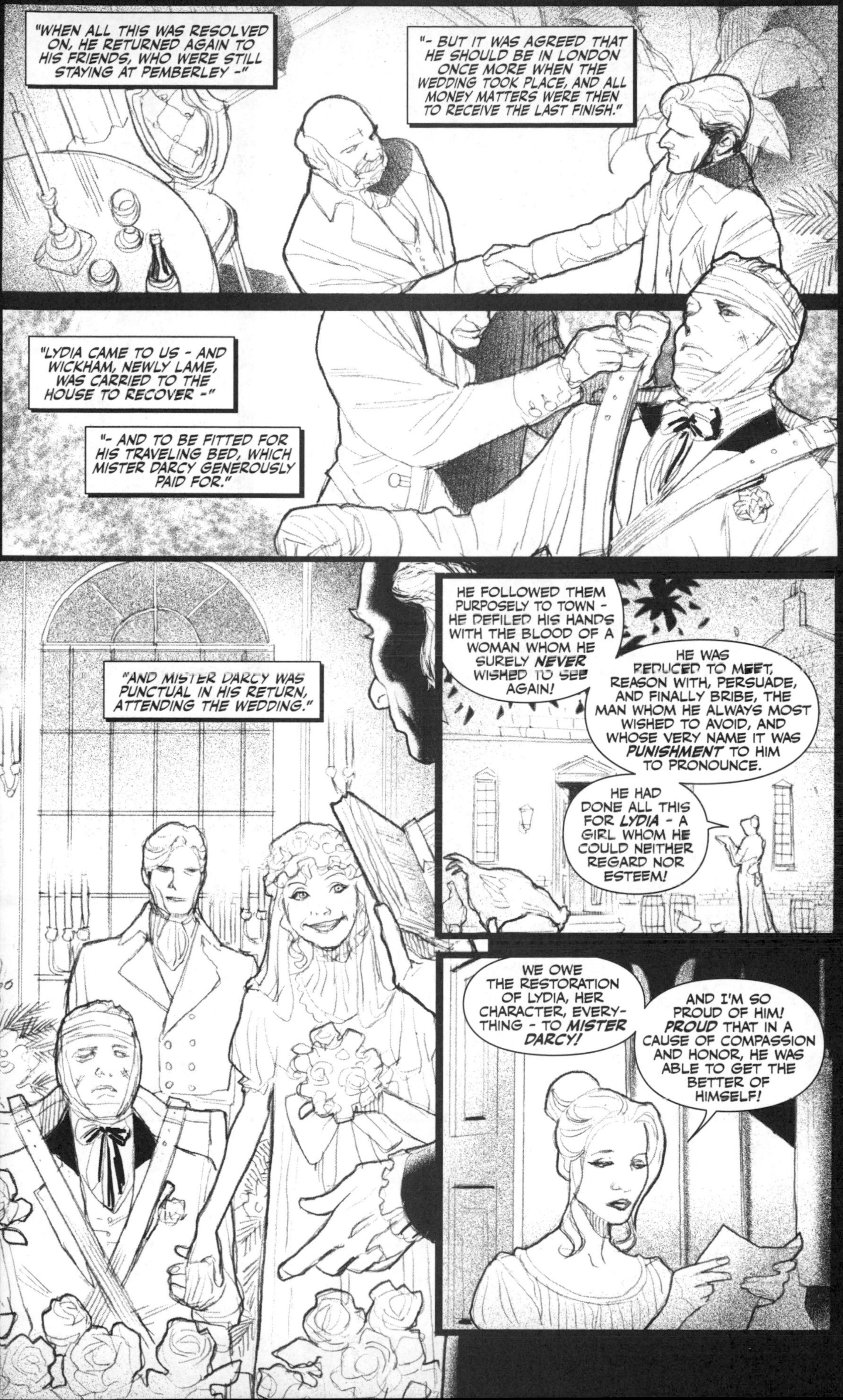
"WHEN ALL THIS WAS RESOLVED ON, HE RETURNED AGAIN TO HIS FRIENDS, WHO WERE STILL STAYING AT PEMBERLEY -"
"- BUT IT WAS AGREED THAT HE SHOULD BE IN LONDON ONCE MORE WHEN THE WEDDING TOOK PLACE, AND ALL MONEY MATTERS WERE THEN TO RECEIVE THE LAST FINISH."
"LYDIA CAME TO US - AND WICKHAM, NEWLY LAME, WAS CARRIED TO THE HOUSE TO RECOVER -"
"- AND TO BE FITTED FOR HIS TRAVELING BED, WHICH MISTER DARCY GENEROUSLY PAID FOR."
"AND MISTER DARCY WAS PUNCTUAL IN HIS RETURN, ATTENDING THE WEDDING."
HE FOLLOWED THEM PURPOSELY TO TOWN - HE DEFILED HIS HANDS WITH THE BLOOD OF A WOMAN WHOM HE SURELY NEVER WISHED TO SEE AGAIN!
HE WAS REDUCED TO MEET, REASON WITH, PERSUADE, AND FINALLY BRIBE, THE MAN WHOM HE ALWAYS MOST WISHED TO AVOID, AND WHOSE VERY NAME IT WAS PUNISHMENT TO HIM TO PRONOUNCE.
HE HAD DONE ALL THIS FOR LYDIA - A GIRL WHOM HE COULD NEITHER REGARD NOR ESTEEM!
WE OWE THE RESTORATION OF LYDIA, HER CHARACTER, EVERY-THING - TO MISTER DARCY!
AND I'M SO PROUD OF HIM! PROUD THAT IN A CAUSE OF COMPASSION AND HONOR, HE WAS ABLE TO GET THE BETTER OF HIMSELF!

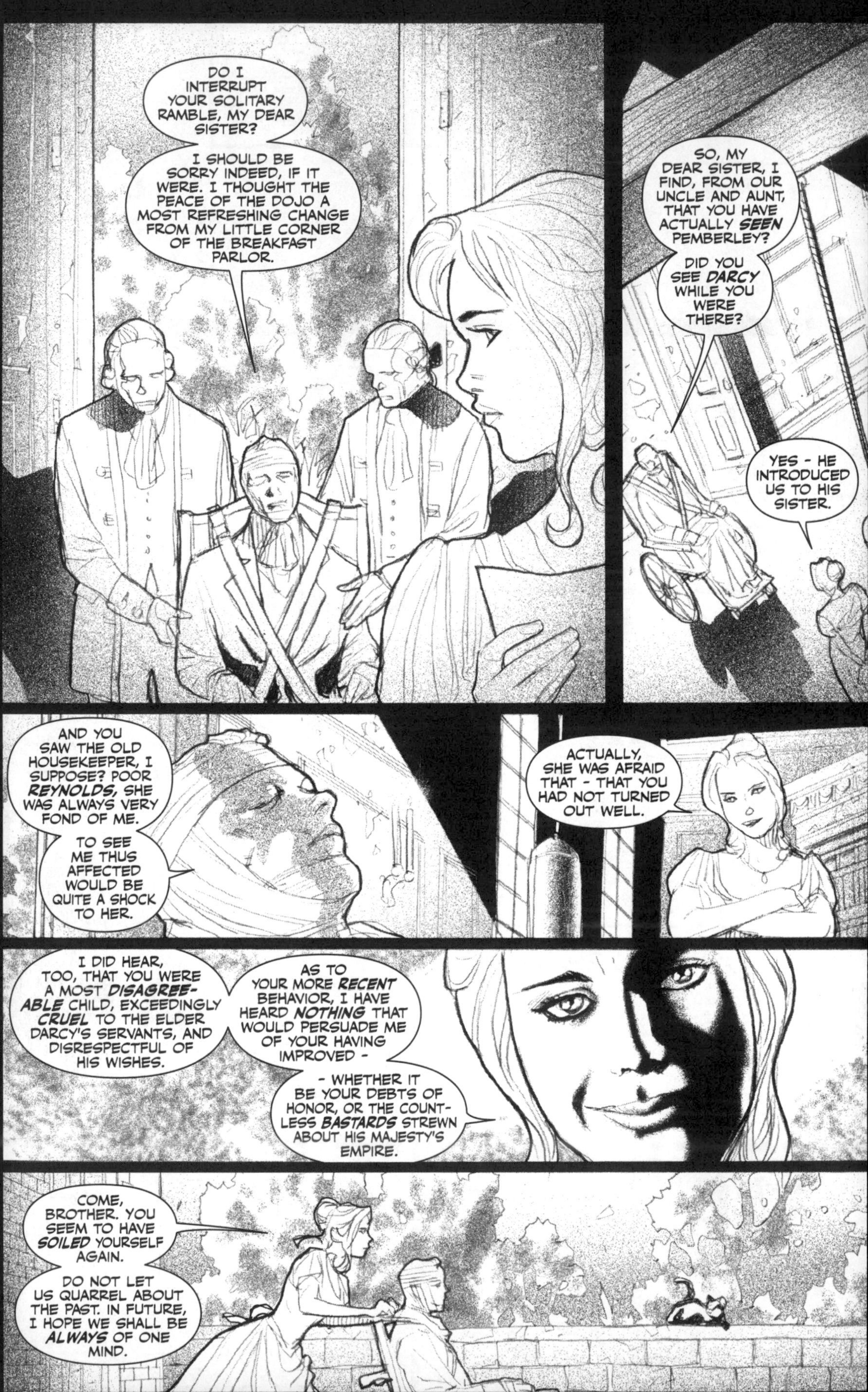
DO I INTERRUPT YOUR SOLITARY RAMBLE, MY DEAR SISTER?
I SHOULD BE SORRY INDEED, IF IT WERE. I THOUGHT THE PEACE OF THE DOJO A MOST REFRESHING CHANGE FROM MY LITTLE CORNER OF THE BREAKFAST PARLOR.
SO, MY DEAR SISTER, I FIND, FROM OUR UNCLE AND AUNT, THAT YOU HAVE ACTUALLY SEEN PEMBERLEY?
DID YOU SEE DARCY WHILE YOU WERE THERE?
YES - HE INTRODUCED US TO HIS SISTER.
AND YOU SAW THE OLD HOUSEKEEPER, I SUPPOSE? POOR REYNOLDS, SHE WAS ALWAYS VERY FOND OF ME.
TO SEE ME THUS AFFECTED WOULD BE QUITE A SHOCK TO HER.
ACTUALLY, SHE WAS AFRAID THAT - THAT YOU HAD NOT TURNED OUT WELL.
I DID HEAR, TOO, THAT YOU WERE A MOST DISAGREE-ABLE CHILD, EXCEEDINGLY CRUEL TO THE ELDER DARCY'S SERVANTS, AND DISRESPECTFUL OF HIS WISHES.
AS TO YOUR MORE RECENT BEHAVIOR, I HAVE HEARD NOTHING THAT WOULD PERSUADE ME OF YOUR HAVING IMPROVED -
- WHETHER IT BE YOUR DEBTS OF HONOR, OR THE COUNT-LESS BASTARDS STREWN ABOUT HIS MAJESTY'S EMPIRE.
COME, BROTHER. YOU SEEM TO HAVE SOILED YOURSELF AGAIN.
DO NOT LET US QUARREL ABOUT THE PAST. IN FUTURE, I HOPE WE SHALL BE ALWAYS OF ONE MIND.

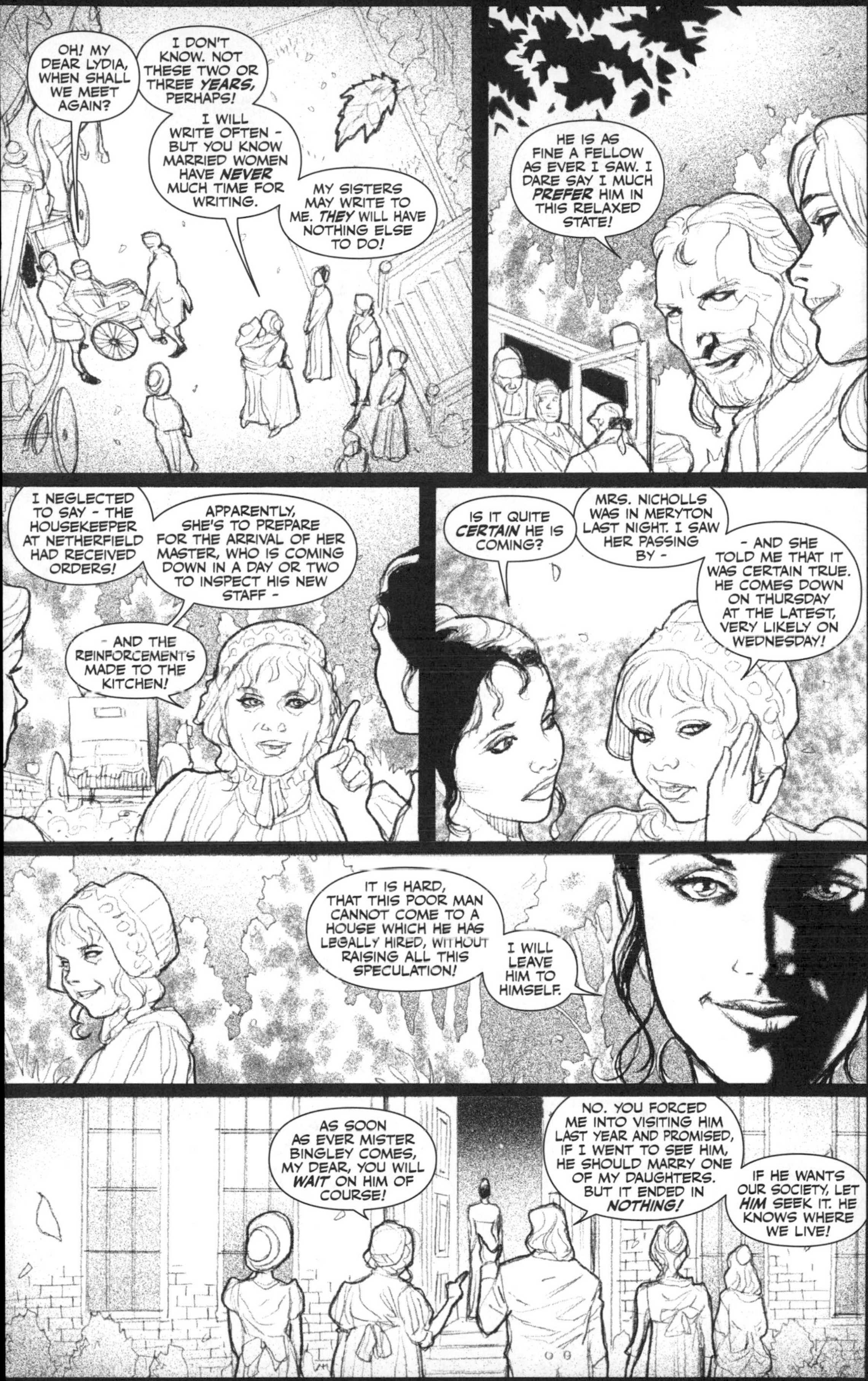
OH! MY DEAR LYDIA, WHEN SHALL WE MEET AGAIN?
I DON'T KNOW. NOT THESE TWO OR THREE YEARS, PERHAPS!
I WILL WRITE OFTEN - BUT YOU KNOW MARRIED WOMEN HAVE NEVER MUCH TIME FOR WRITING.
MY SISTERS MAY WRITE TO ME. THEY WILL HAVE NOTHING ELSE TO DO!
HE IS AS FINE A FELLOW AS EVER I SAW. I DARE SAY I MUCH PREFER HIM IN THIS RELAXED STATE!
I NEGLECTED TO SAY - THE HOUSEKEEPER AT NETHERFIELD HAD RECEIVED ORDERS!
APPARENTLY, SHE'S TO PREPARE FOR THE ARRIVAL OF HER MASTER, WHO IS COMING DOWN IN A DAY OR TWO TO INSPECT HIS NEW STAFF -
- AND THE REINFORCEMENTS MADE TO THE KITCHEN!
IS IT QUITE CERTAIN HE IS COMING?
MRS. NICHOLLS WAS IN MERYTON LAST NIGHT. I SAW HER PASSING BY -
- AND SHE TOLD ME THAT IT WAS CERTAIN TRUE. HE COMES DOWN ON THURSDAY AT THE LATEST, VERY LIKELY ON WEDNESDAY!
IT IS HARD, THAT THIS POOR MAN CANNOT COME TO A HOUSE WHICH HE HAS LEGALLY HIRED, WITHOUT RAISING ALL THIS SPECULATION!
I WILL LEAVE HIM TO HIMSELF.
AS SOON AS EVER MISTER BINGLEY COMES, MY DEAR, YOU WILL WAIT ON HIM OF COURSE!
NO. YOU FORCED ME INTO VISITING HIM LAST YEAR AND PROMISED, IF I WENT TO SEE HIM, HE SHOULD MARRY ONE OF MY DAUGHTERS. BUT IT ENDED IN NOTHING!
IF HE WANTS OUR SOCIETY, LET HIM SEEK IT. HE KNOWS WHERE WE LIVE!

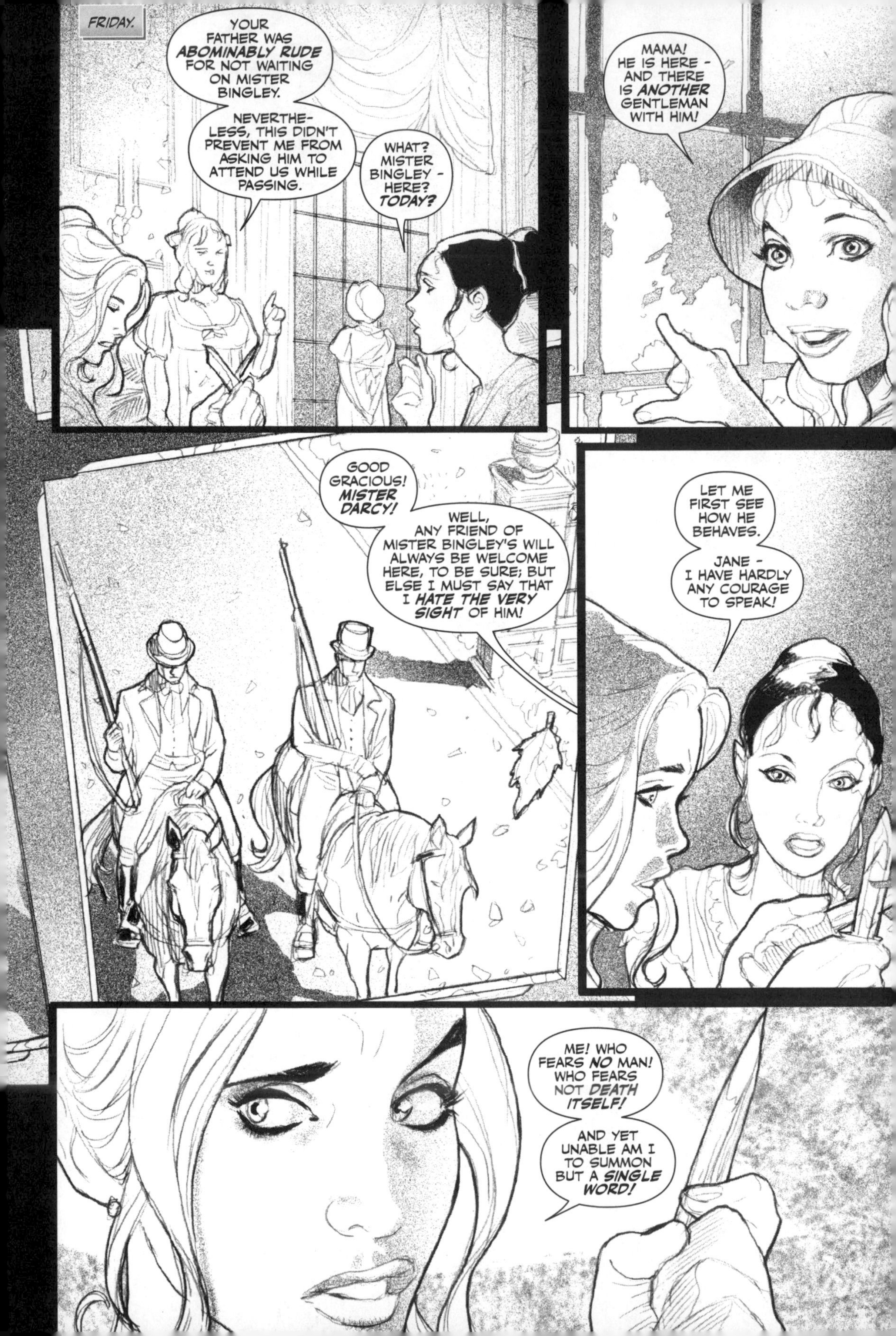
FRIDAY.
YOUR FATHER WAS ABOMINABLY RUDE FOR NOT WAITING ON MISTER BINGLEY.
NEVERTHE-LESS, THIS DIDN'T PREVENT ME FROM ASKING HIM TO ATTEND US WHILE PASSING.
WHAT? MISTER BINGLEY - HERE? TODAY?
MAMA! HE IS HERE - AND THERE IS ANOTHER GENTLEMAN WITH HIM!
GOOD GRACIOUS! MISTER DARCY!
WELL, ANY FRIEND OF MISTER BINGLEY'S WILL ALWAYS BE WELCOME HERE, TO BE SURE; BUT ELSE I MUST SAY THAT I HATE THE VERY SIGHT OF HIM!
LET ME FIRST SEE HOW HE BEHAVES.
JANE - I HAVE HARDLY ANY COURAGE TO SPEAK!
ME! WHO FEARS NO MAN! WHO FEARS NOT DEATH ITSELF!
AND YET UNABLE AM I TO SUMMON BUT A SINGLE WORD!

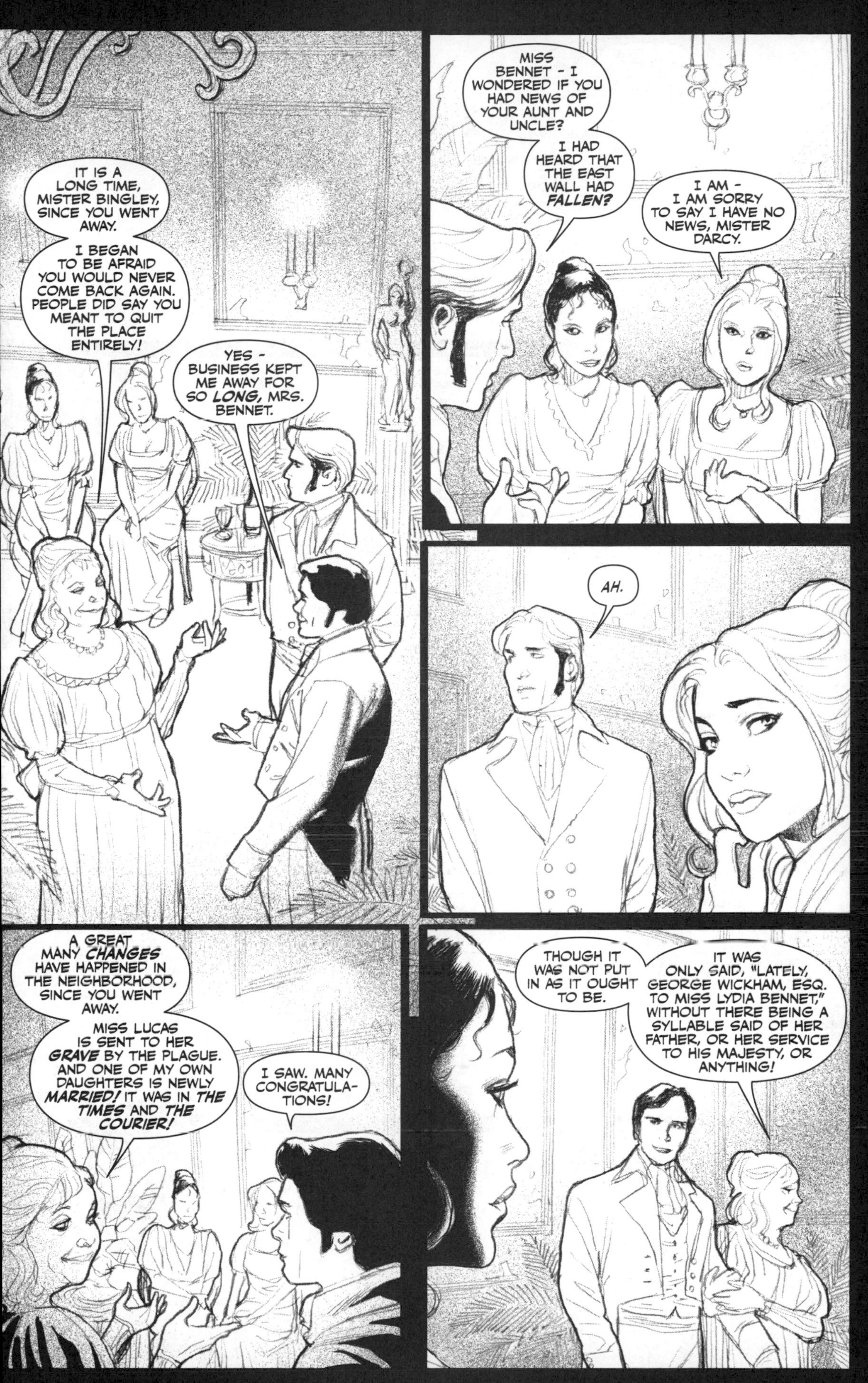
IT IS A LONG TIME, MISTER BINGLEY, SINCE YOU WENT AWAY.
I BEGAN TO BE AFRAID YOU WOULD NEVER COME BACK AGAIN. PEOPLE DID SAY YOU MEANT TO QUIT THE PLACE ENTIRELY!
YES - BUSINESS KEPT ME AWAY FOR SO LONG, MRS. BENNET.
MISS BENNET - I WONDERED IF YOU HAD NEWS OF YOUR AUNT AND UNCLE?
I HAD HEARD THAT THE EAST WALL HAD FALLEN?
I AM - I AM SORRY TO SAY I HAVE NO NEWS, MISTER DARCY.
AH.
A GREAT MANY CHANGES HAVE HAPPENED IN THE NEIGHBORHOOD, SINCE YOU WENT AWAY.
MISS LUCAS IS SENT TO HER GRAVE BY THE PLAGUE. AND ONE OF MY OWN DAUGHTERS IS NEWLY MARRIED! IT WAS IN THE TIMES AND THE COURIER!
I SAW. MANY CONGRATULATIONS!
THOUGH IT WAS NOT PUT IN AS IT OUGHT TO BE.
IT WAS ONLY SAID, "LATELY, GEORGE WICKHAM, ESQ. TO MISS LYDIA BENNET," WITHOUT THERE BEING A SYLLABLE SAID OF HER FATHER, OR HER SERVICE TO HIS MAJESTY, OR ANYTHING!

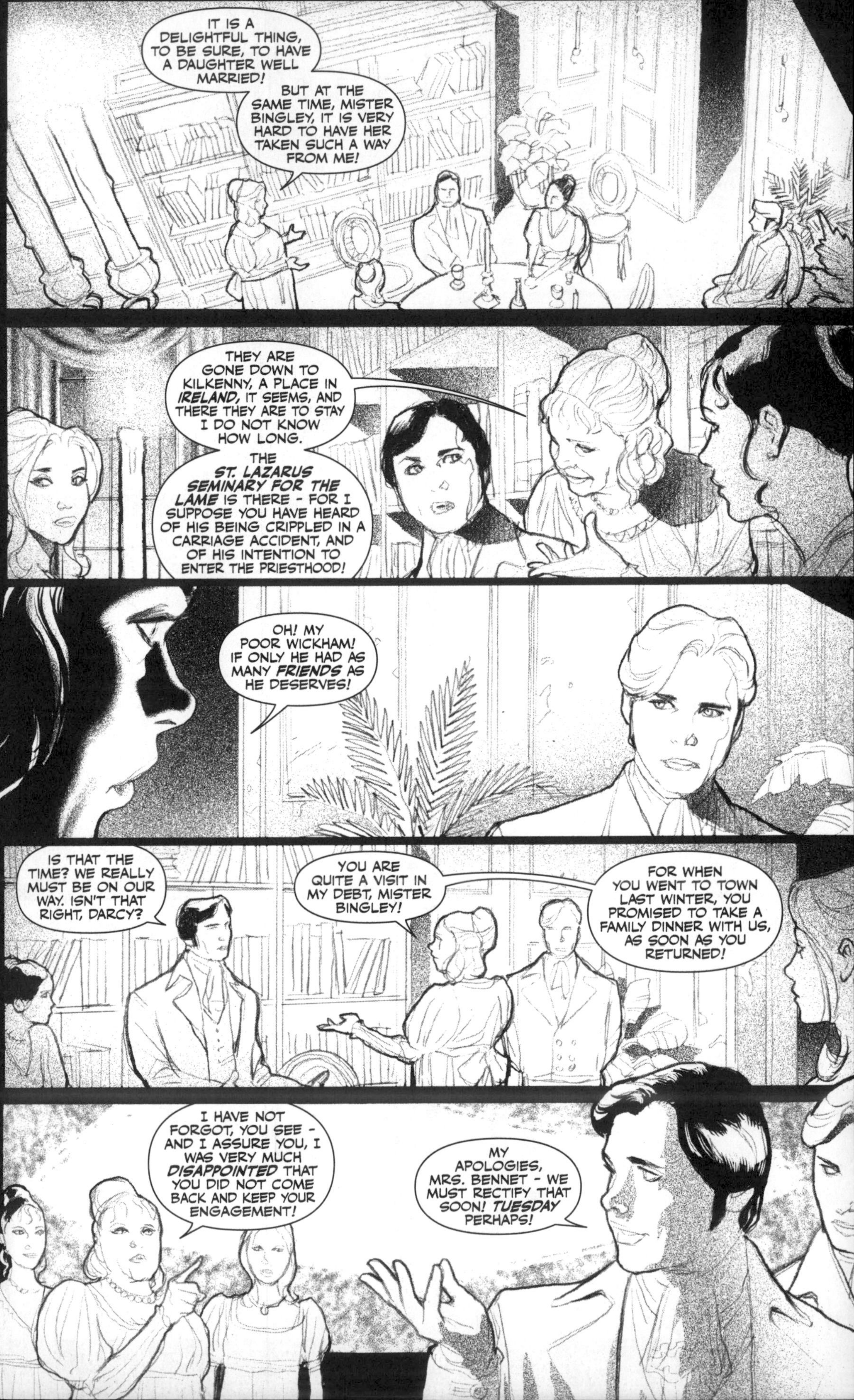
IT IS A DELIGHTFUL THING, TO BE SURE, TO HAVE A DAUGHTER WELL MARRIED!
BUT AT THE SAME TIME, MISTER BINGLEY, IT IS VERY HARD TO HAVE HER TAKEN SUCH A WAY FROM ME!
THEY ARE GONE DOWN TO KILKENNY, A PLACE IN *IRELAND,* IT SEEMS, AND THERE THEY ARE TO STAY I DO NOT KNOW HOW LONG.
THE ***ST. LAZARUS SEMINARY FOR THE LAME*** IS THERE - FOR I SUPPOSE YOU HAVE HEARD OF HIS BEING CRIPPLED IN A CARRIAGE ACCIDENT, AND OF HIS INTENTION TO ENTER THE PRIESTHOOD!
OH! MY POOR WICKHAM! IF ONLY HE HAD AS MANY ***FRIENDS*** AS HE DESERVES!
IS THAT THE TIME? WE REALLY MUST BE ON OUR WAY. ISN'T THAT RIGHT, DARCY?
YOU ARE QUITE A VISIT IN MY DEBT, MISTER BINGLEY!
FOR WHEN YOU WENT TO TOWN LAST WINTER, YOU PROMISED TO TAKE A FAMILY DINNER WITH US, AS SOON AS YOU RETURNED!
I HAVE NOT FORGOT, YOU SEE - AND I ASSURE YOU, I WAS VERY MUCH ***DISAPPOINTED*** THAT YOU DID NOT COME BACK AND KEEP YOUR ENGAGEMENT!
MY APOLOGIES, MRS. BENNET - WE MUST RECTIFY THAT SOON! ***TUESDAY*** PERHAPS!

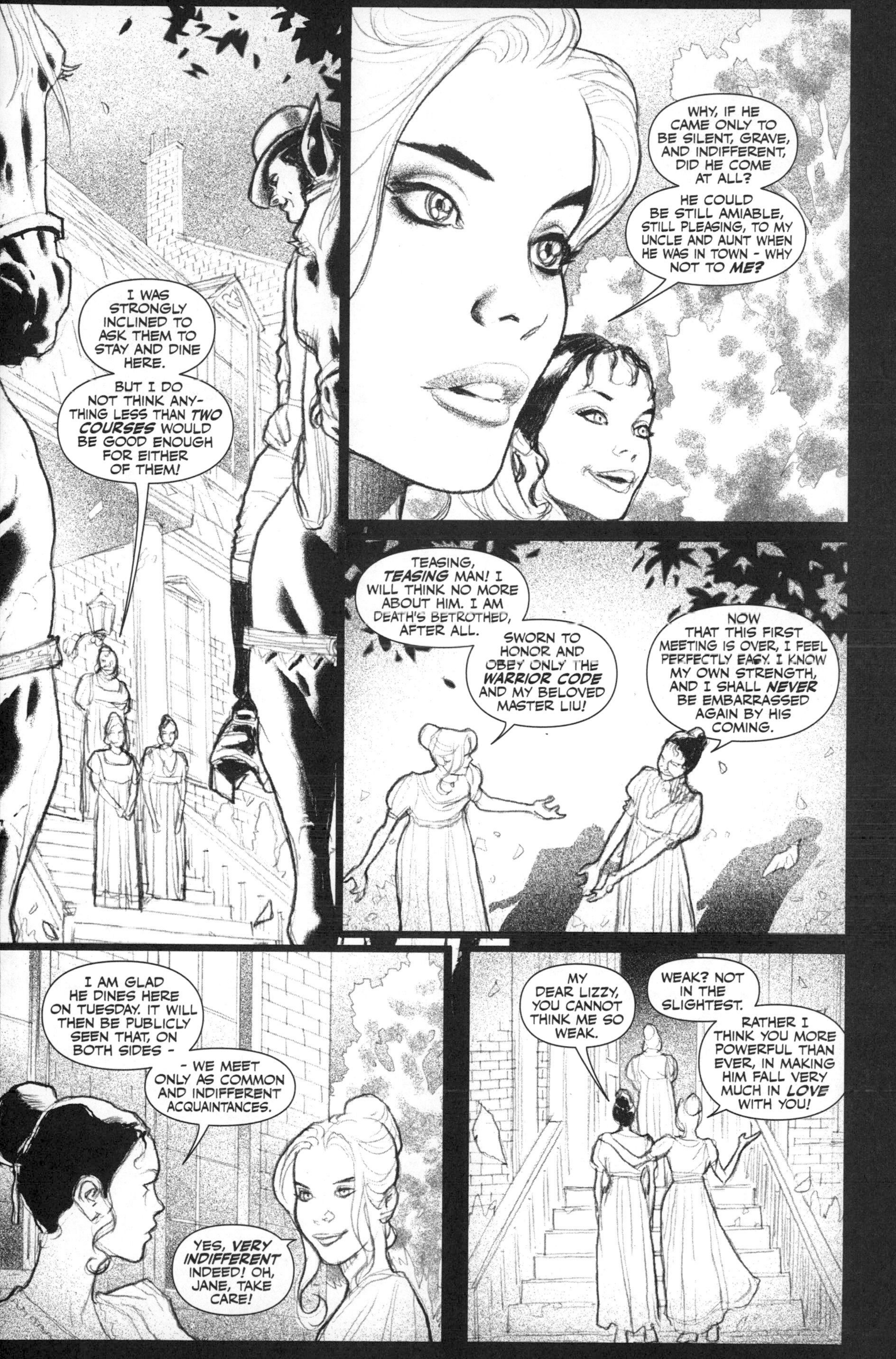
I WAS STRONGLY INCLINED TO ASK THEM TO STAY AND DINE HERE.
BUT I DO NOT THINK ANY-THING LESS THAN TWO COURSES WOULD BE GOOD ENOUGH FOR EITHER OF THEM!
WHY, IF HE CAME ONLY TO BE SILENT, GRAVE, AND INDIFFERENT, DID HE COME AT ALL?
HE COULD BE STILL AMIABLE, STILL PLEASING, TO MY UNCLE AND AUNT WHEN HE WAS IN TOWN - WHY NOT TO ME?
TEASING, TEASING MAN! I WILL THINK NO MORE ABOUT HIM. I AM DEATH'S BETROTHED, AFTER ALL.
SWORN TO HONOR AND OBEY ONLY THE WARRIOR CODE AND MY BELOVED MASTER LIU!
NOW THAT THIS FIRST MEETING IS OVER, I FEEL PERFECTLY EASY. I KNOW MY OWN STRENGTH, AND I SHALL NEVER BE EMBARRASSED AGAIN BY HIS COMING.
I AM GLAD HE DINES HERE ON TUESDAY. IT WILL THEN BE PUBLICLY SEEN THAT, ON BOTH SIDES -
- WE MEET ONLY AS COMMON AND INDIFFERENT ACQUAINTANCES.
YES, VERY INDIFFERENT INDEED! OH, JANE, TAKE CARE!
MY DEAR LIZZY, YOU CANNOT THINK ME SO WEAK.
WEAK? NOT IN THE SLIGHTEST.
RATHER I THINK YOU MORE POWERFUL THAN EVER, IN MAKING HIM FALL VERY MUCH IN LOVE WITH YOU!

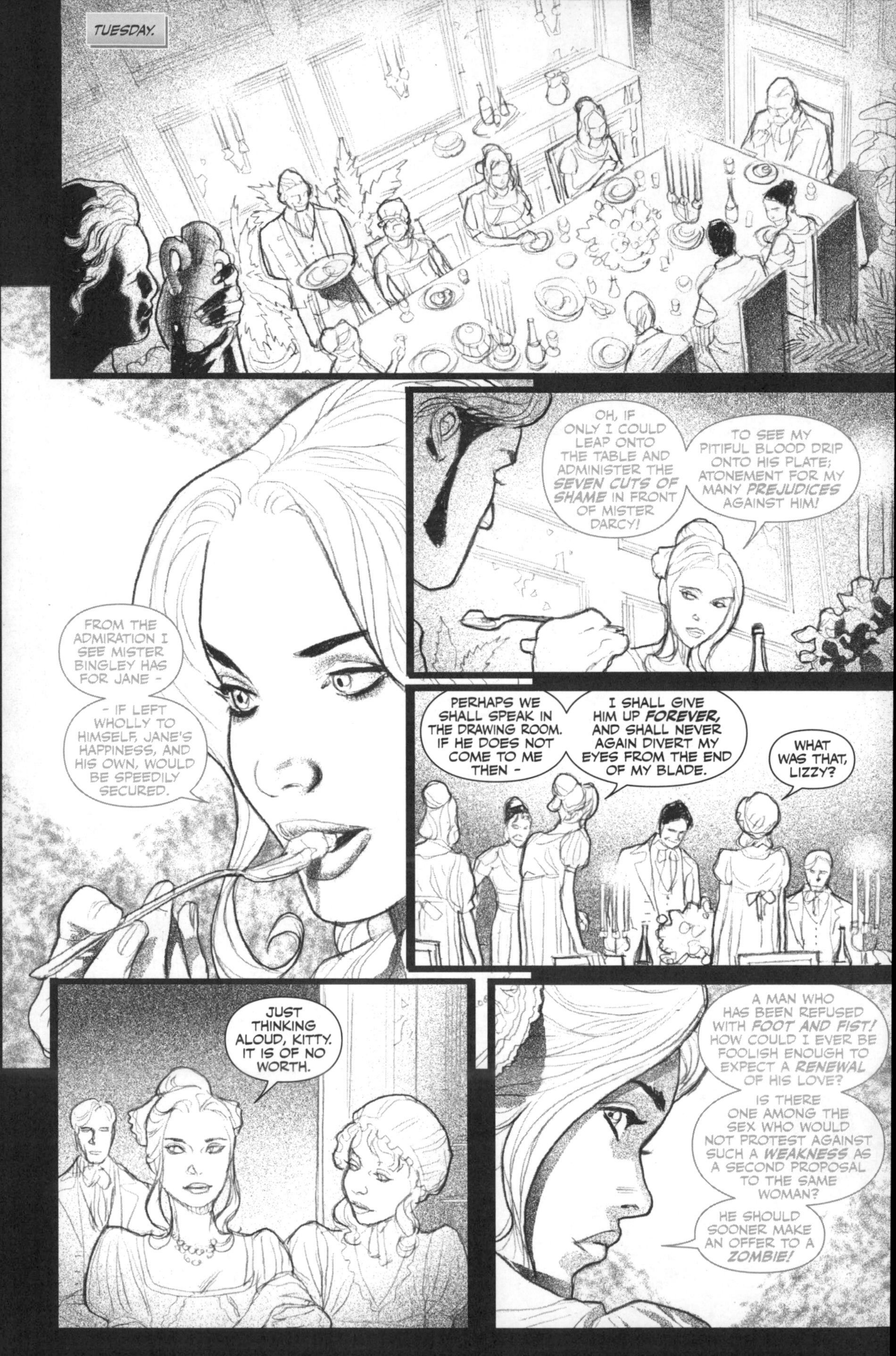
TUESDAY.
OH, IF ONLY I COULD LEAP ONTO THE TABLE AND ADMINISTER THE SEVEN CUTS OF SHAME IN FRONT OF MISTER DARCY!
TO SEE MY PITIFUL BLOOD DRIP ONTO HIS PLATE; ATONEMENT FOR MY MANY PREJUDICES AGAINST HIM!
FROM THE ADMIRATION I SEE MISTER BINGLEY HAS FOR JANE -
- IF LEFT WHOLLY TO HIMSELF, JANE'S HAPPINESS, AND HIS OWN, WOULD BE SPEEDILY SECURED.
PERHAPS WE SHALL SPEAK IN THE DRAWING ROOM. IF HE DOES NOT COME TO ME THEN -
I SHALL GIVE HIM UP FOREVER, AND SHALL NEVER AGAIN DIVERT MY EYES FROM THE END OF MY BLADE.
WHAT WAS THAT, LIZZY?
JUST THINKING ALOUD, KITTY. IT IS OF NO WORTH.
A MAN WHO HAS BEEN REFUSED WITH FOOT AND FIST! HOW COULD I EVER BE FOOLISH ENOUGH TO EXPECT A RENEWAL OF HIS LOVE?
IS THERE ONE AMONG THE SEX WHO WOULD NOT PROTEST AGAINST SUCH A WEAKNESS AS A SECOND PROPOSAL TO THE SAME WOMAN?
HE SHOULD SOONER MAKE AN OFFER TO A ZOMBIE!

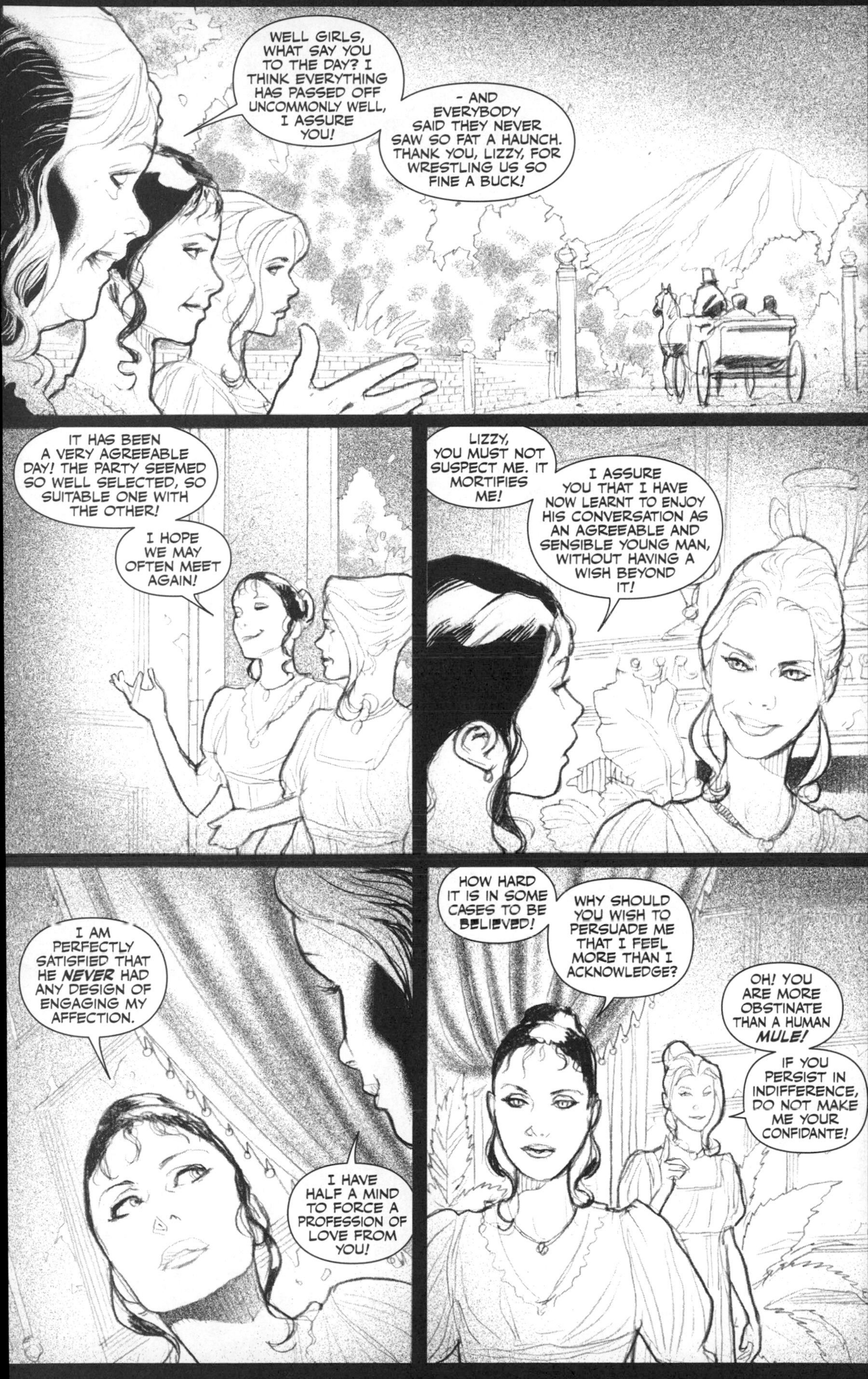

WELL GIRLS, WHAT SAY YOU TO THE DAY? I THINK EVERYTHING HAS PASSED OFF UNCOMMONLY WELL, I ASSURE YOU!
- AND EVERYBODY SAID THEY NEVER SAW SO FAT A HAUNCH. THANK YOU, LIZZY, FOR WRESTLING US SO FINE A BUCK!
IT HAS BEEN A VERY AGREEABLE DAY! THE PARTY SEEMED SO WELL SELECTED, SO SUITABLE ONE WITH THE OTHER!
I HOPE WE MAY OFTEN MEET AGAIN!
LIZZY, YOU MUST NOT SUSPECT ME. IT MORTIFIES ME!
I ASSURE YOU THAT I HAVE NOW LEARNT TO ENJOY HIS CONVERSATION AS AN AGREEABLE AND SENSIBLE YOUNG MAN, WITHOUT HAVING A WISH BEYOND IT!
I AM PERFECTLY SATISFIED THAT HE ***NEVER*** HAD ANY DESIGN OF ENGAGING MY AFFECTION.
I HAVE HALF A MIND TO FORCE A PROFESSION OF LOVE FROM YOU!
HOW HARD IT IS IN SOME CASES TO BE BELIEVED!
WHY SHOULD YOU WISH TO PERSUADE ME THAT I FEEL MORE THAN I ACKNOWLEDGE?
OH! YOU ARE MORE OBSTINATE THAN A HUMAN ***MULE!***
IF YOU PERSIST IN INDIFFERENCE, DO NOT MAKE ME YOUR CONFIDANTE!

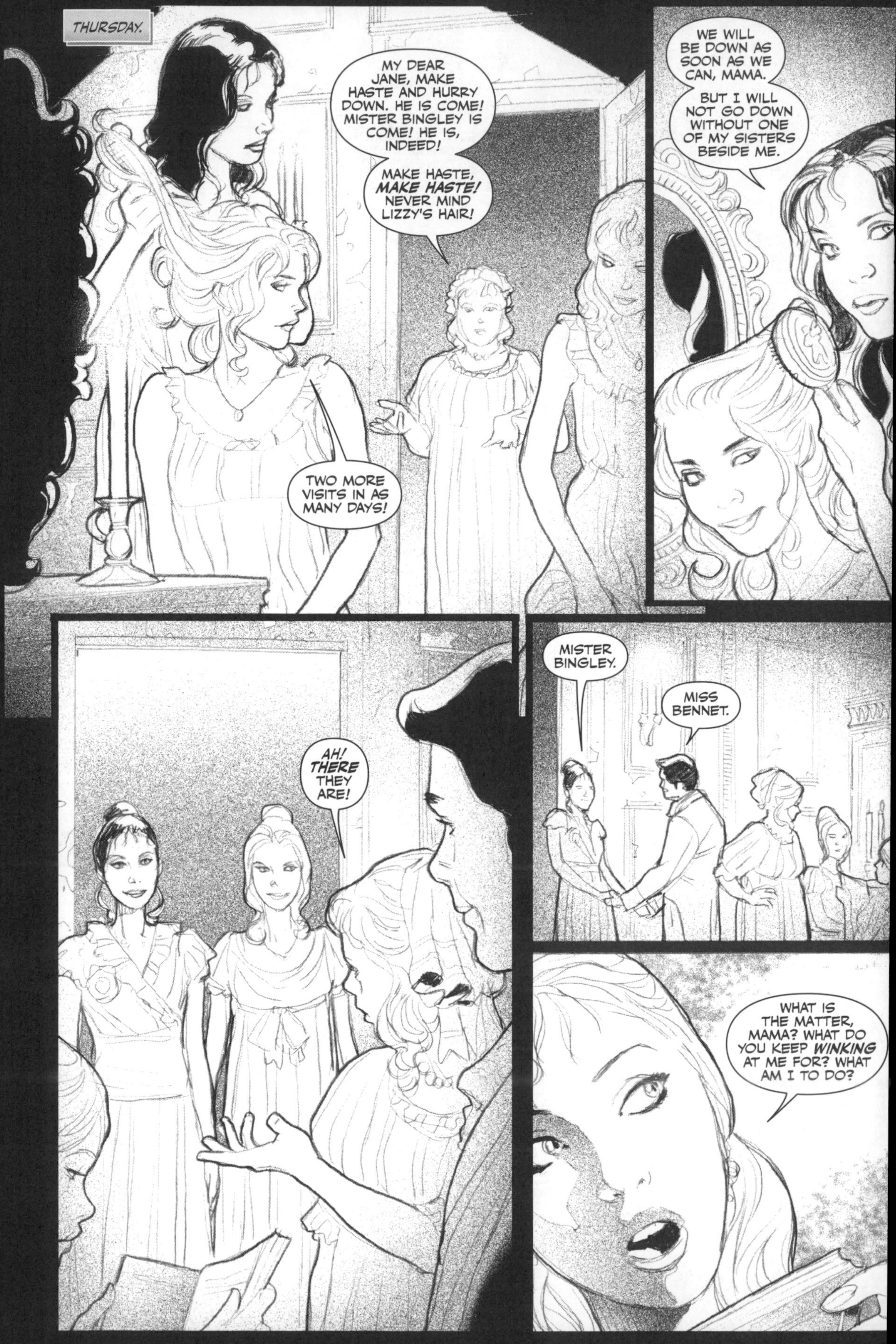
THURSDAY.
MY DEAR JANE, MAKE HASTE AND HURRY DOWN. HE IS COME! MISTER BINGLEY IS COME! HE IS, INDEED!
MAKE HASTE, *MAKE HASTE!* NEVER MIND LIZZY'S HAIR!
TWO MORE VISITS IN AS MANY DAYS!
WE WILL BE DOWN AS SOON AS WE CAN, MAMA.
BUT I WILL NOT GO DOWN WITHOUT ONE OF MY SISTERS BESIDE ME.
AH! *THERE* THEY ARE!
MISTER BINGLEY.
MISS BENNET.
WHAT IS THE MATTER, MAMA? WHAT DO YOU KEEP *WINKING* AT ME FOR? WHAT AM I TO DO?

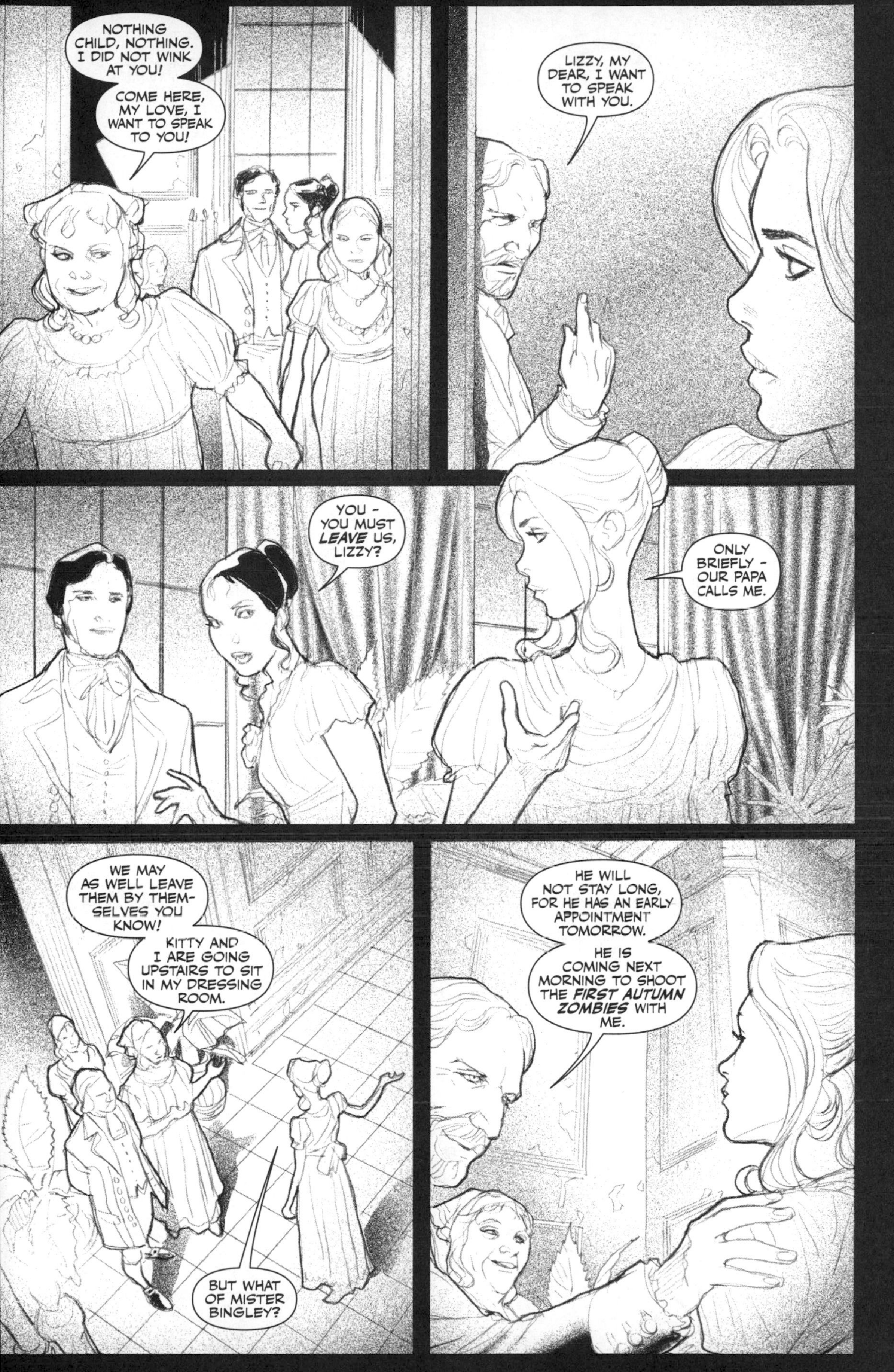
NOTHING CHILD, NOTHING. I DID NOT WINK AT YOU!
COME HERE, MY LOVE, I WANT TO SPEAK TO YOU!
LIZZY, MY DEAR, I WANT TO SPEAK WITH YOU.
YOU - YOU MUST *LEAVE* US, LIZZY?
ONLY BRIEFLY - OUR PAPA CALLS ME.
WE MAY AS WELL LEAVE THEM BY THEMSELVES YOU KNOW!
KITTY AND I ARE GOING UPSTAIRS TO SIT IN MY DRESSING ROOM.
BUT WHAT OF MISTER BINGLEY?
HE WILL NOT STAY LONG, FOR HE HAS AN EARLY APPOINTMENT TOMORROW.
HE IS COMING NEXT MORNING TO SHOOT THE *FIRST AUTUMN ZOMBIES* WITH ME.

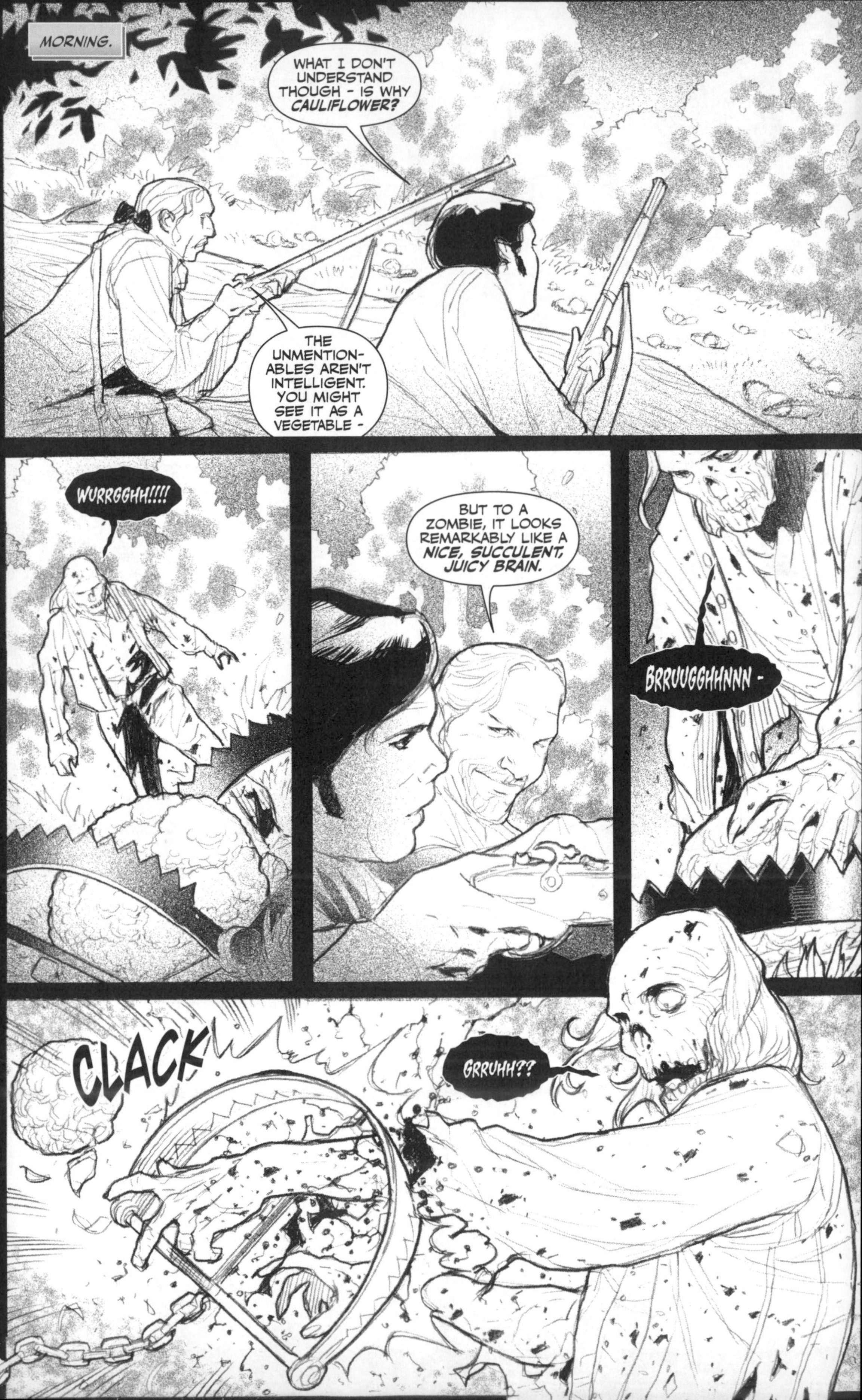
MORNING.
WHAT I DON'T UNDERSTAND THOUGH - IS WHY CAULIFLOWER?
THE UNMENTION-ABLES AREN'T INTELLIGENT. YOU MIGHT SEE IT AS A VEGETABLE -
WURRGGHH!!!!
BUT TO A ZOMBIE, IT LOOKS REMARKABLY LIKE A NICE, SUCCULENT, JUICY BRAIN.
BRRUUGGHHNNN -
CLACK
GRRUHH??

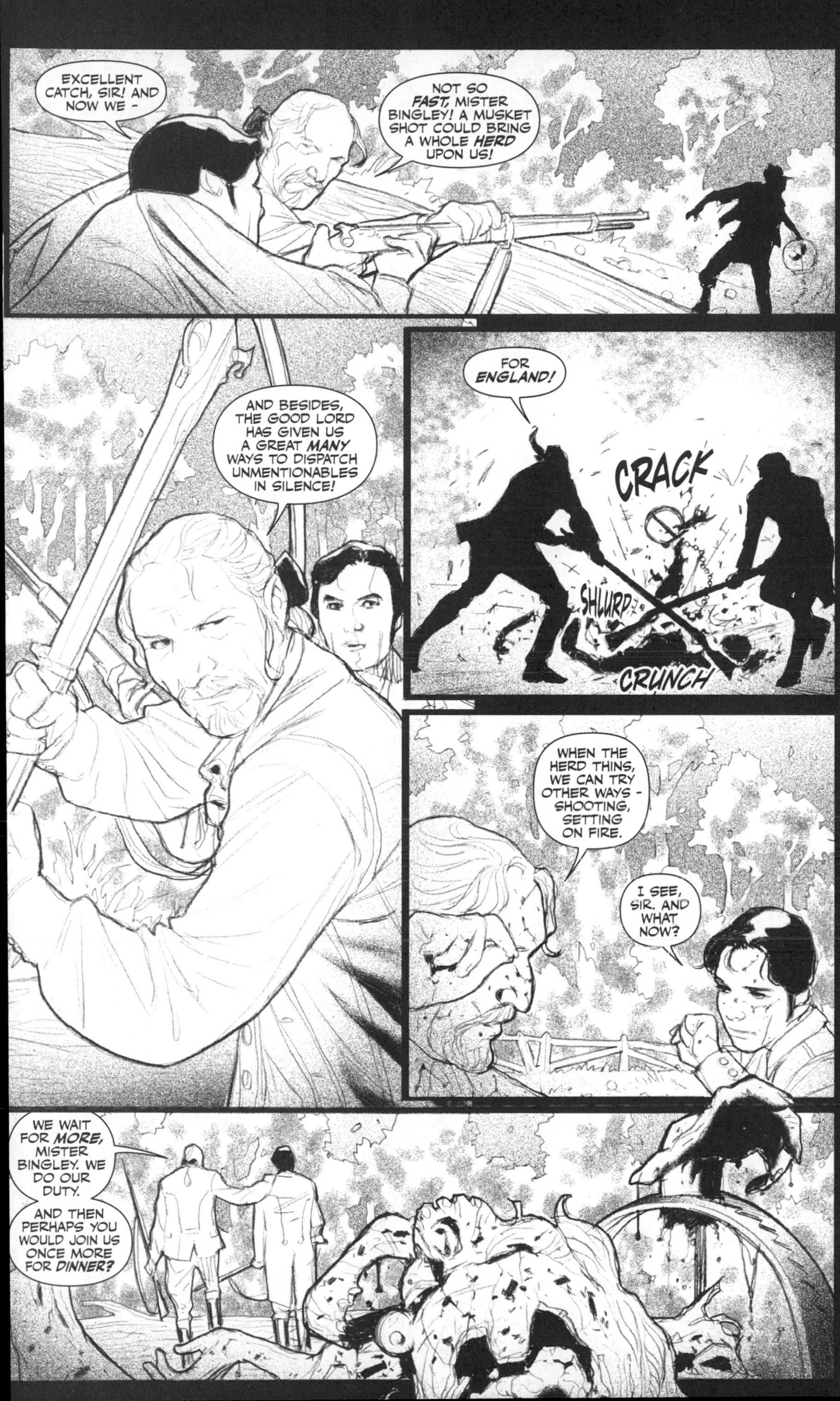
EXCELLENT CATCH, SIR! AND NOW WE -
NOT SO FAST, MISTER BINGLEY! A MUSKET SHOT COULD BRING A WHOLE HERD UPON US!
AND BESIDES, THE GOOD LORD HAS GIVEN US A GREAT MANY WAYS TO DISPATCH UNMENTIONABLES IN SILENCE!
FOR ENGLAND!
CRACK
SHLURP
CRUNCH
WHEN THE HERD THINS, WE CAN TRY OTHER WAYS - SHOOTING, SETTING ON FIRE.
I SEE, SIR. AND WHAT NOW?
WE WAIT FOR MORE, MISTER BINGLEY. WE DO OUR DUTY.
AND THEN PERHAPS YOU WOULD JOIN US ONCE MORE FOR DINNER?

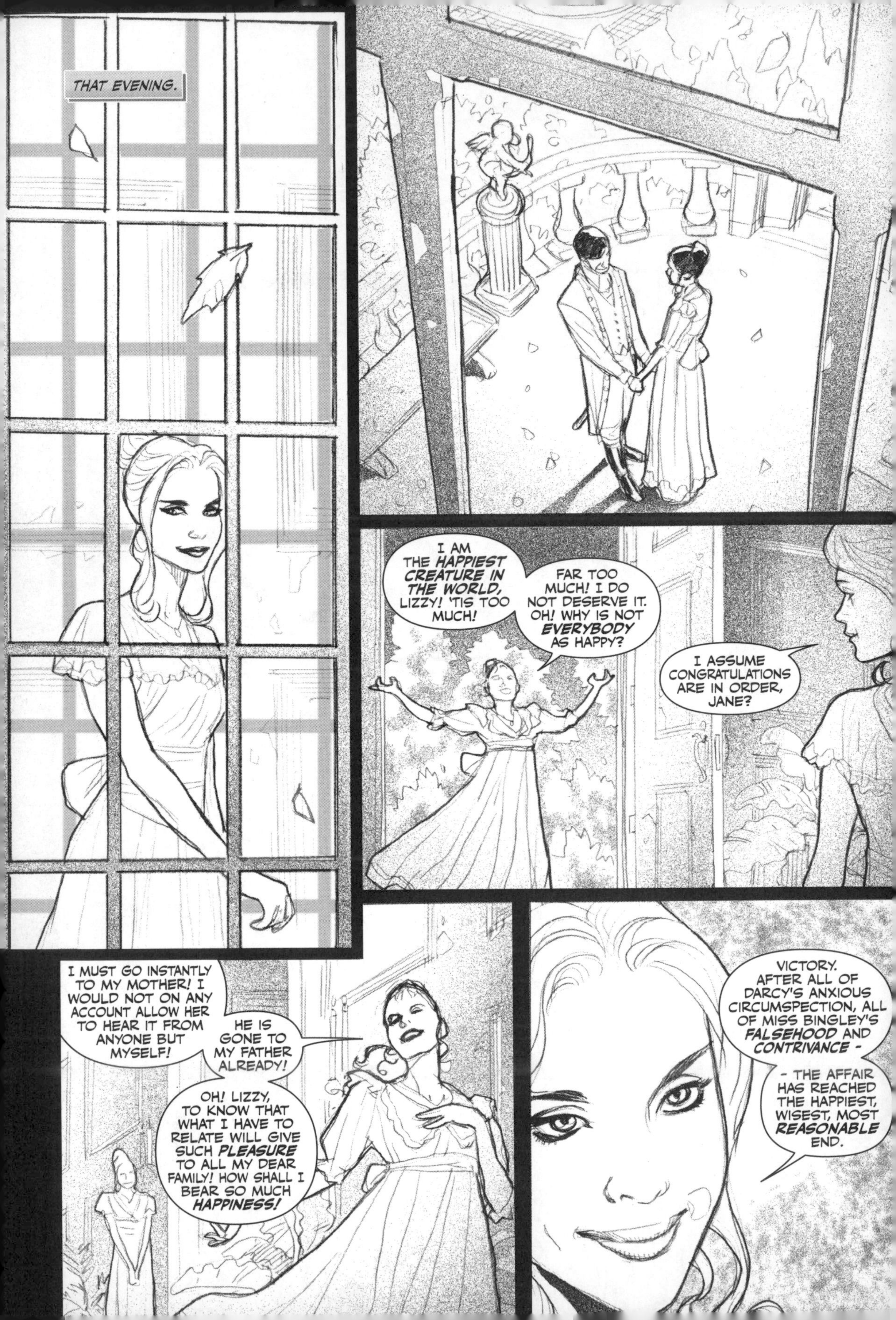

THAT EVENING.
I AM THE HAPPIEST CREATURE IN THE WORLD, LIZZY! 'TIS TOO MUCH!
FAR TOO MUCH! I DO NOT DESERVE IT. OH! WHY IS NOT EVERYBODY AS HAPPY?
I ASSUME CONGRATULATIONS ARE IN ORDER, JANE?
I MUST GO INSTANTLY TO MY MOTHER! I WOULD NOT ON ANY ACCOUNT ALLOW HER TO HEAR IT FROM ANYONE BUT MYSELF!
HE IS GONE TO MY FATHER ALREADY!
OH! LIZZY, TO KNOW THAT WHAT I HAVE TO RELATE WILL GIVE SUCH PLEASURE TO ALL MY DEAR FAMILY! HOW SHALL I BEAR SO MUCH HAPPINESS!
VICTORY. AFTER ALL OF DARCY'S ANXIOUS CIRCUMSPECTION, ALL OF MISS BINGLEY'S FALSEHOOD AND CONTRIVANCE -
- THE AFFAIR HAS REACHED THE HAPPIEST, WISEST, MOST REASONABLE END.

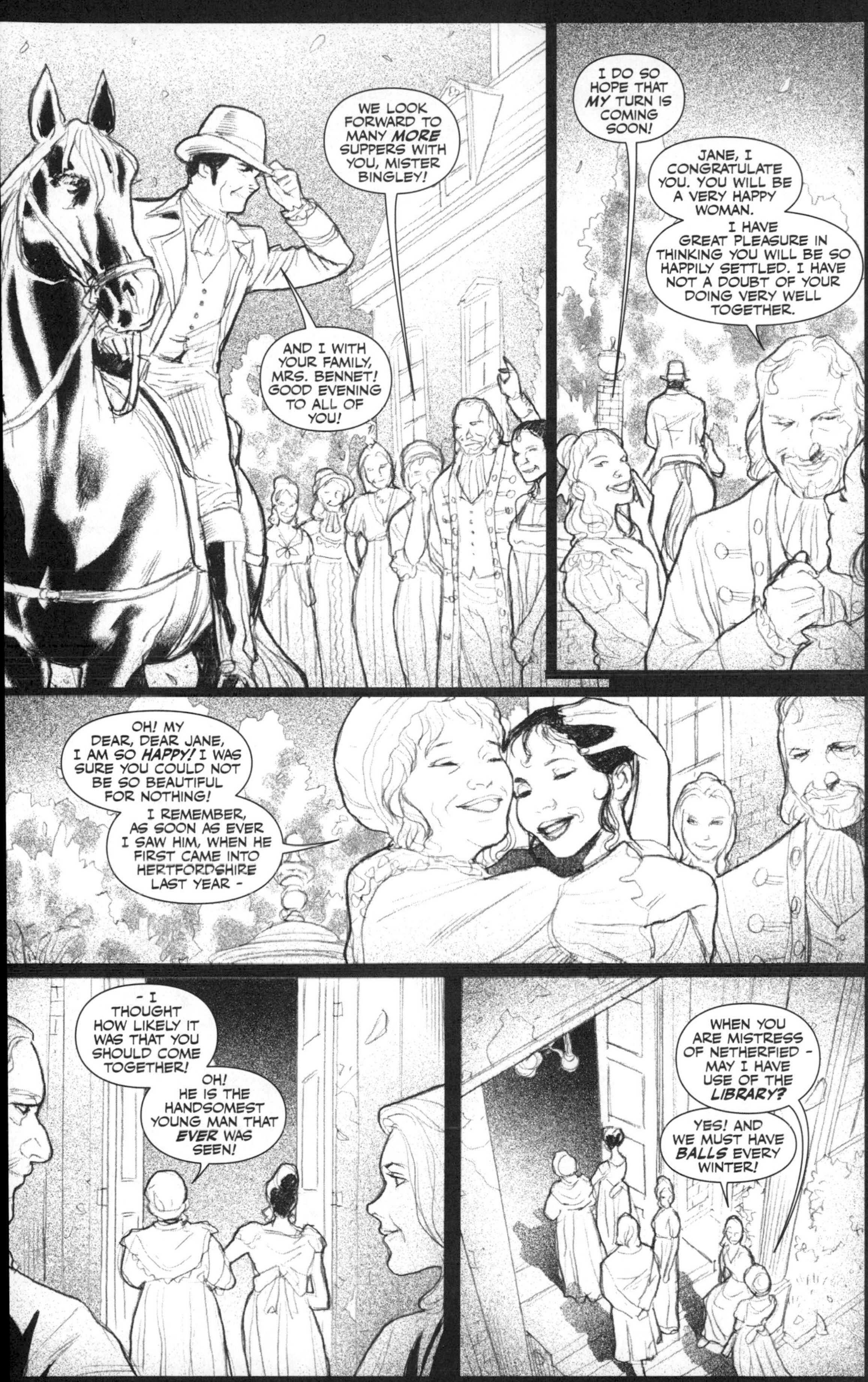

WE LOOK FORWARD TO MANY MORE SUPPERS WITH YOU, MISTER BINGLEY!
AND I WITH YOUR FAMILY, MRS. BENNET! GOOD EVENING TO ALL OF YOU!
I DO SO HOPE THAT MY TURN IS COMING SOON!
JANE, I CONGRATULATE YOU. YOU WILL BE A VERY HAPPY WOMAN.
I HAVE GREAT PLEASURE IN THINKING YOU WILL BE SO HAPPILY SETTLED. I HAVE NOT A DOUBT OF YOUR DOING VERY WELL TOGETHER.
OH! MY DEAR, DEAR JANE, I AM SO HAPPY! I WAS SURE YOU COULD NOT BE SO BEAUTIFUL FOR NOTHING!
I REMEMBER, AS SOON AS EVER I SAW HIM, WHEN HE FIRST CAME INTO HERTFORDSHIRE LAST YEAR -
- I THOUGHT HOW LIKELY IT WAS THAT YOU SHOULD COME TOGETHER!
OH! HE IS THE HANDSOMEST YOUNG MAN THAT EVER WAS SEEN!
WHEN YOU ARE MISTRESS OF NETHERFIED - MAY I HAVE USE OF THE LIBRARY?
YES! AND WE MUST HAVE BALLS EVERY WINTER!

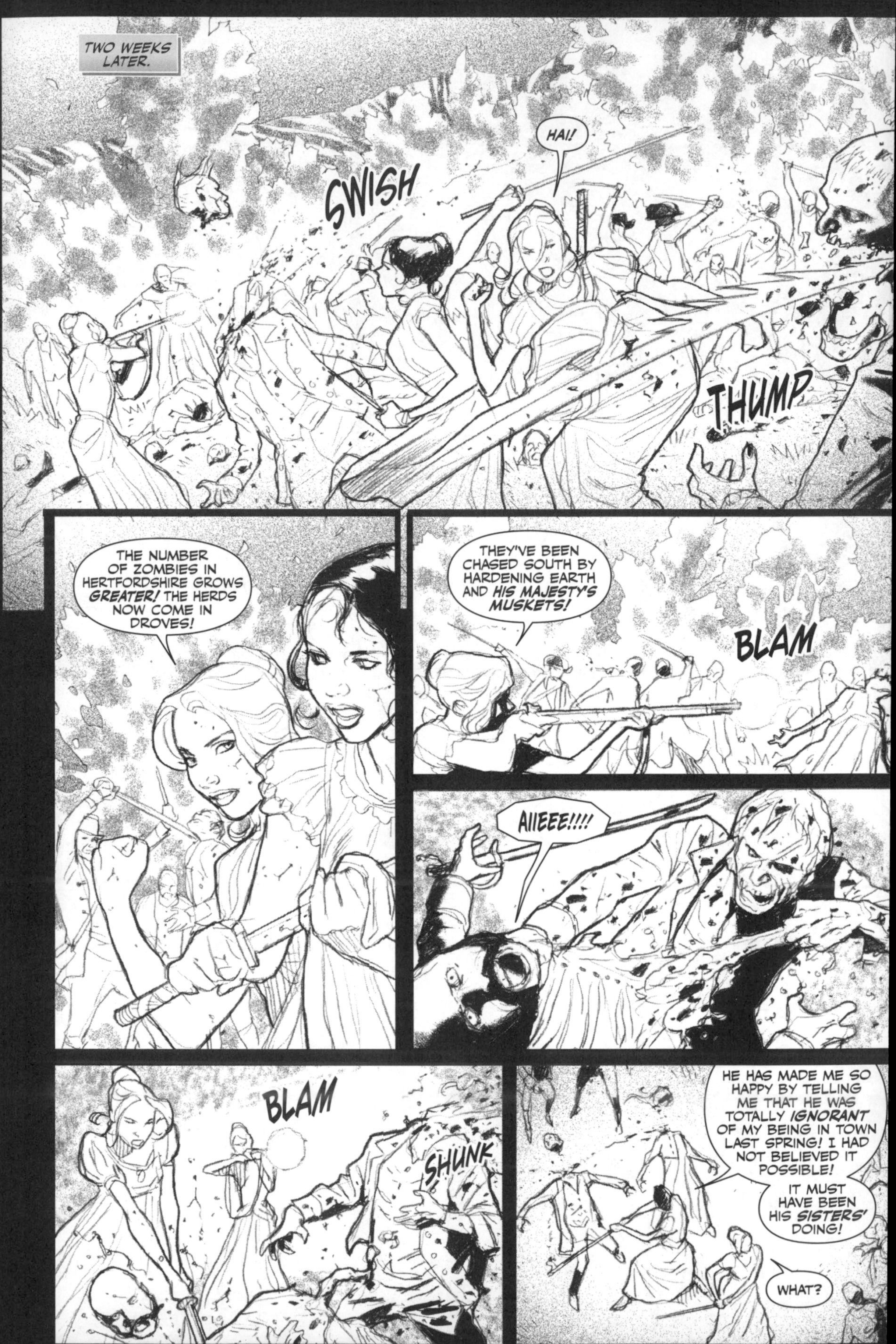
TWO WEEKS LATER.
SWISH
HAI!
THUMP
THE NUMBER OF ZOMBIES IN HERTFORDSHIRE GROWS GREATER! THE HERDS NOW COME IN DROVES!
THEY'VE BEEN CHASED SOUTH BY HARDENING EARTH AND HIS MAJESTY'S MUSKETS!
BLAM
AIIEEE!!!!
BLAM
SHUNK
HE HAS MADE ME SO HAPPY BY TELLING ME THAT HE WAS TOTALLY IGNORANT OF MY BEING IN TOWN LAST SPRING! I HAD NOT BELIEVED IT POSSIBLE!
IT MUST HAVE BEEN HIS SISTERS' DOING!
WHAT?

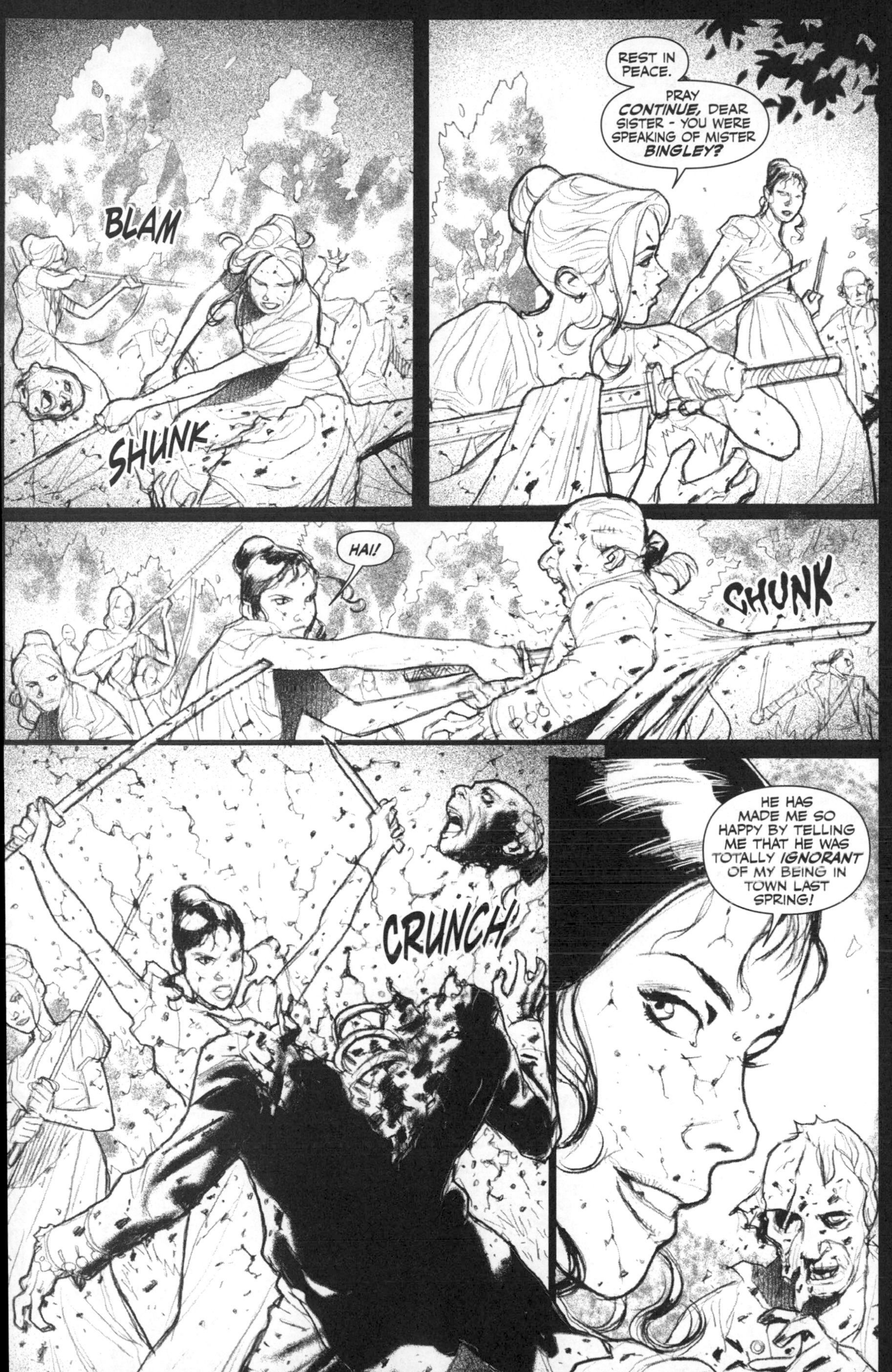
BLAM
SHUNK
REST IN PEACE.
PRAY *CONTINUE,* DEAR SISTER - YOU WERE SPEAKING OF MISTER *BINGLEY?*
HAI!
CHUNK
CRUNCH!
HE HAS MADE ME SO HAPPY BY TELLING ME THAT HE WAS TOTALLY *IGNORANT* OF MY BEING IN TOWN LAST SPRING!

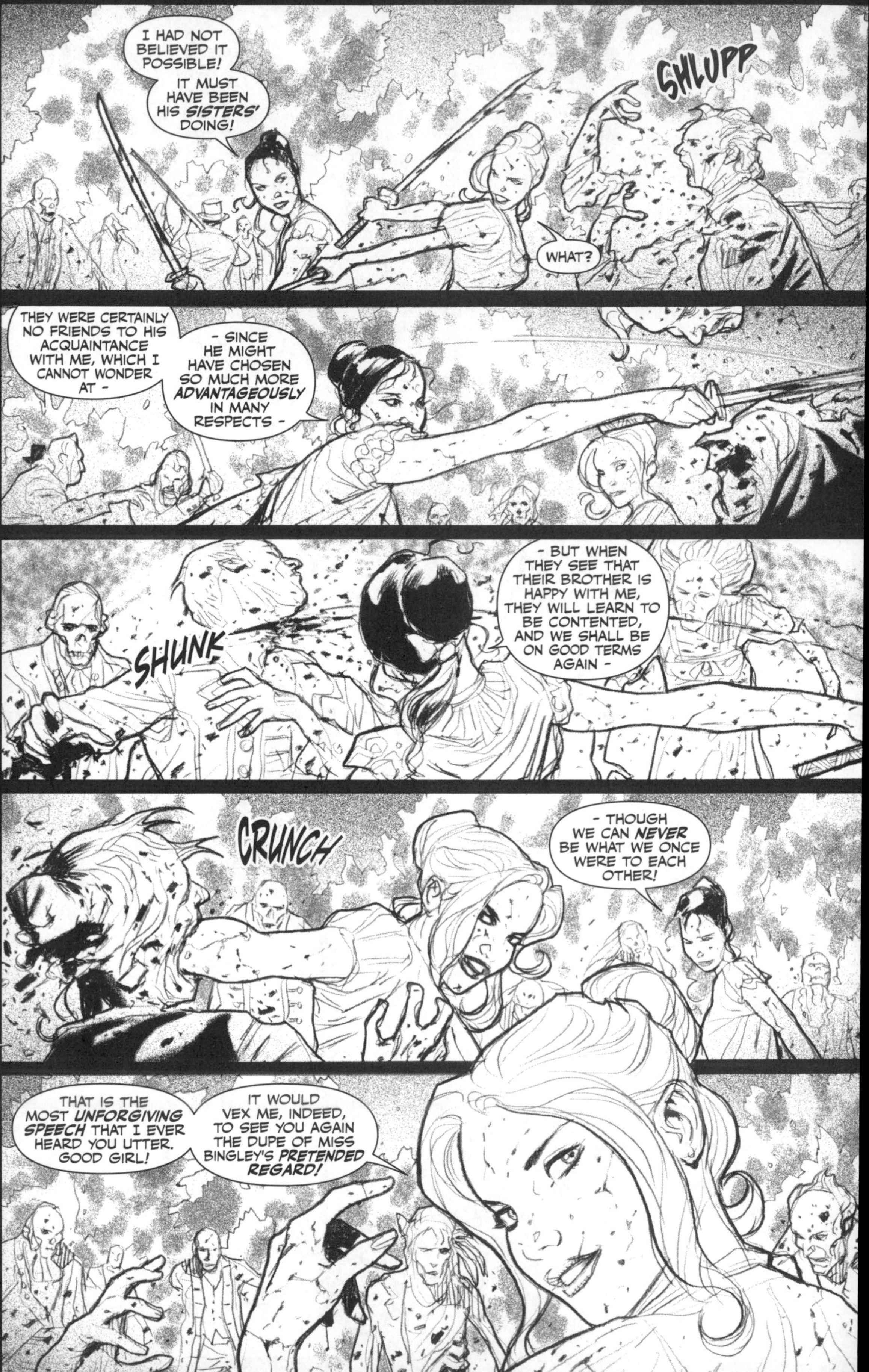
I HAD NOT BELIEVED IT POSSIBLE!
IT MUST HAVE BEEN HIS SISTERS' DOING!
SHLUPP
WHAT?
THEY WERE CERTAINLY NO FRIENDS TO HIS ACQUAINTANCE WITH ME, WHICH I CANNOT WONDER AT -
- SINCE HE MIGHT HAVE CHOSEN SO MUCH MORE ADVANTAGEOUSLY IN MANY RESPECTS -
- BUT WHEN THEY SEE THAT THEIR BROTHER IS HAPPY WITH ME, THEY WILL LEARN TO BE CONTENTED, AND WE SHALL BE ON GOOD TERMS AGAIN -
SHUNK
CRUNCH
- THOUGH WE CAN NEVER BE WHAT WE ONCE WERE TO EACH OTHER!
THAT IS THE MOST UNFORGIVING SPEECH THAT I EVER HEARD YOU UTTER. GOOD GIRL!
IT WOULD VEX ME, INDEED, TO SEE YOU AGAIN THE DUPE OF MISS BINGLEY'S PRETENDED REGARD!

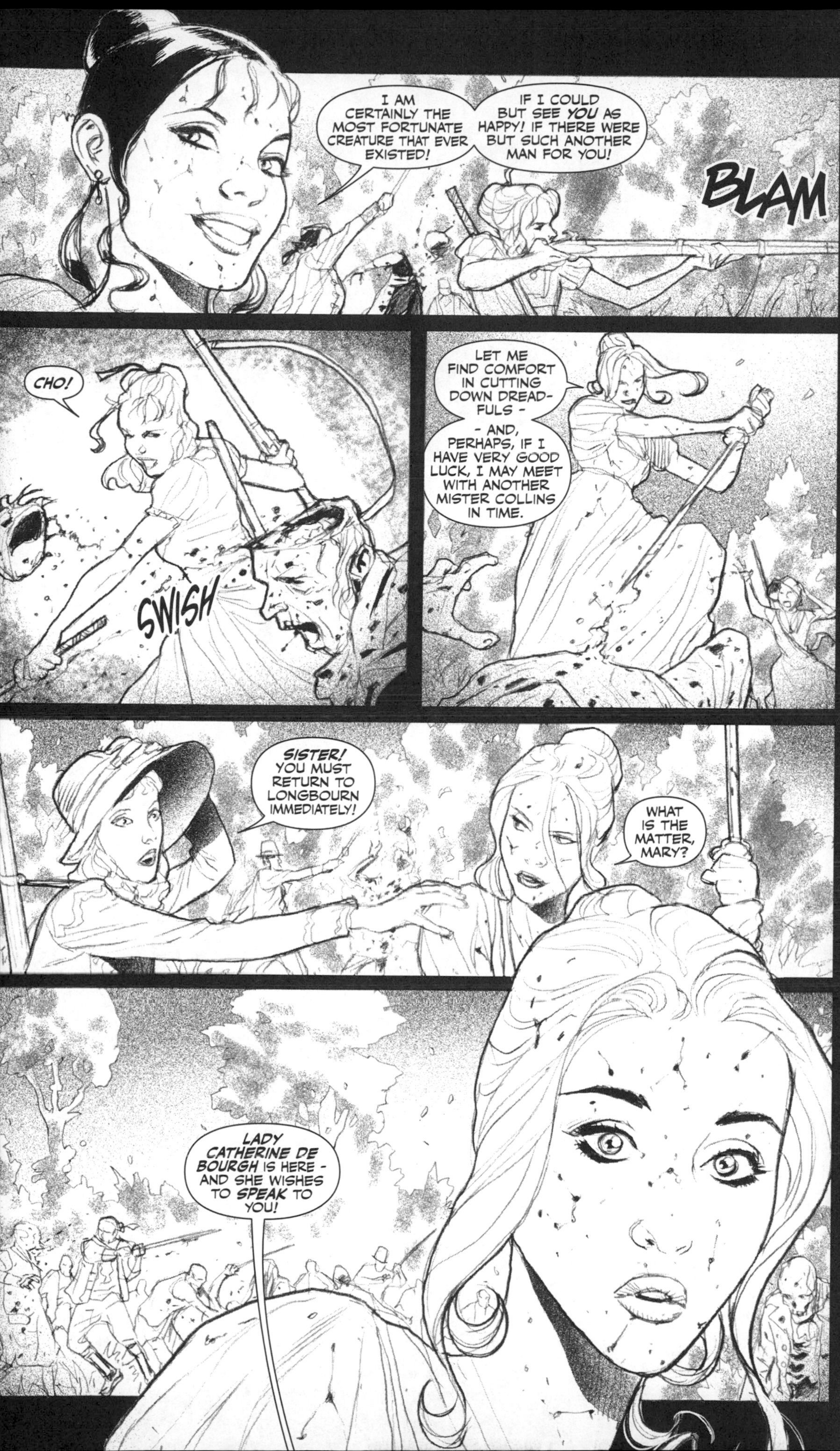
I AM CERTAINLY THE MOST FORTUNATE CREATURE THAT EVER EXISTED!
IF I COULD BUT SEE *YOU* AS HAPPY! IF THERE WERE BUT SUCH ANOTHER MAN FOR YOU!
BLAM
CHO!
SWISH
LET ME FIND COMFORT IN CUTTING DOWN DREAD-FULS -
- AND, PERHAPS, IF I HAVE VERY GOOD LUCK, I MAY MEET WITH ANOTHER MISTER COLLINS IN TIME.
SISTER! YOU MUST RETURN TO LONGBOURN IMMEDIATELY!
WHAT IS THE MATTER, MARY?
LADY CATHERINE DE BOURGH IS HERE - AND SHE WISHES TO *SPEAK* TO YOU!

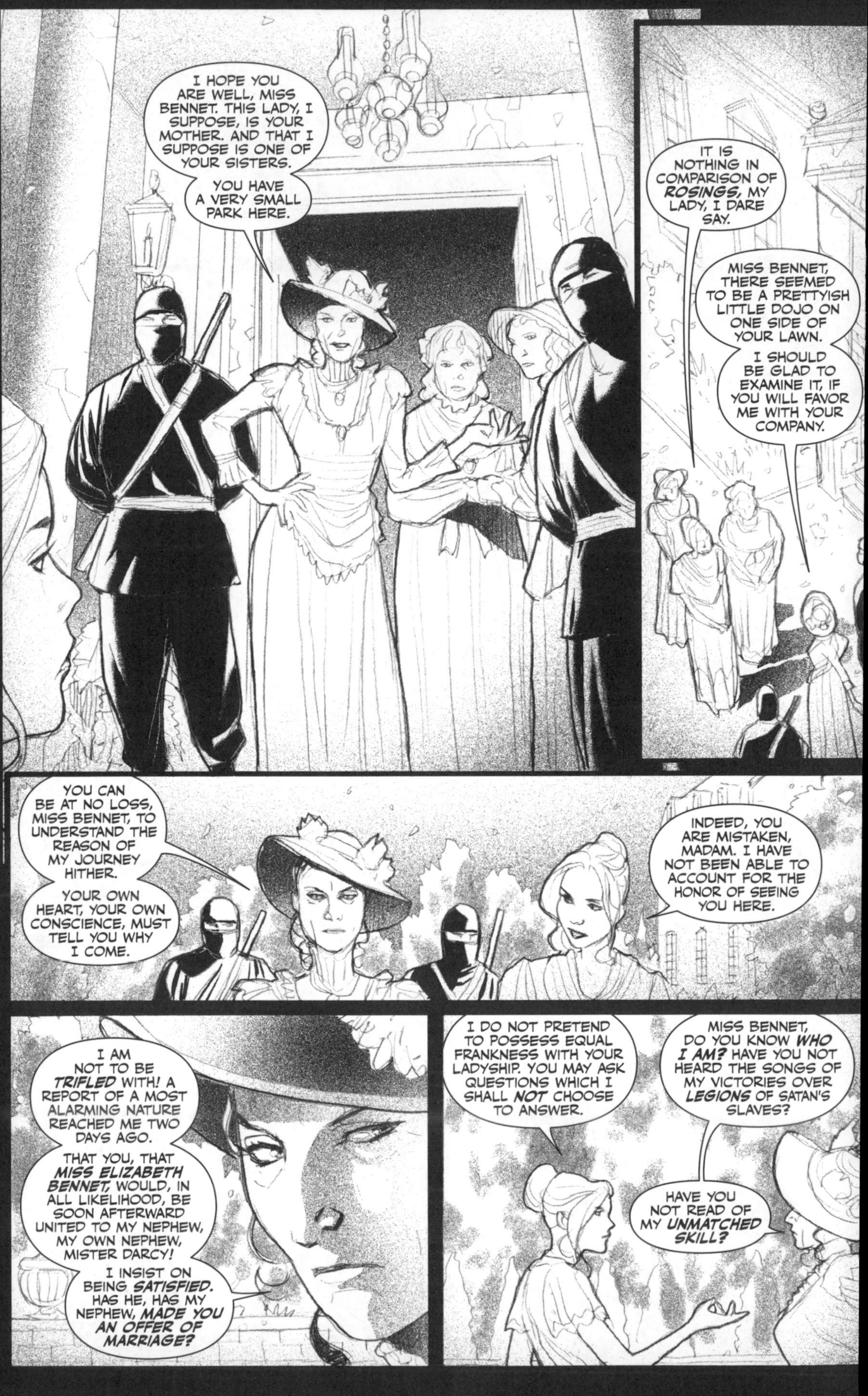
I HOPE YOU ARE WELL, MISS BENNET. THIS LADY, I SUPPOSE, IS YOUR MOTHER. AND THAT I SUPPOSE IS ONE OF YOUR SISTERS.
YOU HAVE A VERY SMALL PARK HERE.
IT IS NOTHING IN COMPARISON OF *ROSINGS,* MY LADY, I DARE SAY.
MISS BENNET, THERE SEEMED TO BE A PRETTYISH LITTLE DOJO ON ONE SIDE OF YOUR LAWN.
I SHOULD BE GLAD TO EXAMINE IT, IF YOU WILL FAVOR ME WITH YOUR COMPANY.
YOU CAN BE AT NO LOSS, MISS BENNET, TO UNDERSTAND THE REASON OF MY JOURNEY HITHER.
YOUR OWN HEART, YOUR OWN CONSCIENCE, MUST TELL YOU WHY I COME.
INDEED, YOU ARE MISTAKEN, MADAM. I HAVE NOT BEEN ABLE TO ACCOUNT FOR THE HONOR OF SEEING YOU HERE.
I AM NOT TO BE *TRIFLED* WITH! A REPORT OF A MOST ALARMING NATURE REACHED ME TWO DAYS AGO.
THAT YOU, THAT ***MISS ELIZABETH BENNET,*** WOULD, IN ALL LIKELIHOOD, BE SOON AFTERWARD UNITED TO MY NEPHEW, MY OWN NEPHEW, MISTER DARCY!
I INSIST ON BEING ***SATISFIED.*** HAS HE, HAS MY NEPHEW, ***MADE YOU AN OFFER OF MARRIAGE?***
I DO NOT PRETEND TO POSSESS EQUAL FRANKNESS WITH YOUR LADYSHIP. YOU MAY ASK QUESTIONS WHICH I SHALL *NOT* CHOOSE TO ANSWER.
MISS BENNET, DO YOU KNOW *WHO I AM?* HAVE YOU NOT HEARD THE SONGS OF MY VICTORIES OVER *LEGIONS* OF SATAN'S SLAVES?
HAVE YOU NOT READ OF MY ***UNMATCHED SKILL?***

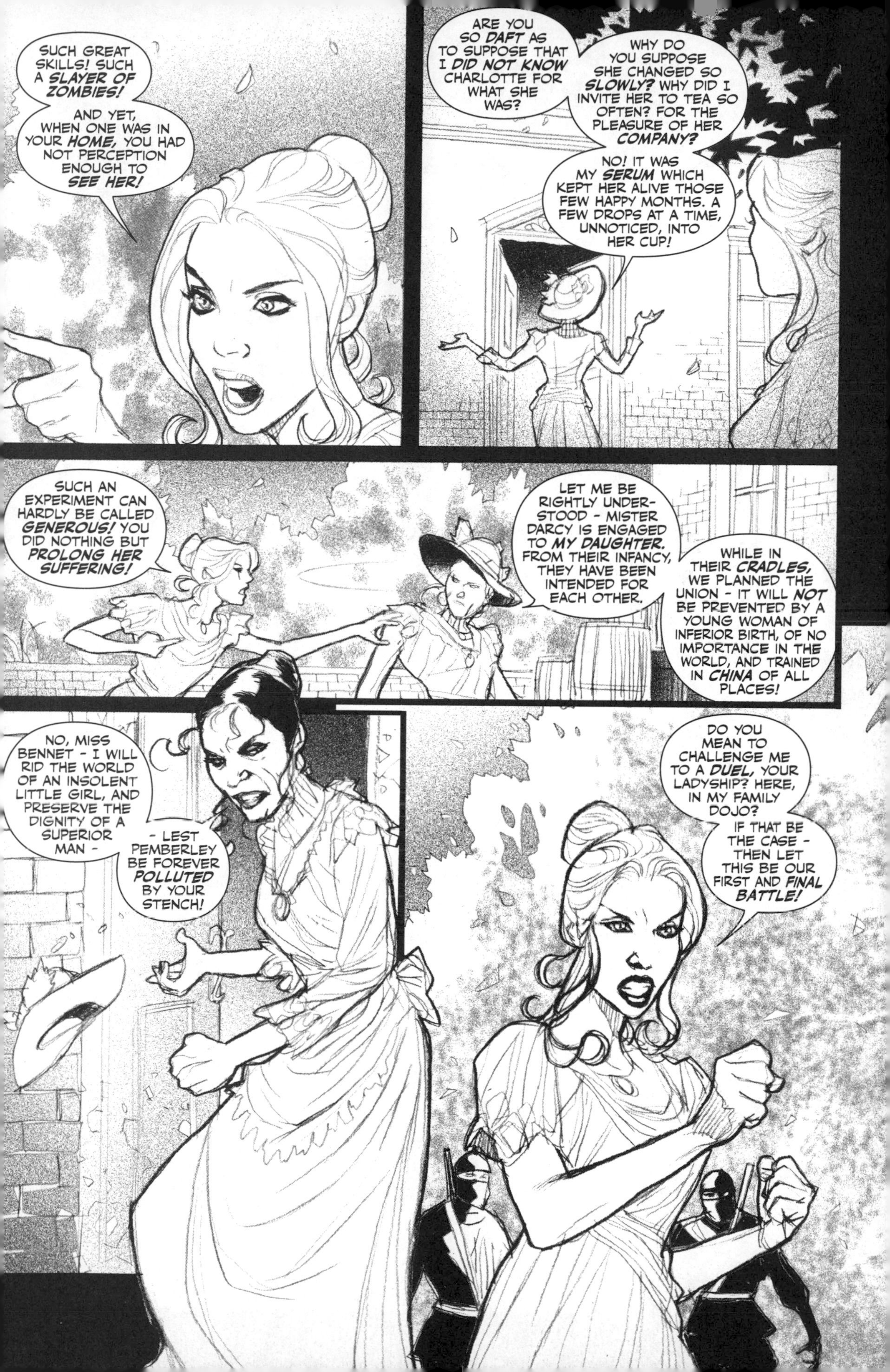
SUCH GREAT SKILLS! SUCH A SLAYER OF ZOMBIES!
AND YET, WHEN ONE WAS IN YOUR HOME, YOU HAD NOT PERCEPTION ENOUGH TO SEE HER!
ARE YOU SO DAFT AS TO SUPPOSE THAT I DID NOT KNOW CHARLOTTE FOR WHAT SHE WAS?
WHY DO YOU SUPPOSE SHE CHANGED SO SLOWLY? WHY DID I INVITE HER TO TEA SO OFTEN? FOR THE PLEASURE OF HER COMPANY?
NO! IT WAS MY SERUM WHICH KEPT HER ALIVE THOSE FEW HAPPY MONTHS. A FEW DROPS AT A TIME, UNNOTICED, INTO HER CUP!
SUCH AN EXPERIMENT CAN HARDLY BE CALLED GENEROUS! YOU DID NOTHING BUT PROLONG HER SUFFERING!
LET ME BE RIGHTLY UNDER-STOOD - MISTER DARCY IS ENGAGED TO MY DAUGHTER. FROM THEIR INFANCY, THEY HAVE BEEN INTENDED FOR EACH OTHER.
WHILE IN THEIR CRADLES, WE PLANNED THE UNION - IT WILL NOT BE PREVENTED BY A YOUNG WOMAN OF INFERIOR BIRTH, OF NO IMPORTANCE IN THE WORLD, AND TRAINED IN CHINA OF ALL PLACES!
NO, MISS BENNET - I WILL RID THE WORLD OF AN INSOLENT LITTLE GIRL, AND PRESERVE THE DIGNITY OF A SUPERIOR MAN -
- LEST PEMBERLEY BE FOREVER POLLUTED BY YOUR STENCH!
DO YOU MEAN TO CHALLENGE ME TO A DUEL, YOUR LADYSHIP? HERE, IN MY FAMILY DOJO?
IF THAT BE THE CASE - THEN LET THIS BE OUR FIRST AND FINAL BATTLE!

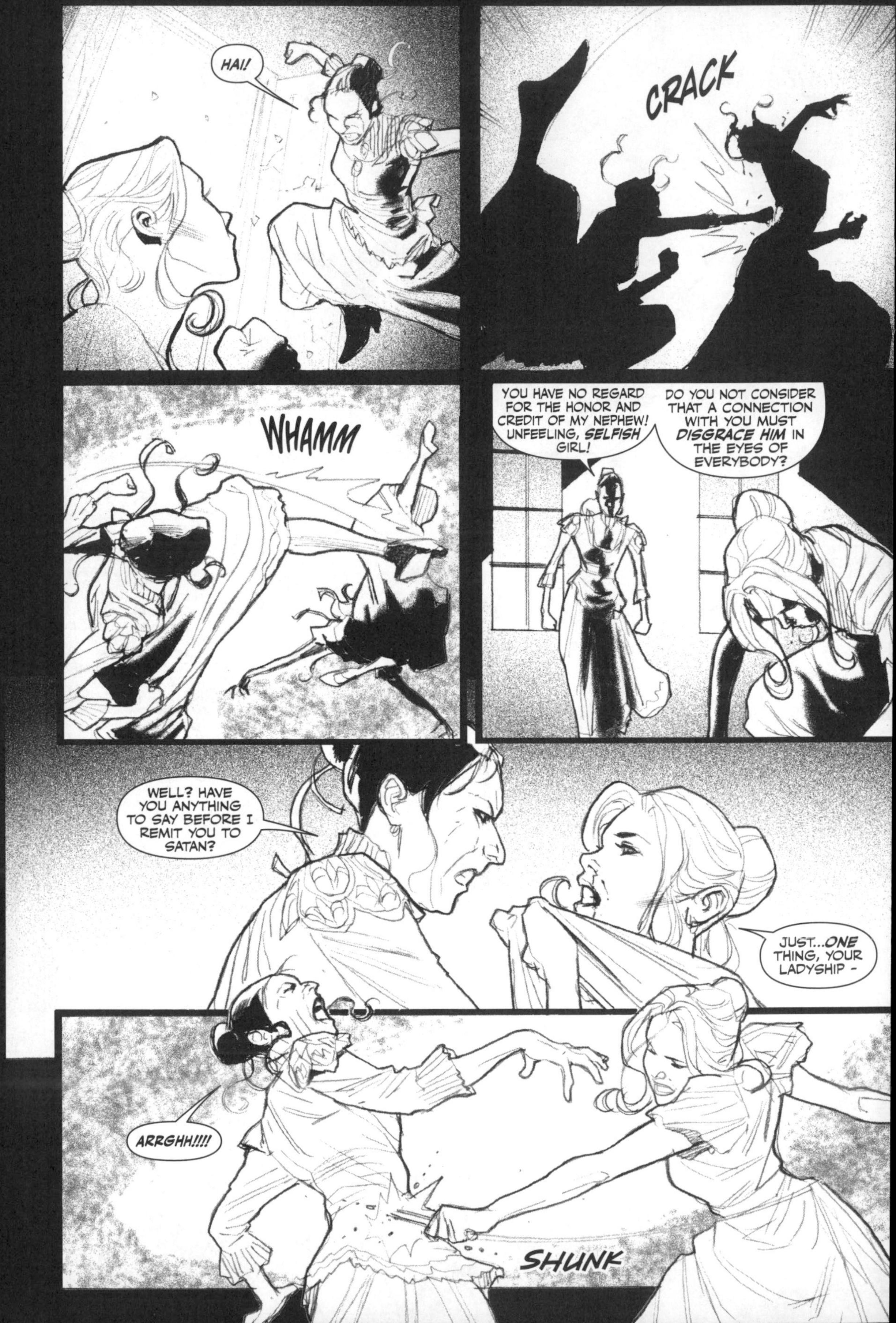
HAI!
CRACK
WHAMM
YOU HAVE NO REGARD FOR THE HONOR AND CREDIT OF MY NEPHEW! UNFEELING, SELFISH GIRL!
DO YOU NOT CONSIDER THAT A CONNECTION WITH YOU MUST DISGRACE HIM IN THE EYES OF EVERYBODY?
WELL? HAVE YOU ANYTHING TO SAY BEFORE I REMIT YOU TO SATAN?
JUST...ONE THING, YOUR LADYSHIP -
ARRGHH!!!!
SHUNK

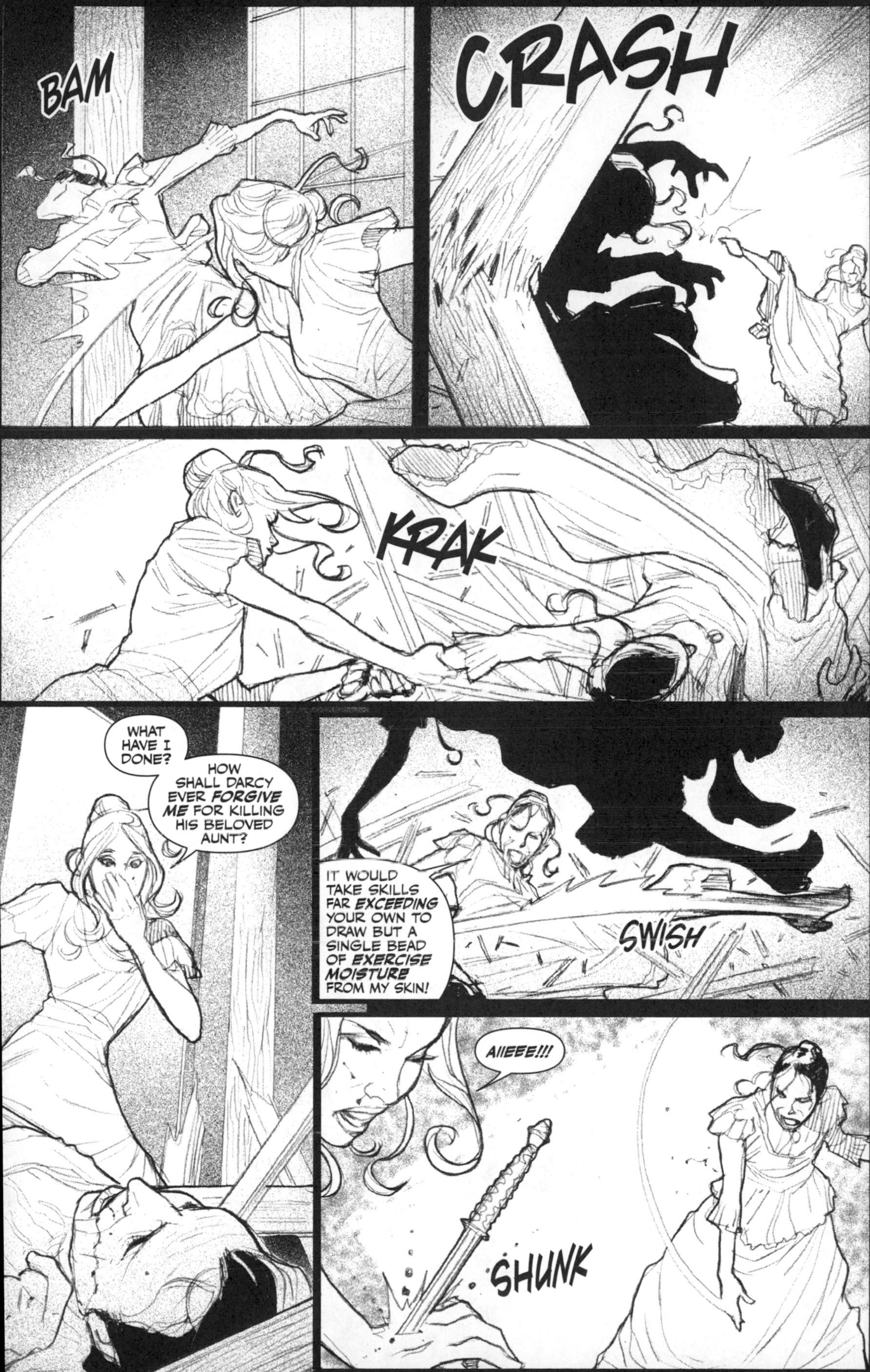
BAM
CRASH
KRAK
WHAT HAVE I DONE?
HOW SHALL DARCY EVER *FORGIVE ME* FOR KILLING HIS BELOVED AUNT?
IT WOULD TAKE SKILLS FAR *EXCEEDING* YOUR OWN TO DRAW BUT A SINGLE BEAD OF *EXERCISE MOISTURE* FROM MY SKIN!
SWISH
AIIEEE!!!
SHUNK

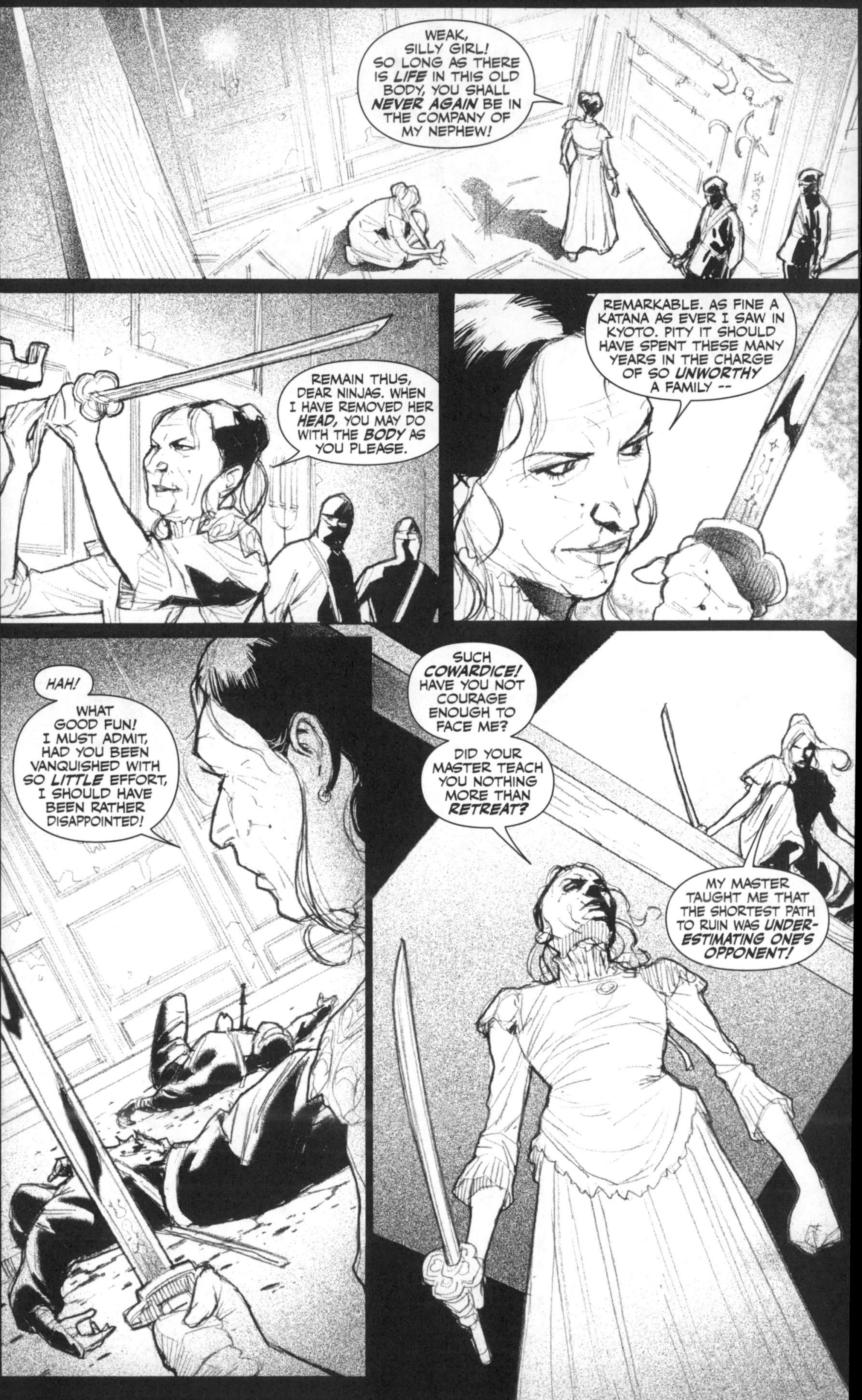
WEAK, SILLY GIRL! SO LONG AS THERE IS LIFE IN THIS OLD BODY, YOU SHALL NEVER AGAIN BE IN THE COMPANY OF MY NEPHEW!
REMAIN THUS, DEAR NINJAS. WHEN I HAVE REMOVED HER HEAD, YOU MAY DO WITH THE BODY AS YOU PLEASE.
REMARKABLE. AS FINE A KATANA AS EVER I SAW IN KYOTO. PITY IT SHOULD HAVE SPENT THESE MANY YEARS IN THE CHARGE OF SO UNWORTHY A FAMILY --
HAH!
WHAT GOOD FUN! I MUST ADMIT, HAD YOU BEEN VANQUISHED WITH SO LITTLE EFFORT, I SHOULD HAVE BEEN RATHER DISAPPOINTED!
SUCH COWARDICE! HAVE YOU NOT COURAGE ENOUGH TO FACE ME?
DID YOUR MASTER TEACH YOU NOTHING MORE THAN RETREAT?
MY MASTER TAUGHT ME THAT THE SHORTEST PATH TO RUIN WAS UNDER-ESTIMATING ONE'S OPPONENT!

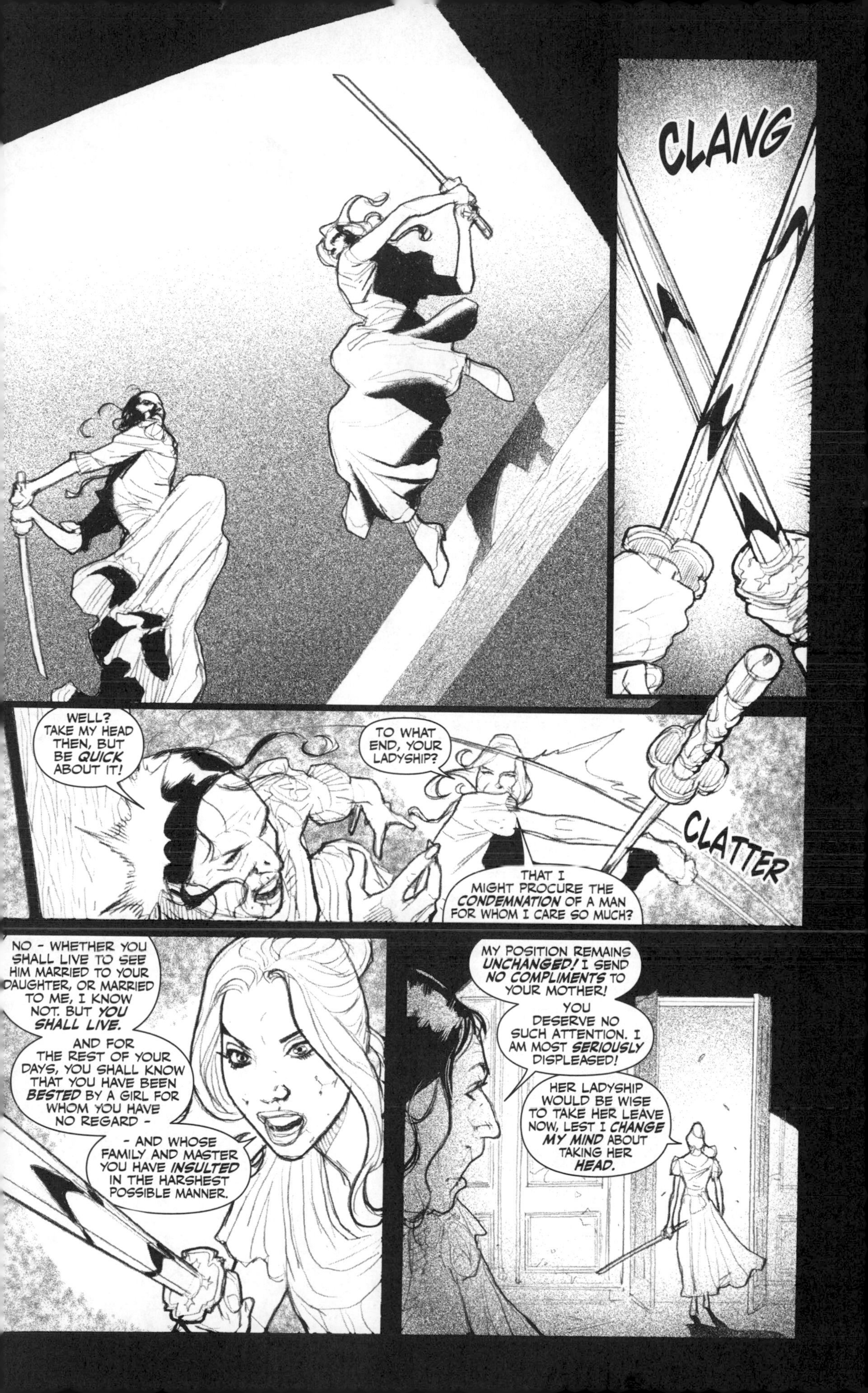
CLANG
WELL? TAKE MY HEAD THEN, BUT BE QUICK ABOUT IT!
TO WHAT END, YOUR LADYSHIP?
CLATTER
THAT I MIGHT PROCURE THE CONDEMNATION OF A MAN FOR WHOM I CARE SO MUCH?
NO - WHETHER YOU SHALL LIVE TO SEE HIM MARRIED TO YOUR DAUGHTER, OR MARRIED TO ME, I KNOW NOT. BUT YOU SHALL LIVE.
AND FOR THE REST OF YOUR DAYS, YOU SHALL KNOW THAT YOU HAVE BEEN BESTED BY A GIRL FOR WHOM YOU HAVE NO REGARD -
- AND WHOSE FAMILY AND MASTER YOU HAVE INSULTED IN THE HARSHEST POSSIBLE MANNER.
MY POSITION REMAINS UNCHANGED! I SEND NO COMPLIMENTS TO YOUR MOTHER!
YOU DESERVE NO SUCH ATTENTION. I AM MOST SERIOUSLY DISPLEASED!
HER LADYSHIP WOULD BE WISE TO TAKE HER LEAVE NOW, LEST I CHANGE MY MIND ABOUT TAKING HER HEAD.

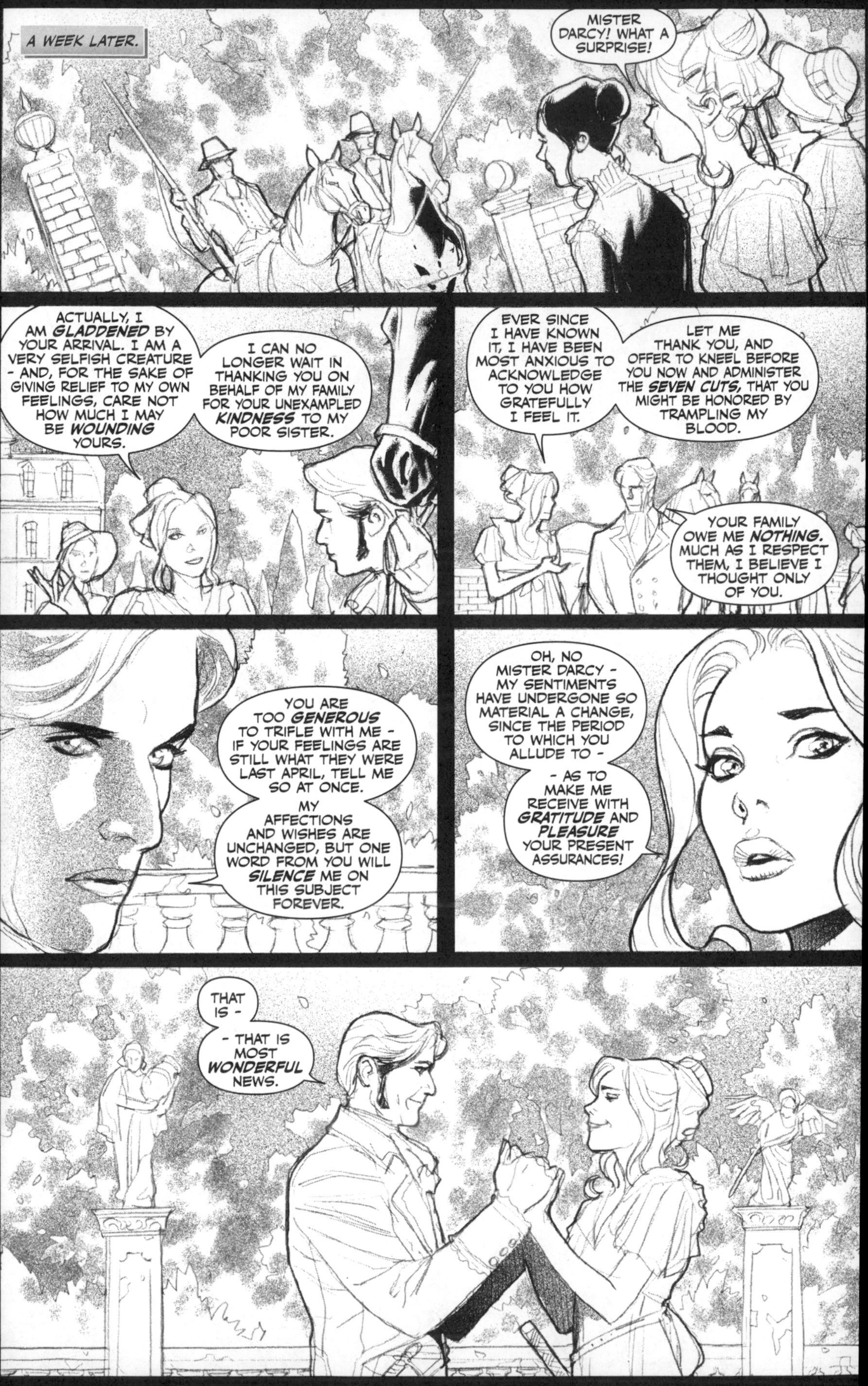
A WEEK LATER.
MISTER DARCY! WHAT A SURPRISE!
ACTUALLY, I AM GLADDENED BY YOUR ARRIVAL. I AM A VERY SELFISH CREATURE - AND, FOR THE SAKE OF GIVING RELIEF TO MY OWN FEELINGS, CARE NOT HOW MUCH I MAY BE WOUNDING YOURS.
I CAN NO LONGER WAIT IN THANKING YOU ON BEHALF OF MY FAMILY FOR YOUR UNEXAMPLED KINDNESS TO MY POOR SISTER.
EVER SINCE I HAVE KNOWN IT, I HAVE BEEN MOST ANXIOUS TO ACKNOWLEDGE TO YOU HOW GRATEFULLY I FEEL IT.
LET ME THANK YOU, AND OFFER TO KNEEL BEFORE YOU NOW AND ADMINISTER THE SEVEN CUTS, THAT YOU MIGHT BE HONORED BY TRAMPLING MY BLOOD.
YOUR FAMILY OWE ME NOTHING. MUCH AS I RESPECT THEM, I BELIEVE I THOUGHT ONLY OF YOU.
YOU ARE TOO GENEROUS TO TRIFLE WITH ME - IF YOUR FEELINGS ARE STILL WHAT THEY WERE LAST APRIL, TELL ME SO AT ONCE.
MY AFFECTIONS AND WISHES ARE UNCHANGED, BUT ONE WORD FROM YOU WILL SILENCE ME ON THIS SUBJECT FOREVER.
OH, NO MISTER DARCY - MY SENTIMENTS HAVE UNDERGONE SO MATERIAL A CHANGE, SINCE THE PERIOD TO WHICH YOU ALLUDE TO -
- AS TO MAKE ME RECEIVE WITH GRATITUDE AND PLEASURE YOUR PRESENT ASSURANCES!
THAT IS -
- THAT IS MOST WONDERFUL NEWS.

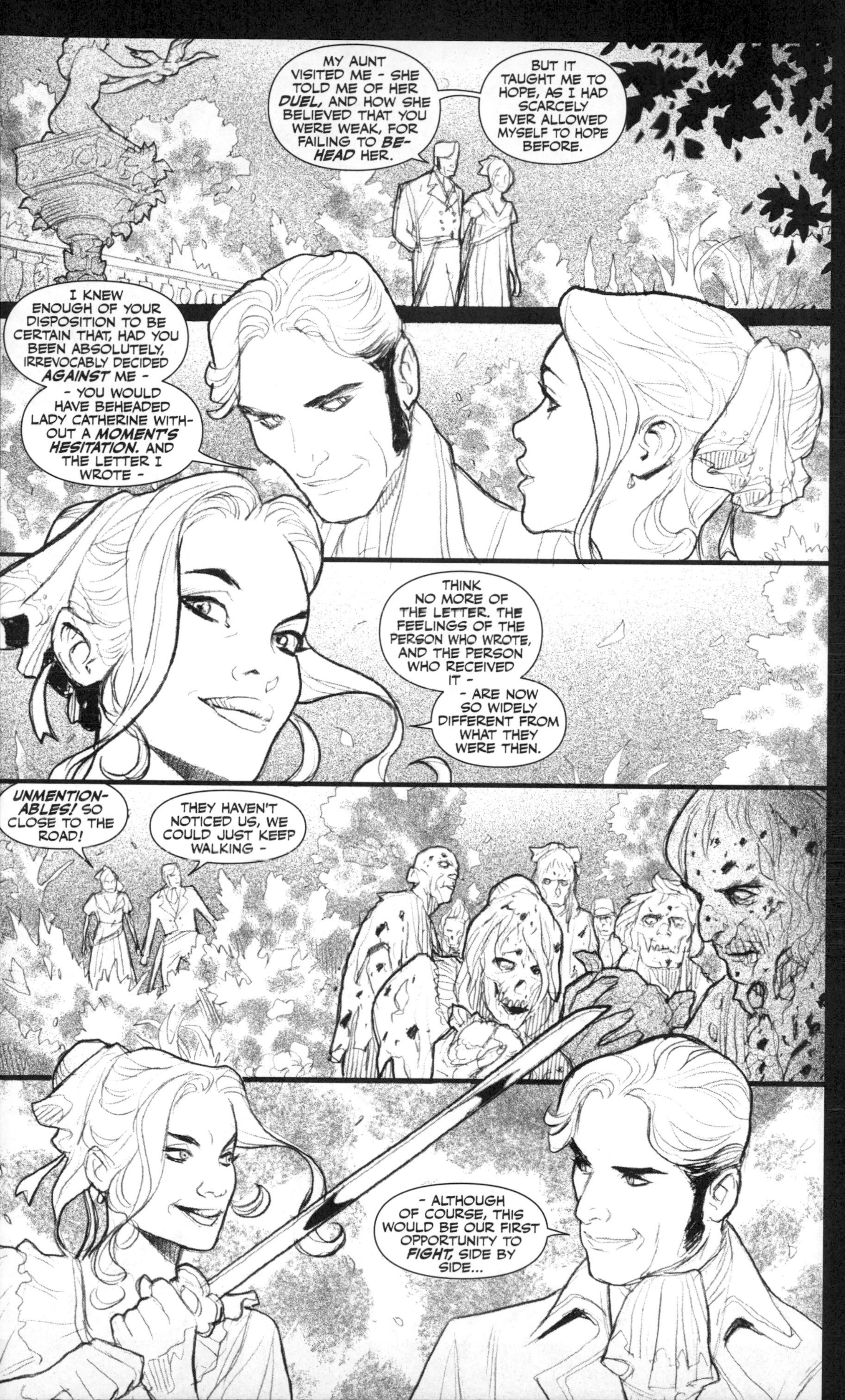
MY AUNT VISITED ME - SHE TOLD ME OF HER DUEL, AND HOW SHE BELIEVED THAT YOU WERE WEAK, FOR FAILING TO BE-HEAD HER.
BUT IT TAUGHT ME TO HOPE, AS I HAD SCARCELY EVER ALLOWED MYSELF TO HOPE BEFORE.
I KNEW ENOUGH OF YOUR DISPOSITION TO BE CERTAIN THAT, HAD YOU BEEN ABSOLUTELY, IRREVOCABLY DECIDED AGAINST ME -
- YOU WOULD HAVE BEHEADED LADY CATHERINE WITH-OUT A MOMENT'S HESITATION. AND THE LETTER I WROTE -
THINK NO MORE OF THE LETTER. THE FEELINGS OF THE PERSON WHO WROTE, AND THE PERSON WHO RECEIVED IT -
- ARE NOW SO WIDELY DIFFERENT FROM WHAT THEY WERE THEN.
UNMENTION-ABLES! SO CLOSE TO THE ROAD!
THEY HAVEN'T NOTICED US, WE COULD JUST KEEP WALKING -
- ALTHOUGH OF COURSE, THIS WOULD BE OUR FIRST OPPORTUNITY TO FIGHT, SIDE BY SIDE...

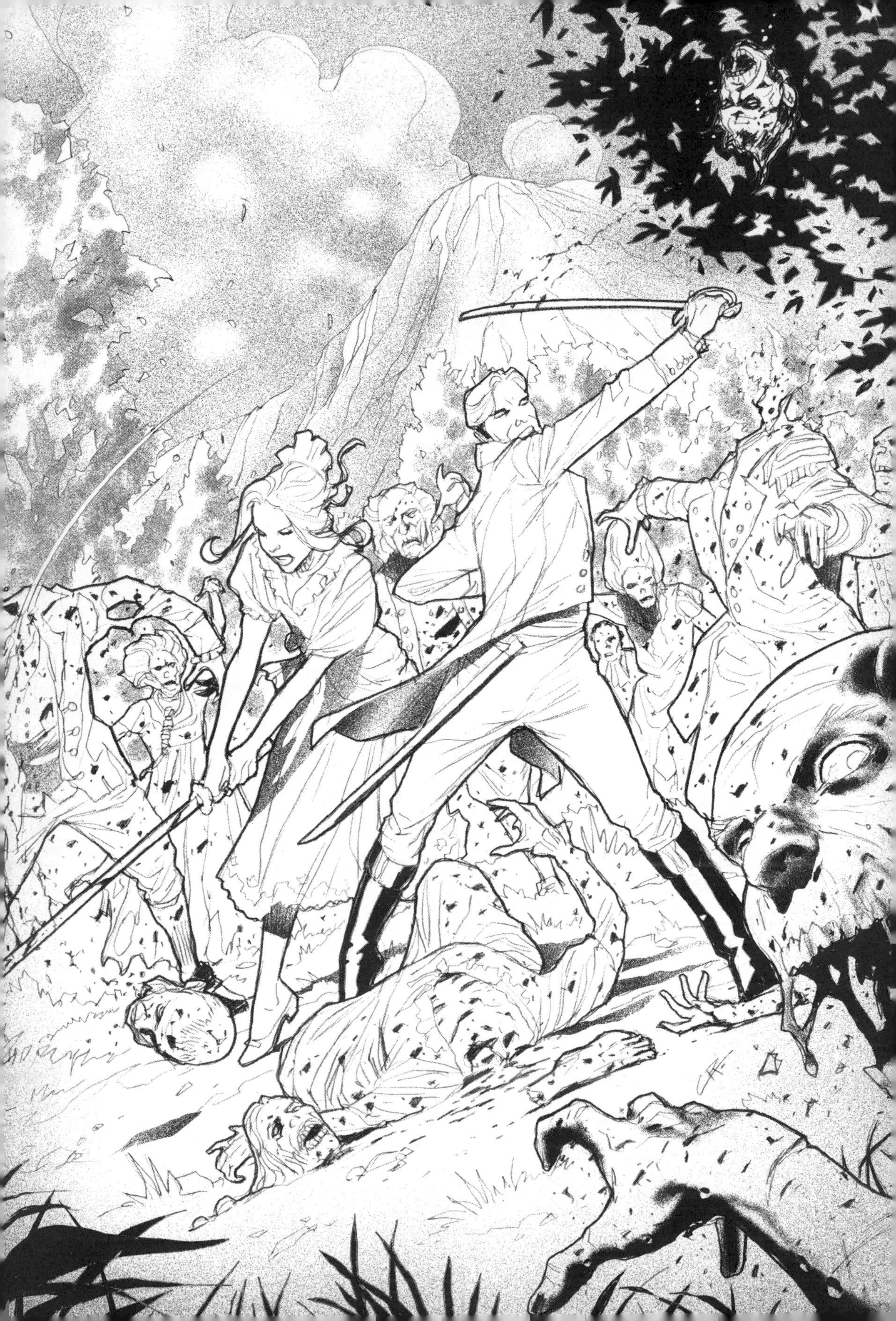

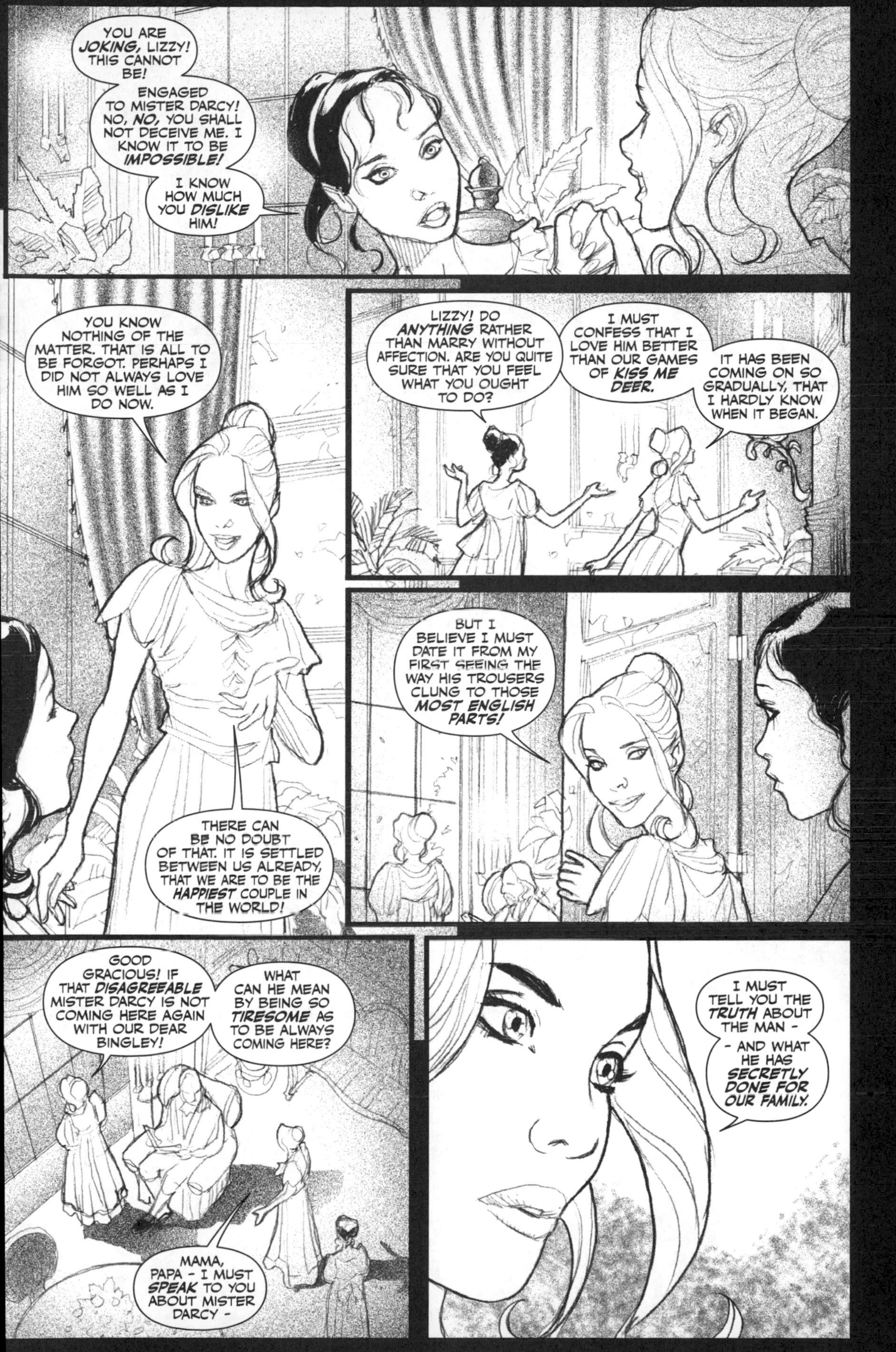
YOU ARE JOKING, LIZZY! THIS CANNOT BE!
ENGAGED TO MISTER DARCY! NO, NO, YOU SHALL NOT DECEIVE ME. I KNOW IT TO BE IMPOSSIBLE!
I KNOW HOW MUCH YOU DISLIKE HIM!
YOU KNOW NOTHING OF THE MATTER. THAT IS ALL TO BE FORGOT. PERHAPS I DID NOT ALWAYS LOVE HIM SO WELL AS I DO NOW.
THERE CAN BE NO DOUBT OF THAT. IT IS SETTLED BETWEEN US ALREADY, THAT WE ARE TO BE THE HAPPIEST COUPLE IN THE WORLD!
LIZZY! DO ANYTHING RATHER THAN MARRY WITHOUT AFFECTION. ARE YOU QUITE SURE THAT YOU FEEL WHAT YOU OUGHT TO DO?
I MUST CONFESS THAT I LOVE HIM BETTER THAN OUR GAMES OF KISS ME DEER.
IT HAS BEEN COMING ON SO GRADUALLY, THAT I HARDLY KNOW WHEN IT BEGAN.
BUT I BELIEVE I MUST DATE IT FROM MY FIRST SEEING THE WAY HIS TROUSERS CLUNG TO THOSE MOST ENGLISH PARTS!
GOOD GRACIOUS! IF THAT DISAGREEABLE MISTER DARCY IS NOT COMING HERE AGAIN WITH OUR DEAR BINGLEY!
WHAT CAN HE MEAN BY BEING SO TIRESOME AS TO BE ALWAYS COMING HERE?
MAMA, PAPA - I MUST SPEAK TO YOU ABOUT MISTER DARCY -
I MUST TELL YOU THE TRUTH ABOUT THE MAN -
- AND WHAT HE HAS SECRETLY DONE FOR OUR FAMILY.

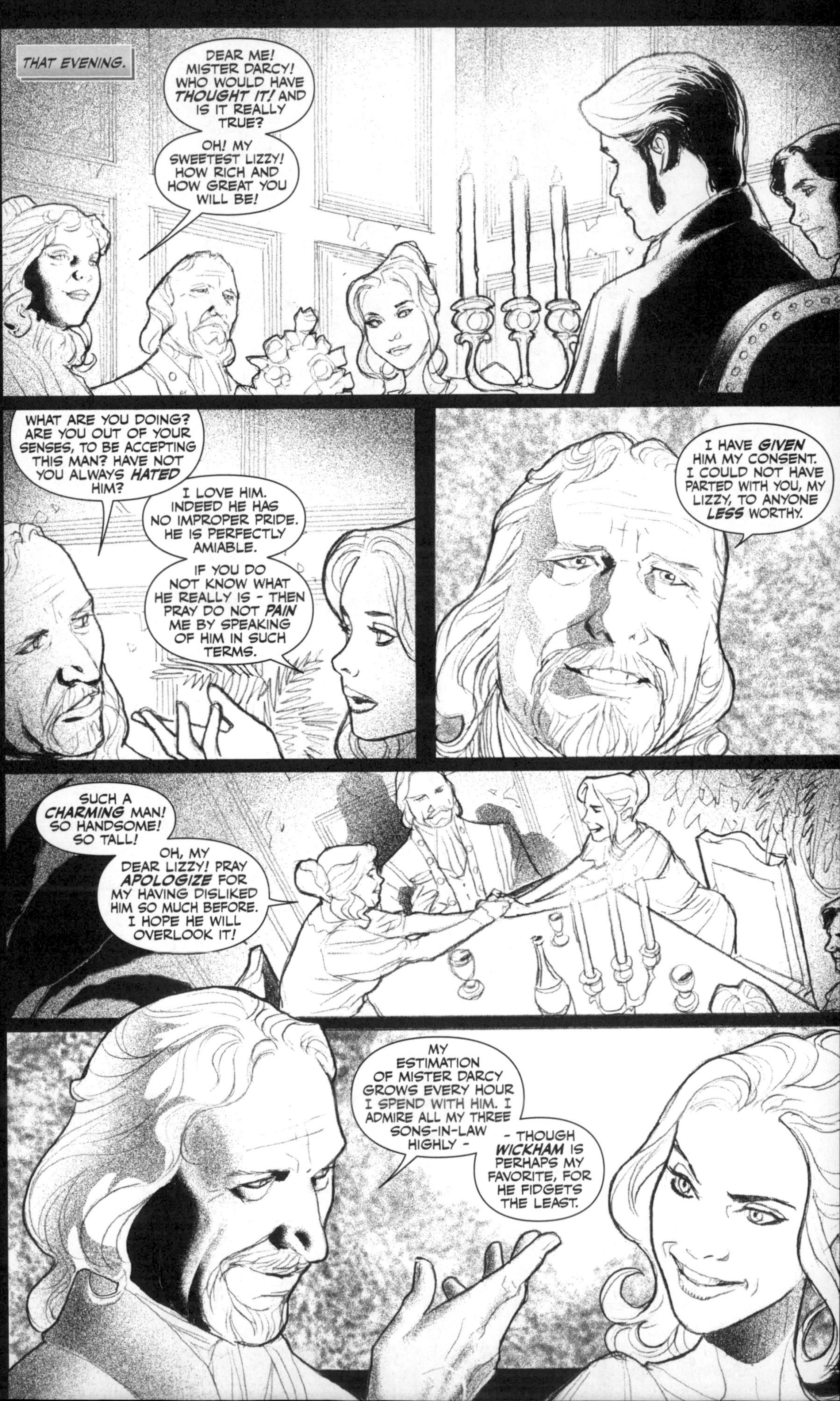
THAT EVENING.
DEAR ME! MISTER DARCY! WHO WOULD HAVE THOUGHT IT! AND IS IT REALLY TRUE?
OH! MY SWEETEST LIZZY! HOW RICH AND HOW GREAT YOU WILL BE!
WHAT ARE YOU DOING? ARE YOU OUT OF YOUR SENSES, TO BE ACCEPTING THIS MAN? HAVE NOT YOU ALWAYS HATED HIM?
I LOVE HIM. INDEED HE HAS NO IMPROPER PRIDE. HE IS PERFECTLY AMIABLE.
IF YOU DO NOT KNOW WHAT HE REALLY IS - THEN PRAY DO NOT PAIN ME BY SPEAKING OF HIM IN SUCH TERMS.
I HAVE GIVEN HIM MY CONSENT. I COULD NOT HAVE PARTED WITH YOU, MY LIZZY, TO ANYONE LESS WORTHY.
SUCH A CHARMING MAN! SO HANDSOME! SO TALL!
OH, MY DEAR LIZZY! PRAY APOLOGIZE FOR MY HAVING DISLIKED HIM SO MUCH BEFORE. I HOPE HE WILL OVERLOOK IT!
MY ESTIMATION OF MISTER DARCY GROWS EVERY HOUR I SPEND WITH HIM. I ADMIRE ALL MY THREE SONS-IN-LAW HIGHLY -
- THOUGH WICKHAM IS PERHAPS MY FAVORITE, FOR HE FIDGETS THE LEAST.

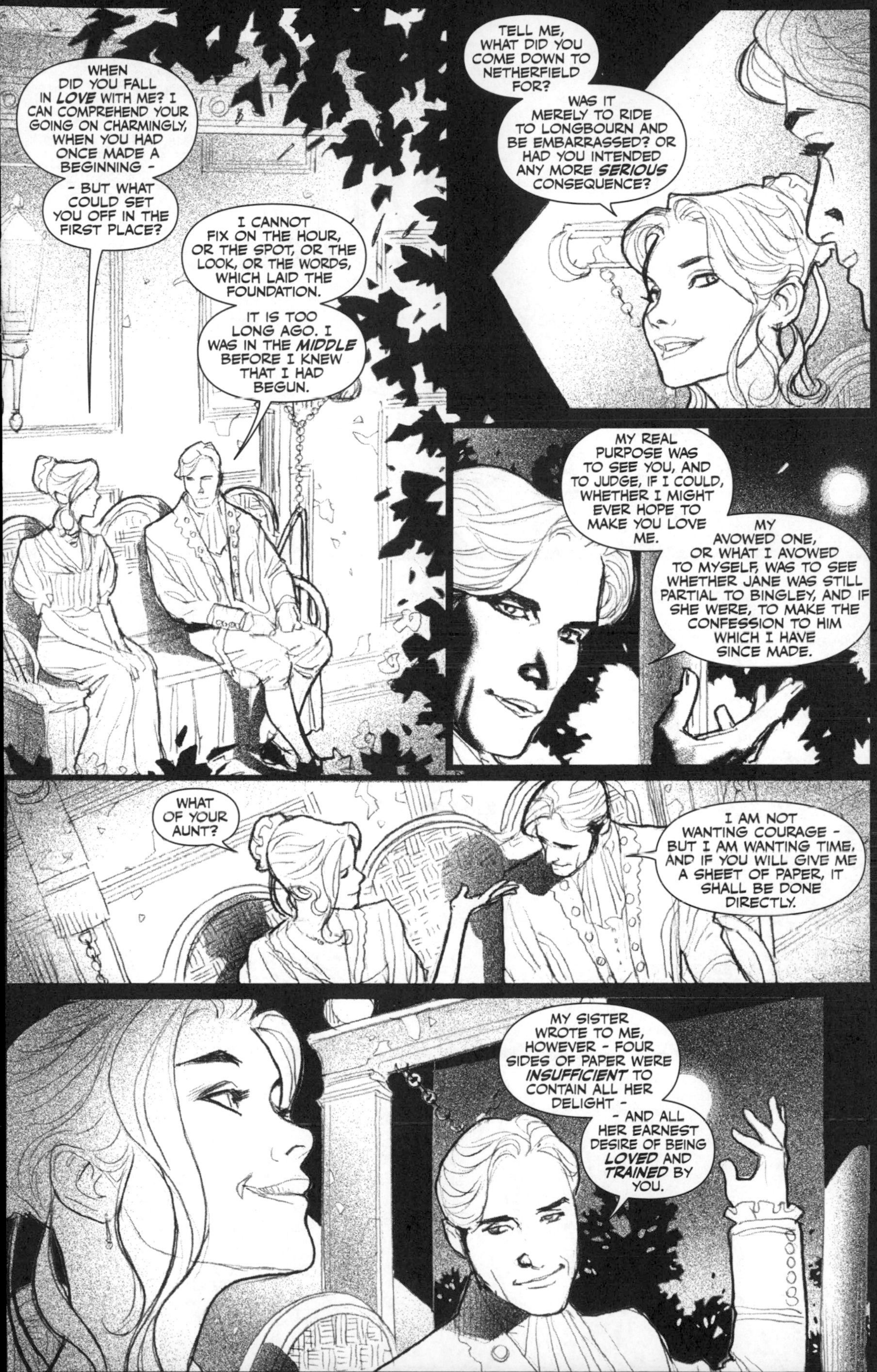
WHEN DID YOU FALL IN LOVE WITH ME? I CAN COMPREHEND YOUR GOING ON CHARMINGLY, WHEN YOU HAD ONCE MADE A BEGINNING -
- BUT WHAT COULD SET YOU OFF IN THE FIRST PLACE?
I CANNOT FIX ON THE HOUR, OR THE SPOT, OR THE LOOK, OR THE WORDS, WHICH LAID THE FOUNDATION.
IT IS TOO LONG AGO. I WAS IN THE MIDDLE BEFORE I KNEW THAT I HAD BEGUN.
TELL ME, WHAT DID YOU COME DOWN TO NETHERFIELD FOR?
WAS IT MERELY TO RIDE TO LONGBOURN AND BE EMBARRASSED? OR HAD YOU INTENDED ANY MORE SERIOUS CONSEQUENCE?
MY REAL PURPOSE WAS TO SEE YOU, AND TO JUDGE, IF I COULD, WHETHER I MIGHT EVER HOPE TO MAKE YOU LOVE ME.
MY AVOWED ONE, OR WHAT I AVOWED TO MYSELF, WAS TO SEE WHETHER JANE WAS STILL PARTIAL TO BINGLEY, AND IF SHE WERE, TO MAKE THE CONFESSION TO HIM WHICH I HAVE SINCE MADE.
WHAT OF YOUR AUNT?
I AM NOT WANTING COURAGE - BUT I AM WANTING TIME, AND IF YOU WILL GIVE ME A SHEET OF PAPER, IT SHALL BE DONE DIRECTLY.
MY SISTER WROTE TO ME, HOWEVER - FOUR SIDES OF PAPER WERE INSUFFICIENT TO CONTAIN ALL HER DELIGHT -
- AND ALL HER EARNEST DESIRE OF BEING LOVED AND TRAINED BY YOU.

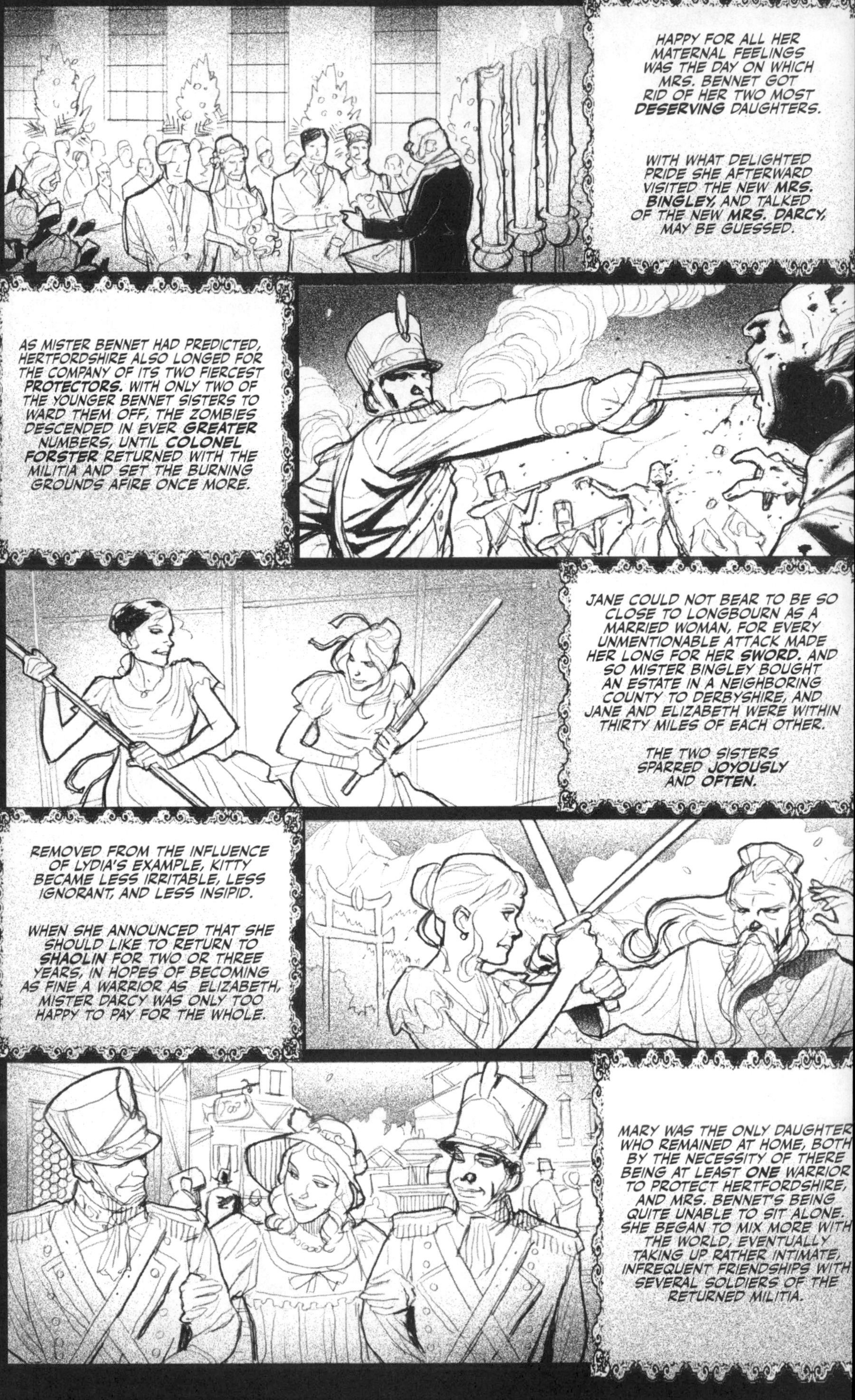
HAPPY FOR ALL HER MATERNAL FEELINGS WAS THE DAY ON WHICH MRS. BENNET GOT RID OF HER TWO MOST **DESERVING** DAUGHTERS.
WITH WHAT DELIGHTED PRIDE SHE AFTERWARD VISITED THE NEW **MRS. BINGLEY**, AND TALKED OF THE NEW **MRS. DARCY**, MAY BE GUESSED.
AS MISTER BENNET HAD PREDICTED, HERTFORDSHIRE ALSO LONGED FOR THE COMPANY OF ITS TWO FIERCEST **PROTECTORS.** WITH ONLY TWO OF THE YOUNGER BENNET SISTERS TO WARD THEM OFF, THE ZOMBIES DESCENDED IN EVER **GREATER** NUMBERS, UNTIL **COLONEL FORSTER** RETURNED WITH THE MILITIA AND SET THE BURNING GROUNDS AFIRE ONCE MORE.
JANE COULD NOT BEAR TO BE SO CLOSE TO LONGBOURN AS A MARRIED WOMAN, FOR EVERY UNMENTIONABLE ATTACK MADE HER LONG FOR HER **SWORD.** AND SO MISTER BINGLEY BOUGHT AN ESTATE IN A NEIGHBORING COUNTY TO DERBYSHIRE, AND JANE AND ELIZABETH WERE WITHIN THIRTY MILES OF EACH OTHER.
THE TWO SISTERS SPARRED **JOYOUSLY** AND **OFTEN.**
REMOVED FROM THE INFLUENCE OF LYDIA'S EXAMPLE, KITTY BECAME LESS IRRITABLE, LESS IGNORANT, AND LESS INSIPID.
WHEN SHE ANNOUNCED THAT SHE SHOULD LIKE TO RETURN TO **SHAOLIN** FOR TWO OR THREE YEARS, IN HOPES OF BECOMING AS FINE A WARRIOR AS ELIZABETH, MISTER DARCY WAS ONLY TOO HAPPY TO PAY FOR THE WHOLE.
MARY WAS THE ONLY DAUGHTER WHO REMAINED AT HOME, BOTH BY THE NECESSITY OF THERE BEING AT LEAST **ONE** WARRIOR TO PROTECT HERTFORDSHIRE, AND MRS. BENNET'S BEING QUITE UNABLE TO SIT ALONE. SHE BEGAN TO MIX MORE WITH THE WORLD, EVENTUALLY TAKING UP RATHER INTIMATE, INFREQUENT FRIENDSHIPS WITH SEVERAL SOLDIERS OF THE RETURNED MILITIA.

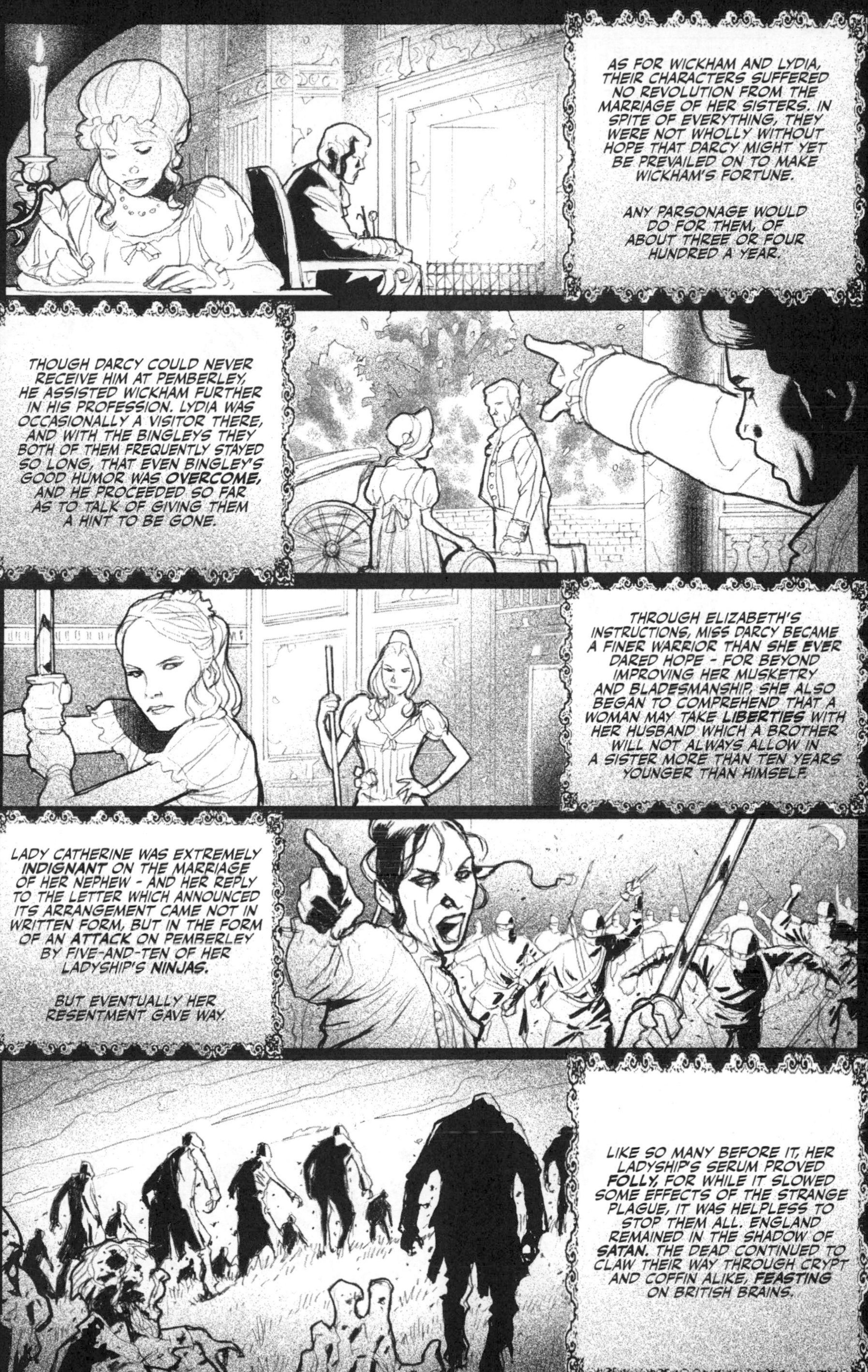
AS FOR WICKHAM AND LYDIA, THEIR CHARACTERS SUFFERED NO REVOLUTION FROM THE MARRIAGE OF HER SISTERS. IN SPITE OF EVERYTHING, THEY WERE NOT WHOLLY WITHOUT HOPE THAT DARCY MIGHT YET BE PREVAILED ON TO MAKE WICKHAM'S FORTUNE.
ANY PARSONAGE WOULD DO FOR THEM, OF ABOUT THREE OR FOUR HUNDRED A YEAR.
THOUGH DARCY COULD NEVER RECEIVE HIM AT PEMBERLEY, HE ASSISTED WICKHAM FURTHER IN HIS PROFESSION. LYDIA WAS OCCASIONALLY A VISITOR THERE, AND WITH THE BINGLEYS THEY BOTH OF THEM FREQUENTLY STAYED SO LONG, THAT EVEN BINGLEY'S GOOD HUMOR WAS **OVERCOME**, AND HE PROCEEDED SO FAR AS TO TALK OF GIVING THEM A HINT TO BE GONE.
THROUGH ELIZABETH'S INSTRUCTIONS, MISS DARCY BECAME A FINER WARRIOR THAN SHE EVER DARED HOPE - FOR BEYOND IMPROVING HER MUSKETRY AND BLADESMANSHIP, SHE ALSO BEGAN TO COMPREHEND THAT A WOMAN MAY TAKE **LIBERTIES** WITH HER HUSBAND WHICH A BROTHER WILL NOT ALWAYS ALLOW IN A SISTER MORE THAN TEN YEARS YOUNGER THAN HIMSELF.
LADY CATHERINE WAS EXTREMELY **INDIGNANT** ON THE MARRIAGE OF HER NEPHEW - AND HER REPLY TO THE LETTER WHICH ANNOUNCED ITS ARRANGEMENT CAME NOT IN WRITTEN FORM, BUT IN THE FORM OF AN **ATTACK** ON PEMBERLEY BY FIVE-AND-TEN OF HER LADYSHIP'S **NINJAS**.
BUT EVENTUALLY HER RESENTMENT GAVE WAY.
LIKE SO MANY BEFORE IT, HER LADYSHIP'S SERUM PROVED **FOLLY**, FOR WHILE IT SLOWED SOME EFFECTS OF THE STRANGE PLAGUE, IT WAS HELPLESS TO STOP THEM ALL. ENGLAND REMAINED IN THE SHADOW OF **SATAN**. THE DEAD CONTINUED TO CLAW THEIR WAY THROUGH CRYPT AND COFFIN ALIKE, **FEASTING** ON BRITISH BRAINS.

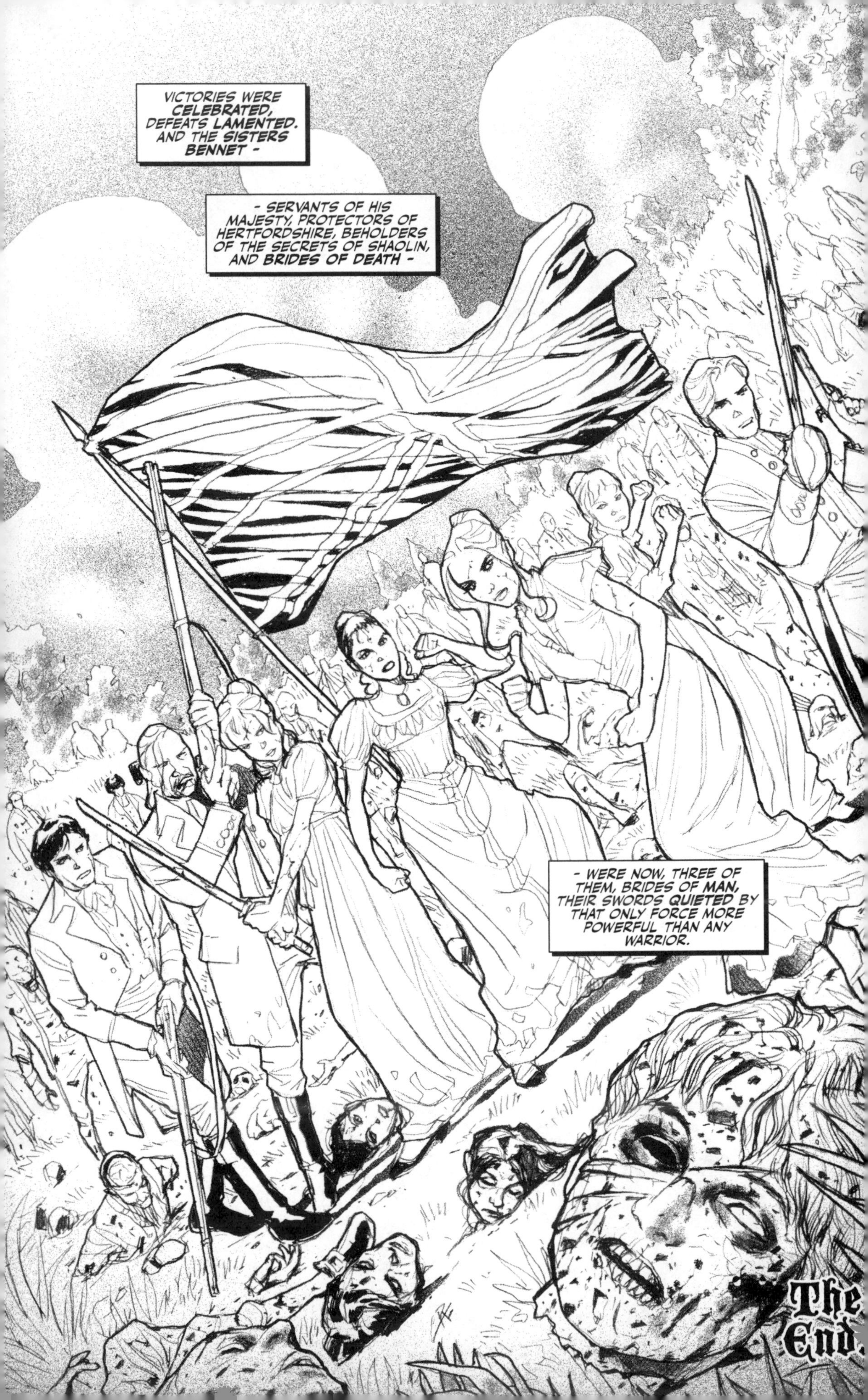
VICTORIES WERE CELEBRATED, DEFEATS LAMENTED. AND THE SISTERS BENNET -
- SERVANTS OF HIS MAJESTY, PROTECTORS OF HERTFORDSHIRE, BEHOLDERS OF THE SECRETS OF SHAOLIN, AND BRIDES OF DEATH -
- WERE NOW, THREE OF THEM, BRIDES OF MAN, THEIR SWORDS QUIETED BY THAT ONLY FORCE MORE POWERFUL THAN ANY WARRIOR.
The End.

About the Creators

TONY LEE

A writer for over twenty years in television, radio, and magazines, for the last six Lee has worked extensively in comics, writing for such licenses as *X-Men, Spider Man, Starship Troopers, Wallace & Gromit, Shrek* and *Doctor Who*. His critically acclaimed graphic novel *Outlaw: The Legend of Robin Hood* has been announced as a Junior Library Guild Selection for 2009.

In addition, he has adapted books by a variety of bestselling authors including Anthony Horowitz and G.P Taylor, and has continued both *Oliver Twist* and *Dracula* in graphic novel format. He lives in London.

CLIFF RICHARDS

Cliff Richards, a veteran artist best known for his five-year run on the *Buffy the Vampire Slayer* comics series, will illustrate the graphic novel. He has also worked on several projects for other comics publishers, including *Birds of Prey, Huntress*, and *Wonder Woman* for DC Comics, and *Rogue, Excalibur,* and *New Thunderbolts* for Marvel Comics.